SIXTH EDITION

PRINCIPLES *of* LANGUAGE LEARNING AND TEACHING

A COURSE IN SECOND LANGUAGE ACQUISITION

H. DOUGLAS BROWN

Principles of Language Learning and Teaching, Sixth Edition

Copyright © 2014 by Pearson Education, Inc.
All rights reserved.

Pearson Education, 10 Bank Street, White Plains, NY 10606

Staff Credits: The people who made up the **Principles of Language Learning and Teaching, Sixth Edition,** team—representing editorial, production, design, and manufacturing—are Tracey Cataldo, Nancy Flaggman, Amy McCormick, Lise Minovitz, Linda Moser, and Jane Townsend.

Project management and text composition: Kelly Ricci/Aptara®, Inc.
Text font: 10.5/12.5, ITC Garamond Std

Library of Congress Cataloging-in-Publication Data

Brown, H. Douglas, 1941-
    Principles of language learning and teaching/H. Douglas Brown.—Sixth Edition.
       pages cm
    "A course in second language acquisition."
    ISBN-13: 978-0-13-304194-1
    ISBN-10: 0-13-304194-8
    1. Language and languages—Study and teaching.   2. Language acquisition.   I. Title.
    P51.B775 2014
    418.0071—dc23   2013045080

ISBN 10:   0-13-304194-8
ISBN 13:   978-0-13-304194-1

Printed by Markono Print Media, Singapore
1 2 3 4 5 6 7 8 9 10—[V056]—22

PEARSON ELT ON THE WEB

PearsonELT.com offers a wide range of classroom resources and professional development materials. Access course-specific websites, product information, and Pearson offices around the world.

Visit us at **www.pearsonELT.com**.

CONTENTS

Chapter 3   Age and Acquisition   51

Chapter 4 Human Learning 78

Chapter 5 Individual Differences 109

Chapter 6   Affective Factors   141

Chapter 7   Language, Culture, and Identity   **174**

Chapter 8   Communicative Competence   **205**

Chapter 9 Interlanguage

Chapter 10   Sorting through Perspectives on SLA   **279**

PREFACE

Nearly three and a half decades ago, when the first edition of *Principles of Language Learning and Teaching* was published in 1980, the field of second language acquisition (SLA) was in what now seems like its infancy. Issues and controversies were manageable, a handful of journals published current studies and theoretical musings, and a budding community of researchers gathered at a smattering of conferences here and there.

Today, as I proudly present the sixth edition of *Principles*, SLA has grown—in complexity and sophistication—to mind-boggling proportions. Hundreds of periodicals now grace the landscape of SLA, along with books and papers and presentations and dissertations from every corner of the world. This rich and diverse field of inquiry has now shed a "beacon of light" (note the cover photograph) on the stormy seas that have perplexed us over the years. Nevertheless, a good deal of research on SLA concludes with the usual caveats: "more research is needed" or "our findings remain tentative."

Still, we have come a long way in six decades or so of concentrated focus on SLA, and this latest edition will reflect those successes, and will—perhaps more so than in previous editions—directly relate what we know about SLA to the language classroom. With a new subtitle, "A Course in Second Language Acquisition," designed to signal the book's primary use as a textbook in SLA, the sixth edition of *Principles* offers practicing teachers and teachers in training opportunities to inform their pedagogical practices.

PURPOSE AND AUDIENCE

As in the previous five editions, the purpose and audience of this sixth edition are as follows:

- *A course in SLA* for students in language-teacher education programs
- *A textbook* on the theoretical foundations of language teaching
- *A summary*, for master's degree candidates, of "everything you need to know" about SLA

- *A handbook,* for experienced language teachers, of current issues, trends, and bibliographic references

For the most part, you don't need to have prior technical knowledge of linguistics or psychology in order to comprehend this book. From the beginning, the textbook builds on what an educated person knows about the world, life, people, and communication. And the book can be used in programs for educating teachers of *any* foreign language, even though many illustrative examples here are in English since that is the language common to all readers.

CHANGES IN THE SIXTH EDITION

Following are some highlights of this edition:

1. **New issues and topics.** The most significant development in SLA research in the last seven years has been an intense focus on the "social turn" in SLA. The research of the previous six decades has come full circle to encompass what is now considered to be the heart of SLA: the intertwining and interdependence of self, identity, social interaction, and language acquisition. This focus is reflected throughout the book, culminating in my six perspectives (seen metaphorically as a color wheel) on SLA in the final chapter. Many of the chapters have been reorganized (new headings and sections, permutations of topics, etc.) to deliver new messages and new ways of thinking.

2. **Updates and new references.** Out of literally thousands of new articles, books, and chapters that have appeared since the last edition, I have added a selection of some 300 new *bibliographic references* that report the latest work in SLA, along with a number of new terms for the end-of-book *glossary*. Almost all of the *suggested readings* at the end of each chapter are new. In order to make way for the new, a good deal of the "old" has been culled, treated now as brief historical backdrops.

3. **More pedagogical focus.** This edition offers more in the way of practical classroom applications. The few *classroom connections* sprinkled through each chapter have multiplied to about a dozen for each chapter, each more simply and briefly worded, and designed to capture the interest of readers who have *not* had teaching experience along with those who have. In the interest of cutting to the chase, some of the detailed descriptions of research studies have been reduced. End of chapter *activities and discussion questions* have some added practicality, and are now addressed to the course instructor. *Journal-writing guidelines* retain their reflective and classroom-based leanings.

4. **Writing style.** You'll notice that my writing style has changed. I think you will soon discern more relaxed, informal, person-to-person prose throughout. I hope you will "hear" me talking with students, with less

academic stuffiness than before. I'm no less serious now, but I hope more approachable. Virtually every paragraph has been rewritten, loosened when needed, tightened in other spots. The final chapter is a complete rewrite—I think you'll like my summation of SLA theories and controversies through several metaphors with, yes, of course, a dash of whimsy here and there.

ACKNOWLEDGMENTS

This book has grown out of graduate courses in SLA that I have taught since 1970. My first debt of gratitude is always to my students, for their insights, enthusiasm, and inquisitiveness. I always learn so much from them! I'm additionally grateful to students scattered around the globe who muster the courage to e-mail me with questions and comments. It's always great to hear from curious readers and yes, many of their comments are reflected in this current edition.

This time around I was the beneficiary of quite a number of formal reviews of the fifth edition, some of them assigned to specific chapters to assess. A huge thank-you to my reviewers for your excellent insights and suggestions: Mahmoud Arani, St. Michael's College, Colchester, VT; Tamara Collins-Parks, San Diego State University, San Diego, CA; Carolyn Duffy, St. Michael's College, Colchester, VT; Mark James, Arizona State University, Tempe, AZ; Youjin Kim, Georgia State University, Atlanta, GA; Heekyeong Lee, Monterey Institute of International Studies, Monterey, CA; Joseph Lee, Ohio University, Athens, OH; Suzanne Medina, California State University, Dominguez Hills, CA; Caroline Payant, Georgia State University, Atlanta, GA; and Luke Plonsky, Northern Arizona University, Flagstaff, AZ. Together you all provided an amazingly coherent collage of commentary! I could not have accomplished what I did here without you.

I'm also grateful to a number of language learners whose interviews and journals provided insightful chapter-opening vignettes. Some remain anonymous, while a special thank you goes to Magdalena Madany and Melody Chen, whose "stories" appear in Chapters 5 and 6.

Another essential link in the culmination of the publication of a book is the publishing team. I feel very fortunate to have worked closely with my editor, Lise Minovitz, and her colleagues at Pearson/Longman, with Kelly Ricci and her editors at Aptara, and with my indexer Sallie Steele.

Finally, on a personal note, I want to say yet another enormous thank-you to my wife, Mary, for once again being so patiently supportive of a sometimes overly driven author as I churned out this sixth edition. The support of loved ones is always an immeasurable but crucial contributor to any successful endeavor.

H. Douglas Brown
Professor Emeritus
San Francisco State University

CHAPTER 1

LANGUAGE, LEARNING, AND TEACHING

Carson, a native Californian, took Spanish as a foreign language for two years in high school and then had two more years in college. As a twenty-year-old, he spent one summer month in Costa Rica helping to build affordable housing for the less fortunate in the city of San José. On arrival, his four years of classroom Spanish were self-described as "somewhat useful in giving me a head start, but for face-to-face conversation, pretty useless." After one month in Costa Rica, making an effort to speak Spanish as much and as often as he could with Costa Rican friends, and as little English as possible, he felt like he came back to the United States with enough Spanish to "get along quite well" in a conversation.

Sonia, from Sao Paulo, Brazil, took German classes all the way through high school, at the prodding of her German-born parents. After two years of college German, reaching an advanced-intermediate level, she dropped the course the next year. She described feeling little sense of ability beyond a lot of "knowledge about German grammar," and a lack of motivation to continue studying German "just to please my mother and father." Ten years later, when asked how her German was, she reported "okay" reading ability (but no practical reason to read in German), "fair" listening ability (with grandparents), "poor" speaking ability (a few phrases with family), and "almost non-existent" writing ability.

What do these two learners tell you about learning a second language? Even without the "whole story" of each learner's journey, can you see that language fluency doesn't happen overnight? And that learning a second language also involves learning a second culture? And that it may mean a whole new way of thinking, feeling, and acting? And that commitment, motivation, and serious effort are involved? And finally, that language learning involves social interaction in a meaningful context?

The two learners above may have benefited from their classroom instruction, but did those classrooms provide optimal communicative opportunities to use their second language (L2)?[1] This book is about both *learning* and *teaching*, and of course teaching is the facilitation of learning. And a major step in learning how to *facilitate* is understanding the intricate web of *principles* that are spun together to affect how and why people learn—or fail to learn—an L2. To begin the process of understanding principles of language learning and teaching, let's ponder some of the questions that you could ask.

QUESTIONS ABOUT SLA

Any complex set of skills brings with it a host of questions. As a means to guide an exploration of second language acquisition[2] (SLA), let's look at some of the questions you might ask, sorted here into some commonly used topical categories.

Learner Characteristics

Who are the learners that you are teaching? What is their ethnic, linguistic, and religious heritage? What are their native languages, levels of education, and socioeconomic characteristics? What life experiences have they had that might affect their learning? What are their intellectual capacities, abilities, and strengths and weaknesses? How would you describe the personality of a student of yours? You can no doubt think of more questions, but these will suffice for starters.

 CLASSROOM CONNECTIONS

In your learning of an L2, how did your own "life experiences" carry over to your SLA process? Among classmates of yours in an L2 class, what are some of their "life experiences" that might make a difference in how you teach your own students or in how well those students will learn the language? For each "experience," what could you do as a teacher to either capitalize on positives in learners' backgrounds or minimize the negatives?

[1, 2]Throughout this book, "second language," abbreviated as L2, refers generically to any *additional* language acquisition beyond the first (L1), including both "foreign" language learning and also subsequent (third, fourth, etc.) languages. Likewise "second language acquisition," abbreviated as SLA, is a generic term referring to L2 acquisition in both natural and instructional settings, as well as to both "foreign" language learning (e.g., learning French in the United States, English in Japan) and "second" language learning (in the L2 culture, e.g., English in the United States and Chinese in China).

Linguistic Factors

What is language? What is communication? What does it mean when we say someone knows how to *use* a language? What are the relevant differences (and similarities) between a learner's first language (L1) and L2? What properties of the L2 might be difficult for a learner to master? These questions are, of course, central to the discipline of *linguistics*. Language teachers need to understand something about the linguistic system of the L2 and some of the possible difficulties a learner might encounter.

Learning Processes

How does learning take place? Are there specific steps to successful learning? What mental or intellectual processes are involved in SLA? What kinds of strategies are available to a learner, and which ones are optimal? What is the optimal interrelationship of mental, emotional, and physical processes for successful SLA?

Age and Acquisition

One of the key issues in L2 research and teaching is a cluster of questions about differences between children and adults. Does the age of learning make a difference? Common observation tells us that children are "better" language learners than adults. Are they, really? What does the research show? How do developmental changes that occur between childhood and adulthood affect SLA?

 CLASSROOM CONNECTIONS

Did you try to learn an L2 as a child? If so, how did that experience differ from learning an L2 as an adult? Suppose you were asked to teach two foreign language classes, one to eight-year-old children and the other to secondary school seniors (about seventeen years old). How would your teaching approach and your materials differ between those two classes?

Classroom Instruction

A good deal of SLA successfully takes place outside of any educational context or classroom. In such "natural" environments, do all people learn a language equally successfully? In what has come to be called "instructed" SLA, many questions arise. What are the effects of varying methodological approaches, textbooks, materials, teacher styles, and institutional factors? Is there an optimal length of *time* required for successful mastery? How can a student best put classroom instruction into action in the "real" world?

Context

Are the learners attempting to acquire the second language within the cultural and linguistic milieu of the second language, that is, in a "second" language situation in the technical sense of the term? Or are they focusing on a "foreign" language context in which the L2 is heard and spoken only in an artificial environment, such as in a language classroom, or an instructional video? How might the sociopolitical conditions of a particular country or its language policy affect the outcome of a learner's mastery of a language? How do inter-cultural contrasts and similarities affect the learning process?

Purpose

Finally, the most encompassing of all questions: Why are learners attempting to acquire the second language? Are they motivated by the achievement of a successful career, or by passing a foreign language requirement, or by wishing to identify closely with the culture and people of the target language?

 CLASSROOM CONNECTIONS

Think back to a time when you were *first* learning an L2, and make a list of all the reasons (purposes) you had in beginning that process. If students in a classroom have many different such purposes, what could you as a teacher do either to refine or develop those purposes, or to redirect purposes that might not be facilitative?

REJOICING IN OUR DEFEATS

The above questions have been posed, in global terms, to give you an inkling of the diversity of issues involved in understanding the principles of language learning and teaching. By addressing such questions carefully and critically, you may actually achieve a surprising number of answers. And with the help of this book, you should be able to hone global questions into finer, subtler questions, which in itself is an important task, for often being able to *ask the right questions* is more valuable than possessing storehouses of knowledge.

At the same time, remember that you may not find *final* answers to all the questions. The field of SLA manifests all the methodological and theoretical problems that come with a developing discipline (Long, 2007; VanPatten & Williams, 2007; Hinkel, 2011; Gass, 2013). Therefore, many of these questions have somewhat tentative answers, or at best, answers that must begin with the phrase, "it depends." Answers must be framed in a context that can vary from one learner to another, and from one moment to another.

The wonderful intricacy of complex facets of human behavior will be very much with us for some time. Roger Brown's (1966, p. 326) wry remark of five decades ago still applies:

> Psychologists find it exciting when a complex mental phenomenon— something intelligent and slippery—seems about to be captured by a mechanical model. We yearn to see the model succeed. But when, at the last minute, the phenomenon proves too much for the model and darts off on some uncapturable tangent, there is something in us that rejoices at the defeat.

We can rejoice in our defeats because we know that it's the very elusiveness of the phenomenon of SLA that makes the quest for answers so exciting. Our field of inquiry is no simple, unidimensional reality. It's "slippery" in every way.

The chapters of this book are designed to give you a picture of both the slipperiness of SLA and the systematic storehouse of reliable knowledge that is now available to us. As you consider the issues, chapter by chapter, you will develop an integrated understanding of how people learn—and sometimes fail to learn—an L2.

That understanding must be *eclectic*: no single theory or hypothesis will provide a magic formula for all learners in all contexts. Your conclusions will need to be *enlightened*: you'll be urged to be as critical as you can in considering the merit of various models and theories and research findings. And you'll have to be a bit *cautious*: don't accept every claim as truth just because someone fervently asserts it to be factual. By the end of the final chapter, with this cautious, enlightened, eclectic approach, you'll no doubt surprise yourself on how many pieces of this giant puzzle you can actually put together!

Thomas Kuhn (1970) referred to "normal science" as a process of puzzle solving in which part of the task of the scientist, in this case the teacher, is to discover the pieces and then to fit the pieces together. Some of the pieces of the SLA puzzle have been located and set in place. Others are not yet discovered, and the careful defining of questions will lead to finding those pieces. We can then undertake the task of fitting the pieces together into what Kuhn called a **paradigm**—an interlocking design, a model, or a theory of SLA.

CLASSROOM CONNECTIONS

How would you describe, in your experience, the current accepted "paradigm," or "approach" to language teaching? As you think about language classes you have taken (and perhaps taught), have you seen a "revolution" in language teaching, or is there one yet to come in the near future?

In order to begin to ask further questions and to find answers to some of those questions, let's first address a fundamental concern in problem-posing: defining the focus of our inquiry. Since this book is about language, learning, and teaching, let's see what happens when we try to define those three terms.

LANGUAGE

A definition is a statement that captures the key features of a concept. Those features may vary, depending on your own understanding of the concept. And, most importantly, your understanding is essentially a "condensed" version of a theory that elaborates on all the facets of the concept. Conversely, a theory could be thought of as an "extended" definition. Defining, therefore, is serious business: it requires choices about which facets of a phenomenon are worthy of being included.

Suppose you were stopped by a reporter on the street, and in the course of an interview about your field of study, you were asked, "Well, since you're interested in second language acquisition, please tell me what *language* is, exactly." You would no doubt probe your memory for a typical dictionary-type definition of language. What would such a definition look like?

According to *Merriam-Webster's Collegiate Dictionary* (2003, p. 699), language is "a systematic means of communicating ideas or feelings by the use of conventionalized signs, sounds, gestures, or marks having understood meanings." If you had read Steven Pinker's *The Language Instinct* (1994), you would find a little more elaboration:

> Language is a complex, specialized skill, which develops in the child spontaneously, without conscious effort or formal instruction, is deployed without awareness of its underlying logic, is qualitatively the same in every individual, and is distinct from more general abilities to process information or behave intelligently (p. 18).

On the other hand, you might, with Ron Scollon (2004, p. 272), also have included some mention of the creativity of language, the presumed primacy of speech over writing, and the universality of language among human beings.

If we were to synthesize a number of definitions of **language**, we might come up with a composite definition represented in the eight items in the left-hand column of Table 1.1. These comprise a reasonably concise "25-word-or-less" definition of language. But the simplicity of the eightfold definition should not mask the sophistication of linguistic research underlying each concept. Enormous fields and subfields, yearlong university courses, and reams of research are suggested in each of the eight categories. Some of these fields of research are listed in the right-hand column of Table 1.1.

Table 1.1 Language definition and related subfields of research

Language	Subfields of Research and Inquiry
1. …is systematic	phonetics; phonology; morphology; syntax; discourse analysis; lexical analysis
2. …uses arbitrary symbols	semiotics; semantics; philosophy & history of language; psycholinguistics
3. …uses symbols that are primarily vocal but may also be visual	phonetics; phonology; writing systems; orthography; nonverbal communication
4. …uses symbols that have conventionalized meanings	semantics; pragmatics; sociolinguistics; psycholinguistics; cognitive linguistics
5. …is used for communication	sentence processing; pragmatics; discourse analysis; conversation analysis
6. …operates in a speech community	sociolinguistics; sociocultural analysis; or culture pragmatics; dialectology; bilingualism
7. …is essentially human, but not limited to humans	innateness; genetics; neurolinguistics; animal communication
8. …has universal characteristics	Universal Grammar; innateness; emergentism; neurolinguistics; cross-cultural analysis

Careful research and extensive study of these eight topics have involved a complex journey through a labyrinth of linguistic science—a maze that continues to be negotiated as many controversies have arisen within these basic concepts.

Your understanding of the components of language determines to a large extent how you teach a language. If, for example, you believe that nonverbal communication is a key to successful second language learning, you will devote some attention in your curriculum to nonverbal systems and cues. If you perceive language as a phenomenon that can be dismantled into thousands of discrete pieces—such as grammar points—and those pieces programmatically taught one by one, you will attend carefully to an understanding of the discrete forms of language. If you think language is essentially cultural and interactive, your classroom methodology will be imbued with sociolinguistic strategies and communicative tasks.

LEARNING AND TEACHING

We can also ask questions about constructs like learning and teaching. Consider again some traditional definitions. A search in contemporary dictionaries reveals that **learning** is "acquiring knowledge of a subject or a skill by study, experience, or instruction." Oddly, an educational psychologist would define learning even more succinctly as "a change in an individual caused by experience" (Slavin, 2003, p. 138).

Similarly, **teaching**, which is implied in the first definition of learning, may be defined as "showing or helping someone to learn how to do something, giving instructions, guiding in the study of something, providing with knowledge, causing to know or understand." Isn't it curious that lexicographers seem to have such difficulty in devising a definition of something as universal as teaching? More than perhaps anything else, such definitions reflect the difficulty of defining complex concepts.

Breaking down the components of the definition of learning, we can extract, as we did with language, domains of research and inquiry. Learning is:

1. Acquisition or "adding"
2. The retention of information or skills
3. The involvement of storage systems, memory, and cognitive organization
4. The application of active, conscious focus, and subconscious attention
5. Relatively permanent but subject to forgetting
6. The result of practice, perhaps reinforced practice
7. A change in behavior

These concepts can also give way to a number of subfields within the discipline of psychology: acquisition processes, perception, memory (storage) systems, short- and long-term memory, recall, motivation, conscious and subconscious attention, learning styles and strategies, theories of forgetting, reinforcement, the role of practice. Very quickly the concept of learning becomes every bit as complex as the concept of language. Yet the second language learner brings all these (and more) variables into play in the learning of a second language.

Teaching cannot be defined apart from learning. Teaching is guiding and facilitating learning, enabling a person to learn, and setting the conditions for learning. Your understanding of how people learn will determine your philosophy of education, your teaching style, approach, lesson design, and classroom techniques. If, like B. F. Skinner (1953), you look at learning as a process of operant conditioning through a carefully paced program of reinforcement, you will teach accordingly. If you view second language learning as a deductive rather than an inductive process, you will probably choose to present rules, lists, and charts to your students rather than let them "discover" those rules inductively.

 CLASSROOM CONNECTIONS

Write your own brief definition of teaching. What are the components of your definition? Take each component and think of how that component was manifested in L2 classes that you took, or if you have taught, how aspects of your definition were apparent in your teaching approach.

An extended definition—or theory—of teaching will spell out governing principles for choosing certain methods and techniques. A theory of teaching, in harmony with your integrated understanding of the learner and of the language to be learned, will point the way to successful procedures on a given day for given learners under the various constraints of the particular context of learning. In other words, your theory of teaching is your theory of learning "stood on its head."

THREE PERSPECTIVES ON SECOND LANGUAGE ACQUISITION

The general definitions of language, learning, and teaching offered frame a beginning of theory-building. However, points of disagreement become apparent after a little probing of details. For example, is L1 acquisition an innately determined process or much like the learning of many other skills? Is language primarily a "system of formal units" or a "means for social interaction"? Can we attribute SLA success to, let's say, simply a matter of comprehensible input, or exposure to meaningful communicative contexts? Differing viewpoints emerge from equally knowledgeable scholars, who usually differ over the extent to which one perspective is more accurate than another.

Yet with all the possible disagreements among applied linguists and SLA researchers, some historical patterns emerge that highlight trends in the study of SLA. These trends will be described here in the form of three different perspectives, or schools of thought in the fields of linguistics and psychology. While each perspective shares historical chronology, bear in mind that such a sketch may risk some overgeneralization

Structural Linguistics and Behavioral Psychology

In the 1940s and 1950s, the **structural**, or **descriptive**, school of linguistics prided itself in a rigorous application of the scientific observation of human languages. Only "publicly observable responses" could be subject to investigation. The linguist's task, according to the **structuralist**, was to *describe* human languages and to identify their structural characteristics. An important axiom of structural linguistics was that languages can differ from each other without limit, and that no preconceptions should apply across languages. Freeman Twaddell (1935), among others, underscored the mandate for the structural linguist to examine only *overtly observable* data, and to ignore any **mentalistic** theorizing that might entertain unobservable guesses, hunches, and intuition about language.

Of further importance to the structural or descriptive linguist was the notion that language could be dismantled into small pieces or units and that these units could be described scientifically, contrasted, and added up again to form the whole. From this principle emerged an unchecked rush of linguists, in the 1940s and 1950s, to the far reaches of the earth to engage in the rigorous production of detailed descriptions of the world's languages, many of them labeled as "exotic."

Similar perspectives were shared by psychologists of this era. For example, B.F. Skinner (1957), Charles Osgood (1957), and others insisted on the rigors of the **scientific method** in studying human behavior. In their **behavioral** paradigm, any notion of "idea" or "meaning" was "explanatory fiction," and in both language and other behavior, the only legitimate "responses" were those that could be objectively perceived, recorded, and measured. The unreliability of observation of states of consciousness, thinking, concept formation, or the acquisition of knowledge made such topics impossible to examine in a behavioral framework.

 CLASSROOM CONNECTIONS

Structural linguistics was best modeled in the classroom by Charles Fries (1945, 1952), whose "structural drills" and "pattern practices" eventually evolved into the Audiolingual Method (see Chapter 4). In your experience learning or teaching a language, what do you think are the advantages and disadvantages of pattern drills and rote memorization in the language classroom? If they should be used at all, how do you place limits on their use?

Generative Linguistics and Cognitive Psychology

In the decade of the 1960s, **generative-transformational linguistics** emerged through the influence of Noam Chomsky and a number of his colleagues. Chomsky was trying to show that human language cannot be scrutinized simply in terms of *observable* stimuli and responses or the volumes of raw data gathered by field linguists. The generative linguist was interested not only in describing language (achieving the level of **descriptive adequacy**) but also in arriving at an **explanatory** level of adequacy in the study of language, that is, a "principled basis, independent of any particular language, for the selection of the descriptively adequate grammar of each language" (Chomsky, 1964, p. 63).

Early seeds of the generative-transformational revolution were planted near the beginning of the twentieth century. Ferdinand de Saussure (1916) claimed that there was a difference between *parole* (what Skinner "observes," and what Chomsky called **performance**), on the one hand, and *langue* (akin to the concept of **competence**, or our underlying and unobservable language ability). A few decades later, however, descriptive linguists chose largely to ignore *langue* and to study *parole*. The revolution brought about by generative linguistics broke with the descriptivists' preoccupation with performance—the outward manifestation of language—and focused on the importance of the underlying (and nonobservable) levels of meaning and thought that give birth to and generate observable linguistic performance.

Similarly, **cognitive** psychologists asserted that meaning, understanding, and knowing were significant data for psychological study. Instead of focusing mechanistically on stimulus-response connections, cognitivists tried to discover psychological principles of organization and functioning. David Ausubel (1965, p. 4), for example, felt that behaviorists "dangerously oversimplified highly complex psychological phenomena." The growth of cognitivism in the 1960s and beyond signaled a distinct change in approaches to the study of human functioning, characterized by assertions that "the mind/brain is, for all intents and purposes, the *necessary* and *sufficient* locus of human thought and learning" (Atkinson, 2011b, p. 3).

Cognitive psychologists, like generative linguists, sought to discover under-lying motivations and deeper structures of human behavior by using a **rational** approach. That is, they freed themselves from the strictly empirical study typical of behaviorists and employed the tools of logic, reason, extrapolation, and inference in order to derive explanations for human behavior. For cognitive psychologists, going beyond merely descriptive adequacy to explanatory power took on the utmost importance.

Both the structural linguist and the behavioral psychologist were interested in description, in answering *what* questions about human behavior by means of objective measurement in controlled circumstances. The generative linguist and cognitive psychologist were, to be sure, interested in the *what* question. But they were far more interested in a more ultimate question: *why?* What underlying factors—innate, psychological, social, or environmental circum-stances—caused a particular behavior in a human being?

Suppose you're blissfully enjoying a meal at a restaurant when another patron across the room starts screaming expletives, stands up from the table, throws his drink into the face of the waitperson, and stomps out of the restaurant. A friend later wants to know what happened, and asks various *what* questions. Which restaurant? What time of day was this? What did the person look like? What did the waiter do? What did the guy say as he walked quickly out of the restaurant? Another friend asks different questions, ones that require your *inference* about the incident. Was the guy angry? Was he mentally disturbed? Why did he throw his drink into the waitperson's face? Were other people shocked? Was the waitperson embarrassed?

The first friend asked objective questions, the answers to which were based on *observable* behavior. But did they probe ultimate answers? The second set of questions was richer, and obviously riskier. By daring to ask some difficult questions about the unobserved, we may lose some objectivity but gain more profound insight into human behavior.

Constructivism: A Multidisciplinary Approach

Constructivism is hardly a new school of thought. Piaget and Vygotsky, names often associated with constructivism, are not by any means new to the scene of language studies. Yet, in a variety of **post-structuralist** theoretical positions, constructivism emerged as a paradigm of intense interest in the last part of the twentieth century. A refreshing characteristic of constructivism is its integration of linguistic, psychological, and sociological paradigms, in contrast to the professional chasms that often divided those disciplines in the previous century. Now, with its emphasis on social interaction and the discovery, or construction, of meaning, the three disciplines have much more common ground.

What is constructivism, and how does it differ from the other two viewpoints described above? First, it will be helpful to think of two branches of constructivism: cognitive and social. In **cognitive constructivism,** emphasis is placed on the importance of learners constructing their own representation of reality. "Learners must individually discover and transform complex information if they are to make it their own, [suggesting] a more active role for students in their own learning than is typical in many classrooms" (Slavin, 2003, pp. 257–258). Such claims are rooted in Piaget's seminal work in the middle of the twentieth century, (Piaget, 1954, 1955, 1970; Piaget & Inhelder, 1969) but have taken a long time to become widely accepted views. For Piaget, "learning is a developmental process that involves change, self-generation, and construction, each building on prior learning experiences" (Kaufman, 2004, p. 304).

Social constructivism emphasizes the importance of social interaction and cooperative learning in ultimate attainment. Spivey (1997, p. 24) noted that constructivist research tends to focus on "individuals engaged in social practices ... on a collaborative group, [or] on a global community." The champion of social constructivism is Lev Vygotsky (1978), who advocated the view that "children's thinking and meaning-making is socially constructed and emerges out of their social interactions with their environment" (Kaufman, 2004, p. 304).

 CLASSROOM CONNECTIONS

Constructivists have championed social interaction, discovery learning, and the active role of a learner as necessary for effective learning. In your own L2 learning (or teaching) experiences, what are some examples of constructivism that successfully contributed to your process of learning (or teaching)?

One of the most popular concepts advanced by Vygotsky was the notion of a **zone of proximal development** (ZPD): the distance between learners' existing developmental state and their potential development. Put another way, the ZPD encompasses tasks that a learner has not yet learned but is capable of learning with appropriate stimuli. The ZPD is an important facet of social constructivism because it involves tasks "that a child cannot yet do alone but could do with the assistance of more competent peers or adults" (Slavin, 2003, p. 44; see also Karpov & Haywood, 1998). A number of applications of Vygotsky's ZPD have been made to foreign language instruction (Lantolf, 2000, 2011; Nassaji & Cumming, 2000; Marchenkova, 2005) in both adult and child second language learning contexts.

Vygotsky's concept of the ZPD contrasted rather sharply with Piaget's theory of learning in that the former saw a *unity* of learning and development while the latter saw stages of development setting a precondition or readiness for learning (Dunn & Lantolf, 1998). Piaget stressed the importance of individual cognitive development as a relatively solitary act. Biological timetables and stages of development were basic; social interaction was claimed only to trigger development at the right moment in time. On the other hand, Vygotsky maintained that social interaction was foundational in cognitive development and rejected the notion of predetermined stages.

Closely allied to a Vygotskian social constructivist perspective is that of Mikhail Bakhtin (1986, 1990), the Russian literary theorist who has now captured the attention of SLA researchers and practitioners (Hall, Vitanova, & Marchenkova, 2005). Bakhtin contended that language is "immersed in a social and cultural context, and its central function is to serve as a medium of communication." In this spirit, the early years of the new millennium have seen increasing emphasis on sociocultural dimensions of SLA, or what Watson-Gegeo (2004) described as a language socialization paradigm for SLA: a new synthesis that "involves a reconsideration of mind, language, and epistemology, and a recognition that cognition originates in social interaction and is shaped by cultural and sociopolitical processes" (Watson-Gegeo, 2004, p. 331).

CLASSROOM CONNECTIONS

In your foreign language learning (or teaching), what "sociocultural dimensions" of the language did you learn? How did you learn them? How did they contrast with the sociocultural dimensions of your native language?

We can see constructivist perspectives in the work of first and second language acquisition researchers who study conversational discourse, sociocultural factors in learning, and interactionist theories. In many ways, constructivist perspectives are a natural successor to cognitively based studies of universal grammar, information processing, memory, artificial intelligence, and interlanguage systematicity.

All three of the historical perspectives described in this section—structural/behavioral, generative/cognitive, and constructivist—must be seen as important in creating balanced descriptions of second language acquisition. Consider for a moment the analogy of a very high mountain, viewed from a distance. From one direction the mountain may have a sharp peak, easily identified glaciers, and jutting rock formations. From another direction, however, the same mountain might appear to have two peaks (the second formerly hidden from view) and different configurations of its slopes. From a slightly different direction but this time with binoculars, yet further characteristics emerge—a forested ravine, rounded rocks, a winding trail. The study of SLA is very much like the viewing of such a mountain: we need multiple vantage points and tools in order to ascertain the whole picture.

Table 1.2 summarizes concepts and approaches in the three perspectives just described. The chronology of the schools of thought illustrates what Kuhn (1970) described as the structure of scientific revolutions. A successful paradigm is followed by a period of anomaly (doubt, uncertainty, questioning of prevailing theory), then crisis (the "fall" of the existing paradigm) with all the

Table 1.2 Three perspectives on second language acquisition

Schools of Thought	Typical Themes
Structural Linguistics/ Behavioral Psychology	Description, Observable performance, Empiricism, Scientific method, Conditioning, Reinforcement
Generative Linguistics/ Cognitive Psychology	Acquisition, Innateness, Language competence, Deep structure, Interlanguage, Systematicity, Variability
Constructivism	Interactive discourse, Sociocultural factors, Construction of identity, ZPD, Cooperative learning, Discovery learning

professional insecurity that comes with it; and then finally a new paradigm, a novel theory, is put together. However, that new paradigm is never unequivocally "new." The "borrowing" from one paradigm to the next underscores the fact that no single paradigm is right or wrong. Some truth can be found in virtually every critical approach to the study of reality.

NINETEEN CENTURIES OF LANGUAGE TEACHING

A survey of research and theoretical trends in SLA could remain unfocused without its practical application to the language classroom. Since most readers of this book are ultimately interested in language pedagogy, I will offer occasional relevant historical commentaries on language *teaching* and link those descriptions to topics and issues being treated. In so doing, I hope to acquaint you progressively with some of the methodological trends and issues on the pedagogical side of the profession.

So far in this chapter, the focus has been on research over the past century or so of linguistics and psychology. What do we know about language teaching in the two or three millennia prior? The answer is not very much.

Louis Kelly's (1969) informative survey of language teaching over "twenty-five centuries," to borrow from his title, revealed interesting anecdotal accounts of L2 instruction, but few if any research-based language teaching methods. In the Western world, foreign language learning in schools was synonymous with the learning of Latin or Greek. Latin, thought to promote intellectuality through "mental gymnastics," was until relatively recently held to be indispensable to an adequate education. Latin was taught by means of what has been called the **Classical Method**: focus on grammatical rules, memorization of vocabulary and grammatical forms, translation of texts, and performance of written exercises.

As other languages began to be taught in educational institutions in the eighteenth and nineteenth centuries, the Classical Method was adopted as the chief means for teaching foreign languages. Little thought was given at the time to teaching oral use of languages; after all, languages were not being taught primarily to learn oral/aural communication, but to learn for the sake of being "scholarly" or, in some instances, for gaining a reading proficiency in a foreign language. Since there was little if any theoretical research on second language acquisition in general, or on the acquisition of reading proficiency, foreign languages were taught as any other skill was taught.

Language teaching before the twentieth century is best depicted as a "tradition" that, in various manifestations and adaptations, has been practiced in language classrooms worldwide even up to the present time. Late in the nineteenth century, the Classical Method came to be known as the **Grammar Translation Method**. There was little to distinguish Grammar Translation from what had gone on in foreign language classrooms for centuries: explanations of grammar points, memorization of lists, and exercises in translation (Prator & Celce-Murcia, 1979). But the Grammar Translation Method remarkably withstood attempts at the outset of the twentieth century to "reform" language teaching methodology, and to this day it remains a standard methodology for language teaching in many educational institutions.

 CLASSROOM CONNECTIONS

Have you ever taken a foreign language that was taught through the Grammar Translation Method? How much of the language did you learn? How did you feel, emotionally, about the class? What, if anything, would you change about that class if you had to take it again (or teach it)?

It is remarkable, in one sense, that this method has been so stalwart among many competing models. It does virtually nothing to enhance a student's communicative ability in the language. It is, according to Jack Richards and Ted Rodgers, "remembered with distaste by thousands of school learners, for whom foreign language learning meant a tedious experience of memorizing endless lists of unusable grammar rules and vocabulary and attempting to produce perfect translations of stilted or literary prose" (Richards & Rodgers, 2001, p. 4).

In another sense, however, one can understand why Grammar Translation has been so popular. It requires few specialized skills on the part of teachers. Tests of grammar rules and of translations are easy to construct and can be objectively scored. Many standardized tests of foreign languages still do not attempt to tap into communicative abilities, so students have little motivation to go beyond grammar analogies, translations, and rote exercises. And it is sometimes successful in leading a student toward a reading knowledge of an L2.

In the final analysis, as Richards and Rodgers (2001, p. 7) pointed out, "It is a method for which there is no theory. There is no literature that offers a rationale or justification for it or that attempts to relate it to issues in linguistics, psychology, or educational theory." As you continue to examine theoretical principles in this book, I'm sure you will understand more fully the "theorylessness" of the Grammar Translation Method.

LANGUAGE TEACHING IN THE TWENTIETH CENTURY

Against the backdrop of the previous nineteen centuries, a glance through the past century or so of language teaching gives us a refreshingly colorful picture of varied interpretations of the "best" way to teach a foreign language. Perhaps beginning with François Gouin's (1880) Series Method, foreign language teaching witnessed some revolutionary trends, all of which in one way or another came under the scrutiny of scientific (or observational) research.

As schools of thought have come and gone, so have language teaching trends waxed and waned in popularity. Albert Marckwardt (1972, p. 5) saw these "changing winds and shifting sands" as a cyclical pattern in which a new para-digm (to use Kuhn's term) of teaching methodology emerged about every quarter of a century, with each new method breaking from the old, but at the same time taking with it some of the positive aspects of the previous paradigm. We might also describe trends across the decades as swings in a pendulum: focus on accuracy vs. focus on fluency, separation of skills vs. integration of skills, and teacher-centered vs. learner-centered approaches. More vividly, we could adopt Mitchell and Vidal's (2001, p. 27) metaphor to depict our journey across time as "that of a major river, constantly flowing, fed by many sources of water—rivers, streams, springs in remote territories, all fed by rain on wide expanses of land."

One of the best examples of both the cyclical (and fluvial) nature of methods is seen in the revolutionary **Audiolingual Method** (ALM) of the late 1940s and 1950s. The ALM, with its overemphasis on oral production drills, bor-rowed tenets from its predecessor by almost half a century, the **Direct Method**, but had essentially sprung from behavioral theories of learning of the time. The ALM rejected its classical predecessor, the Grammar Translation Method, by diminishing if not obliterating the need for metacognitive focus on the forms of language. Within a short time, however, with the increasing popularity of cogni-tive psychology, ALM critics were advocating more attention to rules and to the "cognitive code" of language, which, to some, smacked of a return to Grammar Translation. Shifting sands indeed, and the ebb and flow of paradigms!

 CLASSROOM CONNECTIONS

Have you ever taken a class that used the ALM or pattern drills? If so, was the drilling effective? In what circumstances do you think it is effective to use drills in the classroom?

Since the early 1970s, the symbiotic relationship of theoretical disciplines and teaching methodology has continued to manifest itself (Thomas, 1998). The field of psychology (as noted in this chapter in outlining tenets of construc-tivism) has witnessed a growing interest in interpersonal relationships, the value of group work, and the use of numerous cooperative strategies for attaining desired goals. The same era has seen linguists searching ever more deeply for answers to the nature of communication and communicative competence and for explanations of the interactive, sociocultural process of language acquisition.

The language teaching profession has mirrored these theoretical trends with approaches and techniques that have stressed the importance of self-efficacy, construction of identity, students cooperatively learning together, developing individual strategies for constructing meaning, and above all of focusing on the communicative process in language learning. Some of these methodological innovations will be described in subsequent chapters of this book.

Today, many of the pedagogical springs and rivers of the last few decades are appropriately captured in the term **Communicative Language Teaching** (CLT), now a catchphrase for language teachers. CLT, to be discussed further in Chapter 8, is an eclectic blend of previous methods into the best of what a teacher can provide in authentic uses of the L2 in the classroom. Indeed, the single greatest challenge in the profession is to move significantly beyond the teaching of rules, patterns, definitions, and other knowledge "about" language to the point that we are teaching our students to communicate genuinely, spontaneously, and meaningfully in the L2.

A significant difference between current language teaching practices and those of, perhaps a half a century ago, is the absence of proclaimed "orthodoxies" and "best" methods. We are well aware that **methods**, as they were conceived of forty or fifty years ago, are too narrow and too constrictive to apply to a wide range of learners in an enormous number of situational contexts. There are no instant recipes. No quick and easy method is guaranteed to provide success.

Brown (2001), Kumaravadivelu (2001), and Bell (2003) have all appropriately shown that pedagogical trends in language teaching now spur us to develop a principled basis on which teachers can choose particular designs and techniques for teaching an L2 in a specific context. Mellow (2002) calls this "principled eclecticism," while Richards & Rodgers (2001) refer to an **approach** in which every learner, every teacher, and every context is unique. Your task as a teacher is to understand the properties of those contexts. Then, using a cautious, enlightened, eclectic approach, you can build a set of foundation stones—a theory, or set of coherent perspectives—based on principles of L2 learning and teaching.

SUGGESTED READINGS

Ritchie, W., & Bhatia, T. (2009). (Eds.) *The new handbook of second language acquisition*. Bingley, UK: Emerald Group.

Hinkel, E. (Ed.). (2011). *Handbook of research in second language teaching and learning: Volume II*. New York: Routledge.

Both of these useful research tools offer comprehensive surveys of dozens of different subfields of SLA, written by well-known scholars in their respective fields. The volumes offer a wealth of bibliographic references within each chapter.

Kaufman, D. (2004). Constructivist issues in language learning and teaching. *Annual Review of Applied Linguistics*, 24, 303–319.

A readable summary and synopsis of constructivism in language that a novice in the field can understand.

Modern Language Journal, Fall 2000 (vol. 84, no. 4) and Spring 2001 (vol. 85, no. 1).

An informative picture of the last century of language teaching. Attention is given to the teaching of many different foreign languages

LANGUAGE LEARNING EXPERIENCE: JOURNAL ENTRY 1

In each chapter in this book, a brief set of journal-writing guidelines will be offered. Here, you are strongly encouraged to commit yourself to a process of weekly journal entries that chronicle a *previous* or *concurrent* L2 learning experience. In so doing, you will be better able to connect the issues that you read about in this book with a real-life, personal experience.

Remember, a journal is meant to be "freely" written, without much concern for beautiful prose, rhetorical eloquence, or even grammaticality. It is your diary in which you can spontaneously record feelings, thoughts, reactions, and questions. The prompts that are offered here are not meant to be exhaustive, so feel free to expand on them considerably.

There is one rule of thumb to follow in writing your journal: connect your own experiences learning a second/foreign language with issues and models and studies that are presented in the chapter. Your experiences then become vivid examples of what might otherwise remain somewhat abstract conceptualizations.

If you decide to focus your writing on a previous experience learning a foreign language, you will need to "age regress" yourself to the time that you were learning the language. If at all possible, choose a language you learned (or tried to learn!) as an adult, that is, after the age of twelve or so. Then, describe what you were feeling and thinking and doing then.

If your journal centers on a concurrent experience, so much the better, because your memory of the ongoing events will be more vivid. The journal-writing process may even prompt you to adopt certain strategies for more successful learning.

Guidelines for Entry 1

- As you start(ed) your L2 class, what is your overall emotional feeling? Are you overwhelmed? Scared? Challenged? Motivated? Is the course too easy? Too hard?
- How do you feel about your classmates? The class spirit or mood? Is the class "spirit" upbeat and motivating, or boring and tedious? What are the root causes of this general mood? Is it your own attitude, or the teacher's style, or the makeup of the class?
- Describe activities that you did in the early days of the class that illustrate (1) a behavioral perspective on second language acquisition, (2) a cognitive perspective, and (3) a constructivist perspective.
- Describe your teacher's teaching style. Is it effective? Why or why not? Does your teacher seem to have an approach to language teaching that is consistent with what you've read so far?

FOR THE TEACHER: ACTIVITIES (A) & DISCUSSION (D)

Note: For each of the "Classroom Connections" in this chapter, you may wish to turn them into individual or pair-work discussion questions.

1. (A) At the beginning of this chapter, two language learners are briefly described. Divide the class into pairs and assign one of the two learners to each group, and ask them to brainstorm what they speculate to be the cause(s) of success or failure for their assigned learner. What implications might these causes have for teaching second language learners in the classroom? Ask the groups to report their findings to the rest of the class.

2. (D) Look at the two definitions of language, one from a dictionary and the other from Pinker's (1994) book (page 6). Why are there differences between these two definitions? What assumptions or biases do they reflect on the part of the lexicographer? How do those definitions represent "condensed theories"?

3. (A) Consider the eight subfields of linguistics listed on page 7. Divide the class into pairs or small groups, and assign one subfield to each. Ask each pair to determine the type of approach to second language teaching that might emerge from emphasizing the *exclusive* importance of their particular subfield. Ask groups to report their findings to the rest of the class.

4. (A) Assign one of the three schools of thought described in this chapter to each of several small groups or pairs. Have them suggest some examples of activities in the language classroom that would be derived from their assigned perspective. From those examples, try to derive some simple descriptors of the three schools of thought.

5. (D) In the discussion of constructivism as a school of thought, Vygotsky is cited as a major influence in our understanding of constructivism, especially social constructivism. Ask students to restate Vygotsky's philosophy in their own words (e.g., the ZPD, how social interactions helped or hindered learning) and offer some classroom examples of Vygotsky's theories in action.

6. (A) Richards and Rodgers (2001) said the Grammar Translation Method "is a method for which there is no theory." Ask students in pairs or groups to share any experiences they have had with Grammar Translation in their L2 classes, and to evaluate its effectiveness. Do students agree with the statement? Have them report back to the whole class.

7. (D) At the end of the chapter, twentieth-century language teaching methodology is described as one that evolved into an *approach* rather than a specific accepted *method*, with the Direct Method and Audiolingual Method cited as examples of the latter. What is the difference between approach and method?

CHAPTER 2

FIRST LANGUAGE ACQUISITION

Stefanie, a five-year-old monolingual speaker of English, is excitedly retelling the story of The Wizard of Oz, *just seen on video. Let's listen in.*

. . . and, and then after that she dreamed, um, and then she was in her sleep when she woke up and, know what? she was, she was on her bed but she woke up, and, I didn't see her on her bed cause was dreaming about she woking up, then she dreamed about her, uh, then, know what? she saw (laughing) this is the funny part (laughing gleefully) when the tornado, the tornado blew her mother up she was sewing in a chair (still laughing) that's the funny part, and then, then a witch . . .

What wonderful verbal dynamos children can be! And what a vivid narrative of an amazing scene from a classic American film. Think about all the complexity embedded in her enthusiastic description, the syntactic sophistication, and the threads of discourse being spun into the tale. Oh sure, you can find an oddity here and there, a mish-mash of exploding ideas, but the excitement in Stefanie's story is sheer joy! Listen carefully the next time you hear a small child speak. You'll hear wonderful examples of a creative mind at work.

"Daddy, erase the window!" said a three-year-old child, on seeing a frosted window early in a midwinter morning. Daddy knew exactly what she meant. So did her five-year-old brother, when he declared, "My friend Morgan, she gots a smart phone," and his envious wide-eyed audience understood without blinking an eye. Yes, kids are creative, but they are systematic as well. How do they do this?

The amazing capacity for acquiring one's native language within the first few years of life has been a subject of interest for centuries. In the latter part of the eighteenth century, German philosopher Dietrich Tiedemann recorded his observations of the psychological and linguistic development of his young son. At the end of the nineteenth century, François Gouin observed the language acquisition of his nephew, and from those insights derived what came to be known as the Series Method of foreign language teaching.

But it was not until the second half of the twentieth century that researchers began to analyze child language systematically and to try to discover the nature of the psycholinguistic process that enables children to gain fluent control of an exceedingly complex system of communication. In a matter of a few decades, some giant strides were taken, especially in the generative and cognitive models of language, in describing the acquisition of particular languages as well as in probing universal aspects of acquisition.

Such research soon led language teachers and teacher educators to draw analogies between L1 and L2 acquisition, and even to justifying certain teaching methods and techniques on the basis of L1 learning principles. On the surface, it's entirely reasonable to make the analogy. All children, given a typical developmental environment, acquire their native languages fluently and efficiently. And they acquire them "naturally," without special instruction, although not without significant *effort* and *attention* to language.

However, direct comparisons between first and second language acquisition must be treated with caution. There are dozens of salient differences between L1 and L2 learning. The most obvious difference, in the case of adult SLA, is the tremendous cognitive and affective contrast between adults and children. A detailed examination of these differences is made in Chapter 3.

This chapter will outline issues in L1 learning as a foundation on which you can build an understanding of principles of L2 learning. Let's begin with theoretical models of L1 acquisition.

THEORIES OF FIRST LANGUAGE ACQUISITION

Everyone at some time has witnessed the remarkable ability of children to communicate. Small babies, babble, coo, and cry, sending an extraordinary number of messages and, of course, receiving even more messages. As they reach the end of their first year, children make specific attempts to imitate words and speech sounds they hear around them, and about this time they utter their first "words." By about eighteen months of age, these words have multiplied considerably and are beginning to appear in two-word and three-word "sentences"—commonly referred to as "telegraphic" utterances—such as the following (Clark, 2003):

all gone milk	shoe off	baby go boom
bye-bye Daddy	Mommy sock	put down floor
gimme toy	there cow	this one go bye

The production tempo now begins to increase as more and more words are spoken every day and more and more combinations of multiword sentences are uttered. By two years of age, children comprehend more sophisticated language and their production repertoire is mushrooming, even to forming questions and negatives (Clark, 2003):

where my mitten?	that not rabbits house
what Jeff doing?	I don't need pants off
why not me sleeping?	that not red, that blue

By about age three, children can comprehend an amazing quantity of linguistic input. Their speech and comprehension capacity increases daily as they become the generators of nonstop chattering and incessant conversation. Language thereby becoming a mixed blessing for those around them! Their creativity alone brings smiles to parents and older siblings (O'Grady, 2005; Clark, 2009):

Who deaded that fly? [two-year-old]
Headlights . . . are lights that go on in the head. [three-year-old]
Will you climb me up there and hold me? [three-year-old]
Is this where you get safe? [three-year-old in a "*Safe*way" supermarket]
We have two kinds of corn. Popcorn . . . it crunches. And corn . . . it
    doesn't crunch, its eats. [three-year-old]

This fluency and creativity continues into school age as children internalize increasingly complex structures, expand their vocabulary, and sharpen communicative skills. At school age, children not only learn what to say but what *not* to say as they become more aware of the situated functions of their language.

How can we explain this fantastic journey from that first anguished cry at birth to adult competence in a language? From the first word to tens of thousands? From telegraphese at eighteen months to the complex, cognitively precise, socioculturally appropriate sentences just a few short years later? These are the sorts of questions that research on language acquisition attempts to answer.

One could adopt one of two polarized positions in the study of L1 acquisition. Using the schools of thought referred to in the previous chapter, an extreme behaviorist position would claim that children come into the world with a **tabula rasa**, a clean slate, bearing no preconceived notions about the world or about language. Children are then shaped by their environment and slowly conditioned through various rewards.

At the other extreme is the position that relies on two hypotheses: (1) children come into this world with very specific innate knowledge, predispositions, and biological timetables, and (2) children learn to function in a language chiefly through interaction and discourse.

These perspectives represent opposites on a continuum, with many possible positions in between. Three points are explained in this chapter. The first (behavioral) position is set in contrast to the second (nativist) and third (functional) positions.

Behavioral Approaches

Daddy walks into his house, and his nine-month-old child gleefully exclaims, "Da da!" Daddy grins widely, gives his daughter a big hug, and responds, "Hi, sweetie!"

The process of reinforcement of linguistic utterances is once again played out. A **behavioral** perspective of course easily explains such exchanges as the result of an emitted or stimulated "response" (utterance) that is immediately rewarded (reinforced), thereby encouraging (stimulating) further linguistic attempts from the child.

In examining language "behavior" in children, behavioral psychologists look at immediately perceptible aspects of linguistic behavior—what they might call "publicly observable responses"—and the associations between those responses and perceived rewards in the world surrounding them. "Effective" language behavior is seen as the production of desired responses to stimuli. If a particular response is rewarded, it then becomes habitual, or conditioned.

The model works for comprehension as well as production, although correct comprehension is not, strictly speaking, publicly observable. One must observe context and nonverbal behavior to confirm comprehension. A behavioral view claims that a child demonstrates comprehension of an utterance by responding appropriately to it, and then upon reinforcement of that appropriate response, internalizes (or learns) linguistic meanings. "Want some milk?" asks the mother of an eight-month-old child. The child holds out his cup and says "mi--." Conclusion? The child's verbal and nonverbal response demonstrates correct comprehension of the initial offer.

One of the earliest attempts to construct a behavioral model of language acquisition was embodied in B.F. Skinner's classic, *Verbal Behavior* (1957). Skinner was commonly known for his experiments with animal behavior, but he also gained recognition for his contributions to education through teaching machines and programmed learning (Skinner, 1968). Skinner's theory of verbal behavior was an extension of his general theory of learning by operant conditioning.

Operant conditioning refers to conditioning in which the organism (in this case, a human being) emits a response, or **operant** (a sentence or utterance), without necessarily observable stimuli; that operant is maintained (learned) by reinforcement (for example, a positive verbal or nonverbal response from another person). If a child says "want milk" and a parent gives the child some milk, the operant is reinforced and, over repeated instances, is conditioned. According to Skinner, verbal behavior, like other behavior, is controlled by its consequences. When consequences are rewarding, behavior is maintained and is increased in strength and perhaps frequency. When consequences are punishing, or when there is a total lack of reinforcement, the behavior is weakened and eventually extinguished.

 CLASSROOM CONNECTIONS

What are some examples of operant conditioning techniques that you have experienced in learning or teaching an L2? (Examples include repetition of modeled language, drills of various kinds.) For each technique that you can think of, what is the reinforcement given? How effective was the technique, in your experience?

Challenges to Behavioral Approaches

Skinner's theories attracted a number of critics, not the least among them Chomsky (1959), who penned a highly critical review of *Verbal Behavior*. Some years later, however, MacCorquodale (1970) published a reply to Chomsky's review in which he eloquently defended Skinner's points of view. The controversy raged on.

Today virtually no one would agree that Skinner's model of verbal behavior adequately accounts for the capacity to acquire language, for language development itself, for the abstract nature of language, or for a theory of meaning. A theory based on conditioning and reinforcement is hard-pressed to explain the fact that every sentence you speak or write—with a few trivial exceptions—is novel, never before uttered either by you or by anyone else! These novel utterances are nevertheless created by very young children as they "play" with language, and that same creativity continues into adulthood and throughout one's life.

 CLASSROOM CONNECTIONS

Children are excellent at "playing" with language, experimenting with words and combinations of words. Language play seems to have a positive effect for long-term acquisition. Have you ever played with a language you have taken in a classroom? What kinds of "games" might be useful in teaching a second language to adults?

In an attempt to broaden the base of behavioral theory, some psychologists proposed modified theoretical positions. One of these positions was **mediation theory**, (Osgood, 1953, 1957) in which meaning was accounted for by the claim that the linguistic stimulus (a word or sentence) elicits a "mediating" response that is covert and invisible, acting within the learner.

Mediation theories were criticized on several fronts. There was too much "mentalism" (speculating about unobservable behavior) involved for some, and others saw little relationship between meaning and utterance. Jenkins and Palermo (1964), for example, attempted to synthesize generative and mediational approaches to child language by asserting that the child acquires frames and patterns of sentence elements, and then learns the stimulus-response equivalences that can be substituted within each frame. But this approach also fell short of accounting for the abstract nature of language, for the child's creativity, and for the interactive nature of language acquisition. Oddly, a recent revival of mediation theory (Lantolf, 2000, 2011) is enjoying considerable attention!

As interest in behaviorism waned, generative and cognitive research opened the doors to new approaches that emphasized the presumed innate properties of language, and subsequently the importance of social interaction in child first language acquisition.

The Nativist Approach

The term **nativist** is derived from the fundamental assertion that language acquisition is innately determined, that we are born with a genetic capacity that predisposes us to a systematic perception of language around us, resulting in the construction of an internalized system of language.

Innateness hypotheses spawned several proposals about human language acquisition. Eric Lenneberg (1967) suggested that language is a "species-specific" behavior and that certain modes of perception, categorizing abilities, and other language-related mechanisms are biologically determined. Chomsky (1965) similarly claimed that innate properties of language explained the child's mastery of a native language in such a short time despite the highly abstract nature of the rules of language. This innate knowledge, according to Chomsky, was embodied in a metaphorical "little black box" in the brain, a **language acquisition device** (LAD). David McNeill (1966) described the LAD as consisting of four innate linguistic properties:

1. The ability to distinguish speech sounds from other sounds in the environment
2. The ability to organize linguistic data into various classes that can later be refined
3. Knowledge that only a certain kind of linguistic system is possible and that other kinds are not
4. The ability to engage in constant evaluation of the developing linguistic system so as to construct the simplest possible system out of the available linguistic input

McNeill and others in the Chomskyan tradition composed eloquent arguments for the appropriateness of the LAD proposition, especially in contrast to behavioral stimulus-response (S-R) theory, which could not account for the creativity present in child language. The notion of linguistically-oriented innate predispositions fit perfectly with generative theories of language: children were presumed to use innate abilities to *generate* a potentially infinite number of utterances. Aspects of meaning, abstractness, and creativity were accounted for more adequately. Even though it was readily recognized that the LAD was not literally a cluster of brain cells that could be isolated and neurologically located, such inquiry on the cognitive side of the linguistic-psychological continuum stimulated a great deal of fruitful research.

More recently, researchers in the nativist tradition continued this line of inquiry through a genre of child language acquisition research that focuses on what has come to be known as **Universal Grammar** (Cook, 1993; Mitchell & Myles, 1998; Gass & Selinker, 2001; White, 2003, 2012; Bhatia & Ritchie, 2009).

This line of research expanded the LAD notion by positing a system of universal linguistic rules that went well beyond what was originally proposed for the LAD. Universal Grammar (UG) research attempts to discover what it is that children, regardless of their environmental stimuli (the language[s] they hear around them) bring to the language acquisition process. Such studies have looked at question formation, negation, word order, discontinuity of embedded clauses (The ball that's on the table is blue), subject deletion ("Es mi hermano" —He is my brother), and other grammatical phenomena. (More details about UG are covered in a later section of this chapter.)

One of the more practical contributions of nativist theories is evident if you look at the kinds of discoveries that have been made about how the system of child language works. Research has shown that the child's language, at any given point, is a legitimate system in its own right. The child's linguistic development is not a process of developing fewer and fewer "incorrect" structures—not a language in which earlier stages have more "mistakes" than later stages. Rather, the child's language at any stage is **systematic** in that the child is constantly forming hypotheses on the basis of the input received and then testing those hypotheses in speech (and comprehension). As the child's language develops, those hypotheses are continually revised, reshaped, or sometimes abandoned.

Before generative linguistics came into vogue, Jean Berko (1958) demonstrated that children learn language not as a series of separate discrete items but as an integrated system. Using a simple nonsense-word test, Berko discovered that English-speaking children as young as four years of age applied rules for the formation of plural, present progressive, past tense, third singular, and possessives. She found, for example, that if children saw a drawing of an object labeled as a "wug" they could easily talk about two "wugs," or if they were presented with a person who knows how to "gling," children could talk about a person who "glinged" yesterday, or sometimes who "glang."

 CLASSROOM CONNECTIONS

In your experience learning an L2, do you think you have made "systematic" extrapolations of perceived rules as children do? Do you remember any instances of regularizing irregular verbs? Forming questions with logical but incorrect forms? Using a new word or phrase in what you thought was the appropriate context—but it turned out that you overgeneralized? If so, try to recall them, and analyze the origin of these errors. If you have taught (or are teaching) a second language, in what ways have you seen or heard your students being "creative" with language? And if so, what has been your response?

Nativist studies of child language acquisition were free to construct hypothetical **grammars** (that is, descriptions of linguistic systems) of child language, although such grammars were still solidly based on empirical data. Linguists began to examine child language from early one-, two-, and three-word forms of "telegraphese" (like "allgone milk" and "baby go boom" mentioned earlier) to the complex language of five- to ten-year-olds. Borrowing one tenet of structural and behavioral paradigms, they approached the data with few preconceived notions about what the child's language ought to be, and probed the data for internally consistent systems, in much the same way that a linguist describes a language in the "field."

A generative framework turned out to be ideal for describing such processes. The early grammars of child language were referred to as **pivot grammars**. It was commonly observed that the child's first two-word utterances seemed to manifest two separate word classes, and not simply two words thrown together at random. Consider the following utterances: "my cap"; "that horsie"; "bye-bye Jeff"; "Mommy sock." Linguists noted that the words on the left-hand side seemed to belong to a class that words on the right-hand side generally did not belong to. That is, *my* could co-occur with *cap, horsie, Jeff,* or *sock,* but not with *that* or *bye-bye. Mommy* is, in this case, a word that belongs in both classes. The first class of words was called "pivot," since they could pivot around a number of words in the second, "open" class. Thus the first rule of the generative grammar of the child was described as follows:

Sentence ↦ pivot word + open word

Research data gathered in the generative framework yielded a multitude of such rules. Some of these rules appear to be grounded in the UG of the child. As the child's language matures and finally becomes adult like, the number and complexity of generative rules accounting for language competence, of course, boggles the mind.

Challenges to Nativist Approaches

In subsequent years the generative rule-governed model in the Chomskyan tradition was challenged. The assumption underlying this tradition was that those generative rules, or "items" in a linguistic sense, are connected **serially**, with one connection between each pair of neurons in the brain. A "messier but more fruitful picture" (Spolsky, 1989, p. 149) was provided by what has come to be known as the **parallel distributed processing** (PDP) model, based on the notion that information is processed simultaneously at several levels of attention. As you read the words on this page, your brain is attending to letters, word juncture and meaning, syntactic relationships, textual discourse, as well as background experiences (schemata) that you bring to the text. A child's (or adult's) linguistic performance may be the consequence of many levels of simultaneous neural interconnections rather, than a serial process of one rule being applied, then another, then another, and so forth.

A simple analogy to music may further illustrate this complex notion. Think of an orchestra playing a symphony. The score for the symphony may have, let's say, twelve separate parts that are performed simultaneously. The "symphony" of the human brain enables us to process many segments and levels of language, cognition, affect, and perception all at once—in a parallel configuration. And so, according to the PDP model, a sentence—which has phonological, morphological, syntactic, lexical, semantic, discourse, sociolinguistic, and strategic properties—is not "generated" by a series of rules (Ney & Pearson, 1990; Sokolik, 1990). Rather, sentences are the result of the *simultaneous* interconnection of a multitude of brain cells.

 CLASSROOM CONNECTIONS

Take yourself back to a classroom hour during the first weeks of learning (or attempting to learn) a foreign language. Try to remember a set of sentences that were presented to you (greetings, for example). How many levels, or perceptions—in parallel—was your brain attending to in a simple exchange of greetings? At what point might there be an "overload" at this beginning level, one that would create so many neural interconnections that you would be overwhelmed?

Closely related to the PDP concept is a branch of psycholinguistic inquiry called **connectionism** (Rumelhart & McClelland, 1986), in which neurons in the brain are said to form multiple connections: each of the 100 billion nerve cells in the brain may be linked to thousands of its counterparts. In this approach, experience leads to learning by strengthening particular connections—sometimes at the expense of weakening others.

For example, the L1 acquisition of English regular past tense forms by children may proceed as a series of connections. First, a child may confidently connect the form *went* with the verb *go*. Then, children will often perceive another connection, the regular *-ed* suffix attached to a verb, and start using the word *goed*. Later, with more complex connections, children will perceive *goed* as incorrect, and maintain both connections: the *-ed* form connected to most verbs, and the *went* form as a "special" connection. "According to such accounts, there are no 'rules' of grammar. Instead, the systematicities of syntax emerge from the set of learned associations between language functions and base and past tense forms, with novel responses generated by 'online' generalizations from stored examples" (N. Ellis, 2003, p. 88).

Finally, in recent years a further development of connectionist models of language acquisition is seen in a position that hearkens back to the spirit of behavioral approaches. **Emergentism**, a perspective, espoused by William O'Grady (1999, 2003, 2012), O'Grady, Lee and Kwak (2009), MacWhinney (1999), and others essentially makes the following claim:

> The complexity of language emerges from a relatively simple developmental process being exposed to a massive and complex environment. The interactions that constitute language are associations, billions of connections, which co-exist within a neural system as organisms co-exist within an eco-system. And systematicities emerge as a result of their interactions and mutual constraints (N. Ellis, 2003, p. 81).

This perspective disagrees sharply with earlier nativist views by suggesting that "this "strategy [the search for an 'acquisition device'] is misguided and that language acquisition is a secondary effect of processing amelioration" (O'Grady, 2012, p. 116).

Emergentism represents a more cautious approach to a theory of language acquisition than was evident in the early nativist claims, some arguments (Schwartz, 1999) notwithstanding. First, we must give due attention to the importance of *input* in acquisition (Ellis, 2006b; O'Grady, Lee & Kwak, 2009). Because a child is exposed to a limited sample of language, we are spurred to carefully examine *observable* linguistic performance in the child's environment. We are also reminded of the crucial role of *frequency* of input (Ellis, 2006b). And further, by attending to the identification of neurolinguistic components of language acquisition (Schumann et al., 2004), researchers can be more cautious about making overly "mentalistic" claims about the psychological reality of rule construction in language acquisition.

Research from within the nativist framework, including the challenges just outlined above, has made several important contributions to our understanding of the L1 acquisition process:

1. Freedom from the restrictions of the "scientific method" to explore the unseen, unobservable, underlying, abstract linguistic structures being developed in the child
2. The construction of a number of potential properties of Universal Grammar, through which we can better understand not just language acquisition but the nature of human languages in general
3. Systematic description of the child's linguistic repertoire as either rule-governed, or operating out of parallel distributed processing capacities, or the result of experiential establishment of connections

Functional Approaches

More recently, with an increase in constructivist perspectives on the study of language, we have seen a shift in patterns of research. The shift has not been so much away from the generative/cognitive side of the continuum, but rather a move more deeply into the essence of language. Two emphases have emerged: (1) Researchers began to see that language was just one manifestation of the cognitive and affective ability to deal with the world, with others, and with the self. (2) Moreover, the generative rules that were proposed under the nativist framework were abstract, formal, explicit, and quite logical, yet they dealt specifically with the **forms** of language and not with the deeper **functional** levels of meaning constructed from social interaction. Examples of forms of language are morphemes, words, sentences, and the rules that govern them. Functions are the meaningful, interactive purposes within a social (pragmatic) context that we accomplish with the forms.

Cognition and Language Development

Lois Bloom (1971) cogently illustrated the first issue in her criticism of pivot grammar when she pointed out that the relationships in which words occur in telegraphic utterances are only superficially similar. For example, in the utterance "Mommy sock," which nativists would describe as a sentence consisting of a pivot word and an open word, Bloom found at least three possible underlying relations: agent-action (Mommy is putting the sock on), agent-object (Mommy sees the sock), and possessor-possessed (Mommy's sock). By examining data in reference to contexts, Bloom concluded that children learn underlying structures, and not superficial word order. Thus, depending on the social context, "Mommy sock" could mean a number of different things to a child.

 CLASSROOM CONNECTIONS

Why don't we present "telegraphese" sentences to beginning learners in a foreign language class? Imagine some telegraphic utterances in a foreign language you have learned. How plausible (or ridiculous) would it be to practice those utterances? Would you sound too childlike, or would they work as interim communication strategies?

Bloom's research paved the way for a new wave of child language study, this time centering on the relationship of cognitive development to L1 acquisition. Jean Piaget (1955; Piaget & Inhelder, 1969) described overall development as the result of children's interaction with their environment. According to Piaget, what children learn about language is determined by what they already know about the world. Gleitman and Wanner (1982, p. 13) noted in their review of the state of the art in child language research at that time, "children appear to approach language learning equipped with conceptual interpretive abilities for categorizing the world."

Dan Slobin (1971, 1986, 1997), among others, demonstrated that in all languages, semantic learning depends on cognitive development and that sequences of development are determined more by semantic complexity than by structural complexity. Bloom (1976, p. 37) likewise noted that "what children know will determine what they learn about the code for both speaking and understanding messages." So child language researchers began to tackle the child's acquisition of the *functions* of language, and the relationships of the forms of language to those functions.

Social Interaction and Language Development

In recent years, it has become quite clear that language development is intertwined, not just with cognition and memory, but also with social and functional acquisition. Holzman (1984), Berko-Gleason, (1988), and Lock (1991) all looked at the interaction between the child's language acquisition and the learning of how social systems operate in human behavior. Other investigations of child language (Kuczaj, 1984; Budwig, 1995) centered on one of the thorniest areas of linguistic research: interactive, communicative functions of language. What do children learn about talking with others? About connected pieces of **discourse** (relations between sentences)? The interaction between hearer and speaker? Conversational cues? Within such a perspective, the very heart of language—its communicative and pragmatic function—is being tackled in all its variability (Clark, 2003; O'Grady, 2005).

Of significance in this genre of research is the renewed interest in the *performance* level of language. The overt responses that were so carefully observed by structuralists—and hastily weeded out as "performance variables" by generative linguists in their zeal to get at "competence"—returned to the forefront. Hesitations, pauses, backtracking, and the like are indeed significant conversational cues. Even some of the contextual categories described by—of all people—Skinner, in *Verbal Behavior*, turn out to be relevant! The linguist can no longer deal with abstract, formal rules without dealing with all the minutiae of day-to-day performance that were previously set aside in a search for systematicity.

 CLASSROOM CONNECTIONS

Adult L2 instruction—even in communicative approaches—typically includes an emphasis on the *structure* of the language, and also *vocabulary*. In other words, students are taught the *forms* of language. What has been your experience? Do you think foreign language classrooms should put less emphasis on *form* and more emphasis on communication, social interaction, and discourse? What would be an appropriate "mix" of form and function?

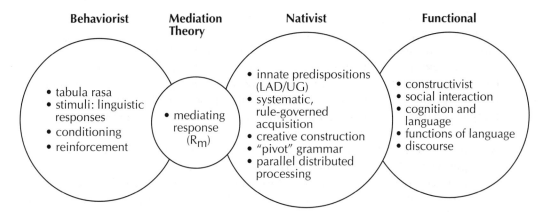

| Behaviorist | Mediation Theory | Nativist | Functional |

- tabula rasa
- stimuli: linguistic responses
- conditioning
- reinforcement

- mediating response (R_m)

- innate predispositions (LAD/UG)
- systematic, rule-governed acquisition
- creative construction
- "pivot" grammar
- parallel distributed processing

- constructivist
- social interaction
- cognition and language
- functions of language
- discourse

Figure 2.1   Theories of first language acquisition

Several perspectives have been sketched out here, as summarized in Figure 2.1. A complete, consistent, unified theory of L1 acquisition is yet on the horizon; however, L1 research has made enormous strides toward that ultimate goal. And even if all the answers are far from evident, maybe we are asking more of the right questions.

ISSUES IN FIRST LANGUAGE ACQUISITION

Intertwining all the above perspectives are issues, questions, and controversies that carry over into quite a number of domains of inquiry in linguistics and psychology. A sketch of these issues will lay the groundwork for understanding some of the variables surrounding SLA that will be taken up in subsequent chapters.

Competence and Performance

Let's go back to Stefanie, the five-year-old monolingual English speaker quoted at the beginning of the chapter. Obviously fond of recounting stories, she is now retelling another story, this time a TV program:

> They heared 'em underground ca-cause they went through a hoyle—a hole—and they pulled a rock from underground and then they saw a wave going in—that the hole—and they brought a table and the wave brought 'em out the k—tunnel and then the—they went away and then, uh, um, ah, back on top and it was, uh, going under a bridge and they went—then the braves hit the—the bridge—they—all of it, th-then they looked there, then they, then they were safe.

The story is replete with what a linguist would call *performance* variables: hesitations, repetitions, false starts, and self-corrections. Is it possible to "weed out" those performance glitches and be left with her basic competence?

For centuries scientists and philosophers have drawn a basic distinction between competence and performance. **Competence** refers to one's underlying knowledge of a system, event, or fact. It is the nonobservable *ability* to do something—to perform something. **Performance** is the overtly observable and concrete manifestation, or realization, of competence. It is the *actual doing* of something: walking, singing, dancing, speaking. The competence–performance distinction is exemplified in all walks of life. In businesses, workers are expected to perform their jobs "competently," that is, to exhibit skills that match their expected competence. In educational circles we have assumed that children possess certain competence in given areas (or standards) and that this competence can be measured by elicited samples of performance called tests and examinations.

Think of language competence and performance in the horticultural metaphor of a tree, as illustrated in Figure 2.2. The "invisible" roots of competence nourish and sustain the outwardly visible branches, leaves, and fruit of production.

In reference to language, competence is one's underlying knowledge of the system of a language—its rules of grammar, vocabulary, all the "pieces" of a language, and how those pieces fit together. Performance is actual production (speaking, writing) or the comprehension (listening, reading) of linguistic events. Chomsky (1965) likened competence to an "idealized" speaker-hearer who does not display such performance variables as memory limitations, distractions, shifts of attention and interest, errors, and hesitation phenomena (e.g., repeats, false starts, pauses, omissions). Chomsky's point was that a theory of language had to be a theory of competence lest the linguist try in vain to categorize an infinite number of performance variables that are not reflective of the underlying linguistic ability of the speaker-hearer.

The distinction is one that linguists and psychologists in the generative/cognitive framework operated under for some time, a mentalistic construct that structuralists and behaviorists obviously discounted, as competence is unobservable. Brown and Bellugi (1964) gave us a delightful example of the difficulty of attempting to extract underlying grammatical knowledge from children. Unlike adults, who can be asked, for example, whether it is better to say "two foots" or "two feet," children exhibit what is called the "pop-go-weasel" effect, as witnessed in the following dialogue between an adult and a two-year-old child:

> **Adult:** Now Adam, listen to what I say. Tell me which is better to say: *some water* or *a water?*
> **Adam:** Pop go weasel.

The child obviously had no interest in—or cognizance of—the adult's grammatical interrogation and therefore said whatever he wanted to! The researcher is thus forced to devise indirect methods of judging competence.

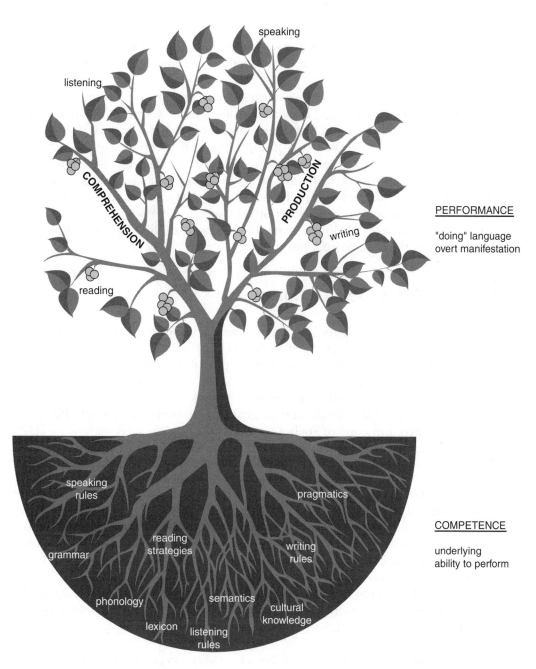

Figure 2.2 Horticultural depiction of language competence and performance

Among those methods are the audio or video recording and transcription of countless hours of speech followed by rigorous analysis, and/or the direct administration of certain imitation, production, or comprehension tests, all with numerous disadvantages.

Now let's return to the five-year-old's narrative at the beginning of this section. On the surface it might appear that Stefanie is severely impaired in her attempts to communicate. In fact, I once presented this same transcript, without identification of the speaker, to a group of speech therapists and asked them to analyze the various possible "disorders" manifested in the data. After they cited quite a number of technical instances of aphasia, I gleefully informed them of the real source! The point is that every day in our processing of linguistic data, we comprehend such strings of speech and comprehend them rather well because we know something about storytelling, hesitation phenomena, and the context of a narrative.

 CLASSROOM CONNECTIONS

Have you ever visited a country where another language is used and tried to make yourself understood by shopkeepers, vendors, or cab drivers? Your attempts were probably riddled with errors as you "butchered" the language. What would you think of a teacher who forced you into such situations (through role-play simulations) in a beginning language *classroom*? What would be the pros and cons of such a technique?

If we were to record many more samples of the five-year-old's speech, we would still be faced with the problem of inferring her competence. What is her knowledge of the verb system? Or her concept of a "sentence"? Even if we administer rather carefully designed tests of comprehension or production to a child, we are still left with the problem of accurately inferring the child's underlying competence. Continued research helps us to confirm those inferences through multiple observations.

Adult talk is often no less fraught with monstrosities, as we can see in the following verbatim transcription of comments made on a talk show by a professional golfer discussing tips on how to improve a golf game.

> Concentration is important. But uh—I also—to go with this of course if you're playing well—if you're playing well then you get up-tight about your game. You get keyed up and it's easy to concentrate. You know you're playing well and you know . . . in with a chance than it's easier, much easier to—to you know get in there and—and start to . . . you don't have to think about it. I mean it's got to be automatic.

Perhaps the guest would have been better off if he had simply uttered the very last sentence and omitted all the previous verbiage!

The competence–performance model has not met with universal acceptance. Major criticisms focus on the notion that competence, as defined by Chomsky, consists of the abilities of an *idealized* hearer-speaker, devoid of any so-called performance variables. Stubbs (1996), reviewing the issue, asserted that the only option for linguists is to study language in *use.* Tarone (1988) pointed out that a child's (or adult's) slips, hesitations, and self-corrections are potentially connected to what she calls **heterogeneous competence**—abilities that are in the process of being formed. So, while we may be tempted to claim that our five-year-old story teller knows the difference, say, between a "hole" and a "hoyle," we must not too quickly pass off the latter as an irrelevant slip of the tongue.

What can we conclude about language acquisition theory based on a competence–performance model? A cautious approach to inferring someone's competence will allow you to draw some conclusions about overall ability while still leaving the door open for the relevance of many linguistic tidbits that might otherwise be discarded.

Comprehension and Production

Look at this typical child-adult exchange:

Three-year-old Lisa:	*My name is Litha.*
Adult:	*Litha?*
Lisa:	*No, Litha.*
Adult:	*Oh, Lisa.*
Lisa:	*Yeah, Litha.*

(Miller 1963, p. 863)

Lisa clearly perceives the contrast between English *s* and *th*, even though she cannot produce the contrast herself, a common characteristic of L1 acquisition. Of course, we know that even adults understand more vocabulary and grammatical structure than they produce in speech and writing. How are we to explain this difference, this apparent "lag" between comprehension and production?

First, let's dispel a myth. **Comprehension** (listening, reading) must *not* be equated with competence, nor should **production** (speaking, writing) be thought of only as performance. Human beings have the *competence* (the internal unobservable mental and physical "wiring") both to understand *and* to produce language. We also *perform* acts of listening and reading just as surely as we perform acts of speaking and writing. Don't let the beginnings of the two pairs of words confuse you!

Second, we can generally concede that for child language, most research evidence points to the superiority of comprehension over production. Children seem to understand "more" than they actually produce. For instance, a four-year-old child may understand a sentence with a relative clause, such as "Give me the ball that's red," but not be able to produce it word for word, "Okay, Daddy, red ball" (Brown, 1970).

Finally, while much of our linguistic competence may "cross over" lines of distinction between comprehension and production, we are compelled to make a distinction between production competence and comprehension competence. A theory of language must include some accounting of the separation of these two broad categories. In fact, linguistic competence no doubt has multiple modes, well beyond the typical "four skills" of speaking, listening, reading, and writing. Within each skill are competencies that range from phonology to discourse, across a variety of sociolinguistic contexts, and encompassing numerous strategic options.

 CLASSROOM CONNECTIONS

Since both children and adults are able to comprehend more language than they produce, Asher (1977) and others advocated a "comprehension approach" to language teaching. This is often in contrast to many language courses that start you off from the first day with practice in *speaking* the language. For a beginning level of language, which do you think should come first? At the same level, how much time do you think should be devoted to comprehension (listening, reading)? Would your answer be different for higher levels of ability?

Nature or Nurture?

Nativists contend that a child is born with an innate knowledge of or predisposition toward language, and that this innate property (the LAD or UG) is universal in all human beings (Pinker, 2007). The innateness hypothesis was a possible resolution of the contradiction between the behavioral notion that language is a set of habits that can be acquired by a process of conditioning and the fact that such conditioning is much too slow and inefficient a process to account for the acquisition of a phenomenon as complex as language.

But the innateness hypothesis presented a conundrum. First, having "explained" language acquisition by means of the LAD, we have to admit that we have little scientific, genetic evidence thus far of such a "device" (Clark, 2009). Then, if you adopt an emergentist perspective, you must challenge the notion that what is innate is grammatical or linguistic at all (O'Grady, 2012). Moreover, fifty years since the LAD was first proposed, we have only scant genetic (scientific) evidence of the transmission of certain abilities, claims about the "FOXP2" gene, notwithstanding (Shenk, 2011). Will we one day find hard evidence of "language genes," thus putting to rest all the conjecture about an innate acquisition device?

Perhaps we should not put all our eggs in the innateness basket. Environmental factors cannot by any means be ignored, as connectionists and emergentists have shown. For years linguists, psychologists, and educators have been embroiled in the "nature-nurture" controversy: What are those behaviors that "nature" provides innately, in some sort of predetermined biological time-table, and what behaviors are internalized by environmental exposure, "nurture," or conscious attention? (Brizendine, 2010) We do observe that language acquisition is universal. But how are the efficiency and success of that learning determined by the environment of the child? Or by the child's individual construction of linguistic reality in interaction with others? The waters of the innateness hypothesis are considerably muddied by such questions.

An interesting line of research on innateness was pursued by Derek Bickerton (1981), who found evidence, across a number of languages, of common patterns of linguistic and cognitive development. He proposed that human beings are "bio-programmed" to proceed from stage to stage. Like flowering plants, people are innately programmed to "release" certain properties of language at certain developmental ages. Just as we cannot make a geranium bloom "before its time," so human beings will "bloom" in predetermined, preprogrammed steps (Bickerton, 2010).

Universals

Closely related to the innateness controversy is the claim that language is universally acquired in the same manner, and moreover, that the deep structure of language may be common to all languages. Decades ago Werner Leopold (1949), who was far ahead of his time, made an eloquent case for certain phonological and grammatical universals in language. Leopold inspired later work by Greenberg (1963, 1966), Bickerton (1981, 2010), Slobin (1986, 1992, 1997), and White (1989, 2003), among others.

Currently, as noted earlier in this chapter, research on Universal Grammar continues this quest. One of the keys to such inquiry lies in research on child language acquisition across many different languages in order to determine the commonalities. Dan Slobin (1986, 1992, 1997) and his colleagues gathered data on language acquisition in, among other languages, Japanese, French, Spanish, German, Polish, Hebrew, and Turkish. Interesting universals of pivot grammar and other telegraphese emerged. Maratsos (1988) enumerated some of the universal linguistic categories under investigation by a number of different researchers:

Word order
Morphological marking tone
Agreement (e.g., of subject and verb)
Reduced reference (e.g., pronouns, ellipsis) nouns and noun classes
Verbs and verb classes
Predication
Negation
Question formation

CLASSROOM CONNECTIONS

Think about a foreign language you are familiar with and as you compare it with your native language, do any of the above categories ring true? For example, does word order make a difference in meaning? Do people make questions by transforming a declarative sentence in some way? If so, how might you capitalize on those universals to help students understand certain variations in the language you are teaching?

Much of current UG research is centered around what have come to be known as principles and parameters. **Principles** are invariable characteristics of human language that appear to apply to all languages universally, such as those listed above. Vivian Cook (1997, pp. 250–251) offered a simple analogy: Rules of the road in driving universally require the driver to keep to one side of the road; this is a principle. But in some countries you must keep to the left (e.g., the United Kingdom, Japan) and in others keep to the right (e.g., the United States, Taiwan); the latter is a parameter.

So, **parameters** vary across languages. Lydia White (2003, p. 9) noted that "UG includes [rules] with a limited number of built-in options (*settings* or *values*), which allow for cross-linguistic variation. Such [rules] are known as *parameters*." If, for example, all languages adhere to the principle of assigning meaning to word order, then depending on the specific language in question, variations in word order (e.g., subject-verb-object; subject-object-verb, etc.) will apply. Or, as Cook and Newson (1996) demonstrated, all languages have "head parameter" constraints in phrases. Some languages are "head first" (e.g., English: "kicked the ball") and others (e.g., Japanese: "wa kabe ni kakkatte imasu"—(something) is hanging on the wall) are "head last."

According to some researchers, the child's initial state is said to "consist of a set of universal principles which specify some limited possibilities of variation, expressible in terms of parameters which need to be fixed in one of a few possible ways" (Saleemi, 1992, p. 58). In simpler terms, this means that the child's task of language learning is manageable because of certain naturally occurring constraints. For example, the principle of structure dependency "states that language is organized in such a way that it crucially depends on the structural relationships between elements in a sentence (such as words, morphemes, etc.)" (Holzman, 1998, p. 49). Take, for example, the following sentences:

1. The boy kicked the ball.
2. The boy that's wearing a red shirt and standing next to my brother kicked the ball.
3. She's a great teacher.
4. Is she a great teacher?

The first two sentences rely on a structural grouping, characteristic of all languages, called "phrase," or more specifically, "noun phrase." Without awareness of such a principle, someone would get all tangled up in sentence (2). Likewise, the principle of word order permutation allows one to perceive the difference between (3) and (4).

Systematicity and Variability

One of the assumptions of a good deal of current research on child language is the **systematicity** of the process of acquisition. From pivot grammar to three- and four-word utterances, and to full sentences of almost indeterminate length, children exhibit a remarkable ability to infer the phonological, structural, lexical, and semantic systems of language. Ever since Berko's (1958) groundbreaking "wug" study, we have been discovering more and more about the systematicity of the acquisition process.

But in the midst of all this systematicity, there is an equally remarkable amount of **variability** in the process of learning! Researchers do not agree on how to define various "stages" of language acquisition, even in English. Certain "typical" patterns appear in child language. The example, cited earlier, of children's learning of past tense forms of verbs like *go* offers an illustration of the difficulty of defining stages. Young children who have not yet mastered the past tense morpheme tend first to learn past tenses as separate items ("walked," "broke," "drank") without knowledge of the difference between regular and irregular verbs. Then, around the age of four or five, they begin to perceive a system in which the *-ed* morpheme is added to a verb, and at this point all verbs become regularized ("breaked," "drinked," "goed"). Finally, after early school age, children perceive that there are two classes of verbs, regular and irregular, and begin to sort out verbs into the two classes, a process that goes on for many years and in some cases persists into young adulthood.

In both L1 acquisition and SLA, the problem of variability is being addressed by researchers (Tarone, 1988; Bayley & Preston, 1996; Gass & Selinker, 2001). One of the major current research objectives is to account for all this variability: to determine if what is now variable in our present point of view can someday be deemed systematic through careful accounting.

Language and Thought

For years researchers have probed the relationship between language and cognition. The behavioral view that cognition is too mentalistic (unobservable) to be studied by the scientific method is diametrically opposed to such positions as that of Jean Piaget (1972), who claimed that cognitive development is at the very center of the human organism and that language is *dependent* upon and springs from cognitive development.

Others emphasized the influence of language on cognitive development. Jerome Bruner (Bruner, Olver, & Greenfield, 1966), for example, singled out sources of language-influenced intellectual development: words shaping concepts, dialogues between parent and child or teacher and child serving to orient and educate, and other sources. Vygotsky (1962, 1978) also differed from Piaget in claiming that social interaction, through language, is a prerequisite to cognitive development. Thought and language were seen as two distinct cognitive operations that grow together (Schinke-Llano, 1993). Moreover, every child reaches his or her potential development, in part, through social interaction with adults and peers, as demonstrated earlier in Vygotsky's (1978) zone of proximal development (ZPD).

In a fascinating study of language and cognition, Graeme Kennedy (1970) tested the hypothesis that perceived conceptual acquisition for eight-, ten-, and twelve-year-olds, as measured by standardized tests of mathematical concepts, could be skewed by language. The ability to grasp comparison of quantities was found to be a factor of how test items were worded. So, for example, "There are more apples than oranges" was found to pose virtually no difficulty, while "There are not as few apples as oranges" and "The number of apples is not less than the number of oranges" posed great difficulty, leading to incorrect answers and to the false conclusion that the concept of comparative quantities had not been acquired.

One of the champions of the position that language affects thought was Benjamin Whorf, who proposed the well-known Whorfian hypothesis of linguistic relativity—namely, that each language imposes on its speaker a particular "worldview." (See Chapter 7 for more discussion of linguistic relativity.) The issue at stake in child language acquisition is to determine how thought affects language, how language affects thought, and how researchers can best account for the interaction of the two. While we do not have complete answers, research confirms that cognitive and linguistic development are inextricably intertwined with dependencies in both directions.

 CLASSROOM CONNECTIONS

In what ways is a foreign language you learned connected with the "worldview" of a culture? Try to think of specific examples. Did those examples prod you to "think" in the language? How helpful are such connections in a language classroom?

Imitation

We always think of children as good imitators. We then—sometimes mistakenly—conclude that imitation is one of the most important strategies a child uses in the acquisition of language. On the one hand, research has shown that *echoing* is a particularly salient strategy in early language learning and an important aspect of early phonological acquisition. Moreover, imitation is consonant with behavioral principles of language acquisition—principles relevant, at least, to the earliest stages.

But on the other hand, it's important to ask what *type* of imitation is implied. In their arguments, behaviorists usually refer to surface-structure imitation, where a person repeats or mimics surface strings, attending to a phonological code rather than a semantic code. It is this level of imitation that enables an adult to repeat random numbers or nonsense syllables, or even to mimic nonsense syllables. In such a case, the semantics, if any, underlying the output are perhaps only peripherally attended to. In L2 classes, rote pattern drills often evoke surface imitation: a repetition of sounds without the slightest understanding of what the sounds might mean.

The earliest stages of child language acquisition may manifest a good deal of surface imitation since very small children do not possess the necessary semantic categories to comprehend the meaning of all utterances that they hear. But as children perceive the importance of the semantic level of language, they attend to a greater extent to a meaningful, deeper level of language. They engage in deep-structure imitation. In fact, the imitation of the deep structure of language can literally block their attention to the surface structure—they become, on the face of it, poor imitators. Look at the following conversation as recorded by McNeill (1966, p. 69):

>**Child:** *Nobody don't like me.*
>**Mother:** *No, say "nobody likes me."*
>**Child:** *Nobody don't like me.* **[eight repetitions of this exchange]**
>**Mother:** *No, now listen carefully; say "nobody likes me."*
>**Child:** *Oh! Nobody don't likes me.*

You can imagine the frustration of both mother and child, for the mother was attending to a surface grammatical distinction and yet the child sought to derive some meaning value. The child was expressing a deep feeling, while the mother was concerned about—of all things—grammar!

Or, consider this delightfully typical exchange between a father and his three-year-old child (O'Grady, 2005, p. 169) that illustrates the ineffectiveness of frequent repetition:

>**Child:** *Want other one spoon, daddy.*
>**Father:** *You mean, you want the other spoon.*
>**Child:** *Yes, I want other one spoon, please daddy.*
>**Father:** *Can you say "the other spoon"?*
>**Child:** *Other . . . one . . . spoon.*
>**Father:** *Say "other"*

> **Child:** *Other.*
> **Father:** *Spoon.*
> **Child:** *Spoon.*
> **Father:** *Other spoon.*
> **Child:** *Other . . . spoon. Now, give me other one spoon?*

These exchanges can make us smile. The teacher of an elementary school class once asked her pupils to write a few sentences on a piece of paper, to which one rather shy pupil meekly responded, "Ain't got no pencil." Disturbed at the nonstandard response, the teacher embarked on a barrage of corrective models for the child: "I *don't have* any pencils, you *don't have* a pencil, they *don't have* pencils. . . . " When the teacher finally ended her monologue of patterns, the intimidated and bewildered child said, "Ain't *nobody* got no pencils?" The teacher's purpose was lost on this child because he too was attending to language as a meaningful and communicative tool, and not to the correctness of certain forms. The child, like the children in the other examples, was attending to the *truth value* of the utterance.

Research has also shown that children, when explicitly asked to repeat a sentence in a test situation, will often repeat the correct underlying deep structure with a change in the surface rendition. For example, sentences such as "The ball that is rolling down the hill is black" and "The boy who's in the sandbox is wearing a red shirt" tend to be repeated back by preschool children as "The black ball is rolling down the hill" and "The red boy is in the sandbox" (Brown, 1970). Children are excellent imitators. It's simply a matter of understanding exactly what it is that they are imitating.

Practice and Frequency

Closely related to the notion of imitation is a somewhat broader question: Do children *practice* their language? If so, how? What is the role of the *frequency* of hearing and producing items in the acquisition of language? It is common to observe children and conclude that they "practice" language constantly, especially in the early stages of single-word and two-word utterances. A behavioral model of first language acquisition would claim that practice—repetition and association—is the key to the formation of habits by operant conditioning.

One unique form of practice by a child was recorded by Ruth Weir (1962). She found that her children produced rather long monologues in bed at night before going to sleep. Here is one example: "What color . . . What color blanket . . . What color mop . . . What color glass . . . Mommy's home sick . . . Mommy's home sick . . . Where's Mommy home sick . . . Where's Mikey sick . . . Mikey sick." Such monologues are not uncommon among children, whose inclination it is to "play" with language just as they do with all objects and events around them. Weir's data show far more structural patterning than has commonly been found in other data. Nevertheless, children's practice seems to be a key to language acquisition.

Practice is usually thought of as referring to speaking only. But one can also think in terms of comprehension practice, which is often considered under the rubric of the *frequency* of linguistic input to the child. Is the acquisition of particular words or structures directly attributable to their frequency in the child's linguistic environment? There is evidence that certain very frequent forms are acquired first: *what* questions, irregular past tense forms, certain common household items and persons. Brown and Hanlon (1970), for example, found that the frequency of occurrence of a linguistic item in the speech of mothers was an overwhelmingly strong predictor of the order of emergence of those items in their children's speech.

There is some conflicting evidence, however. Telegraphic speech is one case in point. Some of the most frequently occurring words in the language are omitted in such two- and three-word utterances. McNeill (1968, p. 416) found that a Japanese child produced the Japanese postposition *ga* far more frequently and more correctly than another contrasting postposition *wa*, even though her mother was recorded as using *wa* twice as often as *ga*. McNeill explained that *ga* as a subject marker may be of more importance, grammatically, to the child, or simply that *ga* is easier to pronounce.

The frequency issue may be summed up by noting that nativists who claim that "the relative frequency of stimuli is of little importance in language acquisition" (Wardhaugh, 1971, p. 12), might in the face of evidence now available (N. Ellis, 2002), be more cautious in their claims. It would appear that frequency of *meaningful* occurrence may well be a more precise refinement of the notion of frequency.

 CLASSROOM CONNECTIONS

The Audiolingual Method, influenced by a behavioral conditioning paradigm, placed almost exclusive value on frequency of input *and output*. Current methods—with their focus on meaning, interaction, and communication—assume that frequency takes a backseat to meaningfulness. In your L2 learning experiences, has frequent repetition been helpful? How, as a teacher, would you balance frequency and meaningfulness?

Input

Input has become a "hot topic" in SLA, and of course the role of input in the child's acquisition of language is undeniably crucial. What sort of linguistic input are children exposed to? Is the speech of parents, caretakers, siblings, and peers grammatical? Research evidence does not provide a conclusive answer. Some linguists have claimed that a child's input is often semi-grammatical and full of performance variables, and that children are exposed to "a haphazard sample" of language (McNeill, 1966, p. 73). Other studies, however, show that input, especially that of parents and other adults, is surprisingly grammatical, lacking the usual hesitations and false starts common in adult-to-adult speech (Bellugi & Brown, 1964; Drach, 1969; Labov, 1970; Landes, 1975; Hladik & Edwards, 1984; Moerk, 1985).

At the same time, it should be remembered that children react very consistently to the deep structure and the communicative function of language, and they do not react overtly to expansions and grammatical corrections, as in the "nobody don't like me" dialogue quoted earlier. Such input is largely ignored unless there is some truth or falsity that the child can attend to. Thus, if a child says "Dat Harry" and the parent says "No, that's *John*," the child might readily self-correct and say "Oh, dat *John*." But what Landes (1975) and others showed is that in the long run, children will, after consistent, repeated models in meaningful contexts, *eventually* transfer correct forms to their own speech and thus correct "dat" to "that's."

It's clear from more recent research that adult and peer input to the child is far more important than nativists earlier believed. Adult input seems to shape the child's acquisition, and the interaction patterns between child and parent change according to the increasing language skill of the child. Nurture and environment in this case are tremendously important, although it remains to be seen just how important parental input is as a proportion of total input.

Discourse

A subfield of applied linguistics that is occupying the attention of an increasing number of child language researchers, especially in an era of social constructivist research, is the area of conversational or discourse analysis. While parental input is a significant part of the child's development of conversational rules, it is only one aspect, as the child also interacts with peers and, of course, with other adults. Jean Berko-Gleason (1982, p. 20) described the perspective:

> While it used to be generally held that mere *exposure* to language is sufficient to set the child's language generating machinery in motion, it is now clear that, in order for successful first language acquisition to take place, *interaction*, rather than exposure, is required; children do not learn language from overhearing the conversations of others or from listening to the radio, and must, instead, acquire it in the context of being spoken to.

How children learn to take part in conversation is very complex. Some answers seem to lie not in sentences and clauses as much as transactions and exchanges (Sinclair & Coulthard, 1975). Children learn not only how to initiate a conversation but also how to respond to another's initiating utterance. Questions are not simply questions, but are recognized functionally as requests for information, for action, or for help. Children learn that utterances have both a literal and an intended or functional meaning. Thus, in the case of the question "You wanna watch the Disney Channel now?" the response "I'm busy" is understood correctly as a negative response.

How do children learn discourse rules? What are the key features children attend to? How do they detect intended meaning? These and other questions about the acquisition of discourse ability are slowly being answered in the research (Holmes, 1995; Tannen, 1996; Clark, 2009). Much remains to be studied in the area of the child's development of conversational knowledge (McTear, 1984; Shatz & McCloskey, 1984). Nevertheless, such development is perhaps the next frontier to be mastered in the quest for answers to the mystery of language acquisition.

 CLASSROOM CONNECTIONS

You may have felt helpless in the first few weeks or even months of learning an L2 when you were forced to interact with other speakers of the language. Did you explicitly learn discourse and conversation rules? Or just eventually "pick them up"? Would it be helpful to *present* such rules in a language classroom?

L1-ACQUISITION-INSPIRED METHODS

Interestingly, the first educators in the "modern" era of research on language teaching drew their insights from *children* learning first and second languages! If you turn your clock back a little over a hundred years, you will happen upon two revolutionaries in language pedagogy, François Gouin and Maximilian Berlitz. Their perceptive observations about language teaching helped set the stage for the development of language teaching methodologies for the century following.

In his *The Art of Learning and Studying Foreign Languages*, Gouin (1880) described a painful set of experiences that finally led to his insights about language teaching. Having decided in midlife to learn German, he took up residency in Hamburg for one year. But rather than attempting to converse with the natives, he engaged in a bizarre sequence of attempts to memorize vocabulary and grammatical paradigms in the privacy of his residence. Only once did he try to "make conversation," but this caused people to laugh at him, so he became too embarrassed to continue. At the end of the year, Gouin was forced to return home a failure!

But there was a happy ending. Upon returning home Gouin discovered that his three-year-old nephew had, during that year, gone through that wonderful stage of *first* language acquisition in which he went from saying virtually nothing to becoming a veritable chatterbox in his native French. How was it that this little child succeeded so easily in a task, mastering a language that Gouin, in a second language, had found impossible? The child must hold the secret to learning a language!

So Gouin devised a teaching method derived from his insights about his nephew. And thus the **Series Method** was created, a method that taught learners directly (without translation) and conceptually (without grammatical rules and explanations), a "series" of connected sentences that are easy to perceive. The first lesson might teach connected sentences such as: "I walk toward the door. I draw near to the door. I draw nearer to the door. I get to the door. I stop at the door."

Such sentences have a number of grammatical forms and vocabulary items, but Gouin was successful with his lessons because the language was easily understood, stored, recalled, acted out, and related to reality. While his "naturalistic" approaches did not catch on immediately, a generation later at the turn of the century, partly through the efforts of visionaries like Maximilian Berlitz, applied linguists finally established the credibility of such approaches in what became known as the **Direct Method**.

The basic premise of Berlitz's method was that L2 learning should be more like L1 learning: lots of active oral interaction, spontaneous use of the language, no translation between first and second languages, and little or no analysis of grammatical rules (Richards & Rodgers, 2001). The Direct Method enjoyed considerable popularity through the end of the nineteenth century and well into the twentieth—and now even into the twenty-first century as Berlitz language schools are known worldwide. We should never downplay the significance of the child's magical L1 journey for insights into the hows and whys of SLA.

SUGGESTED READINGS

Clark, E. (2009). *First language acquisition.* Second Edition. Cambridge, UK: Cambridge University Press.

An authoritative, comprehensive account of L1 acquisition research, written for researchers and teachers alike. The extensive bibliography is extremely useful.

Saxton, Matthew. (2010). *Child language: Acquisition and development.* London: Sage Publications, Ltd.

A delightfully written, engaging textbook, accessible to general readers. It includes exercises, glossary, and suggestions for further reading.

O'Grady, W. (2005). *How children learn language*. New York: Cambridge University Press.

A succinct, readable synopsis of what we know about how children learn their first language, with a wealth of information and appropriate for parents or students.

Pinker, S. (2007). *The language instinct: How the mind creates language (P.S.)*. New York: Harper Perennial Modern Classics.

Steven Pinker's best-selling 1994 book has been revised in this "P.S." that is equally readable by all audiences, providing an update on research on innateness, language, and mind.

LANGUAGE LEARNING EXPERIENCE: JOURNAL ENTRY 2

Note: See journal entry directions in Chapter 1 for general guidelines for writing a journal on a previous or concurrent language learning experience.

- As you learned a second language, did you feel any of the learning was due to a knack (talent, ability) you had for it? Think of some examples to illustrate either the presence or the absence of some ability to pick up the language.
- Is your class focused more on the forms of language than the functions? Illustrate with examples.
- Offer some thoughts about what you see as a relationship between behavioral, nativist, and functional approaches to studying *first* language acquisition and your own experiences in learning or teaching a *second* language. These relationships will be dealt with more thoroughly in Chapter 3, and your present instincts would be worth comparing to your thoughts after you cover Chapter 3.
- Go through the issues discussed in this chapter and ask yourself if, in your foreign language class, you have had opportunities to understand and to speak, to imitate the teacher, to practice your language, especially discourse and conversation?
- Consider how children learn their first languages and speculate (before you go on to Chapter 3) on children's "secrets" that enable them to acquire a language seemingly efficiently.

FOR THE TEACHER: ACTIVITIES (A) & DISCUSSION (D)

Note: For each of the "Classroom Connections" in this chapter, you may wish to turn them into individual or pair-work discussion questions.

1. (A) In a small group, discuss why it is that behavioral theories can account sufficiently well for the earliest utterances of the child, but not for utterances at the sentence and discourse level. Do nativist and

functional approaches provide the necessary tools for accounting for those later, more complex utterances?

2. (A) Give assigned pairs the task of recording some samples of a young child's speech. A child of about three to five years of age is an ideal subject to observe in a study of growing competence in a language. Ask each pair to transcribe a segment of their recording and see if, they can determine some of the rules the child is using. Share findings with the rest of the class.

3. (D) In pairs, as boardwork, ask Ss to write down three to five characteristics of the following positions on L1 acquisition: (1) Universal Grammar; (2) the nativists' concept of LAD; (3) connectionism; and (4) emergentism. As a whole class, discuss the viability of each position.

4. (A) Ask pairs to look at the three samples of speech on pages 21, 33, and 36 (Two by a five-year-old, and the other by a professional golfer). Have them identify what they would consider to be "performance variables" in those transcripts. Then, ask them to try to reconstruct an "idealized" form of the two monologues, and share with the rest of the class.

5. (D) How are competence and performance interdependent? How does competence increase? Can it decrease? Try to illustrate with both language and nonlanguage examples of learning certain skills, such as musical or athletic skills.

6. (A) Ask small groups to recall experiences learning a second language at some point in their past. Share examples of instances when their comprehension exceeded their production abilities. How about the reverse? Share findings with the rest of the class.

7. (D) In what way did Gouin's Series Method reflect some ideas about language and about language acquisition that are now current more than a hundred years later? What aspects of the Series Method and the Direct Method are still effective today?

CHAPTER 3

AGE AND ACQUISITION

"Oh, Doug will be just fine," reasoned my father, on the prospects of enrolling me in the nearby French-speaking school in Leopoldville, Belgian Congo. "He's five now and a new language is no problem for kids. He'll be fluent in French in no time."

And off I went, a frightened little boy, into what was for me a hostile, scary environment in my first schooling experience, in the middle of a kindergarten year that I never had a chance to start earlier—in any language. The emotional scars remain to this day: memories of a monster of a teacher and bratty classmates, mocking the American kid who could hardly speak or understand a word of French.

The story has a happy ending. About eighteen months later, by the end of first grade, my French was fluent—and as flawless as any six-year-old's could be. And I graduated second in my class! Yes, the Belgian system in those days actually ranked children—even first graders—by their test scores!

Does age matter for the ultimate attainment of second language acquisition (SLA)? This is a question we're still sorting out, and we will look at the issues and related research in this chapter. What we do know is that we have all observed children acquiring their first language (L1) easily and well, yet adults learning a second language (L2), particularly in an educational setting, can meet with great difficulty and sometimes failure. We also know that a systematic study of L1 learning experiences has yielded important insights into L2 learning.

What may not be quite as obvious, though, is how the L2 teacher should interpret the many facets and sometimes contradictory findings of L1 research. L1 acquisition starts in very early childhood, but SLA can happen in childhood, early or late, as well as in adulthood. Do childhood and adulthood, and differences between them, hold some keys to SLA models and theories? The purpose of this chapter is to address some of those questions and to set forth explicitly some of the parameters for looking at the effects of age and acquisition.

DISPELLING MYTHS

Let's begin by dispelling some myths about the relationship between L1 and L2 acquisition. Consider some of the flawed arguments that are sometimes given for assuming that L1 and L2 learning are similar processes (Stern, 1970, pp. 57–58):

1. Children learning their first language practice and repeat words and phrases. Therefore, foreign language classes should involve lots of repetition and practice.
2. Child language acquisition is mainly a matter of imitation. Therefore, language classes encourage plenty of imitation.
3. Children practice separate sounds, then words, then sentences. This "natural order" should therefore be used in teaching a foreign language.
4. In a child's speech development, understanding always precedes speaking. Therefore, this must be the correct order of presenting the skills in a foreign language.
5. A very young child listens and speaks, and reading and writing are advanced stages of language development. The natural order for second language learning is listening, speaking, reading, and writing.
6. You did not have to translate when you were a child. If you were able to learn your own language without translation, you should be able to learn a foreign language in the same way.
7. A small child simply uses language, without any instruction in formal grammar. It is equally unnecessary to use grammatical conceptualization in teaching a foreign language.

These statements represented the views of those who felt that "the first language learner was looked upon as the foreign language teacher's dream: a pupil who mysteriously laps up his vocabulary, whose pronunciation, in spite of occasional lapses, is impeccable, while morphology and syntax, instead of being a constant headache, come to him like a dream" (Stern, 1970, p. 58).

There are flaws in each of the seven statements—sometimes in the assumption behind the statement about first language learning, sometimes in the analogy or implication that is drawn, and sometimes in both. Can you detect them? In this chapter, we will eventually touch on all seven pitfalls.

 CLASSROOM CONNECTIONS

Think about the assumption, then the analogy, then the conclusion that is drawn in each of the seven statements about first and second language acquisition. In your experience learning a foreign language, has the methodology ever rested on one or more of the mistaken analogies? What are some specific instances of your teacher using an approach that "rose above" the false analogy?

As cognitive and constructivist research on both L1 and L2 acquisition gathered momentum, researchers and foreign language teachers began to recognize the mistakes in drawing direct global analogies between L1 and L2 acquisition. By the 1970s and 1980s, criticism of earlier direct analogies between L1 and L2 acquisition had peaked. Stern (1970), Cook (1973, 1995), and Schachter (1988), among others, addressed the inconsistencies, but at the same time recognized the legitimate similarities that, if viewed cautiously, allowed one to draw some constructive conclusions about SLA.

TYPES OF COMPARISON AND CONTRAST

Before proceeding further in this discussion, let's clarify the parameters involved. First, it's illogical to compare the *first* language acquisition of a *child* with the *second* language acquisition of an *adult* (Scovel, 1999; Foster-Cohen, 2001; Ortega, 2009; Muñoz & Singleton, 2011). This involves trying to draw analogies not only between first and second language learning contexts, but also between children and adults. We end up manipulating the variable of language (L1 and L2) as well as age (child and adult), which is a basic flaw in most of the seven statements above.

It's more logical to compare *second language* learning in children and adults or to compare first and second language learning in *children*. However, consider this: Do five-year-olds and ten-year-olds exhibit differences in mental and emotional processing? Of course they do! They exhibit a whole array of cognitive, affective, and physical developmental changes, so a further caution should be made about comparing children and adults under any circumstances.

An aside: There have been a few recorded instances of an adult acquiring a first language, all of which are pathological. In one widely publicized case, Curtiss (1977) wrote about Genie, a thirteen-year-old girl who had been socially isolated and abused all her life until she was discovered by the authorities, and who was then faced with the task of acquiring a first language. Accounts of "wolf children" and instances of severe disability fall into this category.

Much of the discussion of the rest of this chapter will be focused on the two types of comparisons described above:

1. SLA in children (of varying ages) and adults
2. Children's L1 and L2 acquisition

In both cases, comparisons will be embedded within a number of issues, controversies, and other topics that have attracted the attention of researchers interested in the relationship of age to acquisition.

THE CRITICAL PERIOD HYPOTHESIS: THE YOUNGER THE BETTER?

Discussions about age and acquisition inevitably consider the question of whether there is a **critical period** (also called a "sensitive period") for language acquisition: a biologically determined period of life when language can be acquired more easily and beyond which time language is increasingly difficult to acquire. The **Critical Period Hypothesis** (CPH) claims that there is such a biological timetable.

Initially the notion of a critical period was connected only to L1 acquisition (Singleton & Ryan, 2004; Clark, 2009). Pathological studies of children who failed to acquire their L1, or aspects thereof, became fuel for arguments of biologically determined predispositions (Lenneberg, 1967; Bickerton, 1981) timed for release, which would wane if the correct environmental stimuli were not present at the crucial stage.

In recent years, a plethora of research has appeared on the possible applications of the CPH to L2 contexts (Birdsong, 1999; Scovel, 2000; Hyltenstam & Abrahamsson, 2003; Moyer, 2004; Singleton & Ryan, 2004; Ioup, 2005; Muñoz & Singleton, 2011; Singleton & Muñoz, 2011). The classic argument is that a critical point for second language acquisition occurs around puberty, beyond which people seem to be relatively incapable of acquiring a second language. This has led some to assume, incorrectly, that by the age of twelve or thirteen you are significantly less capable of successful second language learning. Such an assumption must be viewed in the light of what it means to be "successful" in learning a second language, and particularly the role of *accent* as a component of success. To examine these issues, we will first look at neurological and phonological considerations, then examine cognitive, affective, and linguistic considerations.

 CLASSROOM CONNECTIONS

In your experience learning a language, or knowing others who have learned a foreign language, have you witnessed anecdotal evidence of a critical period for second language acquisition? Do you know adults who have been extremely successful in learning a second language? What does that observational evidence say to you about how you would approach teaching a classroom of elementary-school-age children? And how would that differ from a class of adults?

NEUROBIOLOGICAL CONSIDERATIONS

One of the most interesting areas of inquiry in age and acquisition research has been the study of the function of the brain in the process of acquisition (Obler & Gjerlow, 1999; Schumann et al., 2004; Singleton & Ryan, 2004; Muñoz & Singleton, 2011). How might neurological development affect second language success? Does the maturation of the brain at some stage spell the doom of language acquisition ability?

Hemispheric Lateralization

Several decades ago researchers were favoring **lateralization** of the brain as the key to answering such a question. There is evidence in neurological research that as the human brain matures, certain functions are assigned, or "lateralized," to the left **hemisphere** of the brain, and certain other functions to the right hemisphere. Intellectual, logical, and analytic functions appear to be largely located in the left hemisphere, while the right hemisphere controls functions related to emotional and social needs. (See Chapter 5 for more discussion of left- and right-brain functioning.)

Language functions appear to be controlled primarily, but not exclusively, in the left hemisphere, although there is a good deal of conflicting evidence. For example, patients who have had left hemispherectomies or left hemisphere injuries have been capable of comprehending and producing some language (Zangwill, 1971, p. 220). Other evidence shows right hemisphere lesions to have less impact on language functioning, but Millar and Whitaker (1983) challenged the notion of clear hemispheric divisions in the case of linguistic ability.

More interesting is the question of *when* lateralization takes place, and whether or not that lateralization process affects language acquisition. The evidence is sketchy. Lenneberg (1967) suggested that lateralization is a slow process that begins around the age of two and is completed around puberty. Geschwind (1970) posited a much earlier age of completion, while Krashen (1973) cited research to support the completion of lateralization around age five. But Scovel (1984) cautioned against assuming, with Krashen, that lateralization is *complete* by age five. Adams (1997) found that children up to the age of puberty who suffer injury to the left hemisphere are able to relocalize linguistic functions to the right hemisphere, to "relearn" their first language with relatively little impairment.

What do these arguments and findings say about the relationship between lateralization and language acquisition? Scovel (1969) suggested that the plasticity of the brain prior to puberty enables children to acquire not only their first language but also a second language, and that possibly it is the very accomplishment of lateralization that makes it difficult for people to easily acquire fluent control of a second language. Do we have a resolution? Not according to Muñoz and Singleton (2011, p. 25), who, after reviewing dozens of related studies, concluded that "findings from a number of *neurolinguistic* studies . . . cannot provide decisive evidence concerning the existence of a critical period."

 CLASSROOM CONNECTIONS

Norman Geschwind once interviewed a middle-aged man who had had a left hemispherectomy. After showing some puzzlement over *comprehension* of questions put to him, then faltering on *producing* words and phrases, he then *sang*, in perfect key, "My country 'tis of thee." If you were in a position to help this man to "re-learn" his own native language, how would you reach him?

One branch of neurolinguistic research focused on the role of the right hemisphere in the acquisition of an L2. Obler (1981, p. 58) noted that in SLA, "[significant right hemisphere] participation is particularly active during the early stages of learning the second language." Obler cited the strategy of guessing at meanings, and of using formulaic utterances, as examples of right hemisphere activity. Fred Genesee (1982) concluded that learners in informal contexts use greater right hemisphere processing than left. And Urgesi and Fabbro (2009, p. 361) concluded that the right hemisphere is crucially involved in the processing of *pragmatic* aspects of language use." Such studies seem to suggest that L2 learners, particularly adults, might benefit from more encouragement of right-brain activity in the classroom context.

 CLASSROOM CONNECTIONS

Some approaches to language teaching (for example, Total Physical Response, the Natural Approach) advocate a less analytical approach and a more psychomotor, integrated, social atmosphere in the classroom. What are some typical right-brain-oriented activities that you have experienced—or would use—in the language classroom?

Biological Timetables

Did you know that white-crowned sparrows and other birds exhibit critical periods for the acquisition of their unique birdsong? Can birds teach us something about human language acquisition?

A fascinating argument for an accent-related critical period came from Thomas Scovel's (1988) multidisciplinary review of evidence for a **sociobiological critical period** in various species of mammals and birds. He concluded that the development of a socially bonding accent at puberty enables species (1) to form an identity with their own community as they anticipate roles of parenting and leadership, and (2) to attract mates of "their own kind" in an instinctive drive to maintain their own species.

If the stabilization of an accepted, authentic accent is biologically preprogrammed for baboons and birds, why not for human beings? Scovel (1988) concluded that native accents, and therefore "foreign" accents after puberty, may be a genetic leftover that, in our widespread human practice of mating across dialectal, linguistic, and racial barriers, is no longer necessary for the preservation of the human species. "In other words," explained Scovel, "an accent emerging after puberty is the price we pay for our preordained ability to be articulate apes" (p. 80).

Following another line of research, Walsh and Diller (1981) proposed that different aspects of an L2 are learned optimally at different ages. So, lower-order processes such as pronunciation are dependent on early-maturing brain functions, making foreign accents difficult to overcome after childhood. Higher-order language functions, such as semantic relations, are more dependent on late-maturing neural circuits, which may explain the efficiency of adult learning.

Walsh and Diller's conclusions have been supported in other studies (Hyltenstam & Abrahamsson, 2003; Singleton & Ryan, 2004). We are left, then, with some support for a neurologically based critical period, but principally for the acquisition of an authentic *accent*, and not very strongly for the acquisition of communicative fluency and other higher-order processes. We return to the latter issue later in this chapter.

Anthropological Evidence

Some adults have been known to acquire an authentic accent in a second language after the age of puberty, but such individuals are exceptional (Ortega, 2009). Anthropologist Jane Hill (1970) cited research on non-Western societies that suggested that adults can, in the normal course of their lives, acquire second languages perfectly. Sorenson (1967), for example, studied the Tukano culture of South America, in which at least two dozen languages were spoken. Each tribal group, identified by the language it speaks, is an exogamous unit (people must marry outside their group) and hence almost always marry someone who speaks another language. Sorenson reported that during adolescence, individuals actively and almost suddenly began to speak two or three other languages with no observed trace of a "foreign" accent. What love will do!

Before drawing a hasty conclusion, however, we do well to remember, with Hill (1970), that language acquisition processes in largely monolingual societies are anything but universal. Caution is therefore appropriate in proposing an innatist or cerebral dominance model as a full explanation for adult foreign accents. Subsequent research (Morris & Gerstman, 1986; Flege, 1987; Moyer, 2004; Long, 2007; Muñoz and Singleton, 2011) has pointed to a multitude of cognitive, motivational, affective, social, psychological, and strategic variables affecting the ultimate attainment of proficiency in an L2.

 CLASSROOM CONNECTIONS

Do you know anyone who learned a second language after the age of twelve or thirteen, and who developed a "perfect" command of the language? What do you suppose are the "secrets of their success"? Can you imagine incorporating some of those "secrets" into a foreign language classroom? What kinds of activities would you see in such a classroom?

THE SIGNIFICANCE OF ACCENT

How important is *accent* in assessing overall communicative language ability? This is a question that linguists argued about for decades, but much less so in recent years. Why is that?

Implicit in the comments of the preceding section is the assumption that the emergence of what we commonly call "foreign accent" is of some importance in our arguments about age and acquisition. We can appreciate the fact that given the existence of several hundred muscles (in the throat, larynx, mouth, lips, and tongue) that are used in the articulation of human speech, a tremendous degree of muscular control is required to achieve the fluency of a native speaker of a language. Witness the process of small children developing their speech.

In the middle decades of the twentieth century, research on the acquisition of so-called **authentic** (nativelike) control of the *phonology* of a foreign language supported the notion of a critical period ending at puberty. Possible causes of such an age-based factor have already been discussed: neuromuscular plasticity, neurological development, sociobiological programs, and the environment of sociocultural influences. It is tempting to cite exceptions to the rule: people who have the remarkable ability to achieve a virtually perfect nativelike pronunciation of a foreign language. But in terms of statistical probability, virtually all the research shows that the chances of a person beginning a second language after puberty and achieving a scientifically verifiable authentic *native* accent are slim (Muñoz & Singleton, 2011).

What does the research say? In a series of studies, Gerald Neufeld (1977, 1979, 1980, 2001) tried to determine to what extent adults could approximate native-speaker accents in an L2 never before encountered. Under experimental conditions, adult native English speakers were taught to imitate L2 utterances. Some speakers, but not all, were judged to be native speakers. Others (Scovel, 1988; Long, 1990b), however, noted flaws in Neufeld's experiments. Bongaerts, Planken, and Schils (1995) recorded the speech of a group of adult Dutch speakers of English and again a few of the nonnative performances were judged to have come from native speakers. In contrast, Moyer's (1999) study with native English-speaking graduate students of German found that the subjects were *not* judged to be native speakers.

The findings of these studies are certainly equivocal, leading us again to the question of the significance of *accent* in L2 acquisition. While there is evidence of a critical period for accent, it appears that such evidence *only* applies to accent. Singleton and Ryan (2004), representing the current prevailing view on accent acquisition, prefer to play down the accent issue and look at other proficiency factors, since "the available evidence does not consistently support the hypothesis that younger L2 learners are *globally* more efficient and successful than older learners" (p. 115).

It is important to remember in all these considerations that pronunciation of a language is not by any means the sole criterion for acquisition, nor is it the most important one. We all know people who have nonnative pronunciation but who nevertheless have excellent and fluent control of a second language, control that can even exceed that of many native speakers. The acquisition of the communicative and functional purpose of language is far more important than a "perfect" native accent—unless of course you're planning to be an undercover spy in a foreign country!

A second caveat in viewing research on accent acquisition comes from mounting evidence, especially in the globalization and indigenization of languages, of the inability to define "native" accent at all (Abrahamsson & Hyltenstam, 2009). English users are well acquainted with the concept of "World Englishes," in which many so-called native speakers of English are perceived as having "foreign" accents. The native-speaker ideal of linguistic research in the 1960s is both harder to find and less relevant as time moves on (Birdsong, 2005). Muñoz and Singleton (2011) aptly sum up this view: "The question is whether reliance on [native-speaker] performance is really the best way of exploring age effects and maturational issues. . . . There are better ways of proceeding" (pp. 2–3).

Some of those better ways of proceeding may be seen in more recent studies. Bongaerts et al. (1995) found results that suggested that certain learner characteristics and contexts may work together to override the disadvantages of a late start. Slavoff and Johnson (1995) found that younger children (ages seven to nine) did not have a particular advantage in rate of learning over older (ten- to twelve-year-old) children. Studies on the effects of Universal Grammar (White, 2003), of instructional factors (Singleton & Ryan, 2004), and of contextual and socio-psychological factors (Moyer, 2004; Ortega, 2009) are all highly promising domains of research on age and acquisition.

Hyltenstam and Abrahamsson (2003) reminded us of the positive side of the miracle of second language acquisition: "More surprising, we would like to claim, are the miraculous levels of proficiency that second language learners (at all ages) in fact *can* reach, despite the constraints that are imposed by our biological scheduling" (pp. 578–580).

Perhaps, in our everyday encounters with second language users, we are too quick to criticize the "failure" of adult second language learners by nitpicking at minor pronunciation points or nonintrusive grammatical errors. Cook (1995) warned against "using native accent as the yardstick" (p. 55) in our penchant for holding up monolingualism as the standard. Instead, perhaps we can turn those perspectives into a more positive focus on the "multi-competence" (p. 52) of second language learners. Or, in the words of Marinova-Todd, Marshall, and Snow (2000), we would do well to refrain from too much of "a misemphasis on poor adult learners and an under-emphasis on adults who master L2s to nativelike levels" (p. 9). Instead of being so perplexed and concerned about how bad people are at learning second languages, we should be fascinated with how much those same learners have accomplished.

 CLASSROOM CONNECTIONS

Following up on the more "positive spin" on second language acquisition, in what ways do you think adults might actually have an advantage? In your experience, what have you accomplished as an adult learning a second language that you might not have been able to do as well or as efficiently as a child? How would you put those insights into action in a classroom?

COGNITIVE CONSIDERATIONS

If neurolinguistic research has not yet uncovered empirical evidence of a critical period, might we yield a more fruitful inquiry by looking at the cognitive side of child development?

Human cognition develops rapidly throughout the first sixteen years of life and less rapidly thereafter. Some cognitive changes are critical; others are more gradual and difficult to detect. Piaget (1972; 1955; Piaget & Inhelder, 1969) outlined the course of intellectual development in a child through various stages:

- Sensorimotor stage (birth to two)
- Preoperational stage (ages two to seven)
- Operational stage (ages seven to sixteen)
- Concrete operational stage (ages seven to eleven)
- Formal operational stage (ages eleven to sixteen)

A critical stage for a consideration of the effects of age on second language acquisition appears to occur, in Piaget's outline, at puberty (age eleven in his model). It is here that a person becomes capable of abstraction, of formal thinking which transcends concrete experience and direct perception. Ausubel (1964) hinted at a similar connection in noting the benefit adults might have in performing deductive thinking. Rosansky (1975, p. 96) felt that initial language acquisition takes place when the child is highly egocentric, able to focus on only one dimension at a time, and that this lack of "decentration" may well be a necessity for language acquisition. Singleton and Ryan (2004, pp. 156–159), however, offered a number of objections to connecting Piagetian stages of development with critical period arguments, not the least of which was the lack of empirical data in Piaget's theory.

But cognitive arguments still remain persuasive. Young children are generally not "aware" that they are acquiring a language, nor are they aware of societal values and attitudes placed on one language or another. It is said that "a watched pot never boils." Is it possible that a language learner who is *too* consciously aware of what he or she is doing will have difficulty in learning the second language?

You may be tempted to answer that question affirmatively, but there is both logical and anecdotal counterevidence. Logically, a superior intellect should facilitate what is in one sense a highly complex intellectual activity. Anecdotal evidence shows that some adults who have been successful language learners have been very much aware of the process they were going through, even to the point of utilizing self-made paradigms and other fabricated linguistic devices to facilitate the learning process. So, if mature cognition is a liability to successful second language acquisition, clearly some intervening variables allow some persons to be very successful second language learners after puberty. These variables may in most cases lie outside the cognitive domain entirely, perhaps more centrally in the affective, or emotional, domain.

Are children possibly better language learners because they excel in **implicit learning**, that is, the *incidental* acquisition of linguistic patterns? Robert DeKeyser (2000) thought so, as he contrasted implicit and **explicit learning** (focused attention or instruction). In a study of adult native speakers of Hungarian learning English, he found that certain adults, those with high general verbal ability, were able to use explicit learning mechanisms to bypass the "increasingly inefficient" implicit mechanisms. He went on to conclude that "early age confers an absolute, not a statistical, advantage—that is, there may very well be no exceptions to the age effect" (p. 518). Despite a strong refutation by Bialystok (2002), the implicit/explicit construct nevertheless holds enticing explanatory power.

The lateralization hypothesis may provide another key to cognitive differences between child and adult language acquisition. As the child matures into adulthood, some would maintain, the left hemisphere (which controls the analytical and intellectual functions) becomes more dominant than the right hemisphere (which controls the emotional functions). It is possible that the dominance of the left hemisphere contributes to a tendency to overanalyze and to be too intellectually centered on the task of second language learning (Genesee, 1982).

Another construct that should be considered in examining the cognitive domain is the Piagetian notion of equilibration. **Equilibration** is defined as "progressive interior organization of knowledge in a stepwise fashion" (Sullivan, 1967, p. 12), and is related to the concept of equilibrium. That is, cognition develops as a process of moving from states of doubt and uncertainty (disequilibrium) to stages of resolution and certainty (equilibrium) and then back to further doubt that is, in time, also resolved. And so the cycle continues. Piaget (1970) claimed that conceptual development is a process of progressively moving from states of disequilibrium to equilibrium and that periods of disequilibrium mark virtually all cognitive development up through age fourteen or fifteen when formal operations finally are firmly organized and equilibrium is reached.

It is conceivable that disequilibrium may provide significant motivation for language acquisition: Language interacts with cognition to achieve equilibrium. Perhaps until that state of final equilibrium is reached, the child is cognitively ready and eager to acquire the language necessary for achieving the cognitive equilibrium of adulthood. That same child was, until that time, decreasingly tolerant of cognitive ambiguities.

Children are amazingly indifferent to contradictions, but intellectual growth produces an awareness of ambiguities about them and heightens the need for resolution. Does a general intolerance of contradictions produce an acute awareness of the enormous complexities of acquiring an additional language? If so, perhaps around the age of fourteen or fifteen, the prospect of learning a second language becomes overwhelming, thus discouraging the learner from proceeding a step at a time as a younger child would do.

 CLASSROOM CONNECTIONS

Have you ever felt overwhelmed in the process of learning a foreign language? The sheer quantity of words, grammatical constructions, and conversational know-how just seemed impossible to master? How might you help students in your classroom feel less burdened by the prospects of becoming fluent in a language—less "disequilibrium"? Think of some possible approaches or activities that could accomplish such a goal.

The final consideration in the cognitive domain is the distinction that Ausubel (1964) made between **rote** and **meaningful learning**. Ausubel noted that people of all ages have little use for rote, mechanistic learning that is not related to existing knowledge and experience. Rather, most items are acquired by meaningful learning, by anchoring and relating new items and experiences to knowledge that exists in the cognitive framework.

It's a myth to contend that children are good rote learners, that they make good use of meaningless repetition and mimicking. We have already seen in Chapter 2 that children's practice and imitation is a very meaningful activity that is contextualized and purposeful. Adults have developed even greater concentration and so have greater ability for rote learning, but they usually use rote learning only for short-term memory. By inference, we may conclude that the foreign language classroom should not become the locus of excessive rote drills, pattern repetition, rule recitation, and other activities that are not in the context of meaningful communication.

It is interesting to note that comparisons of child and adult second language acquisition almost always refer, in the case of children, to natural *untutored* learning, and for adults, to the *classroom* learning of a second language. Even so, many foreign language classrooms around the world still utilize an excessive number of rote-learning procedures. So, if adults learning a foreign language by rote methods are compared with children learning a second language in a natural, meaningful context, the child's learning will seem to be superior. The cause of such superiority may not be in the age of the person, but in the context of learning. The child happens to be learning language meaningfully, and the adult is not.

AFFECTIVE CONSIDERATIONS

We turn now to what may be the most complex, yet the most illuminating, perspective on age and acquisition. The affective domain includes many factors: empathy, self-esteem, extroversion, inhibition, imitation, anxiety, attitudes—the list could go on. Some of these may seem at first rather far removed from language learning, but when we consider the pervasive nature of language and the centrality of our emotions, any affective factor can be relevant to L2 learning.

A case in point is the role of **egocentricity** in human development. Very young children are highly egocentric. The world revolves around them, and they see all events as focusing on themselves. As children grow older they become more aware of themselves and more self-conscious as they seek both to define and to understand their self-identity, but their self-awareness is coupled with awareness of others. In preadolescence children develop an acute consciousness of themselves as entities which, in their wavering insecurity, are compared to others.

They develop **inhibitions** to protect this self-identity, fearing to expose too much self-doubt. Inhibitions act as invisible "walls" thrown up verbally or non-verbally to encapsulate a fragile self-concept. At puberty these inhibitions are heightened in the trauma of undergoing physical, cognitive, and emotional changes, and ultimately a totally new physical, cognitive, and emotional identity.

Their egos are affected not only in how they understand themselves, but also in how they reach out beyond themselves, how they relate to others socially, and how they use the communicative process to bring on affective equilibrium.

Isn't it possible that the uninhibited nature of a child yields a more readily absorbable person? One who doesn't suffer as much embarrassment as an adult over making a *faux pas* in the second language?

 CLASSROOM CONNECTIONS

What are some activities that you have experienced, or that you have used in your teaching, to help students to overcome inhibitions? Think of some activities and determine what it is, psychologically, that each activity accomplishes.

Several decades ago, psychologist Alexander Guiora proposed the concept of the **language ego** (Guiora et al., 1972b; Ehrman, 1993; Dörnyei, 2005, 2009) to account for the identity a person develops in reference to the language he or she speaks. For a monolingual person, the language ego involves the interaction of the native language and ego development. A person's self-identity is inextricably bound up with one's language, for it is in the communicative process—the process of sending out messages and having them "bounced" back—that such identities are confirmed, shaped, and reshaped. Guiora suggested that the language ego may account for the difficulties that adults have in learning a second language.

The child's ego is dynamic, growing, and flexible through the age of puberty. Thus a new language at this stage does not pose a substantial "threat" or inhibition to the ego, and adaptation is made relatively easily as long as there are no undue confounding sociocultural factors such as, for example, a damaging attitude toward a language or language group at a young age. Then the simultaneous physical, emotional, and cognitive changes of puberty give rise to a defensive mechanism in which the language ego becomes protective and defensive. The language ego clings to the security of the native language to protect the fragile ego of the young adult.

The language ego, which has now become part and parcel of self-identity, is threatened, and thus a context develops in which one must be willing to "make a fool of oneself" in the trial-and-error struggle of speaking and understanding an L2. Younger children are less frightened because they are less aware of language *forms*. The possibility of making mistakes in those forms— mistakes that one really must make in an attempt to communicate spontaneously—does not concern them greatly.

It is no wonder, then, that the acquisition of a new language ego is an enormous undertaking not only for young adolescents but also for an adult who has grown comfortable and secure in his or her own identity and who possesses inhibitions that serve as a wall of defensive protection around the ego. Making the leap to a new or **second identity** can be daunting. Are children more malleable in accepting the budding new "self" that is emerging? Does the native English-speaking child who has recently relocated to China more readily accept the fascinating little Chinese self that is building within? These considerations will be explored in detail in Chapter 7.

What is the role of **attitude** in examining age-related variables? The research is clear that negative attitudes can certainly affect success in learning a language. Young children, who are not developed enough cognitively to possess feelings about races, cultures, ethnic groups, classes of people, and languages, may be less affected than adults. Macnamara (1975) noted that "a child suddenly transported from Montreal to Berlin will rapidly learn German no matter what he thinks of the Germans" (p. 79). But as children broaden their experiences in school, sports, arts, and travel, they also begin to acquire certain attitudes toward types and stereotypes of people. We will take up this issue again in Chapter 6.

A sometimes neglected factor in considering child–adult comparisons is the power of **peer pressure**. The drive in children to conform to those around them is strong, and usually one that takes on huge significance in the teens. Pressure to conform in a bilingual setting can be a powerful motivator. Conversely, if the child is the only person in a group to try speaking a second language, the resistance to "sounding funny," or being given "the look" by other kids will be an equally powerful motivator.

It is possible that the successful adult language learner is someone who can bridge the ego-related affective gaps. Some of the seeds of success might have been sown early in life: a bilingual neighborhood, parents who gave their children plenty of praise, and who laughed *with* their children when they did something "goofy," or just an environment of "playing" with words and phrases.

A final reminder: In looking at SLA in children, it is important to distinguish younger and older children. Preadolescent children of age ten or eleven, for example, are beginning to develop inhibitions, and it is conceivable that children of this age have a good deal of affective dissonance to overcome as they attempt to learn a second language. Their self-consciousness could work against them.

 CLASSROOM CONNECTIONS

A five- or six-year-old child and a ten- or eleven-year-old are very different emotional and intellectual beings. List some of those differences, especially affective differences, and think about how those differences would affect the way you plan your classroom activities for the two separate groups. What are some specific examples of different approaches you would take for the two age groups?

LINGUISTIC CONSIDERATIONS

What are some *linguistic* considerations in age-related questions about SLA? A growing number of research studies are now available to shed some light on the linguistic processes of second language learning and how those processes differ between children and adults.

Bilingualism

My traumatizing experience upon enrolling midyear in a French-speaking kindergarten wasn't my first "foreign" language. I was bilingual in English and Lontomba until the age of three, and in the Belgian educational system a required "foreign" language was Flemish (Dutch)—which, according to my parents, I learned with relative ease. And by now, because of my parents' relocation, my forgotten Lontomba had to be replaced by Lingala.

So, count them up: five languages before my seventh birthday! The only one I had to "work" at was Flemish, since it was classroom-taught, and I of course promptly forgot Flemish on another relocation at the age of seven.

All four of the other languages were acquired without instruction, implicitly, with motivation that was driven by social and educational necessity. Was it "easy" to do so? I don't remember. Was language acquisition "effortless"? Not at all—I'm sure every fiber of my young boy's being was devoted to the process of learning to communicate.

Research shows that children learning two languages simultaneously acquire them by the use of similar strategies (Lakshmanan, 2009). They are, in essence, learning two first languages, with the added element of distinguishing the appropriate contexts for each language.

Some interesting questions about child **bilingualism** have been pursued in the research. People who learn a second language in separate contexts can often be described as **coordinate bilinguals**—they operate with two meaning systems. In contrast, **compound bilinguals** have one meaning system, that is, one context, in which both languages operate. Children generally do not have problems with language "mixing," regardless of the separate contexts for use of the languages, as "bilinguals are not two monolinguals in the same head" (Cook, 1995, p. 58).

Most bilinguals, however, engage in **code-switching** (the act of inserting words, phrases, or even longer stretches of one language into the other), especially when communicating with another bilingual (Arias & Lakshmanan, 2005). And of course many (but not all) bilinguals will exhibit the dominance of one of the two (or more) languages, which is usually the product of contextual variables.

Another domain of interest has centered on **heritage language** acquisition (Montrul, 2011), which refers to "family lineage" languages acquired by individuals raised in homes where the dominant language of the region, such as English in the United States, is not spoken or not exclusively spoken in the home. Studies of the acquisition of a heritage language involve a fascinating complexity of variables, including motivational factors, attitudes toward the language/culture, peer pressure (or lack thereof), and age. Montrul (2008) described a good deal of heritage language acquisition as "incomplete" acquisition, caused by a number of intervening factors.

Finally, the *rate* of acquisition of both languages in bilingual children is slightly slower than the normal schedule for first language acquisition. However, a respectable stockpile of research (see Schinke-Llano, 1989; Reynolds, 1991) shows a considerable cognitive benefit of early childhood bilingualism, supporting Lambert's (1972) contention that bilingual children are more facile at concept formation and have greater mental flexibility.

Interference Between First and Second Languages

A good deal of the research on children's SLA has focused on the interfering effects of the first and second languages (Natalicio and Ravem, 1968; Natalicio, 1971; Dulay and Burt, 1974a; Ervin-Tripp, 1974; Milon, 1974; Hansen-Bede, 1975; Lakshmanan, 2009). Most are conclusive in showing similar strategies and linguistic features for both first and second language learning in children. Dulay and Burt (1974a) found intralingual strategies, not interference errors from the first language, among Spanish-speaking children learning English. Hansen-Bede's (1975) study of a three-year-old child showed the child used similar strategies and rules for both the first and the second languages.

Adult second language linguistic processes are more vulnerable to the effect of the first language on the second, especially the farther apart the two language-learning events are. What we have learned above all else from this research is that the *saliency* of interference from the first language does not imply that interference is the most *relevant* or most crucial factor in adult second language acquisition. Adults and children both manifest intralingual errors, the result of an attempt to discover the rules of the L2 apart from the rules of the L1. Thus, L1 is a facilitating factor, and not just an interfering factor.

Order of Acquisition

One of the first steps toward demonstrating the importance of factors beyond first language interference in child SLA was taken in a series of research studies by Heidi Dulay and Marina Burt (1972, 1974a, 1974b, 1976). Emphasizing the absence of L1 interference, they claimed that "transfer of L1 syntactic patterns rarely occurs" in child L2 acquisition (1976, p. 72). They claimed that children learning a second language use a **creative construction** process, just as they do in their first language.

This conclusion was supported by research data collected on the acquisition order of eleven English morphemes in children learning English as a second language. Dulay and Burt found a common order of acquisition among children of several native language backgrounds, an order very similar to that found by Roger Brown (1973) using the same morphemes but for children acquiring English as their first language:

1. present progressive (*-ing*)
2. [**and 3.**] *in, on*
3. plural (*-s*)
4. past irregular
5. possessive (*-'s*)
6. uncontractible copula (*is, am, are*)
7. articles (*a, the*)
8. past regular (*-ed*)
9. third-person regular (*-s*)
10. third-person irregular

Support for Dulay and Burt's order of acquisition hypothesis came from Zobl and Liceras (1994, p. 161), but others argued suspect statistical procedures (Rosansky, 1976) and that 11 English morphemes constitute only a minute portion of English syntax (Larsen-Freeman, 1976; Roger Andersen, 1978). Larsen-Freeman (1976), among others, hinted that *frequency* of occurrence in the child's input may be an explanation of the consistent findings.

How do morpheme-order studies shed light on the relevance of age for acquisition? While the *causes* of ostensibly universal patterns of acquisition remain a bit of a mystery, the fact that children manifest such an order raises questions about natural orders for adults. Bardovi-Harlig (1999b) contended that a semantic-oriented approach (as opposed to syntactic) had more explanatory power. In this vein, Goldschneider & DeKeyser (2001, 2005) refined earlier claims about acquisition order by proposing five determinants of acquisition order across numerous languages:

1. Perceptual salience (how easy it is to see or hear a given structure)
2. Semantic complexity (how many meanings are expressed by a particular form)
3. Morpho-phonological regularity (the degree to which language forms are affected by their phonological environment)
4. Syntactic category (grammatical characteristics of forms)
5. Frequency in the input (the number of times a given structure occurs in speech addressed to the learner)

Goldschneider and DeKeyser suggested that "teachers could make the [five determinants] work for them and could potentially increase the rate of acquisition by presenting material . . . in a way that capitalizes on these causes" (2005, p. 63).

 CLASSROOM CONNECTIONS

Can you think of examples, in a foreign language you have learned, of each of the above five determinants? For example, for #2, in English the word *read* can be present or past tense form—how would you present both forms? In #5, what are some frequent forms or words that you might present well before infrequent ones? (Regular and irregular verbs, perhaps?)

At the risk of oversimplifying some complex issues that have been presented here, Table 3.1 is offered as a summary of findings so far on the question of whether or not "younger is better" in SLA. The table distinguishes between acquisition of communicative, interactive *fluency* and the acquisition of a "native" *accent*.

Table 3.1 The Younger the Better? A Summary of Possible Age Effects

Possible Cause	Effect	Plausibility[1]
1. Neurophysiological development	Fluency[2]	NO
	Accent[3]	YES
2. Hemispheric lateralization	Fluency	NO
	Accent	No
3. Critical (sensitive) period	Fluency	NO
	Accent	Yes
4. Cognitive maturation	Fluency	???
	Accent	No
5. Affective factors (inhibition, language ego, identity, attitude)	Fluency	Yes
	Accent	Yes
6. L1-L2 interference	Fluency	???
	Accent	Yes

Scale, from a strong "yes" to a strong "no": YES, yes, ???, no, NO

[1] Does the research show a plausible cause and effect relationship?
[2] Is eventual communicative, interactive fluency a factor of age?
[3] Is the acquisition of an authentic "native" accent a factor of age?

ISSUES IN FIRST LANGUAGE ACQUISITION REVISITED

In Chapter 2, eight issues were cited that could galvanize your awareness of what is at stake in L1 research. How do those issues enlighten our examination of issues in age and acquisition? Here's a brief look.

Competence and Performance

After all these years of research, judging a person's competence under the best of conditions (without intervening variables) relies on *inference* from performance (the actual "doing" of language) data. This fact applies to both children and adults, and explains why the research of the last half-century or so has focused on empirical performance data. We are getting much better at such methodology, with payoffs for the age and acquisition issue in examining neurolinguistic data, contextual factors, and individual cognitive and socio-affective considerations.

Comprehension and Production

When we say, "Do you speak English?" or "Parlez-vous français?" we usually mean "and do you *understand* it, too?" Both child and adult second language learners will normally *hear* a distinction before being able to produce it. Adults are actually better at rote mimicry, especially beyond a few words, but may not comprehend the meaning of what has been mimicked. Adults may be more inhibited and therefore attempt to speak less willingly than children, but because of their more mature cognition, be more willing to attend to longer passages of written or spoken text.

Nature or Nurture?

What happens after puberty to the magic "little black box" (the Language Acquisition Device or LAD)? Does the adult suffer from linguistic "hardening of the arteries"? Does the LAD "grow up" and outlive its usefulness? We don't have complete answers to these questions, but there have been some hints in the discussion of physical, cognitive, and affective factors. What we do know is that adults and children alike appear to have the capacity to acquire a second language at any age. The only trick that nature might play on adults is to make it very difficult to acquire a "native" accent. As you have seen, there is a wide swath of language properties that may actually be more efficiently acquired by an adult. If an adult does not acquire a second language successfully, it is probably because of intervening cognitive or affective variables and not the absence of innate capacities. Defining those intervening variables is clearly more immediately fruitful for researchers and teachers alike.

Universals

Some research on child SLA suggests that children's developing L2 grammars are indeed constrained by Universal Grammar (UG) (Lakshmanan, 1995; Bhatia & Ritchie, 2009). But it is not immediately clear whether this knowledge is available directly from a truly universal "source," or through the mediation of the first language. Some researchers have concluded that second language learners have only "partial access" to UG (O'Grady, 1996), while Bley-Vroman (1988) conjectured that adults acquire second language systems without any reference to UG at all! Cook (1993) concluded that if UG models do not fit L2 learning processes, then it may be "the description of UG that is at fault, and not the L2 learner" (p. 245). With such mixed results (Van Buren, 1996), we are perhaps best served by keeping an open mind on UG-related mysteries.

Systematicity and Variability

Second language linguistic development in "natural" (untutored) contexts appears in many instances to mirror the L1 acquisition process: learners induce rules, generalize across a category, overgeneralize, and proceed in stages of development (more on this in Chapter 9). Recent research has suggested that even the order of acquisition may universally follow certain identifiable determinants (Goldschneider & DeKeyser, 2005). The thorny problems of the variability of L2 data, for both children and adults (R. Ellis, 1987, 1989; Tarone, 1988; Preston, 1996; Gass & Selinker, 2001), are exacerbated by a host of cognitive, affective, cultural, and contextual variables that are sometimes not applicable to a first language learning situation.

Language and Thought

It goes without saying that language helps to shape thinking and vice versa. What happens to this interdependence when a second language is acquired? How does age affect the relationship? Whether one's memory consists of one storage system (compound bilingualism) or two (coordinate bilingualism), we know that language acquisition at any age is also "thought acquisition." The L2 learner must sort out new meanings from old, distinguish thoughts and concepts in one language that are similar but not quite parallel to the L2, or acquire new systems of conceptualization. Age is a factor in all this, but the research is equivocal at best regarding any age advantage one way or another (Muñoz & Singleton, 2011).

CLASSROOM CONNECTIONS

To what extent have you found that learning an L2 has involved "thought acquisition" as well? What are some examples of ways of thinking that were new to you? How would you as a teacher help your students to empathize with new ways of thinking?

Imitation

While children are good deep-structure imitators (centering on meaning, not surface features), adults can fare much better in imitating surface structure (by rote) if they are explicitly directed to do so. Sometimes their ability to center on surface distinctions is a distracting factor; at other times it is helpful. Adults learning a second language might do well to attend consciously to truth value and to be less aware of surface structure as they communicate. The implication is that meaningful contexts for language learning are necessary; L2 learners ought not to become too preoccupied with form lest they lose sight of the function and purpose of language.

Practice and Frequency

Too many language classes are filled with rote practice that centers on surface forms. Most cognitive psychologists agree that the frequency of stimuli and the number of times spent practicing a form are not as highly important as meaningfulness, although some research suggests the importance of frequency (N. Ellis, 2002; Gor & Long, 2009). All sources are unequivocal in advocating contextualized, meaningful communication in the L2 as the best possible "practice."

Input

Input, and how it is processed and acted upon, has emerged as one of the most fundamental keys to acquisition at any age (Gor & Long, 2009). The efficiency of its deliverance, along with related [corrective] feedback, may well prove to be an overriding predictor of successful L2 acquisition in any classroom setting.

Discourse

No doubt a study of children's amazing dexterity in acquiring conversational ability and in perceiving intended meaning will help us find ways of teaching such capacities to second language learners. But we cannot underestimate the superiority of older children's and adults' ability to utilize subtle pragmatic elements of language such as metaphor, humor, "shades" of meaning, double entendres, and nonverbal cues.

AGE-AND-ACQUISITION-INSPIRED TEACHING METHODS

In Chapter 2, we saw that research on language teaching in the modern era may have been sparked by François Gouin's observation of his young nephew's *first* language acquisition. Another look at language teaching methodology in a historical context reveals a number of instances of methods that were inspired by observation of, and research on child *second* language acquisition. Two of these methods are described here as examples of extending an understanding of children's second language acquisition to the adult second language classroom.

Total Physical Response

The founder of the **Total Physical Response** (TPR) method, James Asher (1977), noted that children, in learning their first language, appear to do a lot of listening before they speak, and that their listening is accompanied by physical responses (reaching, grabbing, moving, looking, and so forth). The TPR classroom, then, was one in which students did a great deal of listening and acting. The teacher was very directive in orchestrating a performance: "The instructor is the director of a stage play in which the students are the actors" (Asher, 1977, p. 43).

A typical TPR class utilized the imperative mood, even at more advanced proficiency levels. Commands were an easy way to get learners to get out of their seats and to loosen up: "Open the window," "Pick up the book," "Give it to John." No verbal response was necessary. More complex syntax was incorporated into the imperative: "Draw a rectangle on the chalkboard." "Walk quickly to the door and hit it." Humor was easy to introduce: "Walk slowly to the window and jump." "Put your toothbrush in your book" (Asher, 1977, p. 55). Interrogatives were also easily dealt with: "Where is the book?" "Who is John?" (Students point to the book or to John). Eventually students, one by one, presumably felt comfortable enough to venture verbal responses to questions, then to ask questions themselves, and the process continued.

Like other methods of the twentieth century, TPR had its limitations. It was especially effective in the beginning levels of language proficiency, but lost its distinctiveness as learners advanced in their competence. But today TPR is used more as a type of classroom *activity*, which is a more useful way to view it. Many successful communicative, interactive classrooms utilize TPR activities to provide both auditory input and physical activity.

The Natural Approach

One of the claims of Krashen's (1982) theories of L2 acquisition was that adults should acquire a second language just as children do: They should be given the opportunity to "pick up" a language, and shouldn't be forced to "study" grammar in the classroom. A major methodological offshoot of Krashen's work was the **Natural Approach** (Krashen & Terrell, 1983). Acting on many of the claims that Asher made for TPR, Krashen and Terrell felt that learners would benefit from delaying production until speech "emerges," that learners should be as relaxed as possible in the classroom, and that a great deal of communication and "acquisition" should take place, as opposed to analysis.

The Natural Approach simulated child language acquisition through the use of TPR activities at the beginning level. Everyday language situations were highlighted: shopping, home and health topics, etc. But in advocating teacher-delivered "comprehensible input" (spoken language that is understandable to the learner or just a little beyond the learner's level), this method departed from strictly drawing insights from children's "natural" acquisition. Because learners did not need to say anything until they felt ready to do so, and because the teacher was the (sole) source of the learners' input, the method bore only mild resemblance to child language acquisition—first or second. Richards & Rodgers (2001) noted that the delay of oral production can be pushed too far and that at an early stage it is important for the teacher to step in and encourage students to talk. Language learning is, after all, an interactive process.

We have seen in this chapter that there certainly appear to be some potential advantages to an early age for SLA, but there is absolutely no evidence that an adult cannot overcome *all* of those disadvantages save one, accent, and the latter is hardly the quintessential criterion for effective interpersonal communication. Scovel (1999) says it well: "'The younger, the better' is a myth that has been fueled by media hype and, sometimes, 'junk science.' . . . On at least several planes—literacy, vocabulary, pragmatics, schematic knowledge, and even syntax—adults have been shown to be superior learners" (p. 1).

I began this chapter with an autobiographical account of my French learning experience at the age of five. Two important caveats about child L2 learning are embedded in the story.

One must never assume that young children are emotionally impervious to being thrust into a bilingual learning experience. Yes, they may over time become absorbent sponges, soaking up linguistic data with seemingly little effort. But deep within lies a possibly fragile ego—one that is extremely vulnerable to adults and peers that threaten a perceived strength of self along with the stability of the home language.

Remember, too, that what children learn quickly and naturally is also for-gotten—possibly even more quickly. After my move to another location (and another Bantu language region) on my seventh birthday, I was home-schooled in English and exposed to a Kikongo speech community. I promptly forgot most of my French (except for the retention of a rather good Belgian French accent), along with the Lingala spoken in Léopoldville. I also quickly learned Kikongo, my sixth language, but two years later a one-year stay in the United States managed to obliterate much of that proficiency!

Into my teen years, my Lontomba, Flemish, and Lingala might as well have never surged through my brain cells. A trace of "street" French survived, as I lived in a French-speaking country, but never to the fluency of the end of my first grade. My Kikongo faltered because I was sent at the age of ten to a boarding school in Tshiluba-speaking territory, where I picked up "survival" Tshiluba, my seventh lan-guage. I then ended up being "semi-lingual" in Kikongo, Tshiluba, and French! Mercifully, my English is still okay!

Praise for the child's marvelous ability to learn languages must be miti-gated by recognition of an equally pesky penchant for forgetting!

SUGGESTED READINGS

Birdsong, D. (2009). Age and the end state of second language acquisition. In W. Ritchie & T. Bhatia (Eds.), *The new handbook of second language acqui-sition* (pp. 401–424). Bingley, UK: Emerald Group Publishing, Ltd.

Muñoz, C., & Singleton, D. (2011). A critical review of age-related research on L2 ultimate attainment. *Language Teaching, 44,* 1–35.

Both of these articles provide comprehensive summaries of research over half a century of inquiry, each with an analysis of divergent research find-ings and extensive bibliographic references.

Lakshmanan, U. (2009). Child second language acquisition. In W. Ritchie & T. Bhatia (Eds.), *The new handbook of second language acquisition* (pp. 377–399). Bingley, UK: Emerald Group Publishing, Ltd.

A critical summary and analysis that includes both theoretical and methodological issues, as well as an examination of phonological, lexical, and morphosyntactic acquisition.

Singleton, D., & Ryan, L. (2004). *Language acquisition: The age factor* (2nd ed.). Clevedon, UK: Multilingual Matters.

A detailed book-length discussion of issues and evidence, with separate synopses of first and second language evidence. The comprehensive bib-liography is useful.

LANGUAGE LEARNING EXPERIENCE: JOURNAL ENTRY 3

Note: See Chapter 1 for general guidelines for writing a journal on a previous or concurrent language learning experience.

- How good do you think your pronunciation of your L2 is? How do you feel about your pronunciation—satisfied, dissatisfied, resigned, in need of improvement? Assuming you would not expect to be "perfect," what steps can you take (or could you have taken) to improve your pronunciation to a point of maximum clarity of articulation?
- Given your current age (or your age when you were learning an L2), do you feel you're too old to make much progress? Are you linguistically "beyond your prime" with little hope of achieving your goals? Analyze the roots of your answers to these questions.
- Children might have some secrets of success: not monitoring themselves too much, not analyzing grammar, not being too worried about their egos, shedding inhibitions, not letting the native language interfere much. In what way did you, or could you, put those secrets to use in your own learning?
- In learning an L2, were any aspects (such as listening discrimination exercises, pronunciation drills, learning grammar rules, small group conversations, reading, or writing) easier than others for you? Analyze what made certain procedures easier than others.
- Do you think you might have some advantages over children in learning an L2? Speculate on what those advantages might be. Then make a list of strategies you could use to capitalize on those advantages.

FOR THE TEACHER: ACTIVITIES (A) & DISCUSSION (D)

Note: For each of the "Classroom Connections" in this chapter, you may wish to turn them into individual or pair-work discussion questions.

1. (A) Assign to small groups or pairs (one for each group) the seven common arguments (page 52) cited by Stern (1970) that were used to justify analogies between first language learning and second language teaching. Ask the group to determine what is assumed or presupposed in each statement and to reiterate the flaw in each analogy. Report conclusions back to the whole class for further discussion.
2. (D) Are there any students in the class who have had contact with or who have learned additional languages before puberty? What were the circumstances? What difficulties, if any, were encountered? Has authentic pronunciation in the language remained to this day?
3. (D) Is there anyone in the class, or anyone who knows someone else, who started learning a second language after puberty and who

nevertheless has an almost "perfect" accent. Why was such a person able to be so successful?

4. (D) Explain Scovel's claim that the acquisition of a native accent around the age of puberty is an evolutionary leftover of sociobiological critical periods evident in many species of animals and birds. In view of widely accepted cross-cultural, cross-linguistic, and interracial marriages today, how relevant is the biological claim for mating within the gene pool?

5. (A) In groups or pairs, brainstorm criteria for deciding whether or not someone is an authentic *native* speaker of your native language. In the process, consider the wide variety of dialects of languages spoken today. Talk about occupations, if any, in which a native accent is indispensable. Share with the rest of the class, and try to come to a consensus.

6. (A) In groups, ask Ss to share any cognitive or affective blocks they have experienced in their own attempts to learn an L2. What could they do (or what could they have done) to overcome those barriers? Share findings with the rest of the class.

7. (D) Do you think it is worthwhile to teach children an L2 in the classroom? If so, how might approaches and methods differ between a class of children and a class of adults?

CHAPTER 4

HUMAN LEARNING

Much to the chagrin of his parents, Ethan decides that he will adopt the mynah bird that his Aunt Mary picked up at the animal shelter. He has shown an interest in birds since about the age of three when the same Aunt Mary gave him a bird feeder for Christmas. He is determined to teach the mynah—he has named her Myra—to talk. As an Internet-savvy ten-year-old, he Googles some hints on how to train a mynah to talk, but he's in a bit of a quandary on exactly what steps to take. Short of offering psychological counseling to Ethan's parents, can you help him out?

Ethan's task isn't about *human* learning, but perhaps basic principles of learning will apply. Let's offer Ethan the following steps:

1. First, he will need to specify *entry behavior*—what Myra already "knows." What abilities does she have upon which he can build? What are her drives, needs, motivations, and limitations? Has she ever come close to mimicking a human?
2. Next, Ethan will need to formulate the *goals* of his task. What will his specific objectives be? What words should he start with? How many words or phrases should he teach Myra?
3. Next, he might want to devise *methods of* training. Based on what he determines about entry behavior and goals of the task, the training process might have to be "customized." Where should he begin? Should he start by putting Myra on his finger and talking to her? Offering a favorite snack for Myra's producing anything that sounds like human speech? What alternatives should he have ready if Myra fails to show any signs of talking? (This would delight Ethan's parents.)
4. Finally, Ethan will need some sort of *evaluation procedure*. How should he determine whether or not Myra had indeed learned to talk? It would be a good idea to determine short-term and long-term evaluation measures. If Myra speaks once today, what will happen tomorrow? Will she maintain her talking ability?

Already a somewhat simple task has become quite complex, but we're considering only a species of bird known to be a "talker." If we consider human beings learning a second language, the task is of course much more complex. Nevertheless, the questions and procedures that apply to you, the language teacher, are akin to those that applied to Ethan, the mynah trainer. You must know the person's entry behavior, specify objectives, devise methods that you will employ, and design an evaluation procedure. These steps derive from your conception of how human beings *learn*, and that is what this chapter is all about.

 CLASSROOM CONNECTIONS

In a classroom situation in which you have been a learner or a teacher, what are some of the *entry behaviors* you would count on among students? What sets of abilities, skills, and/or prior language learning experience did you have when you first started learning a foreign language? How would you (as a learner or as a teacher) capitalize on what learners bring to a language class-room before the first lesson has even begun?

In turning now to varied theories of how human beings learn, consider once again the various definitions of learning discussed in Chapter 1. Learning is:

- acquiring or getting of knowledge of a subject or a skill by study, experience, or instruction
- a relatively permanent change in a behavioral tendency
- the result of reinforced practice.

When we consider such definitions, it is clear that one can understand learning in many different ways, which is why there are so many different theories, extended definitions, and schools of thought on the topic of learning.

We'll now focus on how psychologists have defined **learning**, specifically within three broad perspectives: (1) behavioral psychology, (2) cognitive psychology and cognitive linguistics, and (3) social-constructivism. The three positions illustrate not only some of the history of learning theory, but also some of the diverse perspectives that form the foundations of varying language teaching approaches and methods.

BEHAVIORAL PERSPECTIVES

For the first half of the twentieth century, behavioral psychology enjoyed unprecedented popularity as the ultimate explanation of the processes of human (and animal) learning. Emphasizing the supremacy of conditioning paradigms, the crucial role of rewards and punishments, and the scientific nature of experimental evidence, behaviorism went virtually unchallenged until the middle of the twentieth century. Let's look at some of the highlights and champions of this perspective.

The best-known classical behaviorist was the Russian psychologist Ivan Pavlov, who at the turn of the twentieth century conducted numerous **classical conditioning** experiments. For Pavlov the learning process consisted of the formation of associations between stimuli and reflexive responses. Pavlov used the *salivation* response (an **unconditioned response**) to the sight or smell of food in his now famous experiments with dogs. Through repeated occurrences, the dog associated the sound of a bell with food until the dog acquired a **conditioned response**: salivation at the sound of the bell. A previously neutral **stimulus** (the sound of the bell) had acquired the power to elicit a **response** (salivation) that was originally elicited by another stimulus (the smell of meat).

Drawing on Pavlov's findings, John Watson (1913) coined the term **behaviorism,** contending that human behavior should be studied objectively, rejecting nonmeasurable notions of innateness and instinct. He adopted the classical conditioning theory as the explanation for all learning: By the process of conditioning, we build an array of stimulus-response connections, and more complex behaviors are learned by building up series or chains of responses.

Later, E. L. Thorndike (1932) expanded on classical conditioning models by showing that stimuli that occurred *after* a behavior had an influence on future behaviors, known as his **Law of Effect**. Pavlov's, Watson's, and Thorndike's emphasis on the study of overt behavior and rigorous adherence to the scientific method had a tremendous influence on learning theories for decades. Language teaching practices were likewise influenced by the behavioristic tradition.

Thorndike's work paved the way for B. F. Skinner, in his seminal publication, *The Behavior of Organisms* (1938), to establish himself as one of the leading behaviorists in the United States. His approach was more appropriately labeled as **neobehaviorism,** since he added a unique dimension to behavioristic psychology (Anderson & Ausubel, 1965). Pavlov's classical conditioning was, according to Skinner, a highly specialized form of learning utilized mainly by animals with minimal relevance for human conditioning. Skinner called Pavlovian conditioning **respondent conditioning** since it was concerned with behavior that is **elicited** by a preceding stimulus.

Skinner contended that Pavlov's respondent conditioning was inferior to **operant conditioning** in which one "operates" on the environment. Here, the importance of a (preceding) stimulus is deemphasized in favor of rewards that *follow* desired behavior. For example, we cannot identify a specific stimulus leading a baby to rise to a standing position or to take a first step; we therefore need not be concerned about that stimulus, but we should be concerned about the *consequences*—the stimuli (rewards) that follow the response. Linguistically, a child's attempts to produce language are, in Skinner's model, operants that are in turn reinforced by a parent's responses.

Skinner defined **operants** in the learning process as acts (e.g., crying, walking, speaking) that are **emitted** with no observable stimulus, and governed by the consequences they produce. If a baby cries to get a parent's attention, and subsequently receives a comforting hug or smile, the emitted response of crying is reinforced through positive consequences. According to Skinner, if parents ignore crying (when they are certain that it is *operant* crying), eventually the absence of **reinforcement** will extinguish the behavior—perhaps Skinner wasn't a model parent!

According to Skinner, the events or stimuli—the **reinforcers**—that follow a response both strengthen behavior and increase the probability of a recurrence of that response. Such reinforcers are far stronger aspects of learning than is mere association of a prior stimulus with a following response, as in the classical respondent conditioning model. We are governed by the consequences of our behavior, and therefore Skinner felt we ought, in analyzing human behavior, to center on the effect of those consequences.

 CLASSROOM CONNECTIONS

Thorndike and Skinner both emphasized the importance of reinforcement that occurs *after* a desired behavior. Teachers in language classrooms often offer responses or reinforcement after a student performs in the foreign language. What kind of responses have your teachers used to reward your efforts? How would you, as a teacher, *reinforce* students' attempts to produce or comprehend language?

What about negative reinforcement? Skinner believed that **punishment** "works to the disadvantage of both the punished organism and the punishing agency" (1953, p. 183). Punishment can be either the withdrawal of a positive reinforcer (such as food, a hug, or a smile) or the presentation of an aversive stimulus (say, a harsh reprimand). Skinner felt that in the long run, punishment does not actually eliminate behavior, but he did concede that mild punishment may be necessary for temporary suppression of an undesired response (Skinner, 1953). The best method of extinction, said Skinner, is the *absence* of any reinforcement whatsoever.

Skinner was extremely methodical and empirical in his theory of learning, to the point of being preoccupied with scientific controls. While many of his experiments were performed on lower animals, his theories had an impact on our understanding of human learning and on education. His book, *The Technology of Teaching* (1968), was a classic in the field of programmed instruction. Skinner was convinced that virtually any subject matter could be taught effectively by a carefully designed program of step-by-step reinforcement. Skinner's *Verbal Behavior* (1957) described language as a system of verbal operants, and his understanding of the role of conditioning led to a whole new era in educational practices around the middle of the twentieth century.

 CLASSROOM CONNECTIONS

One of the hallmarks of Skinnerian psychology was the emphasis on the power of an *emitted* response—one that comes "willingly" from the learner without an outside stimulus (*elicited* response) from the teacher. What kinds of emitted responses have you experienced in learning or teaching a language? How would a teacher encourage students to *emit* if the teacher doesn't first "tell" the student what to do or say? What kinds of common language classroom activities capitalize on setting the stage for emitted responses by students?

A Skinnerian view of both language and language learning strongly influenced L2 teaching methodology in middle of the century, leading to a heavy reliance in the classroom on the controlled practice of verbal operants under carefully designed schedules of reinforcement. The popular Audiolingual Method, which will be discussed at the end of this chapter, was a prime example of Skinner's impact on American language teaching practices in the decades of the 1950s and 1960s.

There is much in behavioral theory that is true and valuable, but there is another viewpoint to be considered. We've looked at the claim that human behavior can be predicted and controlled and scientifically studied and validated. We have not looked at the notion that human behavior is essentially abstract in nature, composed of such a complex and variable system that most human learning simply *cannot* be accurately predicted or controlled. We turn next to some paradigms that attempted just such a response to behaviorism.

COGNITIVE PERSPECTIVES

Cognitive psychology was in many ways a reaction to the inadequacies of behavioral approaches to human learning. Conditioning paradigms were quite sufficient for animal training but mostly failed to account for the network of neurological processes involved in the acquisition of complex skills, the development of intelligence, the ability of humans to think logically and abstractly, and our enigmatic ability to be creative.

Learning as Meaningful Storage and Retrieval

David Ausubel (1968) was among the first educational cognitive psychologists to frame a theory of learning that was understandable, practical, and applicable to classrooms and teachers. Simply put, he described human learning as a *meaningful* process of relating (associating) new events or items to already existing cognitive structure (Ausubel, 1965). You might say it's like hanging new items onto existing cognitive "pegs." Ausubel's (1968) perspective accounted for the acquisition of new meanings (knowledge), retention, the organization of knowledge in a hierarchical structure, and the eventual occurrence of forgetting.

Meaningful learning is best understood by contrasting it with **rote learning**. Ausubel described rote learning as the process of acquiring material as "discrete and relatively isolated entities" (1968, p. 108) that have little or no association with existing cognitive structure. Most of us, for example, can learn a few necessary phone numbers and postal codes by rote without reference to cognitive hierarchical organization.

On the other hand, meaningful learning, or **subsumption**, may be described as a process of relating and anchoring new material to relevant established entities in cognitive structure. As new material enters our perceptual field, it interacts with, and is appropriately *subsumed* under, a more inclusive conceptual system. If we think of cognitive structure as a system of building blocks, then rote learning is the process of acquiring isolated blocks with no particular relationship to other blocks. Meaningful learning is the process whereby blocks become an integral part of already established categories or systematic clusters of blocks. For the sake of a visual picture of the distinction, consider the graphic representation in Figures 4.1 and 4.2.

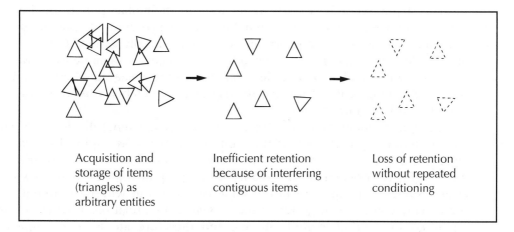

| Acquisition and storage of items (triangles) as arbitrary entities | Inefficient retention because of interfering contiguous items | Loss of retention without repeated conditioning |

Figure 4.1   Schematic representation of rote learning and retention

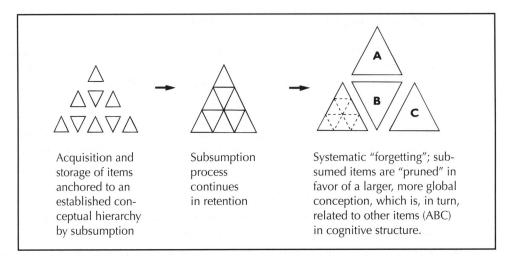

Figure 4.2   Schematic representation of meaningful learning and retention (subsumption)

The significance of the distinction between rote and meaningful learning has tremendous implications for both natural and instructed language acquisition. Recent linguistic research (Ellis & Collins, 2009) has placed emphasis on the role of *frequency* in language acquisition—a role that fits well with behavioral perspectives. But consider the power of *meaningfulness* (importance, significance, relatability) in the eventual retention of cognitive items. If you carelessly run across a crosswalk and narrowly miss getting hit by a car, you won't need frequent repetitions of that scare to teach you to be careful. Once is enough!

Granted, human beings are capable of learning almost any given item within the so-called "magic seven, plus or minus two" (Miller, 1956) units for perhaps a few seconds. We can remember an unfamiliar phone number, for example, long enough to call the number, after which point the phone number is usually extinguished by interfering factors. Arbitrarily assigned, nonsystematically defined numbers are often difficult to retain. To compensate, we can resort to what Smith (1975) called "manufacturing meaningfulness" (p. 162), that is, inventing artificial *mnemonic devices* to remember a list of items, perhaps for an upcoming examination.

Long-term memory is a different matter. A meaningfully learned, subsumed item has greater potential for retention. Area codes, postal codes, and street addresses are sometimes efficiently retained since they bear some meaningful relationship to the reality of geographical areas or houses on a street. Names of people are in the same category, but without frequent reinforcement, could be forgotten. Faces, events, and relationships are clearly anchored in multiple neural circuits, and therefore are good examples of meaningful learning.

CLASSROOM CONNECTIONS

Compile a list of a dozen or so different classroom activities or techniques, e.g., pronunciation drill, grammar explanation, free-writing exercise, information-gap group work. Then decide, on a scale of rote to meaningful, from 1 to 10, where the technique falls. Were all your decisions easy to make? Why or why not?

Systematic Forgetting and Cognitive "Pruning"

Why do we forget things? A behavioral explanation cites *in*frequency of input, the cessation of practice, and lack of reinforcement. A cognitive perspective takes a much broader view, looking at saliency, relevance, emotion, and the strength of anchoring mental sets that capture a trace of memory. As noted above, an infrequently occurring but very scary (or delightful or romantic) event may be indelibly etched in memory.

Once again, Ausubel (1965, 1968) provided a plausible explanation for the universal nature of forgetting. Since rotely learned material is not substantively merged into cognitive structure, its retention is influenced primarily by the interfering effects of similar rote material learned immediately before or after the learning task. The consequence of such effects is referred to as **proactive** and **retroactive inhibition**. In the case of meaningfully learned material, retention is influenced primarily by the properties of "relevant and cumulatively established ideational systems in cognitive structure with which the learning task interacts" (Ausubel, 1968, p. 108). Compared to this kind of extended interaction, concurrent interfering effects have relatively little influence on meaningful learning, and retention is quite efficient. Hence, in a face-to-face conversation, a person's physical features are commonly retained as part of a meaningful set, while phone numbers, as isolated unrelatable entities, are easily forgotten.

We cannot say, of course, that meaningfully learned material is never forgotten. But in the case of such learning, forgetting takes place in a much more intentional and *systematic* manner because it is actually a *continuation* of the very process of subsumption by which one learns. Forgetting is really a second or "obliterative" stage of subsumption, characterized as "memorial reduction to the least common denominator" (Ausubel, 1963, p. 218). Because it is more economical and less burdensome to retain a single inclusive concept than to remember a large number of more specific items, the importance of a specific item tends to be incorporated, or subsumed, into the generalized meaning of the larger item. In this obliterative stage of subsumption, the specific items become progressively less identifiable as entities in their own right until they are finally no longer available and are *said* to be forgotten (see Figure 4.2).

Another way of conceptualizing this second stage of subsumption is in a horticultural metaphor: **cognitive pruning** (Brown, 1972). When you prune a tree, your aim is to eliminate unnecessary clutter and to clear the way for more growth. Mixing metaphors and switching to the building-block analogy, one might say that at the outset, a structure made of blocks is seen as a few individual blocks, but as the mind begins to give the structure a perceived shape, some of the single blocks achieve less and less identity in their own right and become subsumed into the larger structure. Finally, the single blocks are lost to perception, or "pruned" out, and the total structure is perceived as a single whole without clearly defined parts.

Examples of pruning abound in the development of concepts. Learning that a cup of hot coffee, a pan of boiling water, or an iron, for example, can cause excessive pain is a cognitive process. A small child's first exposure to such heat may be either direct contact or a verbal "don't touch!" or "hot!" After a number of exposures to such hot things, the child begins to form a concept of "hotness" by clustering experiences together and forming a generalization. But as time goes on, the bits and pieces of experience that actually built the concept are slowly forgotten—pruned—in favor of the general concept that, in the years that follow, enables the child to avoid burning fingers on hot objects.

An important aspect of the pruning stage of learning is that systematic forgetting, or pruning, is not haphazard or chance. Thus by promoting optimal pruning procedures, we have a potential learning situation that will produce retention beyond that normally expected under more traditional theories of forgetting.

Interestingly, pruned items may not actually be obliterated. They may be difficult to consciously retrieve, but could still be an integral part of "deep" cognitive structure. The notion of **automaticity** in SLA may be a case in point. In the early stages of language learning, certain devices (definitions, paradigms, illustrations, or rules) are often used to facilitate subsumption. But in the process of making language automatic, the devices serve only as "interim" entities, meaningful at a low level of subsumption, and then they are systematically pruned out at later stages of language learning.

We might effectively achieve the goal of communicative competence by removing unnecessary barriers to automaticity. A definition, mnemonic device, or a paraphrase might be initially facilitative, but as its need is minimized by larger and more global conceptualizations, it is pruned. For example, a learner in the early stages of acquisition will perhaps overtly learn the *rule* for when and how to use the present perfect tense. That building block enables the learner to produce past perfect forms correctly and in context, but in later stages the rule ceases to be explicitly retrieved in favor of the automatic production of the correct verb without any recourse to the rule learned earlier. (More on automaticity in Chapter 9.)

CLASSROOM CONNECTIONS

In foreign language classes that you have taken (or taught), what are some specific devices or "tricks" or rules that you used at an early stage, and then no longer needed to "remember" at a later stage? Did you use a mnemonic device, a chart, or an association to recall some aspect of the language? How would your teaching incorporate such pruning as your students move from early to late stages?

Research on **language attrition** has focused on a variety of possible causes for the loss of second language skills (Lambert & Freed, 1982; Weltens, 1987; Weltens & Cohen, 1989; Tomiyama, 2000; Montrul, 2002, 2008, 2011). Some studies have shown that lexical, phonological, or syntactic features may be more vulnerable than idioms, semantic factors, or discourse elements (Andersen, 1982; Nakuma, 1998). Obler (1982) suggested that "neurolinguistic blocking" (left-/right-brain functioning) could contribute to forgetting. Other common reasons for language attrition include the following: (1) the strength and conditions of initial learning, (2) the kind of use that a second language has been put to, (3) motivational factors (Gardner, 1982), and (4) cultural identity (Priven, 2002).

 CLASSROOM CONNECTIONS

Consider the principle of meaningfulness in learning, and the corollary that less relevance or relatability means that forgetting or attrition is likely. What can you do as a learner to help prevent attrition? What kinds of techniques do you think a teacher could use to enhance memory in a language classroom?

Attrition is not limited to second language acquisition (Porte, 1999; Isurin, 2000). Native language forgetting can occur in cases of **subtractive bilingualism** (Siegel, 2003; Montrul, 2008, 2011), when learners rely more and more on a second language, which eventually replaces their first language. Often subtractive bilingualism is the result of members of a minority group learning the language of a majority group because the latter denigrates speakers of the minority language.

Cognitive psychology provides a strong theoretical basis for the rejection of conditioning models of practice and repetition in language teaching. In a meaningful process like second language learning, mindless repetition, imitation, and other rote practices in the language classroom should play only minor short-term roles. Rote learning can be effective on a short-term basis, but for any long-term retention it fails because of a buildup of interference. A case in point was the Audiolingual Method, based almost exclusively on a behavioral theory of conditioning and rote learning. The mechanical "stamping in" of the language through saturation with little reference to meaning was seriously challenged by a more broadly based cognitive view (Ausubel, 1964).

Cognitive Linguistics

In the 1980s, the place of language in cognition, along with the development of linguistic abilities as an integral component of cognition, became a central focus for linguists and applied linguists. We have already referred to some of the issues surrounding language and thought, the place of language acquisition in intellectual development, and cognitive considerations in examining age and acquisition. Such mergers of psychology and linguistics gave rise not only to *psycholinguistics* as a field in its own right, but also to what has come to be called **cognitive linguistics** (Evans & Green, 2006; Verspoor & Tyler, 2009; Holme, 2012), with its standard-bearing journal, *Cognitive Linguistics*, leading the way in related research.

Generative and nativist traditions in the study of L1 acquisition tended to view language as independent of cognitive and social functioning. In a mathematically based model, the child was thought to possess a deep structure of syntactic and phonological rules that in turn generated an infinite variety of strings of language. In contrast, many of today's linguistic researchers are highly attuned to the interrelated dynamics of language and cognition. George Lakoff (1987; Lakoff & Johnson, 1980, 2003) was among the vanguard of such inquiry in examining the rich cognitive and social backdrop of metaphor. Soon, inspired by linguists like Deborah Tannen (1990, 1996) and Leonard Talmy (2003), among others, we could no longer look at a child's or adult's language acquisition as simply the computational generation of language divorced from cognitive, functional, and pragmatic contexts.

 CLASSROOM CONNECTIONS

Metaphor is a pervasive and profound characteristic of human language. Examples: journey metaphors ("I'm on the road to success"); direction metaphors ("Back in 1951 . . ."); war metaphors ("The Yankees battled the Red Sox"). In a language that you have learned, think of a few such metaphors that may have posed some difficulty. What are they? How would you as a teacher help students to conceptualize them?

Several themes characterize cognitive linguistic approaches (Croft & Cruse, 2004; Evans & Green, 2006; Robinson & Ellis, 2008):

1. Language is not an autonomous faculty.
2. Syntax is not simply an arbitrary set of rules but rather is interwoven with conceptualization and knowledge.
3. Language ability cannot be examined without concurrent consideration of language *use.*

In the last part of the twentieth century, as studies in L1 and L2 acquisition continued to probe the place of language in human development, it became increasingly obvious that language is interconnected with cognitive concepts such as perception, memory, categorization, meaning, and attention (Robinson & Ellis, 2008).

Cognitive linguistics was applied to teaching methodology by Holme (2012), who designed a pedagogical model for the L2 classroom. He incorporated concepts of "embodiment" (metaphor), the reality of lexicon and grammar, concept formation, and usage to form cornerstones for understanding classroom approaches and techniques. It is safe to conclude that cognitive linguistics is not so much a radical new field of inquiry as it is the result of a coalescence of research findings and the merging of many strands of research, all of which seek to establish the relationship between language and our complex neural networks.

SOCIAL-CONSTRUCTIVIST PERSPECTIVES

Another manifestation of increasing sophistication in research on language acquisition and human learning was the incorporation of social and affective factors into various theoretical propositions. We have already discussed the importance of the socio-affective domain in previous chapters, and there is more to come in Chapters 6 and 7. For now, a discussion of learning theory would fall short without an examination of what have been called social-constructivist perspectives. We'll highlight three iconic figures here to characterize this side of learning: Carl Rogers, Paolo Freire, and Lev Vygotsky.

Carl Rogers

Rogers is not traditionally thought of as a "learning" psychologist, yet his work had a significant impact on our present understanding of learning, particularly in educational contexts. His views on humanistic psychology emanated from his classic work *Client-Centered Therapy* (1951), an analysis of human behavior in terms of a "phenomenological" perspective, a perspective in sharp contrast to his contemporary, Skinner. Rogers saw the "whole person" as a physical and cognitive, but primarily emotional being. "Fully functioning persons," according to Rogers, live at peace with all of their feelings and reactions; they are able to reach their full potential (Rogers, 1977).

Rogers's position has important implications for education (Curran, 1972; Rogers, 1983; O'Hara, 2003) by focusing away from "teaching" and toward "learning" or, in O'Hara's (2003) terms, "transformative pedagogy." The goal of education is the *facilitation* of change and learning. Learning how to learn is more important than being taught something from the "superior" vantage point of a teacher who unilaterally decides what shall be taught.

Many of our present systems of education, in prescribing curricular goals and dictating objectives, deny persons both freedom and dignity. What is needed, according to Rogers, is for teachers to become facilitators of learning, discarding masks of superiority and omniscience. Teachers also need to have genuine trust and acceptance of the student as a worthy, valuable individual, and to keep open lines of communication between student and teacher.

We can see in Rogers's humanism a radical departure from the scientific analysis of behavioral psychology and even from strictly cognitive theories. Rogers was not as concerned about the actual cognitive process of learning because he felt, if the context for learning is properly created with due attention to students' *affective* states, then they will learn everything they need to.

Of course, teachers could take the nondirective approach too far, to the point that valuable time is lost in the process of allowing students to "discover" facts and principles for themselves. Also, a nonthreatening environment might become so "warm and fuzzy" that the facilitative tension needed for learning is absent. There is ample research documenting the positive effects of competitiveness in a classroom, as long as that competitiveness does not damage self-esteem and hinder motivation to learn (Bailey, 1983).

Paolo Freire

Another giant in educational theory is Brazilian educator Paolo Freire (1970). Freire vigorously objected to traditional "banking" concepts of education in which teachers think of their task as one of "filling" students "by making deposits of information which [they] consider to constitute true knowledge— deposits which are detached from reality" (1970, p. 62). Instead, Freire argued, students should be allowed to negotiate learning outcomes, to cooperate with teachers and other learners in a process of discovery, and to relate everything they do in school to their reality outside the classroom.

It was the need to help students to engage in this real-world reality that gave Freire the impetus to pen his seminal work, *Pedagogy of the Oppressed* (1970), which has since inspired millions of teachers worldwide. Education must be focused on helping students to engage in critical thinking: to look beneath various canons of knowledge and to question that which they are simply told to accept unequivocally. Freire wanted all students to become instruments of their own *empowerment*, "lifting themselves up by their own bootstraps." While such "liberationist" views of education should be approached with some caution (Clarke, 1990), learners may nevertheless be empowered to achieve solutions to real problems in the real world.

 CLASSROOM CONNECTIONS

Rogers and Freire stressed the importance of learner-centered classrooms where the teacher and learners negotiate learning out-comes, engage in discovery learning, and relate the course content to students' reality outside the classroom. How have you observed these ideas in action in your own language learning (or teaching) experience? What kinds of activities emulate such perspectives?

Lev Vygotsky

Russian-born Lev Vygotsky (1962, 1978), author of the seminal 1934 work, *Thought and Language*, went almost unnoticed at the time as the limelight shone on his countryman Pavlov and his behaviorist associates. But in the latter part of the twentieth century, as the shifting sands of psychological research paid due attention to sociocultural and affective factors, Vygotsky's contributions to human learning were lauded for their unique insights.

For Vygotsky the key to understanding higher forms (beyond simply phys-ical reflexes) of human mental activity lay in the **mediation** of symbols, signs, and language. We comprehend the world around us, perceived events, and systems of knowledge through symbolic tools of numbers, music, art, and, of course, language. In Vygotsky's view, the task for psychology is "to understand how human social and mental activity is organized through culturally con-structed artifacts and social relationships" (Lantolf, 2000, p. 80).

Language is not only an instrument for thought, but also, as Vygotsky so ably emphasized, an ability that develops through *social interaction*. Language is primarily a tool for communication with other human beings, and it is this symbiotic relationship that is a driving force in the development and growth of cognition. From this sociocultural perspective, a child's early stages of lan-guage acquisition are an outgrowth of the process of "meaning-making in *col-laborative* activity with other members of a given culture" (Mitchell & Myles, 2004, p. 200).

Interesting, isn't it, how singularly different the two Russian psychologists were—Pavlov and Vygotsky? Of course, the latter cut his scholarly teeth on Pavlov's behavioral paradigm that dominated early twentieth century thinking, and saw in that behavioristic perspective a major flaw in the study of human learning (Vygotsky, 1987).

The work of Rogers, Freire, and Vygotsky contributed significantly to a slow but steady redefinition of the educational process in the last twenty years or so. Educators are increasingly striving to enable learners to understand themselves and to create optimal environments for social interaction and negotiation of meaning. Teachers as facilitators are providing nurturing contexts for learners to face real-world issues and to believe in themselves. When teachers rather programmatically feed students quantities of knowledge, which they subsequently devour, those teachers foster a climate of "defensive" learning in which learners—in competition with classmates—try to *protect* themselves from failure, criticism, and possibly from punishment.

Ancient Greek philosophers reminded their audiences of the importance of body, mind, and soul in their inquiry. Likewise, the three major perspectives that have been described here—behavioral, cognitive, and social constructivist—allow us to put together a comprehensive understanding of human learning and cognition. A behavioral theory helps us to understand some fundamentals of learning for *all* organisms. Cognitive viewpoints have multiplied our appreciation of the intricacies of the uniquely human language-thought connection. And without coming full circle (triangle?) to affectively based sociocultural insights, our understanding would not be balanced. An open-minded twenty-first century view is enriched by considering the benefits and drawbacks of each side of the age-old Greek triangle.

 CLASSROOM CONNECTIONS

Rogers and Freire stressed the importance of learner-centered classrooms where the teacher and learners negotiate learning outcomes, engage in discovery learning, and relate the course content to students' reality outside the classroom. How have you observed these ideas in action in your own language learning (or teaching) experience?

TABLE 4.1 Perspectives on human learning

Behavioral	Cognitive	Social-Constructivist
• Conditioning	• Language-cognition connection	• Learner autonomy
• Rewards	• Meaningful learning	• Whole-person
• Stimulus-response connections	• Subsumption	• Empowerment
• Reinforcement	• Systematic forgetting	• Social interaction
• Emphasis: physical	• Emphasis: mental	• Language as mediation
		• Emphasis: socioaffective

FUNDAMENTAL CONCEPTS IN HUMAN LEARNING

Theories of learning do not capture all of the possible general principles of human learning. In addition to the three theoretical perspectives in the first part of the chapter, there are a number of concepts, categories, and types of human learning applicable to SLA.

Types of Learning

Robert Gagné (1965, pp. 58–59) ably demonstrated the importance of identifying a number of universal *types* of human learning. Let's take a look at how these concepts apply to language acquisition research.

1. **Signal learning.** Attending to something in one's environment (music, animal sounds, human voices, etc.), typical of Pavlovian classical conditioning. *Linguistic application: human beings notice and attend to human language.*
2. **Stimulus–response learning.** The learner makes a response to a "discriminated" stimulus, a specific attendance to a single element in one's perceptual environment. *Linguistic application: Noticing and responding to specific sounds, words, and nonverbal gestures, and receiving a reward for the response.*
3. **Chaining.** Learning a chain of two or more stimulus-response connections. *Linguistic application: Stringing several sounds or words together to attempt to communicate meaning.*
4. **Verbal association.** Attaching meaning to verbal/nonverbal chains. *Linguistic application: Assigning meaning to various verbal stimuli. "Nonsense" syllables become meaningful for communication.*
5. **Multiple discrimination.** Learning to make different responses to many varying stimuli, which may resemble each other. *Linguistic application: Noticing differences between/among sounds, words, or phrases that are similar. For example, minimal pairs (sheep/ship), homonyms (left/left), and synonyms (maybe/perhaps).*
6. **Concept learning.** Learning to make a common response to a class of stimuli even though the individual members of that class may differ widely from each other. *Linguistic application: The word "hot" applies to stoves, candles, and irons; young children learn that four-legged farm animals are not all "horsies."*
7. **Principle learning.** Learning a chain of two or more concepts, a cluster of related concepts. *Linguistic application: Verbs in the past tense are classified into regular and irregular forms, yet both forms express the concept of tense.*
8. **Problem solving.** Previously acquired concepts and principles are combined in a conscious focus on an unresolved or ambiguous set of events.

> *Linguistic application: Learning that metaphorical language is not simply idiosyncratic, but connected to cultural world views and ways of thinking, thus explaining why a dead person is "gone." Also, using language to solve problems, such as information gap exercises in a classroom.*

You may notice that the first five types fit easily into a behavioral framework, while the last three are better explained by cognitive or sociocultural perspectives. Since all eight types of learning are relevant to second language learning, a cautious implication is that certain lower-level aspects of SLA may be more effectively treated by behavioral approaches and methods, while certain higher-order types are more effectively taught by methods derived from cognitive or sociocultural approaches to learning. Methods of teaching, in recognizing different levels of learning, need to be consonant with whichever aspect of language is being taught at a particular time while also recognizing the interrelatedness of all levels of language learning.

 CLASSROOM CONNECTIONS

Can you add some further SLA examples to each of the eight types of learning above? What kinds of classroom activities would be appropriate for teaching each type? So, in #7, how would you teach regular and irregular verbs? What kinds of learning processes would the learner be using?

Transfer and Interference

Human beings approach any new problem by using whatever cognitive structures they possess to attempt a solution, more technically described as the interaction of previously learned material with a present learning event. From the beginning of life, we build a structure of knowledge by the accumulation of experiences and by the storage of aspects of those experiences in memory. Each of those billions of neural bytes become associated with other pieces of our memory, and in the process, some of those connections are bound to facilitate and some are destined to debilitate. Let's consider this phenomenon in terms of three associated concepts in learning: transfer, interference, and overgeneralization.

Transfer usually refers to the carryover of previous performance or knowledge to subsequent learning. (It can also apply to the effect of a current act of learning on previously learned material, which is known as **retroactive transfer**, but we'll deal with that in a moment.) *Positive transfer* occurs when the prior knowledge benefits the learning task—that is, when a previous item is correctly applied to present subject matter. *Negative transfer* occurs when previous performance disrupts or inhibits the performance of a second task. The latter can be referred to as **interference**, in that previously learned material conflicts with subsequent material—a previous item is incorrectly transferred or incorrectly associated with an item to be learned.

A nonlanguage example: Eight-year-old Kaliana has already learned to ride a bicycle, and now attempts to ride her newly acquired skateboard. She *positively* transfers the psychomotor process of keeping her balance on a moving vehicle. So far, so good. However, she *negatively* transfers the experience of steering a front wheel for balance to the skateboard, which results in a skinned knee. Eventually she learns that steering on a skateboard is accomplished by a combination of footwork and leaning the body.

The most salient example in SLA is the effect of the first-learned native language on the second. Many L2 courses warn teachers and students of the perils of such negative transfer, in fact, the L1 is usually an immediately noticeable source of error among learners. The saliency of L1-L2 interference has been so strong that it was once fashionable to view second language learning as exclusively involving overcoming the effects of the native language (Stockwell, Bowen, & Martin, 1965; Wardhaugh, 1970). Is this a fair picture?

One's native language, an obvious set of prior experiences, is frequently negatively transferred. For example, a French native speaker might say in English, "I *am* in New York since January," a perfectly logical transfer of the comparable French sentence "Je *suis* à New York depuis janvier." Because of the negative transfer of the French verb form to English, the French system interfered with production of the correct English form.

However, can we not also claim that the native language of an L2 learner may be positively transferred? In which case, can the learner benefit from the facilitating effects of the first language? Consider the above sentence. The correct one-to-one word order correspondence, personal pronoun, preposition, and cognate "January" have all been *positively* transferred from French to English! A more detailed discussion of the syndrome is provided in Chapter 8.

Equally significant for educators is the positive transfer of previous L2 experience on subsequent L2 experience, both within and across languages (Haskell, 2001; Mestre, 2005). Let's say you studied French in high school and now you take up Spanish in college. One of the goals of your teacher is to help you and your classmates to positively transfer various strategies, mindsets, linguistic tricks, and cross-cultural knowledge to this newest language. Even more commonly, suppose you have been learning English as a second language for a few months now. You are most certainly acquiring pieces of the language that have a *cumulative* effect on your current lessons. You could claim that you are not only building lexical, syntactic, discourse, and other abilities, but you are also "getting the hang of it," as your strategic competence improves.

A final aspect of positive transfer *within* a language pertains to the application of course content to the "real world" outside of the classroom. English for Academic Purposes (EAP), for example, helps students to learn English skills but also to learn the academic "game," which might be quite new to students studying English in an English-speaking university and country. Learning conventions of writing, extensive reading, note-taking, listening to lectures, giving presentations, and taking examinations are all positive side-effects of learning English (James, 2006, 2010; DePalma & Ringer, 2011).

Of significant interest for some linguists is the *retroactive* effect of a second language on the first. It is not uncommon for those who take up residence in a foreign country not only to learn the language of their new home, but also for their native language to be "affected." This phenomenon is found among some bilinguals whose home language is the nondominant language of their country of residence. Spanish in the United States is an example (Montrul, 2011). Also, American professionals who spend perhaps a decade in Japan or Thailand, as a random example, may come back to the United States with "something funny" about the way they talk, according to friends and family.

Overgeneralization

In the literature on SLA, interference is almost as frequent a term as **overgeneralization**, which is simply a form of negative transfer. Generalization involves inferring or deriving a law, rule, or conclusion from the observation of particular instances. In terms of the previously discussed meaningful learning, items are subsumed (generalized) under higher-order categories for meaningful retention. Concept learning for children is the generalization of a principle from experience with particulars. A child learns that ice cream is delicious from a few encounters with the cold, sweet taste. Usually very few encounters are required! The concept of future time, often mediated by language, is a generalization from particulars.

In SLA it is customary to refer to *over*generalization as a process that occurs as the L2 learner acts *within* the target language, generalizing a particular rule or item in the L2—*irrespective* of the L1—beyond legitimate bounds. We have already observed that children acquiring English as a native language overgeneralize regular past tense endings (*walked, opened*) as applicable to all past tense forms (*goed, flied*) until they recognize a subset of verbs that belong in an "irregular" category. L2 learners from all native language backgrounds overgeneralize within the target language: In English, "John doesn't can study" or "He told me when should I get off the train" are common examples. (Again, more on this in Chapter 8.)

CLASSROOM CONNECTIONS

In a language that you have learned, think of instances where you encountered interference (from your L1) and overgeneralization (within the L2). Beyond simply *informing* students of errors and their sources, how would you help students in a classroom to overcome the negative effects of interference and overgeneralization? What activities or pair work or games could be used?

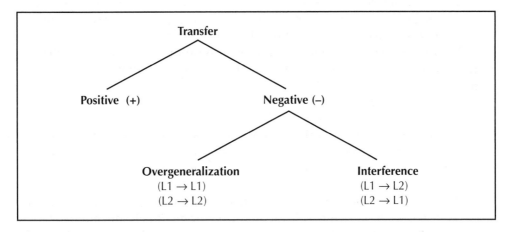

Figure 4.3   Transfer, overgeneralization, and interference

Inductive and Deductive Reasoning

Inductive and deductive reasoning are two polar aspects of the generalization process. In the case of **inductive reasoning**, one stores a number of specific instances and induces a general law or rule or conclusion that governs or subsumes the specific instances. **Deductive reasoning** is a movement from a generalization to specific instances: A general principle allows a person to infer specific facts.

L1 learning and natural or untutored SLA involve a largely inductive process: Learners must infer certain rules and meanings from all the data around them. Most of those rules are learned implicitly, without "conscious," explicit ability to verbalize them.

Classroom language learning tends to rely—more than it should, no doubt—on deductive reasoning. Traditional methods overemphasize the use of deductive reasoning by requiring explicit access to a rule with subsequent attention to its instances. Much of the evidence in communicative L2 learning points to the overall superiority of an inductive approach; however, in the case of *form-focused* instruction (see Chapter 9), learners might reap the benefit of the positive effects of having errors called to their attention.

An interesting extension of the inductive/deductive dichotomy was reported in Peters' (1981) case study of a child learning a first language. Peters found that her subject manifested a number of "Gestalt" characteristics, producing "wholes" in the form of intonation patterns well before speaking the particular words that made up the sentences. Peters cited other evidence of Gestalt learning in children and concluded that such "sentence learners" (vs. "word learners") may be more common than researchers had previously assumed.

In L2 teaching, Wong (1986) capitalized on just such a concept in a discussion of teaching communicative oral production. She advocated explicitly teaching overall intonation patterns for greetings, yes-no questions, and syllable stress before learners had tackled their specific syntactic forms. She was one of the first to advocate the use of kazoos in pronunciation classes so that learners could more easily hear overall sentence stress and intonation.

LANGUAGE APTITUDE

The discussion so far in this chapter has focused on perception, storage, and recall. Little has been said about a related and somewhat controversial issue in SLA, **language aptitude**. A number of questions emerge:

1. Is there an ability or "talent" that we can call foreign language aptitude?
2. If so, what is it, and is it innate or environmentally nurtured?
3. Is it a distinct ability or is it an aspect of general cognitive abilities?
4. Does aptitude vary by age and by whether learning is implicit or explicit?
5. Can aptitude be reliably measured?
6. If so, do such assessments predict success in learning an L2?

Do certain people have a "knack" for learning foreign languages? Anecdotal evidence would suggest that some people are indeed able to learn languages faster and more efficiently than others. One way of looking at such aptitude is the identification of characteristics of successful language learners. Risk-taking behavior, memory efficiency, intelligent guessing, willingness to communicate, low anxiety, and ambiguity tolerance are but a few of the many variables that have been cited (Rubin & Thompson, 1982; Brown, 1991; Dörnyei & Skehan, 2003; Dörnyei, 2005, 2009; Robinson, 2005). Such factors will be the focus of the next chapter in this book.

Historically, research on language aptitude has been a roller-coaster ride. John Carroll's (Carroll & Sapon, 1959) pioneering work on aptitude, embodied in the Modern Language Aptitude Test (MLAT), began the quest. The MLAT asserted the predictability of number learning, sound discrimination, pattern discernment, and memorization for future success in a foreign language. This test, along with the Pimsleur Language Aptitude Battery (PLAB) (Pimsleur, 1966) and the Defense Language Aptitude Battery (DLAB) (Peterson & Al-Haik, 1976) were used for some time in such contexts as Peace Corps volunteer training programs and military communications courses to help predict successful language learners.

The above-mentioned aptitude tests were initially well received by L2 teachers and administrators, especially in view of their reportedly high correlations with ultimate success in language classrooms. But slowly their popularity waned, even in the absence of alternative measures of language aptitude (Parry & Child, 1990; Skehan, 1998). Two factors accounted for the decline. First, even though the paper-and-pencil tests claimed to measure language aptitude, it soon became apparent that they more than likely reflected the general intelligence or academic ability of a student in *any* instructional setting (Skehan, 1989; DeKeyser & Koeth, 2011). At best, they appeared to measure ability to perform focused, analytical, **context-reduced** activities that occupy a student in a traditional language classroom.

They hardly even began to tap into the kinds of learning strategies and styles that subsequent research (Ehrman, 1990; Oxford, 1990b, 1996; Reid, 1995; Chamot, 2005; Cohen, 1998) showed to be crucial in the acquisition of communicative competence in **context-embedded** situations. As we will see in the next chapter, learners can be successful for a multitude of reasons, many of which are much more related to focus and determination than to so-called "native" abilities (Lett & O'Mara, 1990).

Second, how is one to interpret a language aptitude test? Rarely does an institution have the luxury or capability to test people before they take a foreign language in order to counsel certain people out of their decision to do so. And in cases where an aptitude test might be administered, isn't such a test likely to bias both student and teacher? Both are led to believe that they will be successful or unsuccessful, depending on the aptitude test score, and a self-fulfilling prophecy is likely to occur. Isn't it wiser for teachers to be optimistic for *all* their students? By monitoring individual differences and abilities, teachers can steer the student toward strategies that will aid learning and away from those blocking factors that will hinder the process.

In the decades that followed the flurry of administrations of standardized aptitude tests, interest declined. But then, in the late 1990s, we saw renewed efforts to address aptitude factors (Sasaki, 1993a, 1993b; Harley & Hart, 1997). A new era of aptitude research was launched with Skehan's (1998) exposure of the weaknesses of previous aptitude constructs, and his proposal to look at aptitude from a broader view of SLA that incorporates input processing, inductive language learning, output strategies, and fluency.

The birth of the new millennium witnessed a resurgence of interest language aptitude (Grigorenko, Sternberg, & Ehrman, 2000; Robinson, 2001, 2002, 2005; Skehan, 2002; Dörnyei & Skehan, 2003). Grigorenko, Sternberg, and Ehrman (2000) proposed an aptitude battery based on Sternberg's theory of intelligence (see the next section in this chapter), the CANAL-F test (Cognitive Ability for

Novelty in Acquisition of Language—Foreign). This battery differed from previous ones in its involvement of the test taker in a process of learning a simulated language embedded in a multifaceted language context. Further, it was dynamic rather than static in that it measured the ability to learn at the time of taking the test.

Dörnyei and Skehan (2003) followed up on the renewed interest in aptitude with the suggestion that aptitude may be related to varying processes of SLA. So, for example, aptitude constructs such as attention and short-term memory could be relevant for processing input in an L2; phonemic coding ability could contribute to noticing of phonological patterns; and constructs like inductive learning, chunking, and retrieval abilities may allow a learner to identify and integrate grammatical patterns. Dörnyei and Skehan also cite other research to conclude that "aptitude is relevant not simply for conventional, explicit, rule-focused teaching contexts, but also when the learning is implicit [in natural contexts]" (p. 600).

More recently, Robinson (2001, 2002, 2005) and Dörnyei (2005, 2009) suggested that aptitude "has been increasingly seen as too broad an umbrella term, one that refers to an unspecified mixture of cognitive variables" (Dörnyei, 2009, pp. 182–183). DeKeyser and Koeth (2011, p. 396) conceded that "there is no unitary construct of aptitude" and that because it is an encompassing term, one should simply refer to "*aptitudes*, in the plural, for learning a second language." Robinson (2005) suggested that aptitude is a complex of abilities that include processing speed, short- and long-term memory, rote memory, planning time, pragmatic abilities, interactional intelligence, emotional intelligence, and self-efficacy. Dörnyei (2009) noted that motivation, learning styles, learning strategies, anxiety, and other *individual differences* in language learners may also be related to a learner's eventual success in learning an L2.

Robinson and Dörnyei both appear to agree that none of the above "static or linear presuppositions" (Jessner, 2008, p. 270) can be sufficiently singled out as a trait or measurable factor in aptitude. Instead, we are better served by viewing the process of SLA as an involvement of **dynamic systems theory**, "one of complexity, with all parts of the system being interconnected, and of ongoing change that results from the multiple interacting influences" (Dörnyei, 2009, pp. 103–104).

 CLASSROOM CONNECTIONS

The so-called "knack" for learning a language appears to be an elusive factor. But if you were to brainstorm some of what you think are the most important ingredients of language aptitude, what would your "top 5" factors be? Have you invoked any of those abilities within you in your foreign language learning? Using those five factors, how would you, as a teacher, help students to *capitalize* on their "gifts" and to *compensate* for abilities they may not appear to have?

INTELLIGENCE AND LANGUAGE LEARNING

Intelligence, a construct with multiple definitions and theories, has traditionally been defined and measured in terms of linguistic and logical-mathematical abilities. The notion of IQ (Intelligence Quotient) is based on several generations of testing of these two domains, stemming from the early twentieth-century research of Alfred Binet, creator of the famous *Stanford-Binet Intelligence Scales*. Success in educational institutions and in life in general has been shown repeatedly to correlate with high IQ scores (Slavin, 2011).

Does IQ correlate equally well with successful SLA? Will a smart person be capable of learning a second language successfully because of high intelligence? Not according to a good deal of research and observation over the last few decades. It appears that our "language learning IQs" involve more than simply academic "smarts."

Howard Gardner (1983, 1999, 2006, 2011) was the first psychologist to help us to see why IQ is too simplistic a concept to account for a whole host of skills and abilities. Gardner (1983) initially posited seven different intelligences that provided a comprehensive picture of intelligence. He later added one more intelligence, naturalist (Gardner, 1999, 2004), but has rejected adding spiritual or moral intelligence, as they fail, in his view, to meet established criteria. Following are Gardner's eight **multiple intelligences**:

1. Linguistic
2. Logical-mathematical
3. Musical (the ability to perceive and create pitch and rhythmic patterns)
4. Spatial (the ability to find one's way around an environment, to form mental images of reality, and to transform them readily)
5. Bodily-kinesthetic (fine motor movement, athletic prowess)
6. Naturalist (sensitivity to natural objects (plants, animals, clouds))
7. Interpersonal (the ability to understand others, how they feel, what motivates them, how they interact with one another)
8. Intrapersonal intelligence (the ability to see oneself, to develop a sense of self-identity)

Gardner maintained that by looking only at the first two categories we rule out a great number of the human being's mental abilities. And he showed that our traditional definitions of intelligence are culture-bound. The "sixth sense" of a hunter in New Guinea or the navigational abilities of a sailor in Micronesia are not accounted for in Westernized definitions of IQ. His more recent work (Gardner, 2004, 2006, 2011) has focused on applications of his multiple intelligences theory to daily human interactions as we manipulate our environment in order to accomplish a variety of purposes.

In a likewise revolutionary style, Robert Sternberg (1985, 1988) also shook up the world of traditional intelligence measurement. In his **triarchic** view of intelligence, Sternberg proposed three types of "smartness":

1. Componential ability for analytical thinking
2. Experiential ability to engage in creative thinking, combining disparate experiences in insightful ways
3. Contextual ability or "street smartness" that enables people to "play the game" of manipulating their environment (others, situations, institutions, contexts)

 CLASSROOM CONNECTIONS

Consider Gardner's eight intelligences and Sternberg's three factors. In your experience learning a foreign language, what techniques or activities have you experienced that illustrate these different components? If you are teaching a language, to what extent might you help learners to capitalize on strengths and also to compensate for weaknesses?

Sternberg contended that too much of psychometric theory is obsessed with mental speed, and therefore dedicated his research to tests that measure insight, real-life problem solving, "common sense," getting a wider picture of things, and other practical tasks that are closely related to success in the real world. Like Gardner, Sternberg has also recently provided a practical dimension to his research in publications that demonstrate how practical and creative intelligence can determine one's success in life (Sternberg, 1997, 2003, 2007).

Finally, in another effort to remind us of the bias of traditional definitions and tests of intelligence, Daniel Goleman's work on **emotional intelligence** (Goleman, 1995, 1998; Merlevede, Bridoux, & Vandamme, 2001) is persuasive in placing emotion, or what might be called **EQ** (Emotional Quotient), at the seat of intellectual functioning. The management of even a handful of core emotions—anger, fear, enjoyment, love, disgust, shame, and others—drives and controls efficient cognitive processing. Even more to the point, Goleman argued that "the emotional mind is far quicker than the rational mind, springing into action without even pausing to consider what it is doing. Its quickness precludes the deliberate, analytic reflection that is the hallmark of the thinking mind" (1995, p. 291). Goleman has also more recently followed up with work on *social* as well as *ecological* intelligence, in an effort to apply emotional management to practical life situations (Goleman, 2006, 2009).

By expanding our understanding of intelligence, we can more easily discern a relationship between intelligence and second language learning. Gardner's musical intelligence could explain the relative ease that some learners have in perceiving and producing the intonation patterns of a language. Music also appears to facilitate learning, as McGinn, Stokes, and Trier (2005) recently demonstrated. Bodily-kinesthetic modes have already been discussed in connection with the learning of the phonology of a language. Interpersonal intelligence is of obvious importance in the communicative process. (Intrapersonal factors will be discussed in detail in Chapter 6 of this book.) One might even be able to speculate on the extent to which spatial intelligence, especially a "sense of direction," may assist the second culture learner in growing comfortable in a new environment.

Sternberg's experiential and contextual abilities cast further light on components of the "knack" that some people have for quick, efficient, ostensibly "effortless" SLA. After all, successful language learners frequently display their ability to think creatively "outside the box," and thus grasp some of the dynamic complexity of SLA. Finally, Goleman's EQ may be far more important than any other factor in accounting for second language success both in classrooms and in untutored contexts. In Chapter 6 we will expand on the central role of the affective domain in SLA.

Educational institutions have recently been applying multiple intelligence theory to a variety of school-oriented contexts. Thomas Armstrong (1993, 1994), for example, focused teachers and learners on "seven ways of being smart," capitalizing on all forms of intelligence. In foreign language education, Christison (1999, 2005) and others have been successfully applying the concept of multiple intelligences to teaching English as a second or foreign language by showing how each intelligence relates to certain demands in the classroom.

A Post Script: Some time ago, John Oller suggested, in an eloquent essay, that language *is* intelligence. "Language may not be merely a vital link in the social side of intellectual development, it may be the very foundation of intelligence itself" (1981a, p. 466). According to Oller, arguments from genetics and neurology suggest "a deep relationship, perhaps even an identity, between intelligence and language ability" (p. 487). The implications of Oller's hypothesis for SLA are enticing. Both first and second languages must be closely tied to meaning in its deepest sense. Effective L2 learning thus links surface forms of a language with meaningful experiences, as we have already noted in cognitive learning theory. The strength of that link may indeed be a factor in the complex systems that make up what we call intelligence.

LEARNING THEORIES IN THE CLASSROOM: ALM & CLL

Two language teaching methods emerged in the last century of language teaching that bear a singular relationship to certain perspectives on learning. The Audiolingual method, inspired by behavioristic principles, and Community

Language Learning, a direct attempt to apply Carl Rogers's theories, are in stark contrast with each other. We'll look at these two methods here.

The Audiolingual Method

The outbreak of World War II thrust the United States into a worldwide conflict, heightening the need for Americans to become orally proficient in the languages of both their allies and their enemies. The U.S. military, perceiving the need for intensive language courses that focused on aural/oral skills, funded what came to be known as the Army Specialized Training Program (ASTP), or, more colloquially, the "Army Method." The Army Method employed a great deal of oral activity—pronunciation and pattern drills and conversation practice. Oddly, in a rejection of deductive, explicit grammar teaching and translation, virtually none of these characteristics of traditional classes found their way into the method. Soon, spurred by the Army Method's success in military language schools, educational institutions began to adopt the new methodology. In all its variations and adaptations, the Army Method came to be known in the 1950s as the **Audiolingual Method** (ALM).

The ALM was firmly grounded in linguistic and psychological theory. Structural linguists of the 1940s and 1950s had been engaged in what they claimed was a "scientific descriptive analysis" of various languages, and educators saw a direct application of such analysis to teaching linguistic patterns (Fries, 1945). At the same time, behavioral psychologists were advocating conditioning and habit-formation models of learning. The classical and operant conditioning models described earlier in this chapter provided the perfect rationale for the mimicry drills and pattern practices so typical of audiolingual methodology. Students were delighted: "Success" could be more overtly experienced by students as they practiced their dialogs with friends and family in off-hours.

With widespread publication of textbooks and curricula, the ALM enjoyed a number of years of popularity. But the enthusiasm eventually waned, due in part to Wilga Rivers's (1964) eloquent exposure of ALM's ultimate failure to teach long-term communicative proficiency. We discovered that language was not effectively acquired through a process of habit formation and over-learning, that errors were not necessarily to be avoided at all costs, and that structural linguistics did not dictate a course syllabus. While the ALM was a valiant attempt to reap the fruits of language teaching methodologies that had preceded it, in the end it still fell short. Despite its shortcomings, however, we are left today with an important vestige of the ALM: the value of quick, fast-paced drilling routines, even in a communicative classroom.

Community Language Learning

The ALM also lost some of its glamor when the Chomskyan revolution in linguistics turned linguists and language teachers toward the *deep structure* of language and when psychologists began to recognize the fundamentally *interpersonal* nature of language learning. Looking at SLA through the combined lenses of cognitive and affective factors spawned a creative, if somewhat chaotic era during which innovative language teaching methods flourished.

Claims for the success of these revolutionary methods—in the eyes of their proprietary founders and proponents—were often overstated to attract teachers to weekend workshops and seminars, to new books, tapes, and videos, and, of course, to getting their learners to reach the zenith of their potential. Such wild claims of instant satisfaction led Nunan (1989, p. 97) to refer to the methods of the day as "designer" methods: promises of success, one size fits all!

Despite the marketing blitz over designer methods, they remain an important part of our language teaching history, giving us insights into language learning, remnants of which still enlighten our teaching practices. We'll look at one such method here, Community Language Learning (CLL), expressly constructed to put Rogers's theory of learning into action.

In his "Counseling-Learning" model of education, Charles Curran (1972) was inspired by Rogers's (1951) view of education in which students and teacher join together to facilitate learning in a context of valuing and prizing each individual in the group. In such a surrounding, each person lowers the defenses that prevent open, interpersonal communication. The anxiety caused by the educational context is lessened by means of the supportive community. The teacher's presence is not perceived as a threat, nor is it the teacher's purpose to impose limits and boundaries. Rather, as a "counselor," the teacher's role is to center his or her attention on the clients (the students) and their needs.

Curran's model of education was extended to language learning contexts in the form of **Community Language Learning** (CLL) (LaForge, 1971). While particular adaptations of CLL are numerous, the basic methodology was explicit. Students were encouraged to try anything, just as they might do if they had just arrived in a foreign country. They had free rein to inductively "emit" any language forms they wanted to. The teacher could use translation to aid in refinement of production attempts and in comprehension, or explanation when solicited by a student. Learners were encouraged but not forced to respond to one another, always with the supportive role of the teacher to guide them when needed. The rationale was that students slowly move from dependence (on the teacher) to independence.

CLL was a valiant attempt to put Carl Rogers's philosophy into action and to overcome some of the threatening affective factors in second language learning. But practical and theoretical problems emerged. The *non*directive role of the counselor-teacher caused a good deal of "trial by error," much of which was not productive. While inductive struggling can be an invigorating component of L2 learning, days and weeks of floundering can become frustrating. And, the almost exclusive reliance on translation often resulted in linguistic mysteries that could have been avoided.

Despite its weaknesses, CLL offers certain insights to teachers. We are reminded to lower learners' anxiety, to create as much of a supportive group in our classrooms as possible, to allow students to initiate language (up to a point), and to move learners toward autonomy in preparation for the day when they no longer have the teacher to guide them. And while we are certainly offered an example of a method that diverged completely from the behaviorally inspired ALM, we are also reminded that most effective language classrooms manifest bits and pieces of *many* potentially contrasting methods, and that successful teachers are eclectically judicious in their choice of tasks for language lessons.

☆   ☆   ☆   ☆   ☆

Remember young Ethan's mynah training attempt? Unfortunately, he was not successful in teaching his pet bird to talk. She chirped *very* loudly, but never anything that could pass as human speech. Ethan tried all the training tricks that he picked up off the Internet—the right food, attention, cage position, etc. He was as diligent and patient as any busy ten-year-old could be, but with school and soccer and swimming, sometimes Myra was neglected. Avian specialists say not all mynahs talk, and Myra's earlier injury (that placed her in the animal shelter) may have been a factor. Also, the shelter said that Myra was about six months old when they found her, and advised she might be too old to learn to talk (a critical period effect?). So, despite all the good intentions, Ethan and his brother and long-suffering parents remain the proud owners of a very entertaining and very loud non-talking mynah!

SUGGESTED READINGS

Dornyei, Z. (2009). *The psychology of second language acquisition*. Oxford, UK: Oxford University Press.

> A comprehensive review of current theories and models of SLA from a diverse number of psychological perspectives, including applications of Dynamic Systems Theory and Individual Differences research.

Robinson, P. (2005). Aptitude and L2 acquisition. *Annual Review of Applied Linguistics, 25*, 46–73.

Skehan, P. (2002). Theorising and updating aptitude. In P. Robinson (ed.), *Individual differences and instructed language learning* (pp. 69–93). Amsterdam: John Benjamins.

> Both articles offer historical overviews and summaries of developments in research on language aptitude and review alternatives to earlier views on language aptitude.

Gardner, H. (2006). *Multiple intelligences: New horizons in theory and practice.* New York: Basic Books.

Goleman, D. (2006). *Social intelligence: The new science of social relationships.* New York: Bantam Books.

Sternberg, R. (2007). *Wisdom, intelligence, and creativity synthesized.* New York: Cambridge University Press.

The evolution of the work of Gardner, Goleman, and Sternberg on intelligence is manifested in these three practical manuals written for lay audiences and applied to everyday situations, problems, and relationships.

LANGUAGE LEARNING EXPERIENCE: JOURNAL ENTRY 4

Note: See Chapter 1 for general guidelines for writing a journal on a previous or concurrent language learning experience.

- If you had to classify your approach to learning a foreign language, would it be more Skinnerian, Ausubelian, or Rogersian? Or a combination of them?
- Sometimes teachers don't give students opportunities to *emit* language in the classroom, and just keep *eliciting* too much. Sometimes it's the other way around. What is your experience? If you feel (or have felt) that you don't have enough chances to volunteer to speak, what can (could) you do to change that pattern?
- Rogers recommended "nondefensive" learning. Do you feel that you are learning to defend yourself against the teacher's disapproval, or against your classmates, or against bad grades? Are your classmates your allies or competitors?
- Short of actually taking a traditional language aptitude test, how would you assess your own "knack" for learning languages? Whether your self-assessment is high or low, what do you think are key components of high language aptitude? Can you "learn" some of those abilities?
- Do any of Gardner's eight types of intelligence strike you as being crucial to your success in your foreign language? Or how about Sternberg's three views of intelligence? Or Goleman's EQ? Are there any intelligences that you underutilize? What can you do about that?
- Have you been taught with either Audiolingual techniques (rote repetition and drills) or CLL-like activities (small, supportive groups that are encouraged to initiate your own utterances), discussed at the end of the chapter? If so, what is (was) your assessment of their effectiveness?

FOR THE TEACHER: ACTIVITIES (A) & DISCUSSION (D)

Note: For each of the "Classroom Connections" in this chapter, you may wish to turn them into individual or pair-work discussion questions.

1. (A) Divide the class into small groups. Assign each group *one* of the three major perspectives on learning from the first part of the chapter. Tasks for the groups are to "defend" their particular perspective as the most insightful or complete. To do so, each group will need to summarize strengths and to anticipate arguments from other groups. Have each group report findings back to the class and encourage questions or challenges from the other groups.

2. (A) As a follow-up activity, ask the same groups to formulate an integrated understanding of human learning by taking the best of all three points of view. Have them report their thoughts back to the rest of the class.

3. (D) Ask students to reiterate the difference between *elicited* and *emitted* responses. What are some examples of operants that are emitted by the learner in a foreign language class? And some responses that are elicited? Specify some of the reinforcers that are present in language classes. How effective are certain reinforcers?

4. (D) Skinner felt that punishment, or negative reinforcement, was just another way of calling attention to undesired behavior and therefore should be avoided. Do you think correction of student errors in a classroom is negative reinforcement? How can error treatment be given a positive spin, in Skinnerian terms?

5. (A) Ask pairs to list some activities they consider to be rote and others that are meaningful in foreign language classes they have taken (or are teaching). Do some activities fall into a gray area between the two? Evaluate the effectiveness of all the activities your group has listed. Pairs will share conclusions with the rest of the class.

6. (A) Divide the class into small groups. Ask each group to look back at the section on foreign language aptitude and determine what factors they think should be represented in a comprehensive taxonomy of components language aptitude. Use the blackboard to list findings, and to compare various groups' suggestions with those of other groups.

7. (A) Divide the class, numbers permitting, into as many as eight pairs. Assign each pair *one* of Gardner's eight multiple intelligences. Have groups brainstorm typical language classroom activities or techniques that foster their type of intelligence. Ask group representatives to make a list of their activities on the blackboard. Ask the class to evaluate the lists.

CHAPTER 5

INDIVIDUAL DIFFERENCES

Polish-born Magdalena is fluent in four languages: her native Polish; English learned in secondary school on up; Spanish learned as a major in college and then as a resident in Ecuador since age twenty-five; and Italian learned in college studies, from travels in Italy, and from a college romance with an Italian boyfriend. She can "get by" in two other languages: French (learned in college) and Russian, learned as a mandatory subject in primary school.

Magdalena self-reports an intense interest in people and cultures, is on the high end of extroversion, loves the music of various cultures, sings, dances, reads voraciously, mostly in Spanish and English, and has high energy. Her young children are bilingual in Spanish and Polish, and their father is a native Spanish speaker. Magdalena dreams in Spanish, and says her identity is "Spanish."

She taught English in private schools in Poland, and currently works in Quito as a teacher educator and highly successful marketing agent for a publisher of English language textbooks and materials.

What kinds of questions would you like to ask Magdalena about her "secret to success" in becoming so capable in four languages? Was age a factor? Or genetics? How did the support of her parents contribute to her ultimate success? Did she receive remarkable language instruction in school? Did personality, motivation, and intelligence play roles? Did she employ—either consciously or subconsciously—certain strategies, techniques, or other self-regulatory procedures that were significant? What is it that seems to set her apart from those who are monolingual and who struggle a bit with languages? Does she just happen to have a "knack" for learning languages—and if so, what are the components of that knack?

In this chapter we'll address some of these questions under the rubric of *individual differences* (Dewaele, 2009; Dörnyei, 2009) that distinguish one individual from another, along with a close look at *self-regulatory* techniques that have been found to be effective.

SOME HISTORICAL BACKGROUND

As our knowledge of SLA increased markedly during the 1970s, teachers and researchers came to realize that no ultimate method of language teaching would usher in an era of universal success in L2 learning. We even saw that certain learners seemed to be successful *regardless* of methods of teaching. More importantly, we began to see the importance of individual *variation* in language learning. Some people appeared to be endowed with abilities to succeed; others lacked those abilities.

All the apparent individual differences among successful and unsuccessful learners led some linguists, most notably Rubin (1975) and Stern (1975), to ask: What would we discover if we described notable attributes of a group of "good" language learners? That is, what distinguishing techniques and approaches are employed by successful language learners? Rubin and Thompson (1982) later summarized such characteristics, paraphrased and summarized here. Good language learners:

1. Take charge of their own learning, seeking out opportunities to use the language.
2. Are unafraid to creatively experiment with the language and make intelligent guesses.
3. Learn chunks of language and conversational gambits to help them perform "beyond their competence."
4. Use various memory strategies, production tricks, and comprehension techniques.
5. Monitor themselves, allow errors to work *for* them, and learn from mistakes.

Such lists, speculative as they were at the time, spurred quite a string of studies and books that proposed to identify characteristics of "successful" language learners (Naiman et al., 1978; Rubin & Thompson, 1982; Brown, 1989, 1991; Marshall, 1989; Stevick 1989) as well as *un*successful learners (Vann & Abraham, 1990). What ultimately emerged was a collective set of suggestions, or *strategies*, on how to be a successful language learner. As interest grew in what became known as "strategies-based instruction" (SBI), detailed classifications of strategies were drawn up (O'Malley & Chamot, 1990; Oxford, 1990a, 2011b) with a view to providing teachers with a taxonomy of strategic options for their learners.

 CLASSROOM CONNECTIONS

What would you list as your "top five" characteristics of a "good language learner"? How many of those describe you? Has a teacher ever encouraged the development of these abilities or skills in a foreign language class that you have taken? How would you, as a teacher, go about promoting these traits in your students?

More recently, some new perspectives on thirty years of strategy research have emerged. Drawing on the work of Vygotsky (1978) and Bakhtin (1986, 1990), Norton and Toohey (2001) adopted a sociocultural approach that viewed learners as participants in a community of language users in "local contexts in which specific practices create possibilities for them to learn English" (p. 311). Fundamental to their point of view is the *identity* that each learner creates in a socially constructed context. As learners *invest* in their learning process, they create avenues of success.

Harsh criticisms emerged from cognitive linguists who assert that strategies are conceptually ill-defined, too broadly conceived, and not supported by empirical research (Dörnyei & Skehan, 2003; Dörnyei, 2005, 2009). However, Cohen and Macaro (2007) and Oxford (2011b), both giants in the field of strategy research, contend that such "dismissive" criticism is unwarranted. Instead, we can productively, even if cautiously, pursue the value to language pedagogy of attention to strategic options. Oxford (2011b) and others (Zimmerman, 1990, 2000) prefer to capture such pursuits under the rubric of **self-regulation**. We will return to this concept later in the chapter.

Earlier views of successful learners and more recent social constructivist research may merge together in the form of some pedagogical advice: Teachers can benefit from attending to what might indeed be very common strategies for successful learning *across* cultures and contexts, but they also need to be ever mindful of individual needs and variations as well as specific cultural contexts of learning.

LEARNING STYLES

One of the most perplexing problems in language acquisition research is the multiplicity of *individual differences* that bear on attempts to construct a model or theory of SLA. It seems that we humans vary from one another in an infinite number of possible ways, so many that pinpointing the components of such a theory is frustrating, yet at the same time a challenge worth pursuing.

The response to the challenge has so far yielded some great strides toward the construction of a model of SLA. One such step is in a genre of research that identifies **styles** of learning, thinking, and operating on our environment. Styles are what a learner "brings to the table" in learning a language. They are part of the *entry behavior* that was mentioned in Chapter 4.

Styles are general characteristics of intellectual functioning (and personality type, as well) that pertain to you as an individual, and that differentiate you from someone else. They are consistent and rather enduring tendencies or *preferences* within an individual. For example, you might be more visually oriented, more tolerant of ambiguity, or more impulsive than someone else—these would be styles that characterize a general or dominant pattern in your thinking or feeling. So, styles vary *across* individuals, and as such are an important starting point for a teacher in assessing an approach to an individual learner that will be appropriate.

🌐 CLASSROOM CONNECTIONS

Before reading on about styles, try this: Describe yourself as a language learner in a *classroom* setting you have experienced. Who are you? How do you *differ* from other learners you know? Do you tend to speak out easily? Sit in the front or back of the room? Do you need rules and explanations for everything, or are you okay with being a little "lost" for a while? Don't worry about technical terminology right now. Just do your best to describe yourself in a list of items or a short paragraph.

Learning styles differ from **learning strategies** in that the latter are specific methods of approaching a problem or task, techniques for achieving a particular end, or designs for controlling and manipulating certain information. Oxford and Ehrman defined L2 learning strategies as "specific actions, behaviors, steps, or techniques . . . used by students to enhance their own learning" (1988, p. 22). Because they are contextualized "battle plans" that might vary from moment to moment, or from one context to another, or even from one culture to another, they vary *within* an individual. Each of us has a number of possible options for solving a particular problem, from which we choose a particular line of "attack."

Here's a true story:

My flight finally landed in Naples, Italy at 3:00 A.M., after a harrowing day of missed flights, delays, and rerouting that had started early the previous morning in Barcelona. The airport was practically deserted, and to top it off, my luggage was missing! No one around me could speak English and my Italian was limited to phrases like "How much does this cost?" and "Where is the train for Rome?"—these were now useless. What did I do?

With a style that tends to be generally tolerant of ambiguity, I refrained from getting flustered, and remained calm in spite of my fatigue. My left-brain style told me to take practical, logical steps and to focus only on the important details of the moment. Simultaneously, my sometimes equally strong propensity to use a right-brain approach allowed me to empathize with airport personnel and to use numerous alternative communicative strategies (mostly nonverbal gestures and presumed cognates) to get messages across. I was reflective enough to be patient with miscommunications and my inability to communicate well, yet impulsive to the extent that I needed to insist on some action as soon as possible.

The way we learn things in general and the way we address a problem seem to hinge on a rather amorphous link between personality and cognition; this link is referred to as **cognitive style**. When cognitive styles are specifically related to an educational context, where affective and physiological factors are intermingled, they are usually referred to as **learning styles**.

Learning styles might be thought of as "cognitive, affective, and physiological traits that are relatively stable indicators of how learners perceive, interact with, and respond to the learning environment" (Keefe, 1979, p. 4). Or, more simply, Peter Skehan defined learning style as "a general predisposition, voluntary or not, toward processing information in a particular way" (1991, p. 288). In the enormous task of learning a second language, one that so deeply involves affective factors, a study of learning style brings important variables to the forefront.

Learning styles mediate between emotion and cognition, as you will soon discover. For example, a **reflective style** invariably grows out of a reflective personality or a reflective mood. An **impulsive style**, on the other hand, usually arises out of an impulsive emotional state. Some researchers claim that styles are stable traits in adults, while others question such stability (Dörnyei & Skehan, 2003). It would appear that individuals show *general* tendencies toward one style or another, but that differing contexts will evoke differing styles in the same individual. Perhaps an "intelligent" and "successful" person is one who is "bi-cognitive"—one who can manipulate both ends of a style continuum?

Over the decades, educators and psychologists have identified a long list of just about every imaginable sensory, communicative, cultural, affective, cognitive, and intellectual factor among possible styles (Ausubel, 1968; Hill, 1972; Oxford & Anderson, 1995; Reid, 1995; Ehrman, 1996; Cohen, 1998; Wintergerst, DeCapua, & Itzen, 2001; Ehrman & Leaver, 2003). Here are a few of the more salient styles this research has defined:

- Field independence vs. field dependence (sensitivity)
- Random (nonlinear) vs. sequential (linear)
- Global (big picture) vs. particular (attention to details)
- Inductive vs. deductive
- Synthetic (integrative) vs. analytical (systematizing)
- Concrete (attention to physical, literal) vs. abstract
- Impulsive vs. reflective

Other researchers (Stevick, 1982; Chapelle, 1983; Chapelle & Roberts, 1986; Danesi, 1988; Reid, 1995; Brown, 2002) added further factors:

- Left-brain vs. right-brain dominance
- Ambiguity tolerance vs. intolerance
- Visual vs. auditory vs. kinesthetic modalities

The identification and measurement of styles has not met with universal acceptance from researchers. Dörnyei (2005, 2009) has been one of the most strident critics of the literature on cognitive and learning styles. Admitting to the "seemingly straightforward and intuitively convincing" (2005, p. 121) nature of learning styles, and to their potential value in an educational context, Dörnyei posed a number of problematic issues in conceptualizing styles, but in the final analysis, curiously, admits that they constitute an "as yet unrealized potential" (p. 160).

Because of their *historical* value and *intuitive* (if not yet fully theoretically defined) relevance to teaching, five styles have been selected here as illustrative of the significance of learning styles in L2 classroom settings.

Field Independence and Field Sensitivity

In Sunday newspaper comic pages, you will sometimes find two almost identical drawings with the caption: "Find six differences between the two pictures." In a few minutes, careful scrutiny of tiny details reveals very small differences—a smaller lamp, an arm that has moved. The speed and ability to find those differences hinge on **field independence**, the perception of a particular, relevant item or factor in a "field" of distracting items. In general psychological terms, that field may be perceptual, or it may be more abstract, pertaining to a set of thoughts, ideas, or feelings within which you must distinguish specific relevant subsets. **Field dependence** is, conversely, the tendency to be "dependent" on the total field so that the parts embedded within the field are not distracting, as you perceive the total field as a unified whole. Field dependence is synonymous with **field sensitivity**, a term that carries a more positive connotation.

A field independent (FI) style enables you to distinguish parts from a whole, to concentrate on something (like reading a book in a noisy train station), or to analyze separate variables without the contamination of neighboring variables. On the other hand, *too much* FI may result in cognitive "tunnel vision": you see only the parts and not their relationship to the whole. "You can't see the forest for the trees," as the saying goes. Seen in this light, development of a field sensitive (FS) style has positive effects: You perceive the whole picture, the larger view, the general configuration of a problem or idea or event. It is clear, then, that both FI *and* FS are necessary for most of the cognitive and affective problems we face.

Early research on FI/FS (Witkin, 1962; Witkin & Goodenough, 1981) found some interesting relationships. Affectively, persons who were more predominantly FI tended to be generally more independent, competitive, and self-confident. FS persons tended to be more sociable, to derive their self-identity from persons around them, and were usually more empathic and perceptive of the feelings and thoughts of others. The same studies also found FI/FS to be a presumably stable trait in adulthood, a claim that is now widely disputed in view of the difficulty of defining the construct (Dörnyei, 2009), and the implausibility of an L2 learner's manifesting one side of the continuum with no utilization whatsoever of the other side.

How does all this relate to second language learning? Two conflicting hypotheses emerged. First, some studies concluded that FI is closely related to classroom learning that involves analysis, attention to details, and mastering of exercises, drills, and other focused activities (Naiman, Fröhlich, Stern, & Todesco, 1978; Hansen & Stansfield, 1981; Stansfield & Hansen, 1983; Hansen, 1984; Jamieson, 1992; Johnson, Prior, & Artuso, 2000). Other similar findings were reported for FI: success in paper-and-pencil tests (Chapelle & Roberts, 1986); in deductive lessons (Abraham, 1985); and in pronunciation accuracy (Elliott, 1995a, 1995b).

The second hypothesis proposed that an FS style, by virtue of its association with empathy, social outreach, and perception of other people, yields successful acquisition of the *communicative* aspects of a second language. While no one denies the plausibility of this second claim, little empirical evidence has been gathered to support it.

The principal reason for the dearth of such evidence is in the measurement of FI/FS. The standard measure of FI, the Group Embedded Figures Test (Oltman, Raskin, & Witkin, 1971) only measures visual perception; moreover, a high score on FI certainly does not imply a low score on FS! With the absence of a true test of FS, we are left with little hard data on the topic, leading some linguists to be harshly critical of what they called a "theoretically flawed" construct (Griffiths & Sheen, 1992, p. 133). Others were more moderate in recommending "re-conceptualizations" and new measurement tools before drawing conclusions (Chapelle, 1992; Dörnyei & Skehan, 2003).

 CLASSROOM CONNECTIONS

Given that both field independence and field sensitivity can benefit language learners, what are some activities or techniques that you have experienced that rely fairly strongly on FI? And on FS? How might you help students to become aware of this style continuum and to put their awareness into action?

Could FI and FS both be equally important? The two styles deal with two different kinds of language learning. One kind of learning implies natural, face-to-face communication, the kind of communication that occurs too rarely in the average language classroom. The second kind involves familiar classroom activities: drills, exercises, and tests. It is most likely that "natural" language learning in the "field," beyond the constraints of the classroom, is aided by an FS style, and classroom learning is enhanced, conversely, an FI style. Obviously, both styles are facilitative within appropriate contexts.

Left-Brain and Right-Brain Dominance

We have already observed in Chapter 3 that **left-brain and right-brain dominance** is a potentially significant issue in developing a theory of SLA. As the child's brain matures, various functions become lateralized to the left or right hemisphere. The left hemisphere is associated with logical, analytical thought, with mathematical and linear processing of information. The right hemisphere perceives and remembers visual, tactile, and auditory images; it is more efficient in processing holistic, integrative, and emotional information (Urgesi & Fabbro, 2009). A compilation of a variety of characteristics of left-brain (LB) and right-brain (RB) characteristics is listed in Table 5.1 (Edwards, 1979; Torrance, 1980; Joseph, 2012).

While Table 5.1 emphasizes *differences* between LB and RB characteristics, one must not overlook the importance of left and right hemispheres operating *together* as a "team." Through the corpus callosum, messages are sent back and

Table 5.1 Left-brain and right-brain characteristics

Left-Brain Dominance	Right-Brain Dominance
Relies strongly on the intellect	Uses intuitive processes
Remembers names	Remembers faces
Responds to verbal instructions and explanations	Responds to demonstrated, illustrated, or symbolic instructions
Experiments systematically and with control	Experiments randomly and with less restraint
Makes objective judgments	Makes subjective judgments
Is planned and structured	Is fluid and spontaneous
Prefers established, certain information	Is comfortable with elusive, uncertain information
Reads analytically	Reads with synthesis
Relies on language in thinking and remembering	Relies on images in thinking and remembering
Is stronger in talking, writing, and verbal communication	Is stronger in drawing, images, and manipulating objects
Prefers multiple-choice tests	Prefers open-ended questions
Controls feelings	More free with feelings
Deciphers linguistic cues, lexical, and grammatical subtleties	Interprets body language, attends to facial, nonverbal communication
Uses empirical description	Uses metaphors and verbal imagery
Favors logical problem solving	Favors intuitive problem solving

forth so that both hemispheres are involved in much of the neurological activity of the human brain. Most problem solving involves the capacities of both hemispheres, and often the best solutions to problems are those in which each hemisphere has participated optimally (Danesi, 1988).

The LB/RB construct helps to define another useful learning style continuum, with implications for L2 learning and teaching (Scovel, 1982). Danesi (1988) used "neurological bimodality" to analyze the way in which various language teaching methods have failed by appealing too strongly to LB processes. Krashen, Seliger, and Hartnett (1974) found that LB dominant L2 learners preferred a deductive approach to teaching, while RB dominant learners were more successful in inductive techniques. Stevick (1982) concluded that LB dominant second language learners are better at producing separate words, gathering the specifics of language, carrying out sequences of operations, and dealing with classification, labeling, and reorganization. RB dominant learners, on the other hand, appeared to deal better with whole images, generalizations, metaphors, emotional reactions, and artistic expressions.

You may be asking yourself how left- and right-brain functioning differs from FI and FS. While few studies have set out explicitly to correlate the two factors, intuitive observation of learners and conclusions from studies of both hemispheric preference and FI/FS show a strong relationship (Urgesi & Fabbro, 2009; Joseph, 2012). Thus, in dealing with either type of cognitive style, we are dealing with two styles that are highly parallel.

 CLASSROOM CONNECTIONS

In your foreign language learning experiences, what are some examples of left-brain and right-brain activities or techniques that you have experienced? (Examples: LB: explaining a grammatical rule; RB: responding to a piece of poetry.) In the activities you think of, what could you do as a teacher to help students to "cross over" to their less preferred brain orientation? For example, how would you help students who are strongly left-brain-oriented to appreciate and respond to poetry?

Ambiguity Tolerance

How willing are you to tolerate ideas and propositions that run counter to your own belief system or structure of knowledge? Some people—those that are **ambiguity tolerant** (AT)—are relatively open-minded in at least entertaining ideologies, events, and facts that contradict their own views. Others, more closed-minded and dogmatic, tend to reject items that are contradictory or incongruent with their existing system. In their **ambiguity intolerance** (AI), they wish to see every proposition fit into an acceptable place in their cognitive organization, and if they do not, they are rejected.

Again, advantages and disadvantages are present on each end of a continuum. The person who is AT is free to entertain a number of innovative and creative possibilities and not be cognitively or affectively disturbed by uncertainty. In second language learning a great amount of apparently contradictory information is encountered: words that differ from the native language, rules that not only differ but that are internally inconsistent because of certain exceptions, and sometimes a whole cultural system that is distant from that of the native culture. Successful language learning necessitates tolerance of such ambiguities, at least for interim periods or stages, during which time ambiguous items are given a chance to become resolved.

On the other hand, *too much* AT can have a detrimental effect. People can become "wishy-washy," adopting an "anything goes" mentality, accepting virtually every proposition before them, and inefficiently subsuming necessary facts into their cognitive organizational structure. Grammatical rules and word definitions, for example, eventually need to be discarded—pruned—in favor of more-encompassing linguistic conceptualizations.

AI also has its advantages and disadvantages. An optimal level of intolerance enables one to guard against the wishy-washiness referred to above, by closing off avenues of hopeless possibilities, rejecting contradictory material, and dealing with the reality of the system that one has built. On the other hand, AI can close the mind too soon, especially if ambiguity is perceived as a threat, and the result is a rigid, dogmatic, brittle mind that is too narrow to be creative. This may be particularly harmful in second language learning.

Only a few research findings are available on this style in second language learning. Both Naiman et al. (1978) and Chapelle and Roberts (1986) found that learners with high AT were slightly more successful in certain language tasks, suggesting, though not strongly so, that AT may be an important factor in L2 learning. It is hard to imagine a compartmentalizer—a person who sees everything in black and white with no shades of gray—being successful in the overwhelmingly ambiguous process of learning a second language.

 CLASSROOM CONNECTIONS

Foreign language students often want explanations and rules and are sometimes not willing to allow more difficult material to simply and slowly "sink in." For example, in reading, they may insist on looking up every unknown word in a dictionary before continuing to read, rather than moving on in a passage and allowing meanings to be inductively absorbed later. How would you help such students to overcome what you perceive as a block to reading efficiency?

Reflectivity and Impulsivity

Have you ever been tempted to make an impulsive decision to buy a pair of shoes simply because you like them, without carefully calculating their affordability in your budget? Yet another style is an individual's tendency to be comfortable making quick or gambling (**impulsive**) decisions versus a tendency to make slower, more calculated (**reflective**) decisions. Impulsive or *systematic* thinkers tend to weigh all the considerations in a problem, work out all the loopholes, and then, after extensive reflection, venture a solution. An impulsive or *intuitive* style involves making a number of different gambles on the basis of "hunches," with possibly several successive gambles before a solution is achieved (Ewing, 1977).

Educational research reveals that children who are conceptually reflective tend to make fewer errors in reading than impulsive children (Kagan, 1965). However, impulsive persons are usually faster readers, and eventually master the "psycholinguistic guessing game" (Goodman, 1970) of reading. In another study inductive reasoning has also been found to be more effective with reflective persons (Kagan, Pearson, & Welch, 1966). Measurement issues abound, as the only recognized test of reflectivity/impulsivity (R/I) is visually oriented (Kagan, 1965; Cairns & Cammock, 1989), as was the case in measuring FI/FS. Extrapolations of performance on such tests to other cognitive functioning is therefore problematic.

In L2 learning contexts, Doron (1973) found that reflective adults were slower but more accurate than impulsive students in reading. Abraham (1981) concluded that reflection was weakly related to performance on a proofreading task. Jamieson (1992) found that "fast-accurate" learners, or good guessers, were better language learners as measured by the standardized Test of English as a Foreign Language (TOEFL), but warned against assuming that impulsivity always implies accuracy. Some of her subjects were fast and *inaccurate*.

 CLASSROOM CONNECTIONS

Jamieson (1992) concluded that the combination of *speed* and *accuracy* led to success on timed, standardized tests. Time emerges as an important factor in language success: tests, reading, writing (composing), responding to listening, and speaking fluently are all subject to time constraints. In your learning of a foreign language in the classroom, were you fast and *accurate* as well? How might a teacher go about helping students to develop both speed *and* accuracy?

Visual, Auditory, and Kinesthetic Styles

Yet another dimension of learning style—one that is salient in a formal classroom setting—is the preference that learners show toward visual, auditory, and/or kinesthetic input. **Visual** learners tend to prefer reading and studying charts, drawings, and other graphic information. **Auditory** learners prefer listening to lectures and audiotapes. And **kinesthetic** learners will show a preference for demonstrations and physical activity involving bodily movement. Of course, most successful learners utilize both visual and auditory input, but slight preferences one way or the other may distinguish one learner from another, an important factor in examining individual differences in SLA.

In one study of adult learners of ESL, Reid (1987) found some significant cross-cultural differences in visual and auditory styles among Korean, Chinese, Japanese, and Arabic speakers. Reid (1995) later reported a study of kinesthetic styles with results that confirmed the importance of attending to such preferences among learners.

 CLASSROOM CONNECTIONS

In your foreign language classes, how have you been either helped or hindered by an appeal to visual, auditory, and/or kinesthetic modalities? What are some methodological techniques that you could use as a teacher to ensure that students are exposed to all three modalities?

At the risk of some oversimplification, Table 5.2 suggests some SLA advantages to various styles. For each advantage, of course, some disadvantages should also be taken into account.

Measurement of Learning Styles

A number of options are available for helping learners to identify their own styles, preferences, strengths, and weaknesses. The most common method is a self-check questionnaire in which the learner responds to various questions, usually along a scale of points of agreement and disagreement. Examples of such measures include a standard for a number of years, Kolb's (1999) *Learning Style Inventory* (LSI); Oxford's (1995) *Style Analysis Survey*; Wintergerst, DeCapua, and Verna's (2002) *Learning Styles Indicator*; and later in this chapter, a *Styles Awareness Checklist* (Figure 5.1). Similar checklists can be found in Brown's (2002) self-help guide for English language learners.

Measurement of style preferences by means of self-check questionnaires is problematic (Ehrman & Leaver, 2003; Jones, 2009), in that external, objective

Table 5.2 Summary of possible SLA style advantages

Styles	SLA Advantages?
Left-brain processing	Analyzing linguistic systems, rules, structures, definitions Perceiving the logic of language systems
Right-brain processing	Integrating diverse linguistic input Comprehending and producing metaphors
Field Independence	Expressing and comprehending key ideas concisely Remembering lexical and syntactic details
Field Sensitivity	Getting the overall gist of oral and written input "Reading between the lines" of oral and written input
Ambiguity tolerance	Transcending linguistic complexity perceived as difficult Maintaining attention to a difficult conversation or text
Ambiguity intolerance	Ascertaining order and system within complexity Questioning/clarifying misunderstood information
Reflectivity	Taking time to mentally sort through linguistic complexity Speaking out only when certain of linguistic systems
Impulsivity	Taking linguistic risks in the face of possible error Taking initiative in conversations

measures are not available. Then, the fact that learners' styles represent preferred *approaches* rather than immutable stable *traits* means that learners can adapt to varying contexts and situations, regardless of their overall general preferences. As Oxford noted, "Although the learner might have some strong style tendencies, they are not set in stone and are influenced by the sociocultural context" (2011b, p. 40). Styles can be a reflection, if not a direct product, of one's cultural background (Oxford & Anderson, 1995; Wintergerst, DeCapua, & Itzen, 2001), spurring teachers to be sensitive to students' heritage languages and cultures.

With that "grain of salt" added to the consideration of learning styles in SLA, it is nevertheless important for teachers to gauge (even if intuitively) students' preferences, strengths and weaknesses, propensities, and abilities in order to tailor an effective methodological approach.

AUTONOMY AND AWARENESS

A glance at the history of language teaching reveals some interesting "changing winds and shifting sands," as noted in Chapter 1. One way of looking at this history is to consider the extent to which methodological trends have emphasized the respective *roles* of the teacher and the learner. Until some of the "designer" methods appeared in the 1970s, most of language teaching methodology was *teacher-centered.* Students entered a classroom, sat down dutifully in their desks, and waited for the teacher to tell them what to do. Those directives might have been to translate a passage, to memorize a rule, to read aloud, or to repeat a dialogue.

Then, in the last half of the twentieth century, the educational profession began to emphasize the value of learner **autonomy** in the form of *learner-centered* approaches, discovery learning, problem-posing, group work, cooperative learning, and selecting certain goals for individual pursuit (Slavin, 2011). In L2 teaching, methods emphasized allowing learners to initiate oral production, practice language through small-group tasks, and engage in using the language out in the "real world" (Brown, 2007). In keeping with a popular social trend of "self-help" manuals for everything from weight loss to how to feel that you're "okay," the language teaching profession began to encourage learners to "take charge" of their own learning, and to chart their own "pathways to success" (Brown, 1991, 2002).

The process of developing within learners a sense of autonomy required the use of strategies (Wenden, 1992). After all, how many students enter a foreign language class knowing anything at all about the process of language learning, or about the "tricks of the trade" in SLA? With the aid of research on achieving autonomy, language programs and courses have increasingly emphasized the importance of self-starting and of taking responsibility for one's own learning (Riley, 1988; Pemberton, 1996; Benson & Voller, 1997; Pennycook, 1997; Cotterall & Crabbe, 1999; Benson, 2001; Benson & Toogood, 2002; Palfreyman, 2003; Schmenk, 2005; Barfield & Brown, 2007; Lamb & Reinders, 2008; Pemberton, Toogood, & Barfield, 2009). The literature on the topic raises some caution flags. Schmenk (2005) appropriately described the nonuniversality of the concept of autonomy, and Pennycook (1997) warned us about the potential cultural imperialism involved in assuming that every culture equally values and promotes autonomy, especially in educational institutions. For language teaching in sub-Saharan Africa, Sonaiya questioned "the global validity of the so-called *autonomous* method of language learning . . . which has obvious origins in European and North American traditions of individualism" (2002, p. 106).

However, other studies are more encouraging. Dixon's (2011) review of literature on autonomy reveals encouraging signs. Carter suggested that while learners in Trinidad and Tobago traditionally rely heavily on teachers as managers of their learning, autonomy could nevertheless be fostered through what she described as a "context-sensitive" model (2001, p. 26). Similarly, Spratt, Humphreys, and Chan (2002) found that autonomy could be promoted among learners in Hong Kong, as long as an appropriate level of motivation was present. Schmenk recommended a "glocalization" (a combination of both global and local considerations) of the concept of autonomy in non-Western cultures, one that involves "a critical awareness of . . . specific cultural backdrops and impacts" (2005, p. 115).

Closely linked to the concept of autonomy is the demand on learners to become **aware** of their own processes of learning. In your foreign language courses, did your teacher or your textbook help you to become aware of what language learning was all about? Were you encouraged to monitor your own learning process? Or to assess your own strengths and weaknesses, and follow up with strategic action? Probably not.

Until recently, few courses in languages provided such opportunities for learners to become aware of what language learning was all about and what they could do to become better learners. Now, with the backdrop of a good deal of research on awareness and "consciousness raising," language programs are offering more occasions for learners to develop a metacognitive awareness of their ongoing learning (Byram, 2012). The journal *Language Awareness* is, in fact, devoted to the concept. The supporting research stockpile is growing on **awareness-raising** among L2 learners in classrooms around the world: (Lightbown & Spada, 2000; Rosa & Leow, 2004; Simard & Wong, 2004; Nakatani, 2005).

 CLASSROOM CONNECTIONS

Research on learning styles supports learners' becoming *aware* of their preferences, strengths, and weaknesses, and further suggests that they need to distinguish between styles that work *for* them and those that may work *against* them. What are some styles that have worked for you in your foreign language learning experiences? What about styles that worked against you? What could you do as a teacher to capitalize on such self-knowledge?

What are we learning from these studies? Beyond the simple conclusion that learners can indeed benefit from raised awareness of their own processes of learning, one interesting finding is an *optimal* level of awareness that serves learners (Lightbown & Spada, 1990; Rubin, Chamot, Harris, & Anderson, 2007). *Too much* awareness, overattention to monitoring for correctness, or explicit focus on grammar will smother a learner's yearning to simply *use* language. Even too much thinking about strategic options—with too little intuitive, subconscious communication—can block open communication. On the other hand, some levels of awareness are clearly warranted, and in this chapter we will speak to the issue of strategic awareness: the conscious application of appropriate strategies.

SELF-REGULATION

The culmination of research on autonomy coupled with the principle of awareness-raising lies in what researchers (Zimmerman, 1990, 2000; Cohen & Macaro, 2007; Dörnyei, 2009) have called **self-regulation**: the autonomous process of developing awareness, setting goals, monitoring performance, using effective strategies, and holding positive beliefs about oneself. Rebecca Oxford (2011b) expanded Zimmerman's original (1990, 2000) concept to what she calls **strategic self-regulation** (S²R), the self-stimulated application by a learner of cognitive, affective, and sociocultural-interactive strategies. Her S²R model includes a host of practical suggestions for teachers and learners to develop autonomy, awareness, and action.

At the heart of Oxford's **S²R model** is the principle of learners *acting* on their learning. Autonomy and awareness without action would be relatively useless. Once learners can become aware of their predispositions, their styles, and their strengths and weaknesses, they can then take appropriate action in the form of a plethora of self-regulated strategies that are available to them. Not all strategies are appropriate for all learners. A learner who, for example, is already aware of an ambiguity-tolerant, right-brain style surely will not need a battery of new strategies to open up, to be calm in the face of a storm of incomprehensible language, or to take in the big picture. Such strategies are already naturally in place. However, a learner who is intolerant of ambiguity and employs analytical, linear thinking can obviously benefit from an awareness of those proclivities and from taking appropriate strategic action.

What do we know about self-regulated learners? The list of "good language learner" characteristics from Naiman et al. (1978) turns out not to be as passé as one might think. According to Oxford (2011b, p. 15), strategically self-regulated learners do the following:

- Actively participate in their own autonomous learning process
- Control various aspects of their learning for accomplishing specific goals
- Regulate their cognitive and affective states
- Form positive beliefs about themselves
- Use strategies to move from conscious knowledge to automatic procedural knowledge
- Select appropriate strategies for widely differing purposes and contexts
- Make the connection between strategy use and learning outcomes

Does this list sound familiar? Yes, the concepts are more sophisticated and are now better defined than they were in 1978, but we are still attending to what "good language learners" *do* to achieve success.

STRATEGIES

Styles are general characteristics that differentiate one individual from another—they are significant markers of our many *individual differences* (Dewaele, 2009). **Strategies** are those specific actions that we take to solve a given problem, and that vary considerably *within* each individual. Ana Chamot defines strategies quite broadly as "procedures that facilitate a learning task . . . Strategies are most often conscious and goal driven" (2005, p. 112).

Over the last five decades, research on SLA has offered a mélange of *types* of strategies, not to mention hundreds of *specific* strategies, or, in Oxford's (2011b) terminology, **tactics**. Following are just a few examples of general categories of strategy that have at one time or another been employed in researching and teaching SLA (O'Malley et al., 1983, 1985a, 1985b, 1987, 1989; Chamot & O'Malley, 1986, 1987; Chamot, 1990; O'Malley & Oxford, 1990a, 2011b; Chamot, Barnhart, El-Dinary, & Robbins, 1999; Cohen & Macaro, 2007).

- Learning vs. Communication
- Metacognitive
- Memory
- Direct vs. Indirect
- Cognitive
- Affective
- Socio-affective (also, Social)
- Sociocultural-Interactive
- Input (comprehension) vs. Output (production)
- Skill-oriented (relating to the four skills)
- Avoidance
- Compensatory
- Self-regulated

A bewildering array of strategic options, but perhaps such proliferation of typology is simply part of the historical growing pains of a long period of research. As the intricacies of a learner's strategic investment in L2 learning were uncovered, the refining and redefinition process necessitated new frameworks on which to build an increasingly sophisticated science.

In order to simplify where we appear to stand regarding what I like to call **strategic investment** in SLA, I will use Oxford's (2011b) typology to describe the current state of the art. She employed three broad categories (or **meta-strategies**— for general management and control) within which to consider strategic self-regulation (S^2R): cognitive, affective, and sociocultural-interactive strategies. These three categories will be used to summarize an extensive range of work by Chamot, Cohen, Dörnyei, O'Malley, Oxford, Rubin, and others.

Cognitive Strategies

The first of Oxford's (2011b) three overall meta-strategies is a group of **cognitive strategies**, which help the learner "construct, transform, and apply L2 knowledge" (p. 24). Included in this category are a number of subcategories, each of which includes specific **tactics**: "specific manifestations of a strategy or meta-strategy by a particular learner in a given setting for a certain purpose."

Table 5.3 Cognitive strategies and tactics

Cognitive Strategies	Examples of Tactics
Planning	Previewing, reviewing, setting schedules, deciding to attend to a specific aspect of language input, planning for and rehearsing linguistic components necessary to carry out an upcoming language task, deciding to postpone speaking
Organizing	Deciding to attend to specific aspects of language input or situational details that will cue the retention of language input, reordering, classifying, labeling items in the language
Monitoring	Correcting one's speech for accuracy in pronunciation, grammar, vocabulary, imitating a language model, including silent rehearsal, and self-checking
Evaluating	Checking the outcomes of one's own language learning against an internal measure of completeness and accuracy
Using senses	Creating visualizations and pictures to remember, noticing phonological sounds, acting out a word or sentence
Activating knowledge	Using the first language for comparison/contrast to remember words and forms, applying rules by deduction, using translation to remember a new word
Contextualization	Placing a word or phrase in a meaningful language sequence, relating new information to other concepts in memory
Going beyond the data	Guessing meanings of new items, predicting words or forms from the context

Table 5.3 lists some of the possibilities (synthesized from O'Malley et al., 1985 and Oxford, 2011b).

Affective Strategies

The second of Oxford's meta-strategies is a set of **affective strategies** that help the learner to employ beneficial emotional energy, form positive attitudes toward the learning process, and generate and maintain motivation. The list in Table 5.4 is a synthesis of affective strategies from Oxford (1990b, 2011b), Brown (2002), and Cohen and Macaro (2007).

Sociocultural-Interactive Strategies

The third of Oxford's categories contains what others have called **communication** strategies (Dörnyei, 1995) or **socioaffective** strategies (O'Malley et al., 1985b), both of which refer to the learner's tactics for generating and

Table 5.4 Affective strategies and tactics

Affective Strategies	Examples of Tactics
Activating supportive emotions	Encouraging oneself, making positive statements, making lists of one's abilities, rewarding oneself for accomplishments, noticing what one has accomplished to build self-confidence, writing a language learning diary
Minimizing negative emotions	Using relaxation to lower fear or anxiety, using positive self-talk to lower self-doubt, generating interesting charts, images, or dialogues to lower boredom, making a list of "to do" items to avoid feeling overwhelmed
Generating motivation	Learning about the culture of a language, setting personal goals and monitoring their accomplishment, listing specific accomplishments, turning attention away from tests and toward what one can do with the language
Building positive attitudes	Using relaxation to lower fear or anxiety, generating interesting activities to lower boredom, empathizing with others to develop cultural understanding

maintaining interactive communication within a cultural context. Oxford's **sociocultural-interactive (S-I) strategies** "help the learner interact and communicate (despite knowledge gaps) and deal [effectively] with culture" (2011b, p. 24). Let's look at examples (Table 5.5) drawn from several sources, including Dörnyei (1995), Oxford (1990a), and Brown (2002).

Table 5.5 Sociocultural-interactive strategies and tactics

S-I Strategy	Examples of Tactics
Interacting to learn	Cooperating with one or more peers to obtain feedback, pool information, or model a language activity
Overcoming knowledge gaps	Asking a teacher or other native speaker for repetition, paraphrasing, explanation, and/or examples, questioning for clarification, using memorized chunks of language to initiate or maintain communication
Guessing intelligently	Using linguistic clues in lexicon, grammar, or phonology to predict, using discourse markers to comprehend
Generating conversation	Initiating conversation with known discourse gambits, maintaining conversation with affirmations, verbal and nonverbal attention signals, asking questions
Activating sociocultural schemata	Asking questions about culture, customs, etc., reading about culture (customs, history, music, art)

> ### 🌐 CLASSROOM CONNECTIONS
>
> The three lists above enumerate quite a number of tactics that learners have used to successfully learn foreign languages. Have you used any of these tactics in your L2 learning? If you could choose a few of them to highlight, how would you *teach* them to students?

The three classifications of meta-strategies outlined above only begin to capture the complexity of the L2 learner's potential strategic investment in learning the target language. A study of the work of Andrew Cohen (2011), Zoltan Dörnyei (2009), and Rebecca Oxford (2011a, 2011b) is strongly recommended for anyone who wishes to pursue such complexity and to apply it in a comprehensive way to teaching L2s.

Compensatory Strategies

A further note is in order, however, before moving on to a commentary on the research and to pedagogical implications of research on strategies. It is of singular interest that many language learners who possess a "knack" for gaining communicative control of a second language have some special insights into what Dörnyei (1995, 2009) and others have called **compensatory strategies,** a few of which were listed under sociocultural-interactive strategies in Table 5.4. A review of various self-help books and "how to" manuals on learning a foreign language shows a strong emphasis on how the learner can compensate for weaknesses and avoid various pitfalls (Lai, 2009). The "knack" seems to be composed quite prominently of such "tricks" and techniques.

Consider the list of tactics drawn from Dörnyei (1995) and Brown (2002) in Table 5.6.

All of these compensatory strategies are designed to make up for gaps in one's ability. Such communicative or sociocultural-interactive strategies often spell the difference between a person who "survives" in a language and one who does not. What psycholinguistic elements are involved in these tactics?

Avoidance is a tactic for preventing a pitfall, a linguistic weakness that could break down communicative flow. Syntactic, phonological, and lexical avoidance are common tactics in successful learners, as is topic avoidance. Psychologically, avoidance is a combination of face-saving and maintaining communicative interaction. To save embarrassment, the following L2 learner switched to another construction:

    L2 Learner: I lost my road.
Native Speaker: You lost your *road*?
    L2 Learner: Uh, . . . I lost. I lost. I got lost.

Table 5.6 Compensatory strategies

Strategy	Tactic
Avoidance	Avoiding a topic, concept, grammatical construction, or phonological element that poses difficulty
Circumlocution	Describing an object or idea with a definition (e.g., You know, that thing you open bottles with—for corkscrew)
Approximation	Using an alternative term which expresses the meaning of the target lexical item as closely as possible (e.g., ship for sailboat)
Word coinage	Creating a nonexistent L2 word based on a supposed rule (e.g., vegetable-ist for vegetarian)
Nonverbal signals	Mime, gesture, facial expression, or sound imitation
Prefabricated patterns	Using memorized stock phrases, usually for "survival" purposes (e.g., Where is . . .? How much is . . .? (morphological components are not known to the learner)
Code switching	Using an L1 word with L1 pronunciation while speaking in L2 (e.g., Je serais à la rehearsal—for *repetition*)
Appeal to authority	Asking for aid either directly (e.g., What do you call . . .?) or indirectly (e.g., rising intonation, pause, eye contact, puzzled expression)
Keeping the floor	Using fillers or hesitation devices to fill pauses and to gain time to think (e.g., well, now let's see, uh, as a matter of fact)

Another compensatory trick is the memorization of certain stock phrases or sentences without internalized knowledge of their components. These memorized chunks of language, known as **prefabricated patterns**, are often found in pocket bilingual phrase books: "How much does this cost?" "Where is the toilet?" "I don't speak English." Such phrases are memorized by rote to fit a context. In my first few days of Kikongo learning in the Congo, I tried to say, in Kikongo, "I don't know Kikongo" to anyone who attempted conversation. I was later embarrassed to discover that instead of saying *Kizeyi Kikongo ko*, I had said *Kizolele Kikongo ko* (I don't *like* Kikongo)—not a good way to endear yourself to Kikongo speakers!

Code-switching is the use of a first or third language within a stream of speech in the second language. Often code-switching occurs subconsciously between two advanced learners with a common first language, but, in such a case, usually not as a compensatory strategy. Learners in the early stages of acquisition, however, might code-switch—use their native language to fill in missing knowledge—whether the hearer knows that native language or not.

Yet another common compensatory strategy is a direct appeal for help, often termed **appeal to authority**. Learners may, if stuck for a particular word or phrase, directly ask a proficient speaker or teacher for the correct form, or consult a dictionary. An English learner, when asked to introduce himself to the class, said, "Allow me to introduce myself and tell you some of the . . ." At this point he reached for his iPhone bilingual dictionary app, and finding the word he wanted, continued, "some of the *headlights* of my past." Oops, those apps are useful, but language learners beware!

 CLASSROOM CONNECTIONS

Have you used any of these compensatory strategies? Some are difficult to teach, as learners tend to use them subconsciously. Pick a few of the compensatory tactics discussed above and decide how you would "coach" students with advice on compensating for gaps in their competence.

Research on Learning Strategies

The research of the last four decades on L2 strategies has slowly but surely been pushing toward a *theory* of language learning strategies (Griffiths & Parr, 2001; Hsiao & Oxford, 2002; Dörnyei & Skehan, 2003; Cohen & Macaro, 2007; Oxford, 2011b). One of the major conundrums of the hundreds of research studies on strategies has been the identification of the theoretically most parsimonious way of *categorizing* strategies. Oxford's three meta-strategies comprise one lens—among many—through which to view strategies.

Identifying Types of Strategy

Other pedagogically useful studies separate strategies for acquiring the four skills of *listening, speaking, reading, and writing. Learning* (input) strategies, as opposed to *communication* (output) strategies, emphasize differences between learning receptive skills of listening and reading in contrast to producing language in speech and writing. O'Malley, Chamot, and Kupper (1989) found that L2 learners developed effective listening skills through monitoring, elaboration, and inferencing. Selective attention to keywords and advance organizers, inferring from context, prediction, using a worksheet, and taking notes were shown to be teachable (Rost & Ross, 1991; Ozeki, 2000; Carrier, 2003; Vandergrift, 2003). And reading strategies such as bottom-up and top-down processing, predicting, guessing from context, brainstorming, and summarizing have also been shown to be effective (Anderson, 1991; Chamot & El-Dinary, 1999; Pressley, 2000).

Communication or output strategies, defined by Faerch and Kasper as "potentially conscious plans for solving what to an individual presents itself as a problem in reaching a particular communicative goal," (1983a, p. 36) comprise yet another research focus. Attention to communication strategies (Bongaerts & Poulisse, 1989; Oxford & Crookall, 1989; Bialystok, 1990a; Rost & Ross, 1991; Dörnyei, 1995; McDonough, 1999; Anderson, 2005; Chamot, 2005) has been directed in large part to the *compensatory* nature of communication strategies, mentioned above. Other current approaches (Cohen, 2011; Oxford, 2011b) take a more positive view of communication strategies as elements of an overall strategic competence (see Chapter 9) in which learners bring to bear all the possible facets of their growing competence in order to send clear messages in the second language. Such strategies can be consciously self-regulatory (Bongaerts & Poulisse, 1989; Oxford, 2011b) as well as subconscious or implicit.

Cross-Cultural Issues

Another theoretical issue probes the effectiveness of strategy use and instruction *cross-culturally*, which has already been alluded to above in our discussion of autonomy (Oxford & Anderson, 1995; Oxford, 1996; Pemberton, 1996; McDonough, 1999). Do cross-cultural factors facilitate or interfere with strategy use among learners? Conclusions from an extensive number of studies in many countries promise more than a glimmer of hope that strategy instruction and autonomous learning are viable avenues to success: China (Jun Zhang, 2003; Gan, Humphreys, & Hamp-Lyons, 2004); Egypt (Nelson, Carson, Al Batal, & El Bakary, 2002); Italy (Macaro, 2000); Japan (Ozeki, 2000; Taguchi, 2002; Cohen, 2004); Korea (Lee & Oxford, 2005), Kuwait (El-Dib, 2004); Taiwan (Lai, 2009); and Singapore (Wharton, 2000).

 CLASSROOM CONNECTIONS

In your experience, what are some specific cultural issues in either researching or teaching strategies? Do awareness and autonomy fit well with cultures that you know? How would you as a teacher help learners in more traditional educational systems (where learners expect the teacher to control everything and tell them everything they need to know) to act more strategically on their learning?

Measuring Strategy Use

A controversial issue in both research and pedagogy is the measurement of strategy use. One of the most widely used instruments for learners to identify strategies is Oxford's (1990a) *Strategy Inventory for Language Learning* (SILL), a questionnaire that has been tested in many countries and translated into several languages. The SILL's 50 items, divided into six categories, each present a possible strategy (e.g., "I use rhymes to remember new words"), which responders must indicate on a five-point scale of "never true of me" to "always true of me." Once style preferences have been identified, a learner can presumably proceed to take action through strategies.

How adequate are self-reports for identifying strategy use? And is frequency of use (as implied in the SILL and other questionnaires) an appropriate gauge of a learner's ability to select strategies appropriate for many different contexts? Self-report questionnaires may best be taken with a grain of salt, in that learners may not actually understand the strategy being named, may incorrectly claim to use strategies, and could possibly fail to remember strategies they have used (White, Schramm, & Chamot, 2007).

Other forms of identifying styles and strategies, and for raising them to the consciousness of learners, include self-reports through interviews (Macaro, 2001); written diaries and journals (Halbach, 2000; Carson & Longhini, 2002); think-aloud protocols (O'Malley & Chamot, 1990; Macaro, 2000) in which questions like, "Why did you hesitate and restate that verb form?" require a learner response; student portfolios (Chamot, 2005); and inventories that focus on learning the four skills (Cohen, Oxford, & Chi, 2003).

The Effectiveness of Strategy Instruction

We have seen mounting evidence of the usefulness of learners' incorporating strategies into their classroom learning process. Strategy training has appeared in three basic forms: (1) textbook-embedded instruction (with hints and strategic suggestions within a student textbook and a teacher's manual); (2) student manuals that promote autonomous self-help strategy training (e.g., Brown, 2002); and (3) strategies-based advice, hints, and tips within a teacher's planned or impromptu classroom procedures. All three have been demonstrated to be effective for learners in various contexts (Wenden, 1992; Hill, 1994; Cohen, 1998; McDonough, 1999; Dörnyei & Skehan, 2003; Anderson, 2005; Chamot, 2005). We turn to strategies-based instruction (SBI) in the next section.

STRATEGIES-BASED INSTRUCTION

Much of the work of researchers and teachers on the application of strategies to classroom learning has come to be known generically by several terms: *learner strategy training, learning strategy instruction, styles- and strategies-based instruction* (SSBI) (Cohen, 1998; Cohen & Weaver, 2006), and perhaps more simply as **strategies-based instruction** (SBI) (Cohen, 1998; McDonough, 1999). As we seek to make the language classroom an effective milieu for learning, it has become increasingly apparent that "teaching learners how to learn" is crucial. Wenden (1985) was among the first to assert that learner strategies are the key to learner autonomy, and Chamot (2005) stressed the importance of including facilitation of that autonomy through explicit instruction.

Drawing on an understanding of what makes learners successful and unsuccessful, teachers can establish in the classroom an atmosphere for the realization of successful strategies. Teachers cannot always expect instant success in that effort since students often bring with them certain preconceived notions of what "ought" to go on in the classroom (Bialystok, 1985). However, it has been found that students will benefit from SBI if they (1) understand the strategy itself, (2) perceive it to be effective, and (3) do not consider its implementation to be overly difficult (MacIntyre & Noels, 1996). Therefore our efforts to teach students some technical know-how about how to tackle a language are well advised.

 CLASSROOM CONNECTIONS

In what ways have you been helped by a teacher (or through your own effort) to utilize certain strategies or "tricks" for learning a language? What could you do as a teacher to help students to take "action" through strategy use?

Stimulating Awareness

The effective implementation of SBI in language classrooms involves several steps and considerations:

1. identifying learners' styles and linking them with potential strategies
2. incorporating SBI in communicative language courses and classrooms
3. providing extra-class assistance for learners

One way of accomplishing the first of these objectives is to administer a simple checklist to students, with a view to acquainting students with their own preferences in learning. Figure 5.1 shows a *Styles Awareness Checklist* (SAC), a simple scaled questionnaire to familiarize students with their styles (not strategies at this point).

From Awareness to Action

The SAC is an instrument that has immediate practical value. Once students have had a chance, with no advance coaching, to fill out the checklist, you can engage them in any or all of the following:

- a discussion of why they responded as they did
- small-group sharing of feelings underlying their responses
- an informal tabulation of how people responded to each item
- some advice, from your own experience, on why certain practices may be successful or unsuccessful
- reaching the general consensus that responses in the A and B categories are usually indicative of successful approaches to language learning.

Check one box in each item that best describes you. Boxes A and E would indicate that the sentence is very much like you. Boxes B and D would indicate that the sentence is somewhat descriptive of you. Box C would indicate that you have no inclination one way or another.

A   B   C   D   E

1. I don't mind if people laugh at me when I speak.
I get embarrassed if people laugh at me when I speak.

2. I like to try out new words and structures that I'm not completely sure of.
I like to use only language that I am certain is correct.

3. I feel very confident in my ability to succeed in learning this language.
I feel quite uncertain about my ability to succeed in learning this language.

4. I want to learn this language because of what I can personally gain from it.
I am learning this language only because someone else is requiring it.

5. I really enjoy working with other people in groups.
I would much rather work alone than with other people.

6. I like to "absorb" language and get the general "gist" of what is said or written.
I like to analyze the many details of language and understand exactly what is said or written.

7. If there is an abundance of language to master, I just try to take things one step at a time.
I am very annoyed by an abundance of language material presented all at once.

8. I am not overly conscious of myself when I speak.
I "monitor" myself very closely and consciously when I speak.

10. I find ways to continue learning language outside of the classroom.
I look to the teacher and the classroom activities for everything I need to be successful.

Figure 5.1   Styles Awareness Checklist

The SAC is designed so that each item highlights a major tenet in a list of "good language learner" characteristics. Item by item, numbered 1 through 10, the questionnaire reiterates the following 10 "maxims":

1. Lower inhibitions.
2. Encourage risk taking.
3. Build self-confidence.
4. Develop intrinsic motivation.
5. Engage in cooperative learning.
6. Use right-brain processes.
7. Promote ambiguity tolerance.
8. Practice intuition.
9. Process error feedback.
10. Set personal goals.

As mentioned, most current language *textbooks* now include strategy awareness modules. With "Did You Know?" boxes and sections on "Hints for Learning," a standard language course embeds styles and strategy awareness and action into the curriculum. Another option being used by language teachers is to stimulate strategy awareness and practice in their students with the use of short, simple *manuals* written for students, designed to raise their awareness, and to offer multiple strategic options (Ellis & Sinclair, 1989; Brown, 1991, 1989, 2002; Rubin & Thompson, 1994; Murphey, 2006). These practical handbooks are easy to follow, incorporate many self-check inventories, offer practical advice, and in some cases suggest that L2 learning can be *fun* (Murphey, 2006).

Even without such published, predesigned material, teachers can engage in their own SBI as an integral part of their *methodology*. As teachers utilize such techniques as communicative games, rapid reading, fluency exercises, and error analysis, to name a few, they can help students to understand *why* they are doing these activities and help them to extrapolate to the use of successful strategies beyond the classroom. For example, when students are playing a guessing game, performing a skit, or singing songs, the teacher can remind them that they are practicing strategies for lowering inhibitions. Table 5.7 provides a list of ways to "build strategic techniques" in a language classroom.

 CLASSROOM CONNECTIONS

Encouraging students to set their own goals for learning is problematic in any culture. Students almost universally expect teachers to set goals and to inform them of expectations. Have you ever set goals for yourself in learning a foreign language? How could a teacher approach students with a proposal that they set some goals for themselves? How would you, or your students, assess the accomplishment of those goals?

Table 5.7 Building strategic techniques

---

1. To lower inhibitions: Play guessing games and communication games; do role plays and skits; sing songs; use plenty of group work; laugh with your students; have them share their fears in small groups.

---

2. To encourage risk taking: Praise students for making sincere efforts to try out language; use fluency exercises where errors are not corrected at that time; give outside-of-class assignments to speak or write or otherwise try out the language.

---

3. To build students' self-confidence: Tell students explicitly (verbally and nonverbally) that you do indeed believe in them; have them make lists of their strengths, of what they know or have accomplished so far in the course.

---

4. To help students develop intrinsic motivation: Remind them explicitly about the rewards for learning English; describe (or have students look up) jobs that require English; play down the final examination in favor of helping students to see rewards for themselves beyond the final exam.

---

5. To promote cooperative learning: Direct students to share their knowledge; play down competition among students; get your class to think of themselves as a team; do a considerable amount of small-group work.

---

6. To encourage students to use right-brain processing: Use movies and tapes in class; have students read passages rapidly; do skimming exercises; do rapid "free writes"; do oral fluency exercises where the object is to get students to talk (or write) a lot without being corrected.

---

7. To promote ambiguity tolerance: Encourage students to ask you, and each other, questions when they don't understand something; keep your theoretical explanations very simple and brief; deal with just a few rules at a time; occasionally resort to translation into a native language to clarify a word or meaning.

---

8. To help students use their intuition: Praise students for good guesses; do not always give explanations of errors—let a correction suffice; correct only selected errors, preferably just those that interfere with learning.

---

9. To get students to make their mistakes work for them: Tape-record students' oral production and get them to identify errors; let students catch and correct each other's errors—do not always give them the correct form; encourage students to make lists of their common errors and to work on them on their own.

---

10. To get students to set their own goals: Explicitly encourage or direct students to go beyond the classroom goals; have them make lists of what they will accomplish on their own in a particular week; get students to make specific time commitments at home to study the language; give "extra credit" work.

From Classroom Action to Autonomy

Finally, it is important to note that style awareness and strategic action are not and should not be limited to the classroom. Most successful learners reach communicative goals by virtue of their own self-motivated efforts to extend learning well beyond the confines of a classroom. Teachers can help learners to achieve this further step toward *autonomy* by helping learners to see that raising their awareness of styles and strategies aids them in the authentic use of language "out there." The classroom is an opportunity for learners to *begin* the journey toward success, and to grasp the reality that beyond those classroom hours are dozens of hours weekly that can be devoted to practicing meaningful uses of their new language.

★   ★   ★   ★   ★

This chapter has highlighted *individual differences* among learners across both cognitive and affective domains. An awareness of these factors will help you, the teacher, to appreciate that not all learners are alike. No one can be neatly pigeonholed into a cognitive type or style or set of preferred strategies. A potentially infinite number of cognitive/affective "profiles" might be identified among the L2 learners of the world! Perhaps the best moral lesson here is the importance of the "specialness" of each student and our responsibility as teachers to respect all those unique differences that our students manifest. Doing so requires recognizing and understanding a multiplicity of cognitive variables active in the L2 learning process, making appropriate assessments of individual learners, meeting them where they are, and providing them with the best possible opportunities for learning.

Remember Magdalena, described at the beginning of this chapter? Would you like to know what her "secret" to success was? I asked her lots of questions, and her answers are distilled here into some advice from one who is certainly qualified to give it!

"I think some of what you are calling 'success' is simply good fortune. My parents were always very supportive of my quirky interest in language, my crazy questions about words and people and cultures. I mostly attended public schools, so I can't say I received extraordinary attention in school, but I was taught the value of education and even as a child appreciated (and enjoyed?) learning. Being able to learn English and Russian at a very young age helped—because it came more naturally. Falling in love with a handsome Italian at age 21 gave me lots of intrinsic ☺ motivation. From a young age I loved Spanish and Spanish culture, so I majored in Spanish literature in college. Moving to Ecuador was a natural step, and then meeting my future husband propelled my Spanish to perfection! Now in my work teaching English, training English teachers, and working for a major textbook publisher, English is second nature to me now. What can I say? I love words and books and literature and culture and language, so I don't think I have any 'secret' to success, just a growing appreciation for what languages mean to people, and the importance of language for all of us to understand each other around the world."

SUGGESTED READINGS

Cohen, A. (2011). Second language learner strategies. In E. Hinkel (Ed.), *Handbook of research in second language teaching and learning: Volume II.* (pp. 681–698). New York: Routledge.

A concise survey of current issues, definitions, controversies, and pedagogical uses of learning strategies in SLA, including sections on the four skills.

Oxford, R. (2011a). Strategies for learning a second or foreign language. *Language Teaching, 44,* 167–180.

A comprehensive annotated bibliography of virtually every research study on L2 learning strategies over the last four decades.

Oxford, R. (2011b). *Teaching and researching language learning strategies.* Harlow, UK: Pearson.

A description of Rebecca Oxford's model of strategic self-regulation (S^2R) for L2 learners, complete with charts, lists, tables, practical applications, and sections on the four skills.

Cohen, A., & Macaro, E. (Eds.). (2007). *Language learner strategies: Thirty years of research and practice.* Oxford, UK: Oxford University Press.

A survey and update by numerous research experts on researching and teaching strategies, including separate chapters on the four skills.

LANGUAGE LEARNING EXPERIENCE: JOURNAL ENTRY 5

Note: See Chapter 1 for general guidelines for writing a journal on a previous or concurrent language learning experience.

- List each of the five learning styles discussed in the chapter (FI/FS, left-/right-brain dominance, ambiguity tolerance, reflectivity/impulsivity, visual/auditory/kinesthetic). Write a few sentences about which side you think is dominant for you, and list some examples in your language learning to illustrate.
- Which of your preferences, styles, or tendencies, if any, do you think might be working *against* you? Make a short list of specific things you could do to help push yourself to a more favorable position.
- Take the *Styles Awareness Checklist* (Figure 5.1, p. 134). Do you think you should try to change some of your styles, as they are described on the checklist? How would you do that?
- How autonomous are you as a language learner? Make a list of ways that you could become more autonomous. And, for a challenge, write about what a teacher can do to help a learner develop autonomy.

- If you are now taking a foreign language, you are becoming quite aware of your own learning processes. In previous language learning experiences, how overtly aware were you of factors like "good language learner" characteristics, your own styles, and strategies you could consciously apply? What would you have done differently then, knowing what you know now? What can you do differently in a current or future language learning situation, given what you now know about styles and strategies?
- Using the four lists of learning strategies (Tables 5.3, 5.4, 5.5, 5.6), describe examples of two or three strategies that you have already used. Pick one or two that you don't use very much and list them as your challenge for the near future.
- Brainstorm some compensatory strategies that you have used. Does the list in Table 5.6 give you some ideas about what you could be doing to further your communicative success? Write down one or two specific things you will try out in the near future in a foreign language.
- How does your teacher (either now or in the past) measure up as a strategies-based instructor? What does this tell you about how your own teaching might help students to be more successful learners?

FOR THE TEACHER: ACTIVITIES (A) & DISCUSSION (D)

Note: For each of the "Classroom Connections" in this chapter, you may wish to turn them into individual or pair-work discussion questions.

1. (A) Divide students into pairs or small groups. Ask them to share what each of them perceives to be their more dominant learning style along the continua presented here: FI/FS, left/right brain dominance, ambiguity tolerance, reflective/impulsive, and visual/auditory/kinesthetic. Ask them to talk about examples of how they manifest those styles in language classrooms.
2. (A) Ask students to look at the list of differences between left- and right-brain processing in Table 5.1, and individually to check or circle the side that corresponds to their own preference. Then, in pairs, have them compare their preferences and talk about examples in their lives in general, in educational contexts, and in language classes they have taken.
3. (A) As a follow-up to exercise 2 above on left-/right-brain dominance, form four groups, with one of the four *remaining* cognitive styles assigned to each group. Ask each group to list the types of activities or techniques in foreign language classes that illustrate both sides of its style continuum. Have each group share their results with the rest of the class.

4. (D) Ask the class to look at the list of "good language learner" characteristics from 1970s research on page 110. Which ones seem the most important? Which the least? Which ones have students used? Would they be able to add some items to the list, from their own or others' experiences?

5. (A) In small groups, ask students to share their own opinion, from a *cultural* perspective, about the importance of learner autonomy as an avenue to success in learning a foreign language. Can learners from *any* culture develop the autonomy that researchers recommend?

6. (D) Ask the class to share any instances in which they have used any of the compensatory strategies listed on page 129. Ask them to be creative in suggesting other compensatory strategies that have worked for them.

7. (A) Ask students on their own to take the Styles Awareness Checklist on page 134 (Figure 5.1). Then, in pairs, have them look at a partner's responses and find one item on which partners differ greatly (e.g., A vs. E, A vs. D, or B vs. E). Next, ask them to talk about experiences in their own language learning that illustrate their choice. Finally, ask them to decide which side of the continuum (the "A–B" side or the "D–E" side) gives them more of an advantage. Have them share the results with the rest of the class.

CHAPTER 6

AFFECTIVE FACTORS

Beijing-born-and-raised Melody, with encouragement and nurturing from her English-professor mother, was exposed to English as a young child at home and took many years of English classes in school. She excelled in those classes, surpassing all her classmates in all four skills, especially speaking and listening, gaining top marks on examinations. After two years of graduate study in the United States, her English was so nativelike she was hired by her university's intensive language program to teach a full load of academic English courses.

Her friends and teachers will tell you that Melody is a warm, extroverted, friendly person with what all agree is a charming disposition. Since she was a child, her social connections have been important to her. She has shown a strong interest in American history, culture, music, and, of course, her American friends. In school, she always tried to "make learning experiences more positive and fun." Her teachers and friends expected a lot from her because of her mother's profession, which put pressure on her at times. As she developed more English ability, she felt that being able to use English in many contexts (movies, books, music) was its own reward. Culturally, she now identifies with both Chinese and American cultures, appreciates both, but leans toward American culture in her personal tastes.

What can Melody teach us about affective factors in SLA? Did her early childhood experiences make a difference? How did her personality, cultural empathy, and positive outlook contribute to her success? Can we *teach* students to acquire beneficial emotional traits or must they simply be *born* into them—or *raised* as a young child to think, act, and feel a certain way?

An understanding of SLA based only on the somewhat cognitive considerations discussed thus far would fall short. We would be circumventing the most fundamental side of human behavior—as educational psychologist Ernest Hilgard put it: "Purely cognitive theories of learning will be rejected unless a role is assigned to affectivity" (1963, p. 267). And a few decades later there is no doubt at all about the importance of examining personality factors in building a theory of SLA (Arnold, 1999; Dewaele, 2009; Dörnyei & Ushioda, 2011).

The affective domain almost defies empirical description. A large number of variables are implied; operational definitions of constructs vary from one researcher to another; and findings are mixed on the cause and effect interaction of affective factors with L2 success. Some have suggested that it is quite possible that certain personality types are attracted to L2 study (Ortega, 2009, p. 195), even further muddying the waters!

For example, when people are asked to name a "key" to L2 success, often the first thought that comes to mind is *motivation*. To be sure, history tells us that within virtually every successful learner is a significant level of motivation, a drive to attain goals, perceptions of rewards, and more. But does a motive to "win" come first or does the process of little victories generate its own motivation? Perhaps this chicken-or-egg question will never yield a final answer. Nevertheless, the elusive nature of affective concepts need not deter us from seeking answers to questions. Careful, systematic study of the role of personality in SLA has already led to a greater understanding of the language learning process and to improved language teaching designs.

THE AFFECTIVE DOMAIN

Affect refers to emotion or feeling. The **affective domain** is the emotional side of human behavior, and it may, with some caution, be contrasted to the cognitive side. The development of affective states or feelings involves a variety of personality factors, feelings both about ourselves and about others with whom we come into contact.

Half a century ago, educational psychologist Benjamin Bloom (Krathwohl, Bloom, & Masia, 1964) provided a useful extended definition of the affective domain that is still widely used today. In Bloom's conception, in both child development and in adulthood, the internalization of affectivity involves a five-step, hierarchical process:

1. Emotional development begins with *receiving*. We become aware of our surrounding environment and perceive situations, people, and objects, and give a stimulus our selected attention.
2. Next, we *respond*, committing ourselves to an object, person, loved one, or context. Usually this response is voluntary, chosen willingly, followed by receiving satisfaction from that response.
3. The foundations are now in place for *valuing:* seeing the worth of an object, a behavior, or a person. Beliefs and attitudes are internalized as we commit themselves, and finally, to the point of conviction.
4. Our values are now ready to be *organized* into a system of beliefs, as we determine interrelationships and establish a hierarchy of values.
5. Finally, we develop a self-*identity* as we conceptualize ourselves in terms of our value system of values and beliefs. As we mature beyond the stage of abstract thinking, we act in accordance with a relatively self-consistent philosophy or worldview.

CLASSROOM CONNECTIONS

Consider the last step in Bloom's hierarchy, self-identity. To what extent has learning an L2 involved developing a "new" self-identity? How is it different from your native language or native cultural identity? How can teachers help students to recognize such a possible process and to make it as positive and fulfilling as possible?

Is there a connection here with L2 learning? Yes, if language is inextricably woven into the fabric of virtually every aspect of human behavior. And yes, if language is so pervasive a phenomenon in our humanity that it cannot be separated from "who I am" as a human being. Kenneth Pike (1967, p. 26) said that language *is* behavior, constituting "a structural whole . . . that cannot be subdivided into neat 'compartments' with language insulated in character, content, and organization from other behavior." Half a century before, Malinowski (1923) stressed our need for **phatic communion**, language used to express or create an atmosphere of shared feelings, goodwill, or sociability, rather than to impart information.

AFFECTIVE FACTORS IN SLA

In the 1970s, affective factors were a hot topic in SLA. The budding field eagerly made connections between psychological personality constructs and SLA, and offered fruitful implications and applications to classroom teaching methodology. In a field already brimming with interest in the cognitive side of SLA, the "new" dimension of emotion injected some excitement, even to the point of offering hope for the discovery of a set of personality traits that would give us ultimate answers to the causes of success (Guiora, Brannon, & Dull, 1972b; Brown, 1973; Scovel, 1978; Heyde, 1979; Ehrman, 1993).

The search for the ultimate model was, in the words of Dewaele, like the "quest for the Holy Grail . . . [characterized by] researchers, like Arthur's knights, stumbling through the night" (2009, p. 625). But the failure—so far—to devise a unified theory of affective individual differences must not deter researchers and teachers from enriching their perspectives by a composite of variables that completes the "triangle" of body, mind, and soul in theories of SLA. In the words of Imai, "emotions do not merely *facilitate* cognitive functioning; rather, they *mediate* development, especially when learning is embedded in interpersonal transaction" (2010, p. 278).

In that spirit, with due recognition of the thin ice of empirical findings on emotional factors, but with respect for half a century of inquiry and several millennia of intuitive wisdom, let's look at some of the factors at play in successful SLA.

Self-Esteem

Self-esteem is at the heart of virtually every aspect of human behavior. It could easily be claimed that no successful cognitive or affective activity can be carried out without some degree of self-esteem, self-confidence, knowledge of yourself, and **self-efficacy**—belief in your own capabilities to successfully perform an activity. Bloom's taxonomy, referred to above, emphasizes the centrality of growth of a person's concept of self, acceptance of self, and reflection of self as seen in the interaction between self and others.

Rubio referred to self-esteem as "a psychological and social phenomenon in which an individual evaluates his/her competence and own self according to [a set of] values" (2007, p. 5). He adds that self-esteem "is open to variation depending on personal circumstances" (p. 5). Three levels of self-esteem capture such personal circumstances, its multidimensionality, and its relevance to SLA:

1. **Global self-esteem** is relatively stable in a mature adult, quite resistant to change. It is the general or prevailing assessment one makes of one's own worth over time and across a number of situations.
2. **Situational self-esteem** (sometimes called "specific") refers to one's self-appraisals in *particular* life contexts, such as work, education, play, home, or in certain relatively discretely defined skills, such as communicative, athletic, musical, or mathematical ability. The degree of situational self-esteem a person has may vary depending upon the situation in question.
3. **Task self-esteem** relates to particular tasks within specific situations. Within the educational domain, task self-esteem might refer to one subject-matter area. In an athletic context, skill in a sport—or even a facet of a sport such as net play in tennis or pitching in baseball.

Situational self-esteem could be said to pertain to L2 acquisition in general, and task self-esteem might appropriately refer to one's self-evaluation of a particular aspect of the process: speaking, writing, a particular class in a second language, or even certain classroom activities. As early as the 1978 "good language learner" studies, positive attitudes and believing in oneself were at the top of everyone's list. The flip side of that coin was noted by Jane Arnold: "In language learning, more than in most other areas of the curriculum, our self-concept can often be truly endangered. . . . The self is especially vulnerable because it is deprived of its normal, familiar vehicle of expression" (2007, p. 17).

CLASSROOM CONNECTIONS

Have you ever felt deprived, in the words of Arnold (2007), of your "normal, familiar vehicle of expression" in attempting to communicate in an L2? Without the discourse competence of your native language, have you felt less than capable in the L2? How did you cope with those feelings? How can a teacher help students to feel less vulnerable?

Adelaide Heyde (1979) was among the first researchers to look at the effects of three levels of self-esteem in SLA. On an oral production task by American college students learning French, she found that all three levels correlated positively with oral performance, with the strongest effect for task self-esteem. Similarly, Gardner and Lambert (1972), Brodkey and Shore (1976), and Watkins, Biggs, and Regmi (1991) found that self-esteem was an important variable in SLA.

Does high self-esteem cause language success, or does language success cause high self-esteem? Should teachers try to improve self-esteem or simply attend to a learner's proficiency and let self-esteem take care of itself? Heyde (1979) found that certain sections of a beginning college French course had better oral production *and* self-esteem scores than other sections after only eight weeks of instruction. This finding suggests that teachers can have a positive and influential effect on both the linguistic performance and the emotional well-being of a student. Andrés (1999) concurred and suggested classroom techniques that can help learners to "unfold their wings" (p. 91). Perhaps these teachers succeeded because they gave optimal attention both to linguistic goals and to confidence-building in their students.

Attribution Theory and Self-Efficacy

Underlying the issues and questions about the role of self-esteem in language learning are the foundational concepts of attribution and self-efficacy. Based on the seminal work of psychologist Bernard Weiner (1986, 1992, 2000), **attribution theory** focuses on how people explain the causes of their own successes and failures. Weiner and others (Bandura, 1993; Williams & Burden, 1997; Slavin, 2003; Dörnyei & Ushioda, 2011) describe attribution theory in terms of four explanations for success and/or failure in achieving a personal objective: ability, effort, perceived difficulty of a task, and luck. Two of those four factors are internal to the learner: ability and effort; and two are attributable to external circumstances outside of the learner: task difficulty and luck.

According to Weiner, learners tend to *attribute* their success on a task using these four dimensions. Depending on the individual, a number of causal determinants might be cited. Thus, failure to get a high grade on a final exam in a language class might, for some, be judged to be due to their poor ability or effort, and by others to the difficulty of an exam ("That was a 'bear' of an exam!"), and perhaps others to just plain old bad luck!

This is where **self-efficacy** comes in. If a learner feels capable of carrying out a given task—in other words, a high sense of self-efficacy—a commensurate degree of effort is likely to be devoted to achieving success. Falling short of one's personal goals may then be attributable to not enough effort expended, but rarely, in the case of students with high self-efficacy, would an "excuse" be made attributing the bad performance to something like bad luck. Conversely, a learner with low self-efficacy may quite easily attribute failure to external factors, a relatively unhealthy psychological attitude to bring to any task, one that creates a self-fulfilling sense of failure at the outset.

 CLASSROOM CONNECTIONS

Have you ever attributed lack of success to external factors? If so, what factors? Can such attribution be avoided? How can teachers help students to build self-efficacy, even in small steps?

A few empirical data are available on self-efficacy and SLA (Dörnyei & Ushioda, 2011), and those studies show promise of a positive relationship between students' self-efficacy and performance (Mills, Pajares, & Herron, 2006; Gorsuch, 2009). Intuition would also support the conviction that it is essential for learners to believe in their own capability in order to succeed at learning an L2. The prospect of learning a second language is itself potentially so overwhelming that learners can—and often do—lose momentum in the face of a number of forms of self-doubt. One of the most important roles of successful teachers, then, is to facilitate high levels of self-efficacy in their students.

Willingness to Communicate

A factor related to attribution and self-efficacy, one that has seen a surge of interest in the research literature, is the extent to which learners display a **willingness to communicate** as they tackle a second language. Peter MacIntyre defined willingness to communicate (WTC) as "an underlying continuum representing the predisposition toward or away from communicating, given the choice" (MacIntyre et al., 2002, p. 538). Or, more simply put, "the intention to initiate communication, given a choice" (MacIntyre et al., 2001, p. 369). Emerging from studies and assertions about language learners' *un*willingness to communicate and what we commonly label as "shyness," researchers have now been examining the extent to which WTC is a factor not just in second language acquisition, but one that may have its roots in a learner's first language communication patterns (MacIntyre et al., 2002).

An earlier study on WTC (MacIntyre et al., 1998) found that a number of factors appear to contribute to predisposing some learners to seek, and others to avoid, second language communication. Noting that a high level of communicative ability does not necessarily correspond with a high WTC, the researchers proposed a number of cognitive and affective factors that underlie WTC: motivation, personality, self-confidence, and intergroup climate. The latter—intergroup climate—was confirmed in Fushino's (2010) study of the relationship between beliefs about group work and WTC.

 CLASSROOM CONNECTIONS

Current L2 teaching methodology strongly advocates communicative techniques such as group and pair work and related interactive activities, all of which can potentially provide *social support*. What has been the extent of social support in your experiences learning an L2? What techniques has your teacher used—or have you used, if you have taught—to promote social support? To what extent have they led to students' greater willingness to communicate?

Other studies of WTC generally confirm its relationship to self-efficacy and self-confidence (Yashima, Zenuk-Nishide, & Shimizu, 2004). Cross-culturally, some questions have been raised about WTC, especially in what is described by Wen and Clément (2003) as the Confucian culture of China. One can quite easily see that an individualistic, as opposed to a collectivist, culture would view constructs of self-efficacy from markedly different perspectives. Another study (MacIntyre et al., 2001) found that higher levels of WTC were associated with learners who experienced social support, particularly from friends, offering further evidence of the power of socially constructed conceptions of self. And finally, MacIntyre (2007) and later MacIntyre and Legatto (2011) found WTC to be a "dynamic system," one that varies considerably over time.

Inhibition

All human beings, in their understanding of themselves, build sets of defenses to protect the ego. A young child, born with no concept of self, gradually learns to identify a self that is distinct from others, and then in stages of awareness, responding, and valuing, constructs a self-identity. In adolescence, physical, emotional, and cognitive changes bring on mounting defensive inhibitions designed to protect a fragile ego from threats to the organization of values and beliefs on which appraisals of self-esteem have been founded.

The process of building defenses continues into adulthood. Some people—those with higher self-esteem and ego strength—are more able to withstand threats to their existence, and thus their defenses are lower. Those with weaker self-esteem maintain stronger "walls" of **inhibition** to protect what is self-perceived to be a weak or fragile ego or a lack of self-efficacy.

The human ego encompasses what Alexander Guiora (Guiora et al., 1972a) and Madeline Ehrman (1996) referred to as **language ego** or the very personal, egoistic nature of second language acquisition. Most SLA involves some degree of *identity* conflict as learners take on a new identity with their newly acquired competence. An adaptive language ego enables learners to lower the inhibitions that may impede success.

In a classic study, Guiora et al. (1972a) designed an experiment using small quantities of alcohol to induce temporary states of less-than-normal inhibition in an experimental group of subjects who were administered a pronunciation test in Thai. The subjects given *moderate* amounts of alcohol performed significantly better than those receiving higher and lower quantities and the control group, leading to the conclusion that lowered inhibitions enhance pronunciation performance. A second study (Guiora et al., 1980) measured the effect of Valium (a chemical relaxant) on pronunciation, but with mixed results at best.

Critics were quick to point out flaws in these studies. Scovel (2001) questioned the presumably controlled conditions of the study and its experimental design. In addition, we know that alcohol may lower inhibitions, but alcohol and Valium can also lower muscular tension, which may have been a major factor in accounting for superior pronunciation. Further, is pronunciation accuracy an appropriate indicator of overall *communicative* competence?

Some have facetiously suggested that the moral to Guiora's experiments is that we should provide cocktails—or prescribe tranquilizers—for foreign language classes! This would of course delight students, but dismay school treasurers who cannot even boast a "beer budget"!

Did we gain any insight into SLA through these studies? Not directly, but indirectly researchers were later inspired to focus on the inhibitions, the defenses, that we place between ourselves and others as important factors contributing to L2 success. Ehrman (1993, 1999) suggested the significance of **thin** (permeable) **ego boundaries** in some students, and **thick** (not as permeable) **ego boundaries** in others: The openness, vulnerability, and ambiguity tolerance of those with thin ego boundaries create different pathways to success from those with hard-driving, systematic, perfectionistic, thick ego boundaries.

Pedagogical approaches quickly seized the opportunity to reduce inhibition in L2 classrooms by creating a "safe" atmosphere for students to take risks, communicate willingly, and try out their budding language competence. Mistakes are simply part of the acquisition process in SLA as learners test out hypotheses about language by trial and many errors. Both children learning their first language and adults learning a second can learn from their mistakes. If we never ventured to speak a sentence until we were absolutely certain of its total correctness, we would likely never communicate productively at all. But mistakes can be viewed as threats to one's ego. They pose both internal and external threats, to hearken back to attribution theory described earlier. Internally, one's critical self and one's performing self can be in conflict: The learner performs something "wrong" and becomes critical of his or her own mistake. Externally, learners perceive others to be critical, even judging their very person when they blunder in a second language.

 CLASSROOM CONNECTIONS

Have you ever felt your L2 teachers have created inhibition within you? How can teachers create a "safe" atmosphere for student risk-taking and WTC? When you made mistakes in your L2 learning experiences, did your teacher reprimand you or help you to make it a learning experience? What are some examples of the latter?

Earl Stevick (1976b) spoke of language learning as involving a number of forms of alienation: alienation between the critical me and the performing me, between my native culture and my target culture, between me and my teacher, and between me and my fellow students. This alienation arises from the defenses that we build around ourselves. These defenses inhibit learning, and their removal can therefore promote language learning, which involves self-exposure to a degree manifested in few other endeavors.

Risk Taking

In Chapter 5 we saw that one of the prominent characteristics of "good language learners" was the ability to make *intelligent guesses*, something you cannot do without a healthy level of **risk taking**. Learners have to be able to gamble a bit, to be willing to try out hunches about the language and take the risk of being wrong.

Beebe (1983) described some of the negative ramifications that foster fear of risk taking in the classroom: a bad grade, a fail on the exam, a reproach from the teacher, a smirk from a classmate. Outside the classroom, L2 learners fear looking ridiculous, a listener's blank look, failure to communicate, alienation, and perhaps worst of all, they fear a loss of identity. The classroom antidote to such fears, according to Dufeu, is to establish an adequate affective framework so that learners "feel comfortable as they take their first public steps in the strange world of a foreign language" (1994, p. 89).

Should L2 learners become *high* risk-takers? Not necessarily, as Beebe (1983) found, successful L2 learners are usually *moderate* risk-takers. "They do not take wild, frivolous risks or enter into no-win situations" (p. 41). A learner might be too bold in blurting out meaningless verbiage that no one can quite understand, while success lies in an optimum point where calculated guesses are ventured. As Rubin and Thompson (1994) noted, successful language learners make willing and *accurate* guesses.

 CLASSROOM CONNECTIONS

What are some examples of "moderate" risk-taking in an L2 classroom? How does a teacher draw a fine line between promoting risk-taking that is wild and haphazard and risks that are "calculated"?

The implications for teaching are important. In a few uncommon cases, overly high risk-takers, as they dominate the classroom with wild gambles, may need to be "tamed" a bit by the teacher. But most of the time our challenge as teachers will be to encourage students to guess somewhat more willingly than the usual student is prone to do, and to reward them for those risks.

Anxiety

Intricately intertwined with self-esteem, self-efficacy, inhibition, and risk taking, the construct of **anxiety** plays a major affective role in second language acquisition. Even though we all know what anxiety is and we all have experienced feelings of anxiousness, anxiety is still not easy to define in a simple sentence. Spielberger (1983, p. 1) described anxiety as a "subjective feeling of tension, apprehension, nervousness, and worry associated with an arousal of the autonomic nervous system." More simply put, anxiety is associated with feelings of uneasiness, frustration, self-doubt, apprehension, or worry (Scovel, 1978, p. 134).

The research on anxiety suggests that anxiety, like self-esteem, can be experienced at various levels (Oxford, 1999; Horwitz, 2001, 2010). At the deepest, or global, level, **trait anxiety** is a more permanent predisposition to be anxious. At a more momentary, or situational level, **state anxiety** is experienced in relation to some particular event or act. As we learned in the case of self-esteem, it is important in a classroom for a teacher to try to determine whether a student's anxiety stems from a more global trait or whether it comes from a particular context at the moment.

Trait anxiety, because of its global and somewhat ambiguously defined nature, has not proved to be useful in predicting second language achievement (MacIntyre & Gardner, 1991c). However, recent research on **language anxiety**, as it has come to be known, focuses more specifically on the situational nature of state anxiety. Three components of foreign language anxiety have been identified in order to break down the construct into researchable issues (Horwitz, Horwitz, & Cope, 1986; MacIntyre & Gardner, 1989, 1991c; Horwitz, 2010):

1. Communication apprehension, arising from learners' inability to adequately express mature thoughts and ideas
2. Fear of negative social evaluation, arising from a learner's need to make a positive social impression on others
3. Test anxiety, or apprehension over academic evaluation

Two decades of research (summarized in Horwitz, 2010) have now given us useful information on foreign language anxiety. Most studies conclude that "foreign language anxiety can be distinguished from other types of anxiety and that it can have a negative effect on the language learning process" (MacIntyre & Gardner, 1991c, p. 112).

Yet another important insight to be applied to our understanding of anxiety lies in the distinction between **debilitative** and **facilitative anxiety** (Alpert & Haber, 1960; Scovel, 1978), or what Oxford (1999) called "harmful" and "helpful" anxiety. Spielmann and Radnofsky (2001) preferred to identify **tension** as a more neutral concept to describe the possibility of both "dysphoric" (detrimental) and "euphoric" (beneficial) effects in learning a foreign language.

We may be inclined to view anxiety as a negative factor, something to be avoided at all costs. But the notion of facilitative anxiety and euphoric tension is that some concern—some apprehension—over a task to be accomplished is a positive factor. Otherwise, a learner might be inclined to be "wishy-washy," lacking that facilitative tension that keeps one poised, alert, and just slightly unbalanced to the point that one cannot relax entirely. The "butterflies in one's stomach" before giving a public speech could be a sign of facilitative anxiety, a symptom of just enough tension to get the job done.

Several studies have suggested the benefit of facilitative anxiety in learning foreign languages (Horwitz, 1990; Young, 1992; Ehrman & Oxford, 1995; Spielmann & Radnofsky, 2001). In Bailey's (1983) diary study of competitiveness and anxiety in L2 learning, facilitative anxiety was one of the keys to success, as in the case of her inner competitiveness that sometimes motivated her to study harder. So the next time your language students are anxious, you would do well to ask yourself if that anxiety is truly debilitative. Once again, we find that a construct has an optimal point along its continuum: Both too much and too little anxiety may hinder the process of successful second language learning.

A further by-product of ongoing research on language anxiety has been a debate over whether anxiety is the *cause* of poor performance in a second language, or the *product* of less than satisfactory performance. In a series of articles, Sparks, Ganschow, and their colleagues maintained that foreign language anxiety (FLA) is a *consequence* of their foreign language learning difficulties (Sparks,

Ganschow, & Javorsky, 2000; Sparks & Ganschow, 2001). More controversially, they earlier argued (Sparks & Ganschow, 1991, 1993a, 1993b, 1995; Ganschow et al., 1994) that anxiety in a foreign language class could be the result of *first* language deficits, in what they called the **Linguistic Coding Deficit Hypothesis** (LCDH).

Others (MacIntyre, 1995a, 1995b; Horwitz, 2000, 2001) raised strong objections to the validity of the research cited in support of the LCDH. While admitting that FLA could indeed be the *cause* of poor language performance, they flatly rejected the LCDH, showing that anxiety is a common source of interference in all kinds of learning, that highly proficient language learners experience anxiety, and that with over one-third of language learners reporting degrees of anxiety, it is highly implausible to attribute anxiety to *first* language deficits (Horwitz, 2000).

Other studies have improved our understanding of FLA. Anxiety was correlated with low perceived self-worth, competence, and intelligence in a study by Bailey, Onwuegbuzie, and Daley (2000). Spielmann and Radnofsky (2001) found that students of French in Vermont who were able to "reinvent" themselves in their foreign language were able to garner more euphoric tension. Among college students in Japan, Kitano (2001) showed that anxiety levels were higher as learners reported greater fear of negative evaluation. Gregersen and Horwitz (2002) linked anxiousness with perfectionism, suggesting that those who set unrealistically high standards for themselves were likely to develop greater anxiety. Levine (2003) suggested in a study of German as a foreign language that anxiety varied depending on whether students were speaking with other students or with teachers. Rodríguez and Abreu (2003) looked at the stability of anxiety across different foreign languages. In a study of native Spanish speakers learning English, Gregersen (2003) observed that anxious learners made more errors, overestimated the number of their errors, and corrected themselves more than less anxious learners.

In somewhat more recent studies, WTC and FLA were negatively correlated in university students in China (Liu & Jackson, 2008). "The younger the better" maxim held up for Dewaele, Petrides, and Furnham (2008) as they found that students who were younger when they started learning an L2 have lower levels of FLA. These and earlier findings reinforce the assertion that self-efficacy and attribution are keys to other affective variables, especially to anxiety, and that pedagogical attention to FLA is of utmost importance (Sparks & Young, 2009; Horwitz, 2010).

 CLASSROOM CONNECTIONS

In your L2 learning, or in your experience teaching, have you experienced a quest for perfection, fear of negative evaluation, or identity conflict? Or have you identified other sources that could account for anxiety? If your anxieties are debilitative, what approaches and activities can help to alleviate them? How would a teacher embrace a degree of facilitative anxiety in students?

Empathy

Language is social, and the social transactions that L2 learners must navigate are complex endeavours. **Transaction** is the process of reaching out beyond the self to others, and language is a major tool used to accomplish that process. A variety of transactional variables may apply to second language learning: imitation, modeling, identification, empathy, extroversion, aggression, styles of communication, and others. Two of these variables, chosen for their relevance to a comprehensive understanding of SLA, will be treated here: empathy and extroversion.

In common terminology, **empathy** is the process of "putting yourself into someone else's shoes," of reaching beyond the self to understand what another person is feeling. Empathy is a major factor in the harmonious coexistence of individuals in society. Language is one of the primary means of empathizing, but nonverbal communication facilitates the process of empathizing and must not be overlooked.

In more sophisticated terms, empathy is usually described as the projection of one's own personality into the personality of others in order to understand them better. (Note: Empathy and **sympathy** are not synonymous. Sympathy involves a close affinity with another person while empathy implies more possibility of detachment.) Psychologists generally agree that there are two necessary aspects to the development and exercising of empathy: first, an *awareness* and knowledge of one's own feelings, and second, *identification* with another person (Hogan, 1969). In other words, you cannot fully empathize—or know someone else—until you adequately know yourself.

Communication requires a sophisticated degree of empathy. In order to accurately reach out to another person, we need to transcend our own ego boundaries, or, using Guiora's (1972b) term, to "permeate" our ego boundaries so that we can send and receive messages clearly. In oral communication, empathetic perceptions are made through immediate feedback from a hearer. A misunderstood word, phrase, or idea can be questioned by the hearer and then rephrased by the speaker until a clear message is interpreted. Written communication requires a special kind of empathy in which the writer, without the benefit of immediate feedback from the reader, must communicate ideas by means of a very clear empathetic intuition and judgment of the reader's state of mind and structure of knowledge.

 CLASSROOM CONNECTIONS

Writing is difficult even in one's native language, because in most writing your reader is far removed from you and you have to anticipate the accuracy of your message. If you have tried to write something in an L2, you know how difficult that was. How can teachers help L2 students to develop empathy for their audience as they write?

In L2 learning, the problem of a form of "linguistic" empathy becomes acute. Not only must learner-speakers correctly identify cognitive and affective states in the hearer, but they must do so in a language in which they are insecure. Then, learner-hearers, attempting to comprehend an L2, are called upon to correctly interpret potentially garbled messages, and the result can be a tangle of "crossed wires."

Guiora and his colleagues (1972a, 1972b) found that empathy successfully predicted authenticity of pronunciation of a foreign language. On the other hand, in their search for characteristics of "good language learners," Naiman, Fröhlich, Stern, and Todesco (1978) found no significant correlation between empathy and language success. Such conflicting findings are not unexpected, however, because of the difficulty of measuring empathy through either self-check tests (Hogan, 1969) or visually oriented perception tests (e.g., Guiora's Micro-Momentary Expression (MME) Test). It has been shown that such tests appropriately identify personality extremes (schizophrenic, paranoid, or psychotic behavior, for example) but fail to differentiate among the vast normal population.

Extroversion and Introversion

Let's first dispel a myth. We are prone to think of an extroverted person as a gregarious, "life of the party" person, and introverts as quiet, reserved, and reclusive. Our worldwide culture of glitz, glamor, and Hollywood values the stereotypical extrovert. Nowhere is this more evident than in the classroom where teachers praise talkative, outgoing students who participate freely in class discussions. On the other hand, introverts are thought to present "issues" for teachers.

Such a view of extroversion/introversion (E/I) is misleading. **Extroversion** is the extent to which a person has a deep-seated need to receive ego enhancement, self-esteem, and a sense of wholeness *from other people* as opposed to receiving that affirmation within oneself. Extroverts actually need other people in order to feel "good," and are energized by interaction with others. But extroverts are not necessarily loudmouthed and talkative, and one of their weaknesses can be a deep-seated need for affirmation from others.

Introversion, on the other hand, is the extent to which a person derives a sense of wholeness and fulfillment within oneself. Contrary to prevailing stereotypes, introverts can have an inner strength of character, be more attentive to thoughts and concepts, and be "energized by concentration on the inner world" (Wakamoto, 2009, p. 18). Introverts can be pleasantly conversational, but simply require more reflection, and possibly exercise more restraint in social situations.

It is unfortunate that these stereotypes have influenced teachers' perceptions of students. Ausubel noted that introversion and extroversion are a "grossly misleading index of social adjustment" (1968, p. 413), and other educators (Dörnyei, 2005; Wakamoto, 2009) have warned against prejudging students on the basis of presumed extroversion. In language classes, where oral participation is highly valued, it is easy to view active participants with favor and to assume that their visibility in the classroom is due to an extroversion factor (which may not be so). Culturally, American society differs considerably from a number of other societies where it is improper to speak out in the classroom. Teachers need to consider cultural norms in their assessment of a student's presumed "passivity" in the classroom.

Extroversion is commonly thought to be related to empathy, but such may not be the case. The extroverted person may actually behave in an extroverted manner in order to protect his or her own ego, with extroverted behavior being symptomatic of defensive barriers and high ego boundaries. At the same time the introverted, quieter, more reserved person may show high empathy—an intuitive understanding and apprehension of others—and simply be more reserved in the outward and overt expression of empathy.

It is not clear then, that E/I helps or hinders the process of second language acquisition. Naiman et al. (1978) found no significant effect for extroversion in characterizing the good language learner. In a comprehensive study on extroversion, Busch (1982) explored the relationship of E/I to English proficiency in adult Japanese learners of English in Japan. She found that *introverts* were significantly better than extroverts in their pronunciation performance, suggesting that introverts may have the patience and focus to attend to clear articulation in an L2. Wakamoto (2000, 2009) found that junior college English majors in Japan who were extroverted were likely to make better use of learning strategies than introverts. This finding suggests that extroverts may have a strategic edge over introverts, but it masks the possibility that extroverts may simply *need* the strategies in question more than introverts.

 CLASSROOM CONNECTIONS

Do you think introversion was the *cause* of better pronunciation in Busch's (1982) study? If not, what other variables seem to be typical of introverts that could lead them to better pronunciation accuracy? Could those variables be taught in the classroom?

For classroom teaching, one can cautiously say that E/I is a factor in the development of general oral communicative competence (Dewaele & Furnham, 1999; 2000), which requires face-to-face interaction, but *not* in listening, reading, and writing. It is also readily apparent that cross-cultural norms of nonverbal and verbal interaction vary widely, and what in one culture (say, the United States) may appear as introversion is, in another culture (say, Japan), respect and politeness. How culturally loaded are techniques that incorporate group work, drama, pantomime, and role plays? A teacher needs to be sensitive to cultural norms, to a student's willingness to communicate in class, and to strengths and weaknesses of the E/I continuum.

PERSONALITY TYPE

In 1972 Thomas Harris published his best-selling *I'm OK, You're OK*, offering solutions to life's problems to millions of readers through Transactional Analysis. It was not the first or the last of a flurry of thousands of self-help books, magazine articles with self-check quizzes, and weekend seminar retreats, all designed to analyze the "real you" and to assure that your life is being optimized at your fullest potential.

Among this surge of interest in psychological well-being was the widely popularized *Myers-Briggs Type Indicator* (MBTI) (Myers, 1962), commonly referred to as the Myers-Briggs test. Borrowing from some of Carl Jung's (1923) psychological *types*, the Myers-Briggs test proposed to assess one's various prevailing personality styles. To this day, office personnel, athletic teams, church leaders, and school in-service workshops have been holding MBTI sessions in which the participants discover their various idiosyncrasies and share "personality pathways" with their team members.

Four (presumably) dichotomous styles of functioning are covered in the MBTI and a number of related spinoffs (e.g., Keirsey & Bates, 1984; Tieger & Barron-Tieger, 2007): (1) introversion vs. extroversion, (2) sensing vs. intuition, (3) thinking vs. feeling, and (4) judging vs. perceiving. Table 6.1 summarizes the four categories.

Table 6.1 Myers-Briggs character types

Extroversion (E)	Introversion (I)
Interaction	Concentration
Multiplicity of relationships	Limited relationships
Interest in external events	Interest in internal reaction
Sensing (S)	**Intuition (N)**
Experience	Hunches
Realistic	Speculative
Practicality	Ingenuity
Thinking (T)	**Feeling (F)**
Objective	Subjective
Principles	Values
Analysis	Sympathy
Judging (J)	**Perceiving (P)**
Organize one's life	Let life happen
Closure-oriented	Keep options open
Deadline!	What deadline?

With four two-dimensional categories, 16 personality profiles are possible. Disciples of the Myers-Briggs research have described the implications of being an "ISTJ" or an "ENFP," and all the other combinations. ISTJs, for example, presumably make better behind-the-scenes workers, while ENFPs should excel at dealing with the public. Lawrence (1984) stressed the importance of personality types for understanding students: E's will excel in group work; I's will prefer individual work; SJ's are linear learners and need structure; NT's are good at paper-and-pencil tests. The generalizations were myriad.

What might all this have to do with SLA? In the 1980s and 1990s, researchers sought to discover a link between Myers-Briggs types and second language learning (Oxford & Ehrman, 1988; Moody, 1988; Ehrman, 1989, 1990; Ehrman & Oxford, 1989, 1990, 1995; Carrell, Prince, & Astika, 1996). The upshot of these studies was capsulized in research that demonstrated a correlation between Myers-Briggs types and L2 learners' strategy use (Ehrman & Oxford, 1990; Wakamoto, 2000) in predictable ways. Extroverts used social strategies; sensing students showed a liking for memory strategies; thinkers used metacognitive strategies and analysis. More pedagogically useful was Ehrman's (1989) list of both assets and liabilities of each side of the Myers-Briggs continuum (see Table 6.2).

Table 6.2 Assets and liabilities of Myers-Briggs types (adapted from Ehrman, 1989)

Assets

Extroversion	Willing to take conversational risks
Introversion	Concentration, self-sufficiency
Sensing	Systematic work, attention to detail
Intuition	Inferencing, guessing from context
Thinking	Analysis, self-discipline
Feeling	Bonding with teachers, social interaction
Judging	Punctual, complete assignments
Perceiving	Open, flexible, adaptable to new experiences

Liabilities

Extroversion	Dependent on outside interaction, "shoot from the hip"
Introversion	Need processing time before speaking, risk avoidance
Sensing	Hindered by lack of clear objectives, syllabus, structure
Intuition	Inaccuracy, missing important details
Thinking	Performance anxiety, excessive need for control
Feeling	Discouraged if not praised, disrupted by lack of social harmony
Judging	Rigidity, intolerance of ambiguous language and tasks
Perceiving	Missing deadlines, inconsistent pacing, disrupted by schedules

Several theoretical issues are present in defining, measuring, and applying Jung's century-old personality types. (1) The operational definitions of each of the 16 types remain rather tentative and their understanding is based more on experience than on scientific validation. (2) The pairs of types are clearly not dichotomous, as a person can easily manifest characteristics of both sides of the presumed continuum. As we have seen in other affective variables, the most successful learners (and people) are able to *contextualize* their strategic options, regardless of their general proclivities and preferences. (3) The obvious weakness endemic in self-check tests renders the model as difficult, at best, to cross-validate with more indirect or objective assessment. (4) And finally, for classroom use, the feasibility of asking students to take the MBTI—or a scaled-down form thereof—is problematic, as are cross-cultural issues surrounding concepts such as extroversion, intuition, and feeling.

 CLASSROOM CONNECTIONS

Have you ever taken a Myers-Briggs test? Has a teacher ever administered one in your classroom? If a teacher were to do so, how would he or she follow up on the test to students' advantage? What kinds of tips might the teacher offer?

Still, oddly enough, the Myers-Briggs model remains an intriguing and possibly enlightening journey into the human psyche. For all its empirical weaknesses, it helps people to ponder personality differences that they never considered. The model helps teachers to contemplate yet another set of *individual differences* among their students, and to vary their classroom activities to embrace a number of different possible student characteristics. Taken with a grain of salt, and applied with a generous dose of "N" (intuition), the Myers-Briggs model just might be a helpful set of thoughts to keep in your hip pocket.

MOTIVATION

What does it mean to say that someone is "motivated"? How do you create, foster, and maintain motivation? Having considered an almost bewildering number of lenses through which to view affect in SLA, we turn now to one of the most powerful affective variables in accounting for the success or failure of virtually any complex task: motivation.

Motivation is a star player in the cast of characters assigned to L2 learning scenarios around the world. Such assumptions are meritorious: Countless studies and experiments in human learning have shown that motivation is a key to learning in general (Maslow, 1970; Deci, 1975; Weiner, 1986). In the field of SLA, in particular, the subject of motivation has garnered huge amounts of attention (see Dörnyei & Ushioda, 2011, for a comprehensive overview). But broad claims can gloss over a detailed understanding of exactly what motivation is and what the subcomponents of motivation are.

Defining Motivation

Various operational definitions of **motivation** have been proposed over the course of decades of research. Following the historical schools of thought described in Chapter 1, three different perspectives emerge:

1. From a *behavioral* perspective, motivation is quite simply the anticipation of reward. Driven to acquire positive reinforcement and by previous experiences of reward, we act to achieve further reinforcement.
2. In *cognitive* terms, motivation emphasizes the individual's decisions, "the choices people make as to what experiences or goals they will approach or avoid, and the degree of effort they will exert in that respect" (Keller, 1983, p. 389). Some cognitive psychologists see underlying needs or drives as the compelling force behind our decisions, as in Ausubel's (1968, pp. 368–379), list of *needs*:

   - *Exploration*, to see "the other side of the mountain," opening new vistas
   - *Manipulation*, to persuade, and cause change in one's environment
   - *Activity*, for movement and exercise, both physical and mental
   - *Stimulation*, by people, ideas, feelings, and the environment
   - *Knowledge*, to explore, learn, resolve contradictions, and solve problems
   - *Ego enhancement*, to be accepted and approved of by others

3. A *constructivist* view of motivation places prime emphasis on social context as well as individual personal choices (Williams & Burden, 1997). Our choices to expend effort are always carried out within a cultural and social milieu. Maslow's (1970) hierarchy of needs included *community*, *belonging*, and *social status*. Motivation, in a constructivist view, is derived as much from our interactions with others as it is from our self-determination (Dörnyei & Ushioda, 2011).

All three perspectives can be plausibly amalgamated into an integrated understanding of SLA. Consider those who are said to be "motivated" to learn an L2. They are motivated because they perceive the value (reward) of knowing a language. They *choose* to meet needs of exploration, stimulation, knowledge, self-esteem, and autonomy. And they do so in widely differing individual pathways and in the context of a social milieu that values being able to "speak" an L2. Table 6.3 offers a schematic representation of three views of motivation.

As Dörnyei and Ushioda (2011) demonstrated in their comprehensive survey, motivation can and has been subdivided, categorized, dissected, and

Table 6.3 Three views of motivation

Behavioral	Cognitive	Constructivist
Anticipation of reward	Driven by basic human	Social context
Desire to receive positive	needs: e.g., exploration,	Community
reinforcement	manipulation	Social status
External, individual forces in	Degree of effort expended	Security of group
control	Internal, individual forces in	Internal, interactive forces in
	control	control

charted a head-spinning number of times! To comprehend all the proposed hypotheses and theories and perspectives is almost humanly impossible. So can this giant of an affective factor be simply yet eloquently explained and "demythologized" in such a way that L2 teachers can make a few practical and fruitful applications? I think the answer is yes, if we glean a few fundamental insights from a half-century of research on L2 motivation.

Intrinsic and Extrinsic Motivation

Using a historical timeline as a guide, we turn to one of the earliest traditions of research on motivation, carried out in large part by educational psychologists, and then later applied to SLA: the distinction between intrinsic and extrinsic motivation.

Edward Deci (1975, p. 23) defined **intrinsic motivation** as expending effort "for which there is no apparent reward except the activity itself . . . and not because it leads to an extrinsic reward." Intrinsically motivated behaviors are driven by internally rewarding consequences, namely, feelings of *competence* and *self-determination*, and are, like Skinner's (1957) *emitted response*, willingly engaged in through one's own volition. In contrast, **extrinsic motivation** is fueled by the anticipation of a reward from outside and beyond the self. Typical extrinsic rewards are money, prizes, grades, and even certain forms of positive feedback. Behaviors initiated solely to avoid punishment are also extrinsically motivated.

Maslow (1970) claimed that intrinsic motivation is clearly superior to extrinsic. According to his hierarchy of needs mentioned above, motivation is dependent on the satisfaction first of fundamental physical necessities (air, water, food), then of community, security, identity, and self-esteem, the fulfillment of which finally leads to **self-actualization**, or, to use a common phrase, "being all that you can be." Maslow represented these needs in the form of a pyramid with the physical needs at the bottom, or foundation, of the pyramid, and self-actualization—the culmination of human attainment—at the top.

A later offshoot of Maslow's view of motivation was seen in investigations of the effect of "flow" on ultimate attainment (Csikszentmihalyi & Csikszentmihalyi,

1988; Csikszentmihalyi, 1990; Egbert, 2003). **Flow theory** highlights the importance of

> "an experiential state characterized by intense focus and involvement that leads to improved performance on a task. . . . Flow theory claims that as a result of the intrinsically rewarding experience associated with flow, people push themselves to higher levels of performance" (Egbert, 2003, p. 499).

Others have characterized flow as "optimal experience," being "in the groove," when "everything gelled." All of this research supports the ultimate importance of intrinsic involvement of learners in attaining one's proficiency goals in a foreign language.

Bruner (1966b), praising the "autonomy of self-reward," claimed that one of the most effective ways to help students to think and learn is to free them from the control of rewards and punishments. One of the principal weaknesses of extrinsically driven behavior is its *addictive* nature. Once captivated by the lure of an immediate prize or praise, our dependency on those tangible rewards increases, even to the point that their withdrawal can then extinguish the desire to learn. Piaget (1972) and others pointed out that human beings universally view incongruity, uncertainty, and "disequilibrium" as motivating. In other words, we seek out a reasonable challenge. Then we initiate behaviors intended to conquer the challenging situation.

An unpublished study (anonymous) reported an experiment in which two matched groups of junior high school girls were asked to teach a simple game to Kindergarten children. One group was promised a reward in the form of a movie ticket; the other group received no such promise, and was simply asked to teach the game. The results showed that the "no-reward" group did a better job of teaching the game *and* reported greater satisfaction in doing so. Conclusion? The first group was too focused on the reward, and the (presumed) intrinsic motivation in the second group was a stronger motivator.

Which form of motivation is more powerful in SLA contexts? A stockpile of research (Brown, 1990; Crookes & Schmidt, 1991; Dörnyei, 1998, 2001a, 2001b; Dörnyei & Csizér, 1998; Noels, Clément, & Pelletier, 1999; Noels et al., 2000; Wu, 2003) strongly favors intrinsic orientations, especially for *long-term* retention. Ramage (1990) found intrinsic motivation to be positively associated with high school students who were interested in continuing their L2 in college, while those who only wanted to fulfill language requirements exhibited weaker performance.

In non-English-speaking countries (Warden & Lin, 2000; Wu, 2003; Csizér & Dörnyei, 2005) intrinsic and extrinsic factors have been identified across a variety of cultural beliefs and attitudes. For example, in a survey of Hungarian teachers of English, Dörnyei and Csizér (1998) proposed a taxonomy of factors by which teachers could motivate their learners. They cited factors such as developing a relationship with learners, building learners' self-confidence and autonomy, personalizing the learning process, and increasing learners' goal-orientation. In the same vein, Guilloteaux and Dörnyei (2008) found that learners in South Korea showed higher levels of motivation when their teachers specifically focused on "teaching" motivation. And Gao et al. (2007) found that English learners in China displayed a relationship between motivational intensity and changes in self-identity.

 CLASSROOM CONNECTIONS

Successful L2 programs incorporate instances of both extrinsic and intrinsic rewards. Besides the obvious grades and test scores, what are some of the extrinsic rewards you have experienced in learning a language? How useful were they? What kinds of activities or approaches do you think would help to promote intrinsic motivation? How would you promote a balance between extrinsic and intrinsic rewards?

Social-Psychological Perspectives

Instrumental and Integrative Orientations

For the better part of two decades, research on L2 motivation was dominated by Gardner and Lambert's (1972) work with L2 learners in Canada, the United States, and the Philippines to examine attitudinal and motivational factors. Motivation was studied in terms of a number of different kinds of *attitudes*. Two different clusters of attitudes were identified as **instrumental** and **integrative orientations**. An instrumental orientation referred to acquiring a language as a means for attaining practical goals such as furthering a career, reading technical material, or translation. An integrative orientation described learners who wished to integrate themselves into the culture of the second language group and become involved in social interchange in that group.

Gardner and MacIntyre (1991) and Dörnyei (2001b) later argued that instrumentality and integrativeness are not actually types of *motivation*, but rather, more appropriately forms of **orientations**. That is, depending on whether a learner's main focus or purpose is (1) academic or career related (instrumental), or (2) socially or culturally oriented (integrative), different needs might be fulfilled in learning an L2.

One of the problems with examining instrumental and integrative orientations was that they did not constitute a *dichotomy*. One could quite easily be both instrumentally and integratively inclined. Many L2 learners have reported strong interest in learning a language for academic or professional purposes as well as for social or cultural understanding (Dörnyei & Ushioda, 2011). For example, international students learning English in the United States for academic purposes may be relatively balanced in their desire to learn English both for academic (instrumental) purposes and to understand and become somewhat integrated with American cultural norms. This would explain the contradictory results of a number of studies. An integrative orientation appeared to correspond with higher proficiency levels in studies by Gardner and Lambert (1972), and Spolsky (1969), for example. But evidence began to accumulate that challenged such a claim. Both Lukmani (1972) and Kachru (1977, 1992) demonstrated higher proficiency among English learners with instrumental orientations in India.

In the face of claims and counterclaims, Au (1988) reviewed 27 different studies of the integrative–instrumental construct and concluded that both its theoretical underpinnings and the instruments used to measure orientation were suspect. Gardner and MacIntyre (1993b) of course disputed Au's claims, but the waters continued to be muddied by further studies with ambiguous results. Even Gardner found that certain contexts pointed toward instrumental orientation as an effective context for language success (Gardner & MacIntyre, 1991), but that others favored an integrative orientation (Gardner, Day, & MacIntyre, 1992). Warden and Lin (2000) found no support for an integrative orientation among university English majors in Taiwan. Then, Gardner et al. (2004) found integrative and instrumental orientation to have roughly the same impact on university learners of French in Canada. Similarly, Lamb (2004) reported integrative and instrumental constructs to be almost indistinguishable!

CLASSROOM CONNECTIONS

Have you felt *both* academically and culturally inclined to pursue a foreign language? Was one orientation stronger than another in your experience? How could a teacher foster instrumental benefits in an L2 classroom? How about integrative assets?

Motivational Intensity

What were we to make of this confusion? A partial answer was offered by Masgoret and Gardner (2003), who demonstrated that integrativeness was not as significant a factor as **motivational intensity**. Within either orientation, one can have either high or low level of motivation. One learner may be only mildly motivated to learn within, say, a career context, while another learner with the same orientation may be intensely driven to succeed in the same orientation. A clearer pathway for researchers seemed to lie in this concept of the *strength* of one's motivation, and not in what had proved to be ill-defined constructs of orientations.

As researchers looked at and measured motivational intensity, two new concepts emerged that were related to the amount of effort expended: demotivation and amotivation. A simple dictionary definition of **demotivation** refers to the losing of interest that once was present. Dörnyei and Ushioda referred to a demotivated learner as "someone who was once motivated but has lost his or her commitment/interest" (2011, p. 138). Such loss may be the result of external forces (a boring teacher, a dull textbook, poor test results) or internal phenomena (exhaustion, increased interest in more attractive options, feelings of embarrassment over one's competence).

Demotivation is a significant issue in SLA. Learning an L2 is often a long process of endurance through years of study and focus, and the learner must be able to sustain *momentum* and drive in order to "finish the race." The euphoria of learning an L2, especially in the early stages, often wears down if one does not maintain a modicum of self-competition and drive to continue (Bailey, 1983). Teachers are therefore called upon to embrace their learners, to organize a curriculum well, to create exciting classroom experiences, and above all to respect their students (Gorham & Christophel, 1992). Teachers who are aware of their students' potential for such flagging of zeal will also help learners to maintain the joy of learning through a variety of activities, rewards, social interaction, and goal-setting.

Demotivation is not the same as **amotivation**, which, in Deci and Ryan's (1985) self-determination theory, is the absence of motivation entirely, usually caused by an individual's feelings of incompetence and helplessness, and not by initial interest that declines. Amotivation is present when learners feel they lack the ability to perform a task, think the effort expended is not worthwhile, or feel overwhelmed by the perceived enormity of a task (Vallerand, 1997). Learners who are amotivated clearly present a greater challenge to teachers than those who are demotivated.

Other Orientations

Measuring motivational intensity helped researchers to focus on more observable phenomena and to move beyond the elusive false dichotomy of integrativeness and instrumentality. In the meantime, even more orientations were considered. Noels et al. (2000) and Dörnyei (2005) advocated as many as four orientations: *travel, friendship, knowledge,* along with *instrumental* orientations. McClelland (2000) reminded us that one might distinguish between orientations toward a *global community* of speakers as opposed to *native speakers* of a language. And finally, Graham (1984) suggested that some learners experience a deep *assimilative* orientation, that is, a profound need to identify almost exclusively with the target language culture, possibly over a long-term period.

Sociodynamic and Constructivist Approaches

So far, the discussion of motivation has centered historically on a number of approaches to defining and categorizing motivation. All of these constructs offer fruitful ways to understand what it means to be motivated, and ultimately, advice on how teachers can help foster motivation among their students. The intrinsic/extrinsic contrast tells us that the more we can encourage autonomy and self-determination among learners, the higher will be their drive and usually the greater their success. While integrative/instrumental orientations are difficult to pin down, they remind us, along with the afore-mentioned other possible orientations, of how many different possible motives lurk in the mind of a learner—the beauty of the diversity of learners! Intensity is an important concept to weave into a theory of SLA, as *degrees* of motivation may make the difference between success and failure.

We have already seen that SLA involves complex systems, sometimes even "chaotic" systems if we borrow a term from chaos-complexity theory (Larsen-Freeman, 1997, 2012a). We have also seen that every plausible attempt to be *linear* and predictable in isolating cause-and-effect relationships in SLA is as elusive as Roger Brown's (1966) model that "darts off on an uncapturable tangent" (p. 326).

A resolution of this staggering multiplicity of ways to slice the motivational pie seems to be contained in what Dörnyei and Ushioda (2011) describe as a *sociodynamic* perspective. In their relational view of motivation, we are exhorted to focus on individual persons "as thinking, feeling human beings with an identity, personality, a unique history and background, . . . a focus on the interaction between this self-reflective agent and the fluid and complex . . . micro- and macro-systems in which the person is embedded" (Ushioda, 2009, p. 220). Such a viewpoint is expressed in Ellis's (2007, p. 23) *dynamic systems theory*, which "marks the coming of age of SLA research."

By viewing motivation as contextualized and dynamic, we not only avoid the pitfalls of attempting to isolate elusive and possibly ill-defined factors, but we also free our inquiry to celebrate the individual differences among L2 learners. In one sense, motivation is something that can, like self-esteem, be global, situational, or task-oriented. A learner may possess high global motivation (which probably cannot be accurately measured) but then experience low motivation to perform well on, say, the written mode of the L2, or on certain types of activity. Learners may derive their sense of determination from an abundance of different sources and needs. And of course they may have many more orientations (Noels et al., 2000) than the few mentioned above!

 CLASSROOM CONNECTIONS

Try to list a number of possible *sources* of motivation that you have experienced in learning an L2. Which ones of them were "strong," high-priority motives? Which had weaker intensity? Would you change anything about any of those sources? Should a teacher capitalize on students' high-intensity motives and also compensate on lesser motives? Or is there a healthy mix that can work for each unique student?

We are still left with a respect for the power of motivational drives in the affective systems of learners. Instead of hoping, like participants in a quiz show, for a "final answer," we have many potential pathways to success in a classroom full of learners. Each one, in *social* interaction with classmates and teacher, and in a process of *constructing* a dynamic set of motivators for the minute-by-minute challenges of learning the L2, is a unique human being with the potential to succeed. It is the challenge of teachers to blend the best of science with the best of artful intuition to help learners discover those pathways.

THE NEUROBIOLOGY OF AFFECT

Michael Long (1990a) once said that any viable theory of SLA requires the specification of a *mechanism* to account for the acquisition of an L2. There is no more basic a mechanism for language acquisition than the *brain*. The last part of the twentieth century saw significant advances in the empirical study of the brain through such techniques as positron emission tomography (PET) and magnetic resonance imaging (MRI). Using such techniques, some connections have been made between affectivity and neural processing (Schumann & Wood, 2004), involving several areas of interest for SLA, including plasticity, affect, memory and learning.

John Schumann's (1997, 1998, 1999; Schumann & Wood, 2004) work in this area has singled out one section of the temporal lobes of the human brain, the *amygdala*, as a major player in the relationship of affect to language learning. The amygdala is instrumental in our ability to make an *appraisal* of a stimulus. In other words, if you see or hear or taste something, the amygdala helps you decide whether or not your perception is novel, pleasant, relevant to your needs or goals, manageable (you can potentially cope with it), and compatible with your own social norms and self-concept. So, when a teacher in an L2 class suddenly asks you to perform, if your reaction is fear and anxiety, it means that the amygdala has sent neural signals to the rest of the brain indicating that the stimulus is perhaps unpleasant, unmanageable, or a threat to self-esteem.

Looking at motivation as a powerful affective factor, Schumann (1999) examined L2 motivation scales in terms of our *biological appraisal system*. He noted how certain questions about motivation refer to the neural processes of pleasantness ("I enjoy learning English"), goal relevance ("Studying French will allow me to . . ."), coping potential ("I never feel quite sure of myself when . . ."), and self-compatibility ("Being able to speak English will add to my social status"). His conclusion: "positive appraisals of the language learning situation . . . enhance language learning and negative appraisals inhibit second language learning" (p. 32).

Schumann and Wood (2004) provided further explanation of the neurobiological bases of motivation as **sustained deep learning** (SDL), the kind of learning that requires an extended period of time to achieve. SDL, not unlike intrinsic motivation, is rooted in the biological concept of *value*. Value is a bias that leads humans to certain preferences and to choosing among alternatives. We have, for example, what Schumann and Wood call *homeostatic* value that promotes an organism's survival, and *sociostatic* value that leads us to interact with others, and to seek social affiliation.

Perhaps one of the most important applications of neurobiological research to SLA is that brains vary in an almost infinite number of possible ways. So, "it would be difficult to argue that there is any 'right' way to teach a foreign language" (Schumann & Wood, 2004, p. 19), and even more difficult to presume that neurology or psychology will provide a linear model of SLA that fits all learner. One size certainly does not fit all.

MEASURING AFFECTIVE FACTORS

Our examination of dozens of affective factors leads us to probe issues surrounding their measurement, which has always posed a perplexing problem. Some affective factors can be reliably measured by means of indirect measures (such as the famous Rorschach "inkblot" tests) or by formal interviews, but these methods are expensive and require a highly trained expert to administer them.

In a spirit of practicality, the language-teaching profession has quite readily relied on paper-and-pencil tests, such as the MBTI, which require self-ratings by the learner. In Myers-Briggs spinoff tests, for example, we must decide if we tend to "stay late, with increasing energy" at parties or "leave early, with decreased energy," an item designed to measure extroversion vs. introversion. Typical tests of self-esteem ask you to agree or disagree with a statement like "My friends have no confidence in me," and in an empathy test to indicate if the sentence, "I am generally very patient with people" accurately describes you. Such tests can be conveniently administered to hundreds of subjects, scored by computer, and analyzed statistically.

While self-check tests have a number of inherent assessment problems, they have remained a standard for applied linguistics research today. A popular test of anxiety is the Foreign Language Classroom Anxiety Scale (FLCAS), developed by Horwitz, Horwitz, and Cope (1986), which poses situations representing potential anxiety ("Speaking in class makes me feel uneasy") to which the student must agree or disagree. Unlike the MBTI, the FLCAS was specifically designed for use within the field of SLA. Likewise, Gardner's (1985) Attitude/ Motivation Test Battery (AMTB), which had its roots in the original Gardner and Lambert (1972) study, asks learners to judge themselves across a number of categories, including attitudes toward the L2 culture, desire to learn the L2, L2-use anxiety, and integrative instrumental orientation.

CLASSROOM CONNECTIONS

Should tests of affect and personality be the province of research alone, or might they have some use in L2 classrooms? What kinds of problems would a teacher encounter in administering a self-check test to L2 learners? Can those problems be overcome fruitfully?

The above tests have been validated across contexts and cultures. However, they represent a number of inherent shortcomings. Let's look at those drawbacks:

First, the problem of validity is paramount since most tests use a self-rating method, which may lack objectivity. True, external assessments that involve interview, observation, indirect measures, and multiple methods (Campbell & Fiske, 1959) have been shown to be more accurate, but often only at great expense. In Gardner and MacIntyre's (1993b) battery of self-check tests of affective variables, the validity of such tests was upheld. We can conclude, cautiously, that paper-and-pencil self-ratings may be valid if (1) the tests have been widely validated previously and (2) we do not rely on only one instrument or method to identify a level of affectivity.

A second related measurement problem lies in what has been called the "self-flattery" syndrome (Oller, 1981b, 1982). In general, test takers will try to discern answers that make them look "good" or that do not "damage" them, even though test directions say there are no right or wrong answers. In so doing, perceptions of self are likely to be considerably biased toward what the test taker perceives as a highly desirable personality type.

Finally, tests of extroversion, anxiety, motivation, and other factors can be quite culturally ethnocentric, using concepts and references that are difficult to interpret cross-culturally. One item testing empathy, for example, requires the subject to agree or disagree with the following statement: "Disobedience to the government is sometimes justified." In societies where one never under any circumstances criticizes the government, such an item is absurd. The extroversion item mentioned earlier that asks whether you like to "stay late" at parties or "leave early" also requires sociocultural schemata that may vary from culture to culture. Even the concept of "party" carries cultural connotations that may not be understood by all test takers.

What can we conclude about measurement of affective factors? Judging from the above pros and cons, perhaps we should remain cautious in our use of various assessment instruments, especially self-check tests, not to the point of discarding them completely, but taking them with an intuitive grain of salt. We certainly must not deny the presence of affectivity nor its influence on SLA simply because we lack sophisticated instrumentation!

CLASSROOM APPLICATIONS: INTRINSIC MOTIVATION

There are so many applications and implications of affective variables at work (or at play!) in the classroom that it is difficult to know where to begin. You could not begin to instruct a classroom of students without attending to their self-efficacy, anxieties, motivations, and other personality variables. Teacher training courses and books on educational psychology universally cite the importance of emotion as a key factor for success in the classroom (Rogers, 1983; Arnold, 1999; Scovel, 2001; DeCapua & Wintergerst, 2004; Slavin, 2011).

For the sake of simplicity and brevity, let's look at *one* issue presented in this chapter, intrinsic motivation, and consider a few of the applications of this construct in the language classroom.

First, think about the interplay in the classroom between *intrinsic* and *extrinsic* motives. Every educational institution brings with it certain extrinsically driven factors: a prescribed school curriculum, a teacher's course goals and objectives, parental expectations (in the case of younger learners), institutional assessment requirements, and perhaps even messages from society at large that tell us to compete against others and to avoid failure. In a language course, extrinsic pressures are most often manifested in foreign language requirements set by the institution and in established standardized test scores that must be achieved.

How are you, as a teacher, to handle these extrinsic motives that are well established in most students? One attitude that would be useful is to recognize that such extrinsic drives are not necessarily "bad" or harmful, and your job may be to capitalize on such factors through your own innovations. Here are two examples:

- If school policy mandates a certain "boring" teacher-centered textbook, perhaps your own creative efforts can add interesting learner-centered group and pair work that gives students choices in topics and activity.
- If institutional tests are a bit distasteful in their multiple-choice, impersonal format, your innovative action could add some peer evaluation, self-assessment, and/or portfolio compilation that would build intrinsic interest in achieving goals.

In my own SLA class, I *require* students to take a concurrent foreign language—this is my extrinsic demand of students. But I have found that by frequently discussing their successes, failures, happy moments, and frustrations, and by asking students to write a diary of their language learning journey, they tend to develop a good deal of *intrinsic* interest in learning the L2.

A second way to apply issues of intrinsic motivation is to consider how your own array of classroom techniques can have an added dimension of intrinsic motivation. Consider the following suggestions for gauging the intrinsically motivating quality of classroom activities:

1. Does the activity appeal to students' genuine interests? Is it relevant?
2. Do you present the activity in a positive, enthusiastic manner?
3. Are students clearly aware of the purpose of the activity?
4. Do students have some choice in (a) selecting some aspect of the activity?
5. Does the activity encourage students to "discover" on their own?
6. Does it encourage students to use effective strategies?
7. Does it contribute to students' ultimate autonomy and independence?
8. Does it foster interactive negotiation with other students in the class?
9. Does the activity present a "reasonable challenge"?
10. Do students receive sufficient feedback on their performance?

The above suggestions may begin to offer a picture of the direct application of affective factors in the second language classroom, even if in this section only one of many possible subareas within the affective domain has been addressed.

☆   ☆   ☆   ☆   ☆

Remember Melody at the beginning of the chapter? An interview with her about how affective factors played into her English acquisition revealed the following:

She has always felt she was a bit timid, but "the confidence I gained during my years of English learning transformed me from a shy little girl to quite a communicative person." She experienced a normal level of anxiety learning English, especially in her younger years, but by the time she was in graduate school managed to "switch my mind into an English framework" and worry less about things like words she didn't know. Was she a risk-taker in learning English? "I wasn't a risk-taker as a child, but as my confidence built, I became less worried about making mistakes—I know that communication in everyday life is far more important than focusing on errors."

When asked if she felt "determined" to succeed in English, Melody said that in high school and college she believed in "enjoying the process of continuing to learn, and in believing that the process is more important to me than the result." Her motivational intensity has always been very high, with a strong level of intrinsic motivation. "I had the opportunity to use English in real life and I knew it was for communication and learning about people from other cultures, not just for exams."

Now, after all those years of "hard work," English classes in school, and success in graduate school, Melody concludes, "Now, I'm responsible for making my own journey meaningful."

SUGGESTED READINGS

Arnold, J. (Ed.). (1999). *Affect in language learning.* Cambridge, UK: Cambridge University Press.

A compilation of research on the affective domain in SLA from different perspectives. Topics include: anxiety, ego boundaries, neurobiology, self-esteem.

Horwitz, E. (2010). Foreign and second language anxiety. *Language Teaching, 43,* 154–167.

A comprehensive annotated bibliography of research over the last forty years covering foreign language anxiety and related topics.

Dörnyei, Z., & Ushioda, E. (2011). *Teaching and researching motivation.* Harlow, UK: Pearson Education, Ltd.

A thorough examination of research on L2 motivation from multiple theoretical perspectives over decades of inquiry.

Schumann, J., et al. (Eds.). (2004). *The neurobiology of learning: Perspectives from second language acquisition.* Mahwah, NJ: Lawrence Erlbaum Associates.

Two chapters in of this anthology are germane to the affective domain: aptitude and motivation.

LANGUAGE LEARNING EXPERIENCE: JOURNAL ENTRY 6

Note: See Chapter 1 for general guidelines for writing a journal on a previous or concurrent language learning experience.

- Consider each of the following affective factors: self-esteem, willingness to communicate, inhibition, risk taking, anxiety, and empathy. Intuitively assess your own level (from high to low) on each factor. In your journal, write your conclusions in a chart, and follow up with comments about how each factor manifests itself in you in your foreign language class (past or present).
- Look at the section on inhibition and write about the extent to which you have felt or might feel a sense of a second language ego—or second identity—developing within you as you use a foreign language. What are the negative and positive effects of that new language ego?
- Estimate your own Myers-Briggs type by using Table 6.1 as a check list. In your journal, discuss the relevance of your personality type to typical language classroom activities. Evaluate the extent to which your characteristics are in your favor or not, and what you think you can do to lessen the liabilities.
- How can you change affective characteristics that are working against you? For example, if you have low task self-esteem when doing certain

kinds of exercises, how might you change your general affective style so that you could be more successful? Or do you see strengths in your tendencies that you should maintain? Explain.

- Think about any present or past foreign language learning experiences. Pick one of them and assess your *sources* of motivation (or demotivation). What specific experiences developed those sources? Did the experiences promote high (or low) intensity? Is there anything you could do (have done) to change motivational intensity—to get yourself more into the "flow" of learning?
- In your language learning experiences, past or present, to what extent has your teacher promoted *intrinsic* motivation through activities or techniques, or through the teacher's attitude toward students?

FOR THE TEACHER: ACTIVITIES (A) & DISCUSSION (D)

Note: For each of the "Classroom Connections" in this chapter, you may wish to turn them into individual or pair-work discussion questions.

1. (D) Look at Bloom's five levels of affectivity described at the beginning of the chapter (page 142). Ask students to place language into each level and give examples of how language is inextricably bound up in our affective processes of receiving, responding, valuing, organizing values, and creating value systems. How do such examples help to highlight the fact that SLA is more than just the acquisition of language *forms*?

2. (A) Divide the class into pairs or groups, and assign each group one of the following factors: self-efficacy, willingness to communicate, inhibition, risk taking, anxiety, empathy, and extroversion. Ask each group to: (a) define their factor; (b) agree on a generalized conclusion about the relevance of the factor for successful SLA; and (c) discuss the extent to which their factor needs to be qualified by some sort of "it depends" statement about certain contexts. Groups should report findings back to the rest of the class.

3. (D) What are some examples of learning an L2 in an *integrative* orientation and in an *instrumental* orientation? Ask the class for further examples of how within both orientations one's motivation might be either high or low, along with situations where either orientation could contain powerful motives.

4. (A) In pairs, make a quick list of activities and techniques commonly occurring in a foreign language class. Then decide whether each activity fosters *extrinsic* motivation or *intrinsic* motivation, or degrees of both. Through class discussion, make a large composite list on the board. Which activities seem to offer deeper, more long-term success?

5. (A) Ask each student to intuitively decide which side of each of the four Myers-Briggs pairs they fall into (Table 6.1, p. 156). For example, a

student might be an "ENTJ" or an "ISTP" or any of 16 possible types. Then, in small groups of three or four, have students share their personality type and give others in the group examples of how their type manifests itself (or does not) in problem solving, interpersonal relations, the workplace, etc. Then have them offer examples of how their type explains (or doesn't explain) how they might typically behave in an L2 class.

6. (D) Ask students to think of some techniques or activities they have experienced in learning an L2. List them on the board, and then, one by one, ask for an assessment of their appeal to affective factors in SLA.

7. (A) Divide the class into small groups. Assign to each small group a typically extrinsically motivating activity (e.g., a multiple-choice final exam, filling in a cloze passage, a dictation exercise, a repetition drill). Ask the groups to brainstorm how they could *modify* or *add to* the activity with any of the items on the list of ten criteria for intrinsically motivating techniques on page 170. Have groups report their findings to the rest of the class.

CHAPTER **7**

LANGUAGE, CULTURE,

AND IDENTITY

"Who am I?" echoed Robert, in response to a question about his cultural identity. "I have no idea, really. With my parents (U.S. State Department officers) I lived in five different countries in the 18 years before I went to college in Southern California. I was exposed to Serbo-Croatian (Belgrade) and Arabic (Kuwait) in my younger years, then acquired Korean (Pusan) and Japanese (Osaka). And of course, English! I have pretty much forgotten whatever Serbo-Croatian and Arabic I knew. My Korean is fair (ages 8–11 in Korea) and my Japanese (ages 11–18 in Japan) is orally fluent. I went to international schools (English medium) so my reading ability in Japanese is limited to subway signs, store ads, and the like.

"I don't know how to describe my identity. I'm sort of American now, at the age of 41, but for years since my early college days I felt culturally homeless. I always surprised people in Japan with my native-like Japanese accent and Anglo-Saxon skin! I still correspond with and occasionally see my Japanese friends. I have a deep affinity and respect for Japan and its people, but I never felt completely Japanese—maybe because of my racial appearance and American parents.

"I have great appreciation for all countries, races, and ethnicities, and certainly do not feel the USA is any way superior to any other country! I find myself turned off by the xenophobia expressed by (in my opinion) too many Americans. When people sing 'God Bless America,' I want to sing 'God bless our Mother Earth.' I don't think God blesses one country any more than any other."

DEFINING CULTURE

What questions would you like to ask Robert? What is *your* cultural identity? Do you feel you "fit in" to a community of people identified by language, country, history, and customs? Do you resist some of the stereotypes of your culture? How do you view people from very different cultures and languages? Can students be *taught* to be interculturally competent?

Culture is a way of life. It's the context within which we exist, think, feel, and relate to others. It's the "glue" that binds a group of people together. Culture is our continent, our collective identity. Culture is a "blueprint" that guides the behavior of people in a community, is incubated in family life, governs our behavior in groups, and helps us know what others expect of us and the consequences of not living up to those expectations (Larson & Smalley, 1972, p. 39). Culture is the ideas, customs, skills, arts, and tools that characterize a given group of people in a given period of time.

Those are a few of literally hundreds of descriptions of culture that have been handed down over the years by anthropologists and psychologists. But culture is more than the sum of its parts and more than an amalgamation of all possible definitions. According to Matsumoto:

> Culture is a *dynamic* system of rules, explicit and implicit, established by groups in order to ensure their survival, involving attitudes, values, beliefs, norms, and behaviors, shared by a group but harbored differently by each specific unit within the group, communicated across generations, relatively stable but with the potential to change across time (Matsumoto, 2000, p. 24).

Notice that Matsumoto's definition includes some important concepts that have emerged over the last decade or so: culture is *dynamic*. It includes attitudes, values, and beliefs that *vary* within and across cultures, or in his words, are *harbored differently* by each unit. Culture is *relatively* stable, and it has the potential to *change* across time.

While culture establishes a broad context of cognitive and affective behavior and a template for personal and social existence, current research consistently emphasizes the *fluidity* of culture (Norton & Toohey, 2011). Yes, we tend to perceive reality within the context of our own culture, but that is a reality that we have *created*, and therefore not a reality that is empirically defined (Condon, 1973). We must be careful to view culture as a *subjective* phenomenon, and therefore not only to resist the temptation to overgeneralize or reduce our understanding of culture to positivist categorical definitions. A person's perception of community may be real or *imagined*, and the latter is a significant phenomenon being addressed in research (Pavlenko & Norton, 2007).

Over the years, researchers have disagreed on theoretical conceptualizations of the construct of culture (Atkinson, 1999, 2000; Siegal, 2000; Sparrow, 2000; Norton & McKinney, 2011). A few years ago Atkinson (1999) proposed an "ecumenical" approach to culture, as hues and colors covering a wide spectrum. On the other hand, Siegal (2000) and Sparrow (2000) preferred to see culture framed more in constructivist terms, placing greater emphasis on learners' *socially constructed identities* within learning communities and native cultural milieu. Others (Duff & Talmy, 2011; Norton & McKinney, 2011) extend these constructivist views of culture to include a community's stance on morality, social stratification and status, ideology, power, and affect. This more recent research captures the dynamic, contextualized, and personal nature of culture in Wenger's (1998) concept of **communities of practice**. We return to this conceptualization later in this chapter.

 CLASSROOM CONNECTIONS

To what extent have your L2 learning experiences in the classroom involved you in a socially constructed identity? Did the process of relating to new classmates and tackling an L2 at the same time see you becoming a "new *you*"? How can a teacher help students to take this kind of journey into a new identity in an L2 class?

CULTURAL PARAMETERS

Sociologists and anthropologists have for centuries examined the "peoples" of the world through numerous lenses. Traditional approaches have studied a community's beliefs, family practices, religion, rules, art, language, and the list goes on. Such an abstract and elusive phenomenon as culture cannot be defined in essentialist terms nor measured by an objective standard. Instead, we have come to understand culture through a number of useful parameters that help us to have an idea at least of what to look for in this "glue" that holds communities together.

The following cultural dimensions are an amalgamation of research over a number of decades (Hall, 1966; Triandis, 1972; Hofstede, 1986; Buckley, 2000; Carpenter, 2000; Matsumoto, 2000; Matsumoto & Juang, 2013). They should prove to be instructive parameters for identifying what holds cultures together, what separates one culture from another, how people differ *within* a culture, and in later sections of the chapter, how language in general and SLA in particular merge into the cultural landscape.

1. **Individualism** (vs. **collectivism**): the degree to which a culture values the needs of the self over the group. In individualist cultures, personal needs take precedence over those of others, while members of a collectivist culture sacrifice personal wishes in order to satisfy the group. An individualist society is loosely integrated; collectivist society is tightly integrated.

2. **Power distance:** (a.k.a. *status differentiation*) the extent to which the culture fosters equality versus inequality in power among members of the group. In large power distance societies, status is *ascribed* to certain occupations, ranks, and positions in society. People in small power distance cultures gain status through *achievement*, as opposed to family background or rank.

3. **Uncertainty avoidance:** the extent to which people are uncomfortable in unstructured, unclear, or unpredictable situations. Strong uncertainty avoidance implies a need for security, strict rules, and absolute truths; cultures with a weak uncertainty avoidance tend to be more contemplative, accepting of personal risks, and tolerant of change.

4. **Gender role differentiation:** the degree to which gender roles are specific and distinct (*masculinity*) as opposed to relatively overlapping social roles for the sexes (*femininity*). The former advocates maximal distinction between what men and women are expected to do.

5. **Action focus:** differences in valuing of "doing" versus "being." In the former culture, decisiveness and spontaneity are valued over reflectiveness. Responses to problems may be immediate and possibly impulsive. "Being" cultures value contemplation, tradition, and conformity.

6. **Space distance:** differences in standards for touching, proxemics, eye contact, and privacy. Public space cultures accept closer nonverbal distances, touching, and such artifacts as open doors to one's home and office, while private cultures value larger "space bubbles" in conversation, minimal touching, and less transparency.

7. **Time orientation:** the extent to which a culture values fixed vs. fluid time concepts. Fixed time cultures are punctual, acutely aware of passing time, single-focused, goal-fixated, and are more intolerant of interruptions. Fluid time cultures are more flexible with time constraints, slower paced, and see value in the "journey" as much as reaching a goal.

8. **Tightness:** the degree to which a culture is homogeneous. A tight culture is highly integrated, with few differences among members of a community, offering greater validity to generalization. A loose culture exhibits diversity, accepts greater divergence of beliefs, customs, religion, etc., and is therefore harder to "pin down."

Already you can see how difficult it is to describe a culture, group, or community! If you were to pick "Hawaiians," for example, you might begin to agree on very broad-stroke depictions on the basis of these dimensions, but would soon find it frustrating to generalize. You would be forced to offer "it depends" qualifications to assertions, to subdivide—with some difficulty—Hawaiians into several ethnic groups, and then be completely at odds with attributing dimensions to any single individual in the group.

An important disclaimer is imperative, however, lest you take such a list too literally. Each descriptor represents a *continuum* along which cultures (and individuals within a culture) may fall. No culture can be seen as entirely individualistic, for example, with no place for collectivist values. As you use such a list to ask questions about a culture, bear in mind that cultures and social identities lie on points between possible extremes. Nevertheless, with the eight parameters for conceptualizing culture, we can *begin* to understand what a *community of practice* is.

What elements comprise the building blocks of a community? To what extent are certain elements simply *perceived* or imagined (Pavlenko & Norton, 2007), as opposed to objectively observed? How does language embody and express such dimensions? Let's look at some possible answers to these questions.

 CLASSROOM CONNECTIONS

In your L2 learning classes, you have no doubt felt at least a few of the eight parameters for viewing and experiencing cultures other than your own. Among the eight, what have been the easiest to internalize into your cultural identity? The most difficult or complex? What are some linguistic manifestations of those differences? How would you help students in your classroom to bridge some of these gaps?

STEREOTYPES

An anonymous Eurocentric quip goes something like this:

HEAVEN is where the police are British, the cooks French, the mechanics German, the lovers Italian, and it's all organized by the Swiss. HELL is where the cooks are British, the mechanics French, the lovers Swiss, the police German, and it's all organized by the Italians.

What makes this humorous? Or is it? You may even find it offensive. Why? The answer is stereotyping. The quip is funny if you understand the overgeneralizations about certain European countries that have been the butt of barroom jokes. And it's not funny if you are, let's say, British, and you simply hate to see your finest recipe for Shepherd's Pie maligned in any way!

Stereotypes abound: Japanese are inscrutable, eat raw fish, and read anime and manga. Indians eat spicy curry and wear turbans. Saudi Arabians are rich, the women submissive, and the men lecherous. *Within* countries, stereotypes are the source of both amusement and disdain: New Yorkers are in your face, brusque, and drink Manischewitz wine. Californians are wishy-washy, sit in hot tubs, and drink white wine. Southerners are sugar-sweet, right wingers, and drink mint juleps. Such sometimes negatively biased caricatures derive from one's own culture-bound **worldview**, or *Weltanschauung*. We picture other cultures (or other regions) in an oversimplified manner, lumping cultural differences into exaggerated categories, and then view every person in a culture as possessing the same traits.

How do stereotypes form? If people recognize and understand differing worldviews, they will usually adopt a positive and open-minded attitude toward cross-cultural differences. A closed-minded view of such differences often results in the maintenance of a **stereotype**—an oversimplification and blanket assumption. A stereotype assigns group characteristics to individuals purely on the basis of their cultural membership. A stereotype is almost always inaccurate for describing a particular individual in a culture, simply because of the *dynamic,* contextualized nature of culture. To judge a single member of a culture by overall traits of the culture is both to prejudge and to misjudge that person. Worse, stereotypes have a way of potentially devaluing people from other cultures.

Sometimes our oversimplified concepts of members of another culture are at best "built on superficial views of diversity" (Kubota, 2004, p. 33) or simply downright false. Americans sometimes think of Japanese as being unfriendly because of their cultural norms of respect and politeness. According to Kumaravadivelu (2003), common false stereotypes of Asian students are held: they are obedient to authority, lack critical thinking skills, and do not participate in classroom interaction. Such attitudes need to be replaced by "a critical awareness of the complex nature of cultural understanding," or what Kubota (2004, p. 34) called "critical multiculturalism."

On the other hand, cross-cultural research has shown that there are some reasonably predictable characteristics that differentiate cultures (Atkinson, 1999, 2002; Matsumoto & Juang, 2013). Americans traveling in Japan can expect a society that is, in their view, highly punctual, quite formal, face-saving, and (in cities) fast-paced. Conversely, Japanese students in the United States regularly report difficulty adjusting to overly friendly teachers, group discussions in class, independent women, and trains that run late. Travel from the United States to Cairo, Egypt and expect chaotic traffic, street markets and bazaars everywhere, and a 5:00 AM wake-up call from the closest minaret calling for early morning *fajr* prayer.

In the final analysis, both learners and teachers of an L2 need to recognize openly that people are *not* all the same beneath the skin. Language classrooms can celebrate cultural and *individual* differences, and even engage in a critical analysis of the use and origin of stereotypes (Abrams, 2002). As teachers and researchers we must strive to understand the *identities* of our learners in terms of their sociocultural background (Atkinson, 1999, 2011a) and their unique life's experiences. When we are sensitively attuned to perceiving cultural identity, we can then perhaps turn perception into appreciation.

CLASSROOM CONNECTIONS

Have your teachers in your own L2 learning experiences helped you to "celebrate" cultural differences? What are some positive characteristics of the culture of an L2 that you have tried to learn? How would you incorporate an appreciation of those characteristics in your own classroom?

LANGUAGE, THOUGHT, AND CULTURE

How does language coalesce with the development of cultural identity? We have already seen that one's performance of language is crucial to the formation of a self-concept. Remember the phrase, "you are what you speak"? Consider the fact that your *voice* (and to a lesser extent your writing) is so unique that it is instantly recognizable by friends and family. It is how you project yourself to others. Comprehending and producing language in social intercourse is inextricably interwoven into establishing and defining your identity.

It has also been observed that the manner in which an idea or assertion is stated affects the way we conceptualize the idea (Boroditsky, 2011). If language *is* intelligence, then our intellect is framed, shaped, and organized in large part by linguistic entities. On the other hand, many ideas, issues, inventions, and discoveries *create* the need for new language, as annual revisions of standard dictionaries show. Can we tease this interaction apart?

Framing Our Conceptual Universe

Words shape our lives. Lakoff's (2004) poignant book on **framing** reminds us of the importance of language and verbal labels in molding the way people think. The advertising world is a prime example of the use of language to influence, persuade, and dissuade. *Weasel words* tend to glorify very ordinary products into those that are "unsurpassed," "ultimate," and "the right choice." Food that has been sapped of most of its nutrients by the manufacturing process are now "enriched" and "fortified." And isn't it odd that in a grocery store there are no "small" or even "medium" eggs, only "large" (which now seem sort of average), "extra large," and maybe "jumbo"?

Euphemisms abound in every culture. We are persuaded by industry, for example, that "receiving waters" are the lakes or rivers into which industrial wastes are dumped and that "assimilative capacity" refers to how much of the waste can be dumped into the river before it starts to show. Garbage collectors are "sanitary engineers"; toilets are "rest rooms"; slums are "substandard dwellings." And when it comes to reporting on military conflicts, deaths are referred to as "collateral damage," and commando SWAT teams are called "peace-keeping

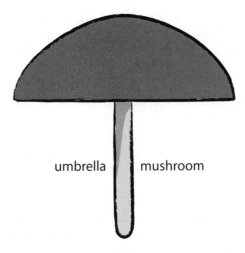

Figure 7.1   Stimulus

forces." Politicians have recently decided that the phrase "tax cuts" does not garner nearly as much sympathy as the phrase "tax relief."

Early linguistic research showed how verbal labels can shape the way we store events for later recall. Carmichael, Hogan, and Walter (1932) found that when subjects were briefly exposed to simple drawings with varying labels, later reproductions of the drawings were influenced by the labels assigned to the figures. For example, if they saw Figure 7.1 with the "umbrella" label, they would reproduce the drawing more like Figure 7.2, but if they saw the "mushroom" label, the reproductions tended to look like Figure 7.3.

Figure 7.2   "Umbrella"   Figure 7.3   "Mushroom"

Lexical items may reflect something about the intersection of culture and cognition. The verbal labeling of *color*, for example, affects the way a cultural group perceives colors. Gleason (1961) noted that the Shona of Rhodesia and the Bassa of Liberia break up the spectrum differently from Western European tradition. Likewise, Zuni has one term for yellow and orange, suggesting that Zuni children conceptualize these two colors as one (Berlin & Kay, 1969; Pitchford & Mullen, 2006).

Lera Boroditsky (2011, p. 64) offered an even more vivid description of language and thought among the Kuuk Thaayorre, an Aboriginal community in Australia:

> Instead of words like "right," "left," "forward," and "back," which, as commonly used in English, define space relative to an observer, the Kuuk Thaayorre, like many other Aboriginal groups, use cardinal-direction terms—north, south, east, and west—to define space. This is done at all scales, which means you have to say things like "There's an ant on your southeast leg" or "Move the cup to the north northwest a little bit." One obvious consequence of speaking such a language is that you have to stay oriented at all times, or else you cannot speak properly. The normal greeting in Kuuk Thaayorre is "Where are you going?" and the answer should be something like "South-southeast, in the middle distance." If you don't know which way you're facing, you can't even get past "Hello."

Beyond words, the way a sentence is structured can affect nuances of meaning. Loftus (1976) discovered that subtle differences in the structure of questions can affect memory. For example, after viewing a film of an automobile accident, subjects were asked questions like "Did you see the broken headlight?" in some cases and in other cases, "Did you see a broken headlight?" Questions using *the* (presupposing a referent) tended to produce more false recognition of events. The presence of the definite article led subjects to believe that there must have been a broken headlight whether they saw it or not.

On the discourse level of language, we are of course familiar with the persuasiveness of an emotional speech or a well-written novel. But in our everyday conversations we conform to conventionalized discourse styles that vary cross-culturally. Consider the "directness" of discourse of some cultures: in the United States, for example, casual conversation is said to be less frank and more concerned about face-saving than conversation in Greece (Kakava, 1995), and therefore a Greek conversation may appear more confrontational than its counterpart in the United States. In Japanese, the relationship of one's interlocutor is almost always expressed explicitly, either verbally and/or nonverbally (Kubota, 2009). Perhaps those forms shape one's perception of others in relation to self.

Some myths and misconceptions about language and thought have crept into our folklore. In considering color terminology across cultures, it is tempting to conclude that a language that does not have, say, a specific color name for "light sea green" predisposes its speakers to lack the ability to perceive varying shades of blue-green. This is not so, as research very clearly shows (Pitchford & Mullen, 2006). The claim that languages like Inuit, spoken near the Arctic Circle, have dozens of different words for *snow* is also a myth (Pinker, 1994; Scovel, 1999). Arguing that Hopi contains no grammatical forms that refer to "time," Whorf suggested that Hopi had "no general notion or intuition of time" (Carroll, 1956, p. 57), which was widely accepted as fact. However, several decades later, Malotki (1983) showed that Hopi speech does indeed contain tense, metaphors for time, units of time, and ways to quantify units of time!

Linguistic Relativity

Does language merely *reflect* a cultural worldview and the way its speakers think, or does language actually *shape* cognition and affect? The answer, according to Boroditsky (2011), is both, which we will see momentarily.

The most famous early proponent of language as the "shaper of ideas" was Benjamin Whorf (1956, pp. 212–213), who made a strong claim for what has come to be called **linguistic determinism**: "The background linguistic system (in other words, the grammar) of each language is not merely a reproducing instrument for voicing ideas but rather is itself the shaper of ideas, the program and guide for the individual's mental activity." And he went on to say, "We dissect nature along lines laid down by our native languages. . . . We cut nature up, organize it into concepts, and ascribe significance as we do, largely because [of] the patterns of our language" (p. 214).

The **Whorfian Hypothesis**, as it came to be known, cited research on Native American languages and cultures in support. However, as already noted above, some researchers (e.g., Guiora, 1981) took issue with Whorf's claims, deeming them to be "extravagant." Others (Clarke, Losoff, McCracken, & Rood, 1984) demonstrated that the Whorfian Hypothesis was not nearly as monolithic or causal as some would interpret it to be. The term **linguistic relativity** is more appropriate to describe this stance. In more recent years, cultural psychologists (Boroditsky & Gaby, 2010; Boroditsky, 2011) have presented compelling evidence of Whorf's initial views with evidence around the world, but they also readily concede the implausibility of a simple unidirectional influence.

Language teachers continue to recognize a more moderate view of linguistic relativity. Wardhaugh (1976, p. 74) ventured a positive outlook:

> "It appears possible to talk about anything in any language, [to make] any observations that need to be made about the world. Every natural language is a rich system which readily allows its speakers to overcome any predispositions that exist."

So, while some aspects of language seem to provide us with potential cognitive mind-sets (e.g., in English, the agentless passive voice, the tense system, "weasel words," and euphemisms), we can also recognize that an L2 learner does not have to learn to think, in general, all over again. As in every other human learning experience, the L2 learner can make positive use of prior experiences to facilitate the process of learning a new language and possibly acquiring a new (or somewhat "reshaped") cultural identity.

 CLASSROOM CONNECTIONS

Has learning an L2, in your experience, involved learning new ways of thinking, feeling, and acting? To what extent have your L2 learning or teaching experiences involved internalizing cultural thought patterns along with the language forms themselves? Were those cultural phenomena explicitly dealt with in your classroom? If not, how would you approach selected cultural "mismatches"?

COMMUNITIES OF PRACTICE

Anthropologists, cultural psychologists, and linguists have all at one time or another disagreed markedly on a measurable standard for defining *culture*, a goal that has become almost unreachable in our current globalization of what once were monolingual and monocultural traits. With billions of tweets and texts and blogs, Facebook interchange, and other Internet-based communications, no "culture" with electricity and a smart phone is isolated. As McKay noted, globalization is a "reformulation of social space in which the global and local are constantly interacting with one another" (2011, p. 122). To analogize from the famous chaos theory quip—a butterfly flapping its wings in the Amazon is linked to a hurricane in Hawaii—a tweet from a teen in Yemen may, through a progression of connections, save the life of a cancer patient in New Zealand. And with John Donne (1624), certainly "no man is an island . . ." and we are *all* "a piece of the continent."

By the late 1990s, with the phenomenal increase in communications media, the ease of travel around the world, and heightened global awareness, it became increasingly difficult to understand sociocultural variables in empirically based positivist terms. A potentially fruitful model for SLA research emerged early in the concept of **communities of practice** (CoP) to more accurately examine issues of identity in L2 learning. Cognitive anthropologist Wenger (1998) not only applied CoP to any group of people who share a craft or profession, but also (Lave & Wenger, 1991) to classrooms of learners in educational settings. Three characteristics of CoP were posited:

1. **Mutual engagement:** Learners in a classroom build collaborative relationships that bind the learners together as a social entity.

2. **Joint enterprise:** Learners (and teacher) negotiate an understanding of what binds them together as a community.
3. **Shared repertoire:** As part of its practice, the community produces a set of commonly used resources and practices.

Conceptualizing learners in a classroom as CoP has opened the doors to SLA teachers and learners to openly recognize the singular contexts of each educational setting (Block, 2007). Rather than learning to acquire a (real or imagined) "second" culture, which may be as diverse as the hues in a rainbow, students can instead participate in **situated learning** (Lave & Wenger, 1991), contextualized to their own particular milieu and individualized to the varying perceptions of identity and culture among the learners.

 CLASSROOM CONNECTIONS

In your language learning or language teaching experiences, to what extent did the students in your classroom form a community of practice? How did the above three characteristics of CoPs manifest themselves (or fail to do so)? By what means might a teacher specifically promote one or all three of the qualities of a CoP?

IDENTITY AND LANGUAGE LEARNING

The revolutionary change in defining and understanding sociocultural dimensions of SLA centers on the concept of **identity**, spearheaded by Bonnie Norton's (2000) seminal book on identity and language learning. Recent follow-up work (Kramsch, 2009; Noels & Giles, 2009; Blackledge & Creese, 2010) turned "a critical pedagogical eye on the relationship between power, identity, and language learning" (Meredith, 2011, p. 551), by examining how identities are constructed and negotiated by learners.

Foreign language learners (learning an L2 in an L1 culture) are not exempt from the construction and negotiation of identity, as Claire Kramsch (2009) aptly illustrated. She not only questioned the image of foreign language learners as monolingual, privileged, and secure in their identities, but also argues against the notion that foreign language learning has little effect on identity. Citing L2 learners' subjective accounts of their language learning experiences, she linked emotion (affect) to the manner in which learners construct their social realities. Blackledge and Creese (2010) further expanded our knowledge of identity and CoP in multilingual students by demonstrating the importance of identity negotiations, and even the development of hybrid identities in learning an L2.

Identity theory represents a marked conceptual shift in research on SLA, one that was inspired by Vygotsky's (1962, 1987) work on sociocultural theory, aptly referenced in Lantolf and Beckett's (2009) research timeline. James Lantolf explained that "the distinguishing concept of sociocultural theory [for Vygotsky] is that forms of human mental activity are *mediated*. . . . We use symbolic tools, or signs, to mediate and regulate our relationships with others and with ourselves" (2000, p. 80). Language is, of course, the primary symbolic tool through which we construct our identity. For children as well as for adults, new concepts are acquired through social or interactional means, and our ultimate autonomous functioning is one that Vygotsky called *self-regulation.*

Norton and Toohey (2011) explain that identity theory views the L2 learner as situated in a larger social world and variable over time and space. The definitions of learners in binary terms (such as those presented in previous chapters of this book, e.g., extroverted-introverted, reflective-impulsive, etc.) are overgeneralized since learners' traits can vary in contradictory ways and even within a single individual. Further, identity theory recognizes the investment of learners in pursuing "a community of the imagination, a desired community that offers possibilities for an enhanced range of identity options in the future" (Norton & Toohey, 2011, p. 415).

By looking at the L2 learning process through the lenses of CoP and identity theory, we turn old models upside down, shake them loose a bit, and remove assumptions and constraints that no longer apply in a twenty-first century world. SLA rarely is a matter of "second culture learning," since that term implies not only a monolithic community (which does not exist), but also that every learner identifies with a "target" culture in the same way. We are reminded of Bakhtin's (1986) view of language as *situated* utterances in which speakers, in dialogue with others, struggle to create meanings. This poststructuralist view is *not* one of L2 learning as a linear path from "point A to point B" on a map, but rather a multidimensional, individualized, and sometimes meandering journey that may never have an "end point."

HISTORICAL LANDMARKS IN CROSS-CULTURAL RESEARCH

For most of the twentieth century, research on the sociocultural elements of SLA centered on issues in acculturation, culture shock, social distance, culture "learning," and attitudes toward cultures beyond one's own, as recently documented in Risager's (2011) comprehensive annotated bibliography of research on the cultural dimensions of language teaching and learning. Most of this research viewed culture in *essentialist* terms: Culture could be defined and understood in terms of various difficulties encountered by learners in "crossing" cultural borders and in what some called "second culture learning" (Seelye, 1974).

While virtually all this history must now be seen in the perspective of sociocultural theory that focuses on identity and communities of practice, the decades-long study of cultural factors gave us important insights and parameters from which every L2 teacher can benefit to some degree. What follows is a sketch of that research with some conclusions about its benefits today in L2 pedagogy.

But first, a caveat. The contexts of SLA learning are myriad. At one extreme on a hypothetical continuum, is learning an L2 in the country of the L2 with the goal of residing there for an extended period of time. At the other end of the scale are "foreign" language classes taken in the country of the learners' L1, with—for many—the goal of merely fulfilling an academic requirement. Between both extremes are many possible scenarios for contact with the culture of the L2, some with very little emotional or psychological investment and others with deep-seated motives for integration or assimilation. It is therefore both simplistic and unrealistic to assume that every instance of SLA is fraught with sociocultural implications.

Acculturation and Culture Shock

L2 learning, as we saw above, almost always involves the phenomenon of developing an *identity*. The creation of a new identity is at the heart of culture learning, or what has commonly been called **acculturation**. In certain L2 contexts, a reorientation of thinking, feeling, and communication may be necessary. For example, in the eyes of some cultures, the generalized impression created by North American culture may be that of "a frantic, perpetual round of actions that leave practically no time for personal feeling and reflection" (Condon, 1973, p. 25). Japanese may appear to others to be overly consumed with punctuality and formality, and some South American cultures could leave the impression of a place where people are way too laid back, lack a work ethic, or are much too jubilant.

For an L2 learner, understanding a new culture, even in a "foreign" language classroom, can clash with a person's worldview, self-identity, and systems of thinking, acting, feeling, and communication. When that disruption is severe (usually *not* in a "foreign" language situation), a learner may experience **culture shock**, a phenomenon ranging from mild irritability to deep psychological crisis. Culture shock may be experienced by feelings of estrangement, anger, hostility, indecision, frustration, unhappiness, sadness, loneliness, homesickness, and even physical illness.

Edward Hall once noted that when visiting another country, "at first, things in the cities look pretty much alike. But the longer one stays, the more enigmatic the new country looks" (1959, p. 59). People in a new culture may initially be delighted with the "exotic" surroundings. As long as they can perceptually filter their surroundings and internalize the environment in their own worldview, they feel at ease. But as soon as this newness wears off and the cognitive and affective contradictions of the foreign culture mount up, they become disoriented.

It is common to describe culture shock as the second of four successive *stages* of culture acquisition:

1. an initial period of excitement and euphoria
2. culture stress or culture shock, erosion of self-esteem and security
3. gradual recovery, adjustment to new ways of thinking, feeling, and acting
4. a final stage of adaptation/integration, acceptance of a new identity

In describing the third recovery stage of culture acquisition, Lambert's (1967) research on acculturation cited Durkheim's (1897) concept of **anomie**—feelings of social uncertainty, homelessness, or dissatisfaction, in which one may feel neither bound firmly to one's native culture nor fully adapted to the second culture. Lambert claimed that the strongest dose of anomie is experienced when linguistically a person begins to "master" the foreign language and a new culture simultaneously. In Lambert's (1967) study when English-speaking Canadians became so skilled in French that they began to "think" in French and even dream in French, feelings of anomie were markedly high. It was suggested that the very feelings of uncertainty had the potential to propel learners onward into L2 mastery.

 CLASSROOM CONNECTIONS

Consider your own cross-cultural and L2 learning experiences. To what extent have you felt degrees of culture shock, or at least culture stress? How did those feelings manifest themselves in your L2 classroom? How did your teacher help you to deal with your psychological states? How would you, as a teacher, help your learners to develop an awareness of acculturation issues and to understand a possible changing social identity within you?

Social Distance

The concept of social distance emerged as an affective construct to explain various degrees of acculturation. **Social distance** refers—metaphorically—to the cognitive and affective proximity of two cultures that come into contact within an individual. On a very superficial level one might observe, for example, that people from the United States are culturally similar to Canadians, while U.S. natives and Chinese are, by comparison, relatively dissimilar. We could say that the social distance of the latter case exceeds the former.

John Schumann (1976c) described social distance as consisting of the several possible parameters, including the following:

1. *Dominance*, power relationships across two cultures
2. The extent to which *integration* into a second culture is possible
3. The *congruency* of the two cultures in question

Schumann used the above factors to describe hypothetically positive or negative language learning situations. So, for example, if two cultures are not congruent, the negative attitudes toward each other could work against acculturation. A positive language learning situation would be one in which the L2 group is nondominant in relation to the target language group, assimilation (or at least accommodation) is desirable, and both groups have positive attitudes toward each other, a hypothesis that was later supported by Lybeck (2002).

Schumann's hypothesis was that the greater the social distance between two cultures, the greater the difficulty the learner will have in learning the L2, and conversely, the smaller the social distance, the better will be the language learning situation. But Schumann's social distance hypothesis was difficult, if not impossible to measure empirically. To this day the construct has remained a rather subjectively defined phenomenon that defies definition even though one can intuitively grasp the sense of what is meant.

Bill Acton (1979) proposed a solution to the dilemma. Instead of trying to measure *actual* social distance, he devised a measure of **perceived social distance**. His contention was that the actual distance between cultures is not particularly relevant since it is what learners *perceive* that forms their own reality, and in response he devised the Professed Difference in Attitude Questionnaire (PDAQ), which asked learners to quantify what they perceived to be the differences in attitude between two cultures. Acton found that in the case of some learners there was an *optimal* perceived social distance ratio (neither too close nor too far from the target culture) that typified the successful language learners.

Acton's theory of optimal perceived social distance supported Lambert's (1967) contention that mastery of the foreign language takes place hand in hand with feelings of anomie or homelessness, where learners have moved away from their native culture but are still not completely adjusted to the target culture. Acton's findings led to another study (Brown, 1980) that proposed an **optimal distance model** of SLA: An adult who fails to master a second language in a second culture may for a host of reasons have failed to *synchronize* linguistic and cultural development. A delay, well into a stage of adaptation or integration, in achieving communicative success in the L2 may result in lower motivation to succeed and possibly fossilization of language. What was suggested could be seen as a culturally based *critical period* that is independent of the age of the learner.

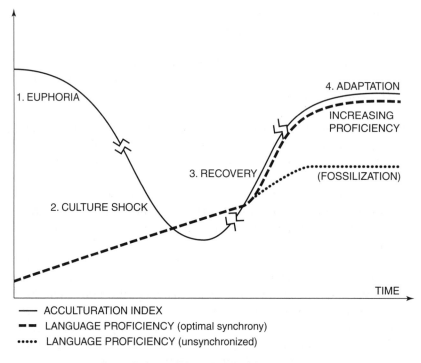

Figure 7.4   Hypothetical optimal distance model

Figure 7.4 illustrates the hypothetical link between stages of acculturation and L2 acquisition. When the L2 learner "seizes the day" in stage 3 to redouble efforts to learn the L2, then linguistic effort and social-psychological state merge to propel the learner simultaneously toward recovery and communicative competence. If the learner moves toward recovery *without* the benefit of increasing L2 proficiency (as is the case in many immigrant L2 learners), the L2 may fossilize. Adapting to the new culture without a comparable increase in linguistic ability may give rise to low motivation to improve one's L2 ability, and the L2 learner "survives" without ever achieving full proficiency.

Some research evidence was gathered in support of the optimal distance construct. In a study of returning Peace Corps volunteers who had remained in their assigned countries for two or more years, Day (1982) garnered some observational evidence of the coinciding of critical leaps in language fluency and cultural anomie. And Svanes (1987, 1988) found that university international students studying in Norway appeared to achieve higher language proficiency if they had "a balanced and critical attitude to the host people" (1988, p. 368) as opposed to uncritical admiration for all aspects of the target culture. The informal testimony of many L2 teachers also confirms the plausibility of a motivational tension created by the need to "move along" in the sometimes lengthy process of adaptation to a new culture.

CLASSROOM CONNECTIONS

Have you ever experienced a period of time when you felt culturally homeless? A time when you were confused about your sociocultural identity? Did those feelings help or hinder your progress
in an L2? How would you as a teacher help your students to use
anomie as a positive motivator to keep pushing toward your goals?

Attitudes

The postulation of theories of social distance to account for acculturation presupposed the significance of **attitudes** toward other cultures. In Gardner and
Lambert's (1972) studies of the effect of attitudes on language learning, they
defined motivation as a construct made up of certain attitudes. The most
important of these is group-specific, the attitude learners have toward the
members of the cultural group whose language they are learning. Positive
attitudes, they surmised, would aid in successful L2 learning.

John Oller and colleagues conducted several large-scale studies of the relationship between attitudes and language success (Oller, Hudson, & Liu, 1977;
Chihara & Oller, 1978; Oller, Baca, & Vigil, 1978). They looked at the relationship
between Chinese, Japanese, and Mexican students' achievement in English and
their attitudes toward self, the native language group, the target language group,
their reasons for learning English, and their reasons for traveling to the United
States. For the most part, positive attitudes toward self, the native language group,
and the target language group enhanced proficiency. There were mixed results on
the relative advantages and disadvantages of integrative and instrumental orientations. For example, in one study they found that better proficiency was attained
by students who did not want to stay in the United States permanently.

It seems clear that L2 learners benefit from positive attitudes. Negative attitudes usually emerge from one's indirect exposure to a culture or group through
television, movies, news media, books, and other sources that may be less than
reliable. Teachers can aid in dispelling myths about other cultures, and replacing
them with an accurate understanding of the other culture as one that is different
from one's own, yet to be respected and valued. Learners can thus move through
the hierarchy of affectivity as described by Bloom in Chapter 6, through awareness and responding, to valuing, and finally to an organized and systematic
understanding and appreciation of the foreign culture.

IDEOLOGY, POLICY, AND POLITICS

Upon due consideration of the variables of identity and acculturation, the next
logical leap is to the relationship of **ideology** to language and the construction of
identity in communities of practice. Ideology is the body of assertions, beliefs, and

aims that constitute a sociopolitical system within a group, culture, or country. We saw in our discussion of stereotypes earlier in this chapter how they can be misleading in their overgeneralization of sociocultural characteristics. Worse, in ideological terms, negative stereotypes "help to maintain existing, unequal social relationships that favor powerful, dominant groups" (Tollefson, 2011, p. 802).

Because identity construction "always implies inclusionary and exclusionary processes, i.e., the definition of *oneself* and *others*" (Wodak, 2012, p. 216), we are inevitably faced with issues of *power*. Who decides the *official* national language? Who decides on national *standards* of language? Who decides on *norms* of language use? Who are the *gatekeepers* who determine language policy?

The relationship between language and culture cannot overlook or underestimate the ideological ramifications of language and language policy. Every country has some form of explicit (official) or implicit (unofficial) policy affecting the status of its native language(s), and many countries include one or more foreign languages in these policies. Ultimately those language policies become politicized as special interest groups vie for power and economic gain, all of which may deeply affect an L2 learner's identity.

 CLASSROOM CONNECTIONS

In an L2 that you have taken, how aware were you of ideology and issues of power and politics regarding language? How, if at all, did it affect your own attitude toward the speakers of the L2? If you took an L2 in the country of the L2, perhaps you were more aware of ideology? How did your teacher bring such issues into your L2 classroom?

English as an International *Lingua Franca*

Into this mix, English, now the major worldwide *lingua franca*, is the subject of international debate as policy makers struggle over the legitimization of varieties of English. Some strands of research even suggest that English teaching worldwide threatens to form an elitist cultural hegemony, widening the gap between "haves" and "have nots" (Tsui & Tollefson, 2007; Kumaravadivelu, 2008; Tollefson, 2011).

The rapid growth of **English as an international language** (EIL) stimulated interesting but often controversial discussion about the status of English in its varieties of what came to be called **world Englishes** (Kachru, 2005, 2011; Dogancay-Aktuna & Hardman, 2008; Seargeant, 2009; McKay, 2011). Learning English in India, for example, really does not involve taking on a new culture since one is acquiring *Indian* English in India. According to Kachru (2005), the "Indianization" of English in India has led to a situation in which English has few if any British cultural attributes.

This process of **nativization** or "indigenization" (Richards, 1979) of English has spread from the **inner circle** of countries (such as the United States, United Kingdom, Australia, New Zealand) to an **outer circle** (Kachru, 1985) of countries that includes India, Singapore, the Philippines, Nigeria, Ghana, and others. In such contexts English is commonly learned by children at school age and is the medium for most of their primary, secondary, and tertiary education.

The stratification of EIL led researchers (Quirk, 1988; Davies, 1989; Phillipson, 1992; Tollefson, 1995; McKay, 2002; Higgins, 2003; Nunan, 2003; Major et al., 2005) to a new conceptualization of contexts of English language use. "The traditional dichotomy between native and non-native is functionally un-insightful and linguistically questionable, particularly when discussing the functions of English in multilingual societies," as Kachru (1992, p. 3) noted. Earlier distinctions among English as a native language (ENL), second language (ESL), and foreign language (EFL) became blurred with the spread of English as a *lingua franca*. Instead, we now tend to view English in terms of a broad range of its functions and the degree of its penetration into a country's society.

The question of whether or not to distinguish between **native** and **non-native** speakers in the teaching profession spurred a productive discussion. For many decades the English language teaching profession assumed that **native English-speaking teachers** (NESTs), by virtue of their superior model of oral production and familiarity with their L1 culture, comprised the ideal English language teacher. Then, Medgyes (1994), among others, showed that **nonnative English-speaking teachers** (non-NESTs) offered as many if not more inherent advantages. Others (Crystal, 1997, 1999; Cook, 1999; Liu, 1999; Pakir, 1999; McArthur, 2001; Higgins, 2003) concurred by noting not only that multiple varieties of English are now considered legitimate and acceptable, but also that teachers who have actually gone through the process of learning English possess distinct advantages over native speakers.

CLASSROOM CONNECTIONS

In your experiences learning an L2, do you think that you were better taught by a native speaker of the L2 than someone who had, like you, learned that language as an L2? Or did that factor make a difference? In your current or future teaching practice, how would you capitalize on the advantages and disadvantages of the two scenarios, depending on what your situation is?

How do questions about EIL and global *lingua francas* relate to sociocultural issues of identity and CoP? One can quite easily see that the blurring of lines of distinction between native and nonnative speakers of a language, between the inner and outer circle, and the widening of the purposes for learning L2s all contributed to the paradigmatic change from "culture learning" to construction of identities in contextualized communities of practice. The emergence of world Englishes is a symptom of the socio-psychological impact of the globalization of cultures. We no longer live in isolated communities where a person in one little corner of the earth must relocate to experience exotic new surroundings. English is a language for texting in Turkey, for Facebook in Finland, for education in Ecuador—along with, of course, commerce in China and politics in the United Nations.

"Second" and "Foreign" Language Acquisition

As the above discussion shows, the spread of EIL muddied the formerly clear waters that separated what we referred to as **English as a second language** (ESL) and **English as a foreign language** (EFL). Learning ESL—English within a culture where English is spoken natively—may be clearly defined in the case of, say, an Arabic speaker learning English in the United States or the United Kingdom, but not as easily identified where English is already an accepted and widely used language for education, government, or business within the country (for example, learning English in the Philippines or India). Nayar (1997), went a step further by citing yet another ESL context, English in regions like Scandinavia, where English has no official status but occupies such a high profile that virtually every educated person can communicate competently in English.

Learning EFL, or learning any L2 in an L1 culture with few opportunities to use the language within the environment of that culture (for example, a Japanese learning English in Japan), may at first also appear to be easy to define. Two global developments, however, mitigate the clarity of identifying a simple "EFL" context: (1) The establishment of immigrant communities within various countries (e.g., Spanish, Chinese, or Russian communities in a large city in the United States) provides ready access to users of so-called foreign languages. (2) In the case of English, the penetration of English language media (especially Internet-based communication, television, and movies) provides further ready access to English even in somewhat isolated settings.

The problem with the ESL/EFL terminology, as Nayar (1997, p. 22) pointed out, is that it

> "seems to have created a worldview that being a native speaker of English will somehow bestow on people not only unquestionable competence in the use and teaching of the language but also expertise in telling others how English ought to be taught."

As we saw in earlier chapters and in the preceding discussion, native-speaker models do not necessarily exemplify the idealized competence that was once claimed for them.

Linguistic Imperialism and Language Rights

One of the most controversial issues to appear in the global spread of EIL was the extent to which the propagation of English as a medium of education, commerce, and government "impeded literacy in mother tongue languages . . . and thwarted social and economic progress for those who do not learn it" (Phillipson, 1992, 1994, 2009; Skutnabb-Kangas & Phillipson, 1994; Canagarajah, 1999; Skutnabb-Kangas, 2009), called attention to the potential consequences of English teaching worldwide when Eurocentric ideologies are embedded in instruction, having the effect of legitimizing colonial or establishment power and resources, and of reconstituting "cultural inequalities between English and other languages" (Phillipson, 1992, p. 47).

A central issue in the linguistic imperialism debate was the devaluing, if not "genocide" (Skutnabb-Kangas, 2000, 2009), of native languages through the colonial spread of English. For more than a century, according to Phillipson (1992), there was little or no recognition of the imperialistic effect of the spread of English (and French) in colonial contexts. Some signs of hope for the preservation of indigenous languages were seen in the Council of Europe's 1988 *European Charter for Regional and Minority Languages*, which assumed a multilingual context and support for minority languages. Likewise, within the United Nations, the *Universal Declaration of Linguistic Rights* endorsed the right of all people to develop and promote their own languages and to offer children access to education in their own languages (Ricento, 1994).

As teachers venture into the far corners of the earth and teach English, one of our primary tenets should be the highest respect for the languages and cultures of our students. One of the most worthy causes we can espouse is the preservation of diversity among human beings. At every turn in our curricula, we must beware of imposing our own personal value system on learners for the sake of bringing a common language to all (Canagarajah, 1999; Skutnabb-Kangas, 2009). We can indeed break down barriers of communication with English, but we are reminded that the two-edged sword of EIL carries with it the danger of the imperialistic erosion of a global ecology of languages and cultures.

 CLASSROOM CONNECTIONS

Should educational institutions in non-English-speaking countries refrain from teaching English so that *heritage* languages and cultures can be preserved? Probably not, if Ricento (1994) and others are correct. Has your L2 learning or teaching experience valued— or devalued—home languages and/or cultures? If so, how did that come about?

Language Policy

Yet another manifestation of the sociopolitical domain of second language acquisition is found in **language policy** (including *language planning*) around the world (Kamwangamalu, 2011; Kheng & Baldauf, 2011; Nekvapil, 2011). The language of the education of children, for example, is a matter for policy: the decision by a political entity (e.g., a ministry of education, a state board of education) to offer education in a designated language or languages. Such decisions inevitably require a judgment on the part of the policy-making body on which language(s) is (are) deemed to be of value for the future generation of wage earners (and voters) in that society. A clash of value systems is brought to bear on the ultimate decision: linguistic diversity, cultural pluralism, ethnicity, race, power, status, politics, and economics. Ironically, as Thomas noted, "such legislation rarely results in a unified society speaking solely the mandated language(s)" (1996, p. 129).

In the United States, one of the most misunderstood issues in recent years was the widespread move to establish English as an official language. Noting that the United States had never declared English to be official, proponents of "**English only**" ballots across many states argued that an official English policy was needed to unify the country and end decades-long debates over bilingual education. The campaigns to pass such ballots, heavily funded by well-heeled right-wing organizations, painted a glowing picture of the unity and harmony of people communicating in a common tongue. What could be more patriotic than everyone in the country speaking the same language?

What those campaigns did not reveal was the covert agenda of the ultimate devaluing of minority languages and culture (Auerbach, 1995; Tollefson, 1995; Thomas, 1996; Crawford, 1998). In related legislative debates across the United States, bilingual education was singled out by its opponents as a waste of time and money. In 1998, for example, in the state of California, a well-financed campaign to severely restrict bilingual education programs managed to seduce the public by promoting myths and misunderstandings about language acquisition and multilingualism (Scovel, 1999). Once again, those who end up suffering from such moves toward "English only" are the already disenfranchised minority cultures.

TEACHING INTERCULTURAL COMPETENCE

Issues of culture, social identity, and concomitant ideological ramifications, as ingrained sets of behaviors and modes of perception, become highly important in the learning of an L2. Except perhaps for highly specialized, instrumental acquisition (as may be the case, say, in acquiring a reading knowledge of a language for examining scientific texts), SLA is intertwined with sociocultural identity (Dlaska, 2000; Hinenoya & Gatbonton, 2000; Littlewood, 2001; Schecter & Bayley, 2002; Uber Grosse, 2004; Tsui & Tollefson, 2007; Kramsch, 2011; Wodak, 2012; Matsumoto & Juang, 2013). But with all the complexities of understanding sociocultural identity, we must remember that language, thought, and culture are indeed a "package" that the L2 learner must grapple with in the journey to successful acquisition.

Both Scarino (2009) and Kramsch (2011) offered the perspective that while much of our attention as teachers in SLA classrooms is focused on *communicative* competence, we must also be mindful of the place of *intercultural* competence. "Intercultural competence has to do with far less negotiable discourse worlds, the circulation of values and identities across cultures, the inversions, even inventions of meaning, often hidden behind a common illusion of effective communication" (Kramsch, 2011, p. 354). Kramsch went on to explain that the self that is engaged in intercultural communication is a symbolic self that is constituted by symbolic systems such as language. How is an L2 learner of English, for example, to understand the lines of Dr. Martin Luther King, Jr., who, in his famous "I have a dream" speech, said, "This sweltering summer of the negro's discontent will not pass until there is an invigorating autumn of freedom and equality"?

Boroditsky and Gaby (2010) and others have reminded us that linguistic relativity (if not determinism) is alive and well in the twenty-first century and thriving in the languages and communities of the world. So, to some extent second *language* learning is also "second" *culture* learning, and the communicative use of an L2 is interwoven with developing intercultural competence. This process is not always euphoric. Stevick (1976b) cautioned that learners can feel alienation in the process of learning an L2—alienation from people in their home culture, from the target culture, and from themselves. In acquiring an "alien" language, the fragility of students is a factor for teachers to address.

On the other hand, Robinson-Stuart and Nocon, observing that culture learning is neither a "magic carpet ride," nor "a list of facts to be cognitively consumed" (1996, p. 434), suggested that language learners undergo culture learning as a "process, that is, as a way of perceiving, interpreting, feeling, being in the world, . . . and relating to where one is and who one meets" (p. 432). Culture learning is a process of creating shared meaning between cultural representatives and constructing a social identity within the learner's CoP. It is experiential, a process that continues over years of language learning, and penetrates deeply into one's patterns of thinking, feeling, and acting.

 CLASSROOM CONNECTIONS

In what way have your L2 learning experiences involved the "creating shared meaning between cultural representatives and constructing a social identity"? If you belong to one culture and your L2 represents another culture, isn't your job simply to learn what that other culture is all about? What is a *shared* meaning and who are the cultural *representatives* in your classroom?

Intercultural Language Learning

Liddicoat recently reminded us that the role of language educators is to "prepare language learners for meaningful communication outside their own cultural environment and to develop in language learners a sense of themselves as *mediators between languages and cultures*" (2011, p. 837). The positive effects of incorporating cultural awareness in language classrooms are well documented (Byram & Feng, 2005; Scarino, 2009; Kramsch, 2011).

Guidelines, practical activities, and tips, all grounded in research on sociocultural awareness, are offered in DeCapua and Wintergerst's (2004) as well as Wintergerst and McVeigh's (2011) reference books for teachers. In the latter, Wintergerst and McVeigh include a chapter on "culture and identity," which helps teachers to explore personal identity in their students. Through emphasizing students' uniqueness and the "sentiments and information an individual has regarding her or his personal self-images" (Ting-Toomey, 1999, p. 35), Wintergerst and McVeigh guide teachers through an exploration of their students' primary (stable) and secondary (changeable, situated) identities.

Research on SLA around the world has confirmed such approaches. Savignon and Sysoyev (2002) promoted sociocultural competence in their learners of English in Russia by introducing sociocultural strategies such as initiating contact, anticipating cultural misunderstandings, and using diplomacy in discussions. Wright (2000) found that using process-oriented tasks promoted cross-cultural adaptability. Abrams (2002) successfully used Internet-based culture portfolios to promote cultural awareness and to defuse cultural stereotypes. Interviews of native speakers of the target language helped learners in Bateman's (2002) study to develop more positive attitudes toward the target culture. Choi (2003) used drama as a "gateway" to intercultural awareness and understanding for her Korean students of English as a second language.

The above studies complement earlier work along the same lines. Teachers who followed an *experiential* model (Robinson-Stuart & Nocon, 1996) of culture learning in the classroom were able to help students to increase cultural- and self-awareness. Donahue and Parsons (1982) examined the use of role-play in ESL classrooms as a means of helping students to overcome cultural "fatigue" while engaging in oral communication. Readings, films, simulation games, culture assimilators, "culture capsules," and "culturgrams" [sic] are also available to language teachers to assist them in the process of sociocultural awareness in the classroom (Kohls, 1984; McGroarty & Galvan, 1985; Levine, Baxter, & McNulty, 1987; Ramirez, 1995; Fantini, 1997).

Perhaps the most deeply personal model of the acquisition of intercultural competence is found among students and immigrants who learn an L2 in a country where the L2 is spoken natively. They bring with them the cultural mores and patterns of acceptable behavior acquired in their home culture and tend to apply those expectations to their new cultural milieu. Sometimes there are difficult and embarrassing mismatches. Let's look at one learner's situated context, Kenji, a university student from Japan who was studying at a pre-university language institute in the United States. A few years later, reflecting on his first few months in the United States, he writes in his journal:

> During my 12 years schooling in Japan, I was taught to give utmost respect to my teacher. I must never contradict my teacher; never to speak in class unless I am asked by teacher to speak; never call a teacher by first name; and respect older teachers even more than younger teacher. But in my new U.S.A. language school, my young teachers (graduate students at university) were friendly and want me to call them by a first-name! They ask students to do small group work, which I never did in Japan, and they wanted students to give the answer to problems, rather than them just giving us answer themselves! This made me very confused at first.

We have already seen how cultural constructs such as individualism and power distance can be difficult concepts to internalize in situations such as Kenji's. Even more deeply personal are the feelings encountered by immigrants in a new country, who must now make a living, possibly together with a family, with no prospect of returning to their homeland. Baran (2010) noted that letters from immigrants often express deep emotions, such as loneliness or even grief. One immigrant wrote in eloquent words:

> My heart is closed, locked in a tight veil, from which that sweet softness of one time is inhibited from transpiring. It no longer has those beats of joy. It's dry. I cannot say more, beyond these words, about this painful story. It tears at my throat.

The road is rocky and the burdens not always light for students—of all ages and many possible situational contexts—whose cultural backgrounds differ from that of the country they now reside in. In the L2 classroom, the climate for effective language acquisition may be considerably clouded by what students see as contradictory expectations for their participation or seemingly insurmountable emotions. Our charge as teachers is to be fully aware of such factors and to facilitate the construction of whatever new identities are necessary for successful L2 acquisition.

CLASSROOM CONNECTIONS

The construction of a social identity is clearly not a simple matter of a few fast steps across a metaphorical cultural border. In the case of L2 students whose psyche is fragile and whose sense of cultural equilibrium is teetering, what can a teacher do in the classroom to spur awareness and positive action toward wholeness? What kinds of activities can aid immigrants, for example, whose families are left behind, whose homes are in rubble, and possibly whose family members have been killed in war-torn countries?

CLASSROOM APPLICATIONS: TIPS FOR TEACHING CULTURE

An excellent resource to direct you in treating cultural issues in your class-room is in Wintergerst and McVeigh's (2011) *Tips for Teaching Culture*. In this practical resource guide for teachers, the authors provide direct training in designing lessons and activities in terms of defining culture, exploring nonverbal communication, constructing social identity, dealing with culture shock, and a challenge to link intercultural learning with social responsibility.

I borrow from their title here to offer further "tips" for intercultural teaching. The checklist below illustrates how lessons and activities may be generated, shaped, and revised according to principles of intercultural language learning.

1. Does the activity value the customs and belief systems that are presumed to be a part of the culture(s) of the students?
2. Does the activity refrain from promoting demeaning stereotypes of any culture, including the culture(s) of your students?
3. Does the activity refrain from any devaluing of the students' native language(s)?
4. Does the activity recognize varying degrees of willingness of students to participate openly due to possible inhibiting cultural factors, such as power distance or collectivism/individualism?
5. If the activity requires students to go beyond the comfort zone of uncertainty avoidance in their culture(s), does it do so empathetically and tactfully?
6. Is the activity sensitive to the perceived (and sometimes deeply ingrained) roles of males and females in the culture(s) of your students?

7. Does the activity sufficiently connect specific language features (e.g., grammatical categories, lexicon, discourse) to cultural ways of thinking, feeling, and acting?
8. Does the activity in some way draw on the rich background experiences of the students in their own culture, as well as their experiences in other cultures?
9. Where possible, does the activity promote critical intercultural thinking and awareness, helping students to appreciate heritages and values different from their own?
10. Does the activity help students to construct their own social identities within an embracing community of practice?

The ten criteria in the checklist represent various facets of the language-culture connection as discussed in this chapter. As each item is applied to an activity that is either being planned or has already been taught, evaluation takes place and the activity thereby becomes a manifestation of a principled approach. All of the principles in your approach could easily lead to similar checklists for the validation of activities.

In the process of actual teaching in the classroom, it is quite possible that you will be led to modify certain aspects of your approach. For example, suppose you were a secondary school teacher in a country in which the concept of equal rights for men and women was simply never discussed openly. How would you design an activity that calls for reading and interpreting a passage that describes the women's suffrage movement in the United States? Or suppose a group-work task in your textbook calls for a description of people from different countries. How would you prepare your students for this, in light of the need to avoid demeaning stereotypes? You can see that items on the checklist might lead you to redesign or alter an activity. Classroom experience then might stir you to further refinement.

SUGGESTED READINGS

Matsumoto, D., & Juang, L. (2013). *Culture and psychology* (5th ed.). Stamford, CT: Wadsworth Publishing.

Now in its fifth edition, a comprehensive survey of issues, with treatment of ethnocentrism, stereotypes, prejudice, gender, emotion, nonverbal behavior, personality, social behavior, and more.

Risager, K. (2011). The cultural dimensions of language teaching and learning. *Language Teaching, 44,* 485–499.

A useful compendium of annotated bibliographic references on intercultural dimensions of SLA over more than five decades of work.

Tollefson, J. (2011). Ideology in second language acquisition. In E. Hinkel (Ed.), *Handbook of research in second language teaching and learning: Volume II* (pp. 801–816). New York: Routledge.

A treatment of the many complex issues, problems, and research on ideological issues in teaching languages in a number of contexts around the world.

Kachru, Y. (2011). World Englishes: Contexts and relevance for language education. In E. Hinkel (Ed.), *Handbook of research in second language teaching and learning: Volume II* (pp. 155–172). New York: Routledge.

A useful summary of research on the globalization of English, specifically how evolving understandings of World Englishes have impacted the teaching of English.

Wintergerst, A., & McVeigh, J. (2011). *Tips for teaching culture: Practical approaches to intercultural communication*. White Plains, NY: Pearson Education.

A practical reference book for teachers on treating culture in the L2 classroom, including issues of identity, culture shock, and social responsibility. Thirty-five pages of photocopiable handouts are included.

LANGUAGE LEARNING EXPERIENCE: JOURNAL ENTRY 7

Note: See Chapter 1 for general guidelines for writing a journal on a previous or concurrent language learning experience.

- In your journal, describe any cross-cultural living experiences you have had, even just a brief visit in another country. Describe any feelings of euphoria, uneasiness or stress, culture shock, and a sense of recovery if you felt such. How did those feelings mesh with any language learning processes?
- Think of one or two languages with which you are familiar or that you have tried to learn. How do you feel about the people of the culture of that language? Any mixed feelings?
- Look at the eight cultural parameters on pages 176–177 and write about a personal example of how you experienced one or more of the eight categories in your own current or past experiences in language classrooms.
- Make a list of words, phrases, or language rules in your foreign language that are good examples of the linguistic relativity (or linguistic determinism). Take a few of those and write about whether or not you think the language itself shapes the way speakers of that language think or feel.

- Why do many linguists say the spread of English in the colonial era had imperialistic overtones? How can you as an L2 teacher in this new millennium avoid cultural imperialism?
- In a foreign language you are taking (or have taken), how, if at all, has your teacher incorporated culture learning into the curriculum?

FOR THE TEACHER: ACTIVITIES (A) & DISCUSSION (D)

Note: For each of the "Classroom Connections" in this chapter, you may wish to turn them into individual or pair-work discussion questions.

1. (D) Direct the class to the cultural parameters on pages 176–177. Ask students to share examples of these parameters in their own past experiences in L2 classrooms (or in any other classroom).
2. (A) Divide the class randomly into small groups. Assign to each group a country (countries should be as widely varying as possible and familiar to the students). First, ask each group to suspend their usual tact and diplomacy for the sake of making this activity more interesting and frank. The task is for each group to brainstorm stereotypes for the people of their assigned country. The stereotypes can be negative and demeaning and/or positive and complimentary.
3. (A) Ask the groups in item 2 to write their list of stereotypes on the blackboard. In each group's comments, they should recount (a) any difficulties they had in agreeing on stereotypes, (b) any *guilty* feelings about some of the negative items on the list, and (c) any inhibitions they had in the activity because of awareness of classmates' feelings.
4. (D) In foreign languages represented in the class, find examples that support the contention that language (specific vocabulary items, perhaps) seems to shape the way the speaker of a language views the world. On the other hand, in what way does the Whorfian hypothesis present yet another chicken-or-egg issue?
5. (D) Ask the class to give examples of an L2 classroom as an example of a community of practice (CoP). How does the concept of constructing a negotiated social identity differ from simply "learning a second culture"? Ask students to give examples of their own construction of identity within a CoP.
6. (D) Ask anyone in the class who has lived for a year or more in another country (and who has used another language) to share with the class the extent to which he or she experienced any or all of the stages of acculturation discussed in this chapter. Were the stages easily identifiable? Was there an optimal period for language breakthrough?

7. (D) Ask the students why language learning and teaching is a political issue. In countries with which they are familiar, discuss the extent to which government dictates language policies either in education in particular or in the country in general.

8. (D) Review the contention that English teaching efforts around the world can be viewed as fostering *linguistic imperialism*. Ask the students if they agree. What examples and/or counterexamples can they suggest?

9. (A) Name some typical intermediate to advanced classroom techniques (e.g., information gap, open discussion of a reading, freewriting after a video, responding to a lecture, practicing disagreement discourse, collaborating on a group project, etc.). Assign groups, and give one type of activity to each group, and ask them to analyze their technique in terms of each of the points on the checklist for *culturally appropriate* activities on pages 200–201. Report your findings to the rest of the class.

CHAPTER 8

COMMUNICATIVE COMPETENCE

Kathy is a forty-year-old adult who until the age of twenty-three spent all her life in California, at which point, after college graduation, she traveled to a few South American and Asian countries. Upon receiving her MA degree in TESOL at the age of twenty-six, she taught English in Japan, Thailand, and Turkey for about five years each. She just returned to the United States. When asked about her communicative competence in Japanese, Thai, and Turkish, she wrote the following in her journal:

"I had completely different experiences linguistically in each country. Oddly enough, I feel more conversationally competent in Thai than in my other two lan-guages. Why? Perhaps because I felt like I 'became' Thai in my years in Chiang Mai. I felt accepted by Thais, I felt a part of my neighborhood, I got to know people at the local markets, I rode busses and tuk-tuks with them. I felt that it was 'home' for me, almost more than the USA. So, I dove into Thai with an uninhibited spirit of 'trial and error.' If I goofed, which I did often, it would elicit a smile and an empathetic correction. After about three years, my pronunciation was really very good (so I was told) and no conversational situation was too much for me.

"My reading proficiency in Thai was marginal—I didn't need it for my teaching job, so I survived with being able to read signs, advertisements, and the like. But I loved the Thai people, customs, religion (among those of my friends who were religious—Buddhists). They seemed warmly welcoming and genuinely gracious. My white skin didn't seem to faze the Thais. They took me in as one of their own. I would go back there in a flash!"

Why do you suppose Kathy became so communicatively competent in Thai, but not to the same degree in the other two languages? What would you like to ask her about her social interaction, her "picking up" conversational ability, and no doubt her keen sense of pragmatics in Thai?

Communicative competence is a construct that has been the subject of interest since the early 1970s, at which time language practitioners and researchers began to see too much emphasis on the structural and cognitive trends of the 1950s and 1960s. In the 1970s, a distinction was made between *linguistic* and *communicative* competence (Hymes, 1972; Paulston, 1974) to highlight the

205

difference between knowledge *about* language forms and abilities that enable a person to communicate *functionally* and interactively. In the last two decades, there has been even more emphasis on the myriad social, cultural, and pragmatic implications of what it means to communicate in a second language.

As Mondada and Doehler stated it, "If interactional activities are the fundamental organizational tissue of learners' experience, then their competence cannot be defined in purely individual terms as a series of potentialities located in the mind/brain of a lone individual" (2004, pp. 502–503). Zuengler and Cole (2005) asserted that the concept of language *socialization* in SLA is of paramount importance in researching L2 learning, while Watson-Gegeo and Nielsen (2003) agreed, saying that it "stands to contribute the most to an understanding of the cognitive, cultural, social, and political complexity of language learning" (p. 155).

This turn-of-the-century wave of interest brought social constructivist perspectives into central focus and drew our attention to language as interactive communication among individuals, each with a *sociocultural identity*, as we saw in the last chapter. Researchers are looking at discourse, interaction, pragmatics, and negotiation of meaning, among other things. Teachers and materials writers are treating the language classroom as a locus of meaningful, authentic exchanges among users of a language. SLA is viewed not just as a potentially predictable developmental process but also as the creation of meaning through interpersonal negotiation among learners.

DEFINING COMMUNICATIVE COMPETENCE

The term **communicative competence** (CC) was coined by sociolinguist Dell Hymes (1972), who asserted that Chomsky's (1965) notion of competence (see Chapter 2) was too limited. Chomsky's "rule-governed creativity" that so aptly described a child's mushrooming grammar at the age of three or four did not, according to Hymes, account sufficiently for the social and functional rules of language. So Hymes referred to CC as that aspect of our competence that enables us to convey and interpret messages and to negotiate meanings interpersonally within specific contexts.

Sandra Savignon (1983) followed a decade later with the claim that "communicative competence is relative, not absolute, and depends on the cooperation of all the participants involved" (p. 9). It is not so much an *intra*personal developmental process, as we saw in Chomsky's early writings, but rather a dynamic, interpersonal construct that can be examined only by means of the overt performance of two or more individuals engaging in communication.

BICS and CALP

In the process of examining components of CC, James Cummins (1979, 1980) proposed a distinction between **basic interpersonal communicative skills** (BICS) and **cognitive/academic language proficiency** (CALP). BICS is the communicative capacity that all human beings use to function in daily interpersonal exchanges. CALP is a specialized dimension of communication used to negotiate typical educational tasks and activities, and often involves a conscious focus on language forms. It is what learners use in classroom exercises, reading assignments, written work, and tests.

BICS is language used for friendly exchanges, often with peers, in informal settings, and involving more slang and conversational metaphor. Here are some examples:

- "Hey, dude, what's up?" "Not much, and you?" "I'm good."
- "Well, my boyfriend is like, you know, I mean, um, he's all . . ., I dunno."
- "What? OMG! RU serious? LOL. BTW, I'm LMAO now. CU."
- "My grandma is sweet as honey, you know, but I was really in the doghouse."
- "Okay, so the Giants bit the dust—don't rub it in!"

CALP typically involves language used, in both comprehension and production modes, for such purposes as the following:

- to manage classrooms ("Everyone be seated." "Get into small groups and discuss this question." "What page did you ask us to look at?")
- to convey information through academic prose ("The following research methodology was used to examine the three hypotheses.")
- to frame test questions ("According to the reading passage, do you feel John is (a) guilty or (b) innocent? Choose (a) or (b).")
- to engage in classroom discourse ("I see your point, but I think . . .")

Cummins later (1981) modified the notion of BICS and CALP in the form of **context-embedded** and **context-reduced** communication, where the former resembles BICS, with the added dimension of considering the context in which language is used, and the latter is similar to CALP. A good share of face-to-face communication with people, because of its social back-and-forth, is context-embedded, while school-oriented language tends to be more context reduced. The last three of the above examples of BICS require some context to understand what the speaker is saying.

 CLASSROOM CONNECTIONS

In your L2 learning experiences, how easy was it to learn to understand and produce interpersonal "BICS" language to teacher or classmates? Did your teacher specifically teach you "CALP" language to make classroom discourse more communicative? As a teacher, what are some ways you might teach your students to engage in classroom discourse, especially in small group work?

Canale and Swain's Framework

Seminal work on defining CC was carried out by Michael Canale and Merrill Swain (1980), and is still a primary reference point for discussions of CC in relation to second language teaching. In Canale and Swain's and later in Canale's (1983) definition, four different components, or subcategories, made up the construct of CC. The first two subcategories reflected the use of the *linguistic system* itself; the last two defined the functional aspects of *communication*.

1. **Grammatical competence:** "Knowledge of lexical items and of rules of morphology, syntax, sentence-grammar semantics, and phonology" (Canale & Swain, 1980, p. 29). It is the competence that we associate with mastering the linguistic code of a language, the linguistic competence referred to by Hymes (1972) and Paulston (1974).
2. **Discourse competence:** The ability to connect sentences in stretches of discourse and to form a meaningful whole out of a series of utterances. With its inter-sentential relationships, discourse encompasses everything from simple spoken conversations to lengthy written texts (articles, books, etc.).
3. **Sociolinguistic competence:** The ability to follow sociocultural rules of language. This type of competence "requires an understanding of the social context in which language is used: the roles of the participants, the information they share, and the function of the interaction." (Savignon, 1983, p. 37).
4. **Strategic competence:** The ability to use verbal and nonverbal communicative techniques to compensate for breakdowns in communication or insufficient competence. It includes the ability to make "repairs" and to sustain communication through paraphrase, circumlocution, repetition, avoidance, and guessing.

The fourth category, in its original conception, limiting strategic competence to the notion of *compensatory* strategies, fell short of encompassing the full spectrum of the construct. In a follow-up article, Swain amended the earlier notion of strategic competence to include, in addition, "strategies to enhance the effectiveness of communication" (1984, p. 189). Yule and Tarone also referred to strategic competence as "an ability to *select* an effective means of performing a communicative act" (1990, p. 181).

 CLASSROOM CONNECTIONS

Were you taught to develop your strategic competence in learning an L2? To what extent were you explicitly introduced to "tricks" like paraphrasing, circumlocution, avoidance, and guessing strategies? Or did you just have to pick those up on your own? Would you teach your students in an L2 classroom how to compensate for breakdowns in communication? If so, can you think of techniques that would accomplish this?

All communication strategies—such as those discussed in Chapter 5—may be thought of as arising out of a person's strategic competence. In fact, strategic competence may be defined as the way we "manipulate" language in order to meet communicative goals. An eloquent public speaker possesses and uses a sophisticated strategic competence. A salesperson utilizes certain strategies of communication to make a product seem irresistible. A friend persuades you to do something extraordinary because he or she has mustered communicative strategies for the occasion.

Later Modifications of CC Models

The conceptualization of CC through the years saw a number of different interpretations, each of which contributed to seeing a different side of the total picture. One promising version of CC was offered by Lyle Bachman (1990), who proposed a reclassification of Canale and Swain's (1980) model under an overarching node, *language competence*, or language *ability*.

Bachman placed grammatical and discourse (renamed "textual") competence under **organizational competence**: the rules and systems that govern what we can do with the *forms* of language, whether they be sentence-level (grammatical) rules or rules that specify how we "string" sentences together (discourse). Canale and Swain's sociolinguistic competence was divided into two separate **pragmatic** categories: *functional* aspects of language (**illocutionary competence**, pertaining to sending and receiving *intended* meanings) and *sociolinguistic* aspects (which deal with such considerations as politeness, formality, metaphor, register, and culturally related aspects of language).

Bachman considered *strategic* competence to be an entirely separate element of communicative language ability, serving an "executive" function of making the final "decision," among many possible options, on wording, phrasing, and other productive and receptive means for negotiating meaning. In such a model, a user of a language utilizes both organizational and pragmatic knowledge in the moment-by-moment (strategic) decisions about how exactly to word an utterance or written communication, and how to interpret linguistic strings perceived through listening or reading competencies.

When John F. Kennedy exhorted listeners in his 1961 inaugural address to "Ask not what your country can do for you, but ask what you can do for your country," his strategic competence—with strings of words planned well in advance—enabled him to utter grammatical sentences, to juxtapose certain rhetorical elements, to use a heuristic device for a memorable catch phrase, apply appropriate oratorical style, and to use appropriate inflections and pauses, all for maximum effect. On a less melodramatic level, when the car salesman says, "This is the absolute rock-bottom offer I can make on this car," you have a choice to respond with a number of strategic options to serve your own purposes: "Oh, I was looking for a lower price." "What? I know from looking online that your dealer's cost is way lower than that!" "Well, that's it then—I'm out of here."

In more recent years, William Littlewood (2011) provided yet another conceptualization of CC using five separate dimensions, mostly a rearrangement of Canale and Swain's and Bachman's definitions. Three competencies are borrowed from the previous concepts, *linguistic*, *discourse*, and *sociolinguistic*, with virtually no redefinition. However, Littlewood added *pragmatic* competence as a separate node: the ability to "use linguistic resources to convey and interpret meanings in real situations, including those where they encounter problems due to gaps in their knowledge" (p. 546). In other words, he prefers the concept of "pragmatic" to "strategic." And a fifth dimension, *sociocultural*, is added to include "cultural knowledge and assumptions that affect the exchange of meanings" (p. 546).

What we have with these three conceptions is a comprehensive picture of what is meant, in broad strokes, by communicative competence. The classifications and redefinitions should not be a cause for confusion if one understands that there are no major theoretical disagreements among the three. Table 8.1 summarizes the three positions.

Table 8.1 Models of communicative competence compared.

Canale and Swain (1980)

1. Grammatical
2. Discourse
3. Sociolinguistic
4. Strategic

Bachman (1990)

Language Competence (with Strategic Competence as an "executive" function):
  A. Organizational competence
    1. Grammatical
    2. Textual (= Discourse)
  B. Pragmatic competence
    3. Illocutionary (= Functions of language)
    4. Sociolinguistic

Littlewood (2011)

1. Linguistic (= Grammatical)
2. Discourse (= Textual)
3. Pragmatic (= Strategic)
4. Sociolinguistic
5. Sociocultural

LANGUAGE FUNCTIONS

Bachman's model of CC included *illocutionary* competence, which is the ability to manipulate the functions of language, a component that Canale and Swain (1980) subsumed under discourse and sociolinguistic competence. **Functions** are essentially the *purposes* that we accomplish with language, e.g., stating, requesting, responding, greeting, parting, etc. Functions cannot be accomplished, of course, without the **forms** of language: morphemes, words, grammar rules, discourse rules, and other organizational competencies. While forms are the outward manifestation of language, functions are the realization of those forms.

Functions are sometimes directly related to forms. "How much does that cost?" is usually a form functioning as a question, and "He bought a car" functions as a statement. But linguistic forms are not always unambiguous in their function. Consider the following examples:

- "I can't find my umbrella!" uttered in a high-pitched voice by a frustrated adult who is late for work on a rainy day is most likely a frantic *demand* for all in the household to join in a search.
- A child who says "I want some ice cream" is rarely stating a simple fact or observation but rather *requesting* ice cream in the child's own intimate style.
- A waiter asks if you would like more coffee, to which you respond, "I'm okay." The latter phrase functions as a *response* that says, "no thank you."
- A sign in a church parking lot in a busy downtown area was subtle in form but direct in function: "We forgive those who trespass against us, but we also tow them." That sign functioned effectively—and humorously—to *prohibit* unauthorized cars from parking there!

 CLASSROOM CONNECTIONS

In an L2 that you learned in a classroom, what are some examples of *forms* (words, phrases) that you learned whose *functions* were quite different from the outward appearance of the form? Did your instructor teach them to you, or point them out, or did you just have to "pick them up" on your own? How would you teach some of these "mismatches" in an L2 classroom?

Speech Acts

Communication may be regarded as a series of linguistic "events" with meaning and intent. Communication is functional, purposive, and designed to bring about some effect—some change, however subtle or unobservable—on the environment of hearers (and readers) and speakers (and writers). Communication is a series of communicative acts or **speech acts**, to use John Austin's (1962) term, or minimal units of analysis in conversational interaction. Hymes (1974) classified speech acts in terms of a number of components, including the following:

> **sender**: speaker, writer
> **message channel:** speech, writing, nonverbal gestures
> **language form:** sequencing or hierarchy of selected words and sentences
> **topic:** what the message is about
> **receiver:** hearer, reader
> **context:** place, time, situation

Austin (1962) stressed three different meanings, or "forces," of speech acts, each of which constitutes a component of CC that L2 learners might find difficult to distinguish:

1. **Locutionary** meaning: The basic literal or propositional meaning of an utterance (or written text) that is conveyed by its words and structure.
2. **Illocutionary** force: The *intended* effect that an utterance or text has on the hearer or reader. This is what the sender assumes to be the message, but may vary from the message that the hearer *receives*.
3. **Perlocutionary** force: The actual effect the utterance has on the hearer. This is the received message and includes the consequences of the delivered message.

In the above examples, "I can't find my umbrella!" literally was a statement of fact, but its illocutionary force was the intention to get everyone in the house to search for the umbrella. The perlocutionary force—we certainly hope—served to locate the umbrella for the harried worker. L2 learners are frequently puzzled by such apparent linguistic contradictions, but once they grasp the form-function relationship, they can more readily avoid these misunderstandings:

An American and Brazilian student were waiting in a hallway to enter a classroom. To make small talk, Adam said, "What's happening, Fernando?" To which Fernando, with a quizzical look, glancing at other students standing quietly in the hallway, replied, "Uh, em, ah, I, uh, think nothing is happening right now, Adam. We are just standing here."

Halliday's Seven Functions of Language

The functional approach to describing language is one that has its roots in the traditions of British linguist J. R. Firth, who viewed language as interactive and interpersonal, "a way of behaving and making others behave" (quoted by Berns, 1984a, p. 5). Since then the term "function" has been variously interpreted. Michael Halliday (1973), who provided one of the best expositions of language functions, used the term to mean the purposive nature of communication, and outlined seven different functions of language:

1. **Instrumental:** To manipulate the environment, to cause certain events to happen, including communicative acts that have a specific *perlocutionary* force—they bring about a particular condition. Examples: "This court finds you guilty." "On your mark, get set, go!" "Don't touch the stove."
2. **Regulatory:** To control events, to set limits and parameters, and to maintain regulations through approval, disapproval, or setting laws and rules. Examples: "Upon good behavior, you will be eligible for parole in ten months." "Eat your broccoli or there's no ice cream for dessert."
3. **Representational:** To make statements, convey information and knowledge, or "represent" reality. Examples: "The sun is hot." "The president gave a speech last night." "The world is flat." (The latter, obviously, a *mis*representation!)
4. **Interactional:** To ensure social maintenance, phatic communion, to keep channels of communication open. Examples: "Oh, I see." "That's interesting." "Hey, how's it going?" "Nice weather today."
5. **Personal:** to express feelings, emotions, personality, reactions. Examples: "I love you." "I resent that remark." "I feel your pain."
6. **Heuristic:** To acquire knowledge, learn, seek (and provide) information, and to form questions designed to elicit information. "Why does water bubble when it gets hot?" "How many planets are in our universe?"
7. **Imaginative:** To create imaginary images, stories, conceptions, or ideas. Examples: fairy tales, jokes, novels, poetry, tongue twisters, puns; going beyond the real world, exploring the beauty of language, creating dreams.

 CLASSROOM CONNECTIONS

Can you think of examples of how you would verbalize some of the seven functions in an L2 that you took in a classroom? How would you teach language that, say, accomplishes interactional or personal functions?

Halliday's seven functions of language are neither mutually exclusive nor exhaustive. A single sentence or conversation might incorporate many different functions simultaneously, and a multiplicity of other functions may also be served through language. Typical courses in SLA cover such functions, each distinctly more specific than Halliday's:

- Apologizing and thanking
- Asking for and offering help
- Complaining politely
- Confirming and correcting
- Expressing a wish; making suggestions
- Giving advice
- Giving commands
- Making small talk

L2 textbooks (see the next section) offer language for accomplishing dozens of other functions, so that learners understand lexical, grammatical, rhetorical, and discourse constraints and possibilities for accomplishing many different objectives in a language. It is the understanding of how to use linguistic *forms* to achieve these functions of language that comprises a major accomplishment in SLA. A learner might acquire correct word order, syntax, and lexical items, but not understand how to achieve a desired and intended function through careful selection of words, structure, intonation, nonverbal signals, and astute perception of the context of a particular stretch of discourse.

Functional Approaches to Language Teaching

The most popular practical classroom application of functional descriptions of language was found in the development of functional curricula, also known as **notional-functional syllabuses.** (*Syllabus*, in this case, is a term used mainly in the United Kingdom to refer to what is commonly known as a "curriculum" in the United States.) Beginning with the work of the Council of Europe (Van Ek & Alexander, 1975) and later followed by numerous interpretations of *notional syllabuses* (Wilkins, 1976), notional-functional syllabuses attended to functions as organizing elements of an L2 curriculum. Grammar, which was the primary element in the historically preceding **structural syllabus**, was relegated to a secondary focus. "Notions" referred both to abstract concepts such as existence, space, time, quantity, and quality and to what we also call "contexts" or "situations," such as travel, health, education, shopping, and free time.

The "functional" part of the notional-functional syllabus corresponded to what we have defined above as language functions. Curricula were organized around such functions as identifying, reporting, denying, declining an invitation, asking permission, apologizing, etc. Van Ek and Alexander's (1975) exhaustive list of language functions became a basic reference for notional-functional syllabuses, now simply referred to as **functional syllabuses**, which remain today in modified form.

Typical L2 textbooks today customarily list communicative functions that are covered. For example, the following functions are featured in a "false" beginner's English textbook, *Top Notch 1* (Saslow & Ascher, 2011):

1. Introducing self and other people
2. Providing personal information
3. Identifying and describing people
4. Accepting and declining an invitation
5. Ordering from a menu
6. Giving directions
7. Booking travel services

Units in this textbook include an eclectic blend of interactive group work, grammar, vocabulary, and pronunciation focus exercises, listening modules, and writing practice. Activities are designed to facilitate the learning of various forms of language to accomplish designated functions.

In the early days of functional syllabuses, there was some controversy over their effectiveness. Russell Campbell (1978, p. 18) wryly observed that some language courses could turn out to be "structural lamb served up as notional-functional mutton." And Margie Berns (1984b) echoed some of Henry Widdowson's (1978a) earlier complaints when she warned teachers that textbooks that claim to have a functional base may be "sorely inadequate and even misleading in their representation of language as interaction" (p. 15). Berns went on to show how *context* is the real key to giving meaning to both form and function, and therefore just because a function is "covered" does not mean that learners have internalized it for authentic, unrehearsed use in the real world. Communication is qualitative and infinite; a syllabus is quantitative and finite.

 CLASSROOM CONNECTIONS

Have you used a textbook on your own L2 classes that follows a functional approach? If so, how helpful was it in helping you to learn different grammatical ways of communicating various functions? In "apologizing and thanking," for example, what are some forms you would use to express yourself in your L2? Can you think of some techniques that you could use as a teacher to teach a variety of ways to apologize or thank someone, in various contexts in the L2?

INTERACTIONAL COMPETENCE

Underscoring the insufficiency of a command of *forms* alone for successful communication, Richard Young (2008, 2011) proposed that a number of crucial components of CC are appropriately subsumed under the term **interactional competence.** The concept of interaction is appropriate to highlight in view of current trends of viewing language in terms of its sociocultural basis and putting SLA into a social constructivist perspective.

Consider the following exchange in a kindergarten classroom on a Navajo reservation in the southwestern United States (Saville-Troike, 1989, pp. 131–132):

> A Navajo man opened the door to the classroom and stood silently, looking at the floor. The Anglo-American teacher said, "Good morning," and waited expectantly, but the man did not respond. The teacher then said, "My name is Mrs. Jones," and again waited for a response. There was none.
>
> In the meantime, a child in the room put away his crayons and got his coat from the rack. The teacher, noting this, said to the man, "Oh, are you taking Billy now?" He said, "Yes."
>
> The teacher continued to talk to the man while Billy got ready to leave, saying, "Billy is such a good boy," "I'm so happy to have him in class," etc.
>
> Billy walked towards the man (his father), stopping to turn around and wave at the teacher on his way out and saying, "Bye-bye." The teacher responded, "Bye-bye." The man remained silent as he left.

From a Navajo cultural viewpoint, silence is respectful, and if the father had said his own name he would have violated a cultural taboo. While the teacher, mindful of Navajo culture, respected the man's behavior, the child, who was familiar by now with standard schoolroom discourse, was able to bridge the gap with a parting "bye-bye." All three, in their respective ways, displayed *interactional* competence.

What is it that enables us to engage in social interaction? The following abilities are adapted from Young (2011, p. 429–430):

1. **Participation framework**: Identifying the participants in interaction, including gender, social class, status, familiarity, etc.
2. **Register**: Accounting for the context of the interaction in terms of style factors, including intimate, casual, deliberative, etc. (see below for further information).
3. **Selection of forms in modes of meaning:** Choosing among linguistic (grammatical, lexical, rhetorical) options to create a desired meaning and effect.
4. **Speech acts:** Using appropriate forms to accomplish such purposes as requesting, answering, greeting, agreeing, disagreeing, etc.

5. **Turn-taking:** Following conventions of maintaining the floor, giving up the floor, selecting the next speaker, interrupting, etc.
6. **Repair:** Responding to misunderstandings, clarifying, requesting restatements, dealing with interactional "trouble."
7. **Boundaries:** Distinguishing one topic from another, topic initiation and change, closing a topic, ending a conversation.

Interactional competence is, according to Young, more than simply pragmatic competence (see below). The ability to interact implies what Kramsch (1986) called *intersubjectivity*, or in simpler terms, empathy—putting oneself in the shoes of those with whom you are interacting. Effective interaction involves collaboration, the establishment of a triangular relationship between sender, receiver, and context, the latter consisting of all the variables of who the participants are, why they are communicating, and what the purpose of the communication is.

DISCOURSE ANALYSIS

Successful interaction requires the use of language forms to accomplish purposes. The construct of interactional competence provides a context for understanding a number of aspects of communication: the nature of discourse, conversation, styles, pragmatic conventions, and even the place of nonverbal communication. We'll attempt to unravel the sometimes tangled threads of social constructivist views of CC by examining some of these variables, and begin with a look at **discourse analysis**, "the heart of which is the interrelation between form and function" (Silberstein, 2011, p. 274).

In technical terms, discourse is any string of words that extends *beyond* the sentence. A single sentence can seldom be fully analyzed without considering its context, and since virtually no *interactive* communication is a single sentence, we string sentences together in interrelated, cohesive stretches of discourse. In most oral language, our discourse is marked by exchanges with another person or persons, in which a sentence or sentences spoken by one participant are followed and built upon by sentence(s) spoken by another. Both the production and comprehension of language are a factor of our ability to perceive and process stretches of discourse, to formulate representations of meaning not just from a single sentence but from referents in both preceding and following sentences.

Consider the following three different exchanges:

1. **Doug:**   Got the time?
   Mary: Ten-fifteen.
2. **Husband:** Bad day?
   Wife: Don't get me started.
3. **Parent:**   Dinner!
   Child: Just a minute!

In so many of our everyday exchanges, a single sentence (or even a phrase) sometimes contains presuppositions or entailments that are not overtly apparent in the sentence-level surface structure, but that are clear from the context. All three of the above conversations contained such presuppositions (how to ask what time of day it is; how to respond when one is too flustered to talk; how to announce that dinner is ready and then indicate one will be there in a minute). So while linguistic science in the 1950s to 1980s centered on the *sentence* for the purpose of analysis, more recently trends in linguistics have emphasized the importance of *inter-sentential* relations in discourse. In written language, similar discourse relations hold true as the writer builds a network of ideas or feelings and the reader interprets them (Eggins, 2004).

 CLASSROOM CONNECTIONS

In the three sample exchanges above, what would happen if you were to directly and literally translate those exchanges into your L2? Does it work equally well? For example, if you said "Don't get me started," in your L2, would it *mean* what it means in English? How would you explain these exchanges to an English learner? Would those explanations help your students to understand such expressions?

Without the pragmatic contexts of discourse, our communications would be extraordinarily ambiguous. A stand-alone sentence such as "I didn't like that casserole" could, depending on context, be agreement, disagreement, argument, complaint, apology, insult, or simply a comment. An L2 learner of English might utter such a sentence with perfect pronunciation and grammar, but fail to achieve the illocutionary effect of, say, apologizing to a dinner host or hostess, and instead the perlocutionary effect would be seeing the speaker as an unrefined boor who most certainly would not be invited back!

With the increasing communicative emphasis on the discourse level of language in classrooms, we saw that approaches that emphasized only the formal aspects of learner language overlooked important discourse functions. Wagner-Gough (1975), for example, noted that acquisition by a learner of the *-ing* morpheme of the present progressive tense does not necessarily mean acquisition of varying functions of the morpheme: to indicate present action, action about to occur immediately, future action, or repeated actions.

Traditional theories of SLA assumed that learners proceed from parts (words, structures) to wholes (sentences in discourse). Evelyn Hatch (1978) suggested otherwise: "We would like to consider the possibility that just the reverse happens. One learns how to do conversation, one learns how to interact verbally, and out of this interaction syntactic structures are developed" (p. 404). More recently, Stefan Frazier (2007) advocated the use of *discourse-based* grammar *practices* rather than the sentence-level grammar *rules* that are part of a long tradition of L2 pedagogy.

Of equal interest to L2 pedagogy is the discourse of the written word. In teaching reading, *strategies* are seldom taught with a simple progression of reading a passage, then doing comprehension questions, and ending with vocabulary exercises. Text attack skills now include sophisticated strategies for recognizing and interpreting cohesive devices (for example, reference and ellipsis), discourse markers (*then, moreover, therefore*), rhetorical organization, and other textual discourse features (Nuttall, 1996). Cohesion and coherence are common terms that need to be considered in teaching reading. Likewise the analysis of writing skills has progressed to recognizing the full range of pragmatic and organizational competence that is necessary to write effectively in a second language.

Conversation Analysis

At the close of the last century, Firth and Wagner's (1997) seminal critique of SLA research turned many eyes (and microscopes) away from objectified empirical cognitive analysis and toward social and contextual orientations in language and language acquisition. Part of what Silberstein (2011, p. 275) calls the "social turn" in L2 research was an intense sociocultural, ethno-methodological enterprise that brought *conversation* to the foreground.

Conversation is not only one of the most salient and significant modes of discourse, but also an excellent way to probe the social and interactive nature of communication. "Conversations are cooperative ventures" (Hatch & Long, 1980, p. 4). What are the rules that govern our conversations? How do we get someone's attention? How do we initiate topics? Hold the floor? Yield the floor? Terminate topics? Avoid topics? How does a person interrupt, correct, or seek clarification? Until recently, few efforts had been made to conduct research in conversation analysis (Markee & Kasper, 2004; Markee, 2005; Seedhouse, 2011; Silberstein, 2011), an area that "invites the reconceptualization of language" (Larsen-Freeman, 2004, p. 603). Let's look at some of the fundamental components of conversational competence.

1. **Attention getting**. Early in life, children learn their first rule of conversation: get the attention of the hearer. Initially, children resort to crying, yelling, banging a toy on the floor—anything to turn a parent's attention to themselves. As the years go by, both verbal and nonverbal attention-getting conventions are assimilated. Simple greetings, certain small-talk conventions, or questions may suffice to attract the desired attention. Techniques include verbal gambits like "Excuse me," "Say," "By the way," "Got a minute?" and nonverbal signals such as eye contact, gestures, and

proxemics. Without knowledge and use of such conventions, L2 learners may be reluctant to participate in a conversation because of their own inhibitions, or they may become obnoxious in securing attention in ways that "turn off" their hearer.

2. **Topic nomination** (initiating conversation). Once speakers have secured the hearer's attention, their task becomes one of initiating an exchange. If the topic is as simple as, say, the weather, then a speaker may employ such gambits as, "Sure is hot today, isn't it?" Or sports: "How 'bout those Giants?" Or more seriously, "Did you see that program on global warming?"

3. **Topic development** (and "holding the floor"). After a topic is nominated, participants in a conversation then use strategies for continuing the conversation, which sometimes involves discourse that holds the floor (as opposed to yielding the floor to another speaker). Techniques include using hesitation signals ("uh," "um," "and, well, like, I mean . . .") when otherwise pauses might suffice.

4. **Turn-taking.** The counterpart of the conversational ability to hold the floor is to yield it to another speaker. Allwright (1980) showed how students of English as a second language failed to use appropriate turn-taking signals in their interactions with each other and with the teacher. Turn-taking is another culturally oriented set of rules that require finely tuned perceptions in order to communicate effectively.

5. **Topic clarification.** A list of components of interactional and conversational competence includes the ability to ask questions for clarification, which may arise from inaudibility ("What did you just say?"), lack of understanding ("What does 'eco-justice' mean?"), or disagreement ("I see your point, but have you considered . . .").

6. **Repair**. In the case of conversations between second language learners and native speakers, topic clarification often involves seeking *or* giving repair of linguistic forms that contain errors. These techniques range along a continuum of possibilities from indirect signals to outright correction. It is part of Canale and Swain's (1980) strategic competence.

7. **Shifting**, **avoiding**, and **interrupting.** These are among numerous conversational abilities that may be effected through both verbal and nonverbal signals. Changing a topic ("Well, speaking of music . . ."), dancing around certain topics, and interrupting politely are especially difficult for an L2 learner to acquire, the rules for which vary widely across cultures and languages. Moreover, as Silberstein (2011, p. 276) noted, L2 learners may be reluctant to display their confusion or misunderstanding in a conversation, relying instead on feigning comprehension.

8. **Topic termination.** You know what it is like to be in a conversation that has stretched beyond your limit. The art of closing a conversation with a glance at a watch, a polite smile, or a "Well, I have to be going now," is not an easy one for an L2 learner to master.

🌐 CLASSROOM CONNECTIONS

It is no simple matter to acquire the ability to "get into" conversations, interrupt, take turns, and end conversations. How often in your learning or teaching of an L2 have you specifically been taught language forms that enable you to carry on a conversation? What language forms do you think would be useful for teaching learners of your target L2 how to negotiate a conversation?

One aspect of the acquisition of conversation competence is the recognition and production of conventions for accomplishing certain functions. L2 researchers have studied such varied conversational purposes as retaining control in classroom situations (Markee, 2004), compensating for lack of lexical knowledge (Mori, 2004), nonverbal aspects of conversations (Roth & Lawless, 2002), turn-taking (Ford, 2002), apologizing (Olshtain & Cohen, 1983), complimenting (Wolfson, 1981), disapproving (D'Amico-Reisner, 1983), inviting (Wolfson, D'Amico-Reisner, & Huber, 1983), and even "how to tell when someone is saying 'no'" (Rubin, 1976).

The applications to teaching are equally numerous, apparent in a perusal of publications that have appeared in the last decade or so. Seedhouse (2011) aptly shows how conversation analysis can be applied to the pedagogical issues methodology, stimulating interaction, assessment, and languages for special purposes. Wong and Waring (2011) offer practical advice on teaching interactional skills by using insights from research on conversation analysis. And Seedhouse's (2004) book explains basic principles of conversation analysis, reviews the literature on L2 classroom interaction, and shows how teachers can deal with such complexities as turn-taking, maintaining the floor, and giving and accepting repair.

Styles

A final lens through which to view interactional competence is composed of a set of **styles** of discourse. Speech (and writing) can be examined in terms of accepted *conventions* for selecting words, phrases, discourse, and nonverbal language in certain contexts. Those contexts include subject matter, audience, occasion, shared experience, and purpose of communication. Styles are *not* social or regional dialects, but they vary considerably within a single language user's idiolect. So, for example, an informal conversation with a friend employs a different style from that which you might use in a job interview.

Native speakers, as they mature into adulthood, learn to adopt appropriate styles for widely different contexts. An important difference between a child's and an adult's fluency in a native language is the degree to which an adult is able to vary styles for different occasions and persons. Adult L2 learners must acquire stylistic adaptability in order to be able to encode and decode the discourse around them correctly.

Martin Joos (1967) provided one of the most common classifications of speech styles using the criterion of *formality*, which subsumes subject matter, audience, and occasion:

1. **Oratorical:** Language conventions used in public speaking before a large audience. Wording is carefully planned in advance, intonation is somewhat exaggerated, and numerous rhetorical devices are utilized.
2. **Deliberative:** Conventions employed in more impromptu contexts in front of audiences. A formal news interview and a classroom lecture are typical examples.
3. **Consultative:** A dialogue, formal enough that words are chosen with some care. Examples: business transactions, doctor-patient conversations, teacher-student conferences.
4. **Casual:** Language used in conversations between friends, colleagues, or sometimes members of a family. In this context, words need not be guarded and social barriers are moderately low.
5. **Intimate/personal:** Language characterized by complete absence of social inhibitions. Talks with family, lovers, loved ones, and very close friends are examples.

Categories of style can apply to written discourse as well. Most writing is addressed to readers who cannot respond immediately; that is, stretches of discourse—books, essays, letters, e-mails—are read from beginning to end before the reader gives a response. Written style is therefore usually more deliberative with the exception of friendly letters, notes, e-mails, or literature intended to capture a more personal style. With the notable exceptions e-mails, phone texts, and tweets, these more common every day written genres usually imply conventional expectations of reasonably well-chosen wording with relatively few performance variables.

Verbal variations in style range from discourse conventions to phonological choices. Syntax in many languages is characterized by contractions and other deletions in intimate and casual styles. At the level of word choice, Bolinger (1975) gave a somewhat tongue-in-cheek illustration of a single semantic meaning in each of the five styles: *on the ball, smart, intelligent, perceptive,* and *astute*—from intimate to oratorical, respectively. Style distinctions in pronunciation are likely to be most noticeable in the form of voice quality, volume, intonation, hesitations and articulatory slips, and perhaps a more "affected" pronunciation in formal language.

Of course, styles have nonverbal features as well. Differences in style can be conveyed in body language, gestures, eye contact, and the like—all very difficult nuances of "language" for a learner to acquire. (Nonverbal communication is further discussed below.)

CLASSROOM CONNECTIONS

What are some examples in an L2 you have taken (or taught) of different discourse conventions applying to different styles/contexts? What kinds of classroom techniques have you experienced in attempting to learn such differences? Can you think of some techniques for teaching styles (e.g., asking students to role-play different contexts)?

Related to stylistic variation is **register**, at times incorrectly used as a synonym for style. Registers, which enable people to identify with a particular group and to maintain solidarity, are identified by phonological variants, vocabulary, idioms, and other expressions that are associated with different occupational or sometimes socioeconomic groups. Colleagues in the same occupation or profession will use certain jargon to communicate with each other, sometimes to the exclusion of outsiders. Truckers, airline pilots, salespersons, and farmers, for example, use words and phrases unique to their own group. Register is also sometimes associated with social class distinctions, but here the line between register and *dialect* is difficult to distinguish (Chaika, 1989; Wardhaugh, 1992).

The acquisition of styles and registers poses no simple problem for L2 learners. Cross-cultural variation is a primary barrier—that is, understanding cognitively and affectively what levels of formality are appropriate or not. North American cultural conventions are typified by more informal styles than those of some other cultures. So, English learners in the United States can experience difficulty in gauging appropriate formality distinctions and tend to be overly formal. Such students are often surprised by the level of informality expressed by their American professors. The acquisition of both styles and registers thus combines a linguistic and sociocultural learning process.

Written Discourse: Intercultural Rhetoric

Discourse is, of course, not by any means limited to oral-aural interchange. The written word, with its potential for premeditated structuring, its permanence, and its power has long attracted the attention of linguists and literary scholars. Learning to write in a second language is arguably the most difficult mode for L2 learners to master, perhaps because, as Ulla Connor (1996) noted, writing is a cultural phenomenon, and learning to write in an L2 "is not just idiosyncratic variation but involves [overcoming] recurring patterns of organization and rhetorical conventions . . . from the students' native language and culture" (Connor, 1996, p. 5).

New York Times editor Eva Hoffman, author of the best-seller *Lost in Translation: Life in a New Language*, wrote about trying to find appropriate words in a new language:

> The words I learn now don't stand for things in the same unquestioned way they did in my native tongue. "River" in Polish was a vital sound, energized with the essence of riverhood, of my rivers, of my being immersed in rivers. "River" in English is cold—a word without an aura. It has no accumulated associations for me, and it does not give off the radiating haze of connotation. It does not evoke. (Hoffman, 1990, p. 106)

To capture the unique nature of L2 writing, Robert Kaplan (1966) coined the term **contrastive rhetoric**, which for several decades was the standard for describing the cultural roots of writing conventions in a language. Launching a now decades-long investigation of writing conventions across different languages and cultures, Kaplan prodded others (Connor & Kaplan, 1987; Connor, 1996, 2002; Li, 1996; Connor, Nagelhout, & Rozycki, 2008) to scrutinize cross-cultural aspects of writing, and in particular the difficulties learners may experience in acquiring conventions of writing in a second language. More recently, with the "social turn" alluded to above, SLA researchers are using the term **intercultural rhetoric** to more appropriately "account for the richness of rhetorical variation or written texts and the varying contexts in which they are constructed" (Connor, Nagelhout, & Rozycki, 2008, p. 9).

In his original article, Kaplan (1966) presented a schematic diagram of how three language families conventionally organize an essay. English and Russian (languages) and Semitic, Oriental, and Romance (language families) were described through what have now been dubbed "doodles" to characterize the structure of an essay. English was depicted as a straight line from one point to another, Semitic languages as a jagged set of lines, and Oriental languages as a spiral. Kaplan's descriptions were clearly inspired by the Whorfian Hypothesis, and as Connor (2002) attests, the writing conventions of a language in many ways *define* a culture.

 CLASSROOM CONNECTIONS

In what ways does writing in an L2 that you have taken define the culture of the language? What are some specific conventions or ways of organizing that you feel are reflective of the culture? How would you teach those conventions to learners of English or learners of another L2 you are familiar with?

The doodles, graphically interesting but overgeneralized, became the object of a good deal of criticism (Raimes, 1998; Leki, 2000) for being ethnocentric and culturally deterministic, among other problems. But even by Kaplan's own admission, his characterizations were "notions" (Connor & Kaplan, 1987), and according to Kaplan himself, "much more detailed and accurate descriptions would be needed before a meaningful contrastive rhetorical system could be developed" (Kaplan, 2005, p. 388).

Leki (1991), Grabe and Kaplan (1996), Panetta (2001), Connor (2002, 1996), and Connor, Nagelhout, and Rozycki (2008) were among those who have taken significant steps to explore the possibility of such a meaningful system, and to take a comprehensive look at intercultural rhetoric from multiple perspectives, not the least of which is a social constructivist perspective. One difficulty in such research is describing conventions for writing that are truly language specific. Every language has genres of writing, and even within, say, an academic genre, disciplines vary in their views of acceptable writing. Writing contexts (who is writing, to whom, and for what purpose) and specific conventions within subgroups of genres (e.g., a scientific laboratory report; a personal narrative essay) may prove to be far more important for learners to attend to than a possible contrasting native language convention.

Another difficulty lies in the assumption that the second language writer's task is to follow certain conventional models, as opposed to engaging in a "socially grounded framework" (Hedgcock, 2005, p. 601) that more creatively encourages writers to develop their own voice as they simultaneously develop the kind of empathy toward the specific intended audience. LoCastro's (2008) study of Mexican students' rhetorical practices within given sociocultural contexts was illustrative of such socially grounded frameworks.

PRAGMATICS

Implicit in the above discussions of interactional competence, language functions, speech acts, conversation analysis, and intercultural rhetoric is the importance of **pragmatics** in conveying and interpreting meaning. Pragmatic constraints on language comprehension and production may be loosely thought of as the effect of *context* on strings of linguistic events. Consider the following conversation:

[Phone rings, a ten-year-old child answers the phone]

  Stefanie: Hello.
   Voice: Hi, Stef, is your Mom there?
  Stefanie: Just a minute. [cups the phone and yells] Mom! Phone!
    Mom: [from upstairs] I'm in the tub!
  Stefanie: [returning to the phone] She can't talk now. Wanna leave a message?
   Voice: Uh, [pause] I'll call back later. Bye.

Pragmatic considerations allowed all three participants to interpret what would otherwise be ambiguous sentences:

- "Is your Mom there?" is not, in a telephone context, a question that *requires* a yes or no answer.
- Stefanie's "Just a minute" confirmed to the caller that her mother was indeed home, and let the caller know that she would either (1) check to see if she was home and/or (2) get her to come to the phone.
- Stefanie's "Mom! Phone!" was easily interpreted by her mother as "Someone is on the phone who wants to talk with you."
- Mom's response, otherwise a rather worthless bit of information, in fact informed Stefanie that she was "indisposed," which was then conveyed to the caller.
- The caller didn't explicitly respond "no" to Stefanie's offer to take a message, but implicitly did so with "I'll call back later."

Undoubtedly it's these kinds of pragmatic elements that drive L2 learners crazy!

Sociopragmatics and Pragmalinguistics

Second language acquisition becomes an exceedingly difficult task when **sociopragmatic** (the interface between pragmatics and social organization) and **pragmalinguistic** (the intersection of pragmatics and linguistic forms) features are brought to bear. The difficulty of acquiring these forms of pragmatics, particularly due to intercultural factors, has been widely demonstrated in research (Turner, 1995, 1996; LoCastro, 1997, 2011; Kasper, 1998, 2009; Bardovi-Harlig, 1999a; Kasper & Rose, 2002; Kasper & Roever, 2005; Riddiford & Joe, 2010; Barron, 2012).

Variations in politeness and formality are particularly touchy:

> **American:** What an unusual necklace. It's beautiful!
> **Samoan:** Please take it. (Holmes & Brown, 1987, p. 526)

> **American teacher:** Would you like to read?
> **Russian student:** No, I would not. (Harlow, 1990, p. 328)

In both cases the nonnative English speakers misunderstood the illocutionary force (intended meaning) of the utterance within the contexts.

Grammatical knowledge, or in Bachman's terms, the *organizational* rules of a language, are fundamental to learning the pragmalinguistic features of an L2 (Bardovi-Harlig, 1999a). But grammar is just one dimension among many when compared to the complexity of catching on to a seemingly never-ending list of pragmatic constraints. Consider the following examples:

1. **Address** forms (how to address another person in conversation) can prove to be problematic for English speakers learning a language like German (Belz & Kinginger, 2003), and other languages that distinguish between formal and informal forms of "you" (German: *Sie* and *du*).
2. **Apologizing**, **complimenting**, and **face-saving** conventions (Turner, 1995) often prove to be difficult for second language learners to acquire.
3. Expressing **gratitude** becomes complex for Japanese learners of English who may express gratitude by saying "I'm sorry," a direct transfer from *Sumimasen,* which in Japanese commonly conveys a sense of gratitude, especially to persons of higher status (Kasper, 1998, p. 194).
4. **Cooperation** principles are especially difficult to master: the difference between "Rake the leaves" and "Don't you think you could rake the leaves?" (Turner, 1996, p. 1) is an example of how, in English, cooperation is sometimes given precedence over directness.
5. **Politeness** conventions are a complex set of pragmalinguistic factors that are difficult to learn, especially considering the possible range of politeness from extremely so, in formal situations ("I humbly beg you to consider . . ."), to casual ("Oh, sorry"), matter of fact expressions, to *im*politeness, "Would you *please* remove your feet?) (LoCastro, 2011, p. 328).

 CLASSROOM CONNECTIONS

One pragmatic element of language that is useful for classroom learners of an L2 is how to *disagree* politely. Have you ever been taught forms such as, "I see your point, but . . ." or "I think I understand what you are saying, but have you considered . . ."? What other phrases or sentences do we commonly use to politely disagree? How would you teach such classroom language?

Language and Gender

One of the major pragmatic factors affecting the acquisition of CC in virtually every language, and one that has received considerable attention over the last few decades, is the effect of one's sex on both production and reception of language. Differences between the way males and females speak have been noted for some time now (Lakoff, 1975; Nilsen et al., 1977; Holmes, 1989, 1991; Tannen, 1990, 1996; Sunderland, 2000; Davis & Skilton-Sylvester, 2004; McKay, 2005).

Among American English speakers, girls have been found to produce more *standard* language than boys. Women appear to use language that expresses more *uncertainty* (hedges, tag questions, rising intonation on declaratives, etc.) than men, suggesting less confidence in what they say. Men have been reported to *interrupt* more than women, and to use stronger *expletives*, while the latter use more *polite* forms. Tannen (1996) and others have found that in conversational interaction, males place more value on *status* and competing for the floor, while females value connection and *rapport*, fulfilling their role as more "cooperative and facilitative conversationalists, concerned for their partner's positive face needs" (Holmes, 1991, p. 210).

Studies of language and gender that were conducted in English-speaking cultures do not even begin to deal with some of the more overtly formal patterns for men's and women's talk in other languages. Among the Carib Indians in the Lesser Antilles, for example, males and females must use entirely different gender markings for abstract nouns (Allaire, 1997). In Japanese and Thai, women's and men's language is differentiated by formal (syntactic) variants, intonation patterns, and nonverbal expressions (Wintergerst & McVeigh, 2011). It is not uncommon for American men who learned Japanese from a female native-speaking Japanese teacher to inadvertently "say things like a woman" when conducting business with Japanese men, much to their embarrassment! (Dresser, 1996)

In English, another twist on the language and gender issue has been directed toward "sexist" language: language that either calls unnecessary attention to gender or is demeaning to one gender. Writers are cautioned to refrain from using what we used to call the "generic" *he* and instead to pluralize or to use *he or she*. What used to be *stewardesses, chairmen,* and *policemen* are now called *flight attendants, chairs,* and *police officers*. It is no longer considered appropriate to address a married woman as "Mrs. Robert Wilson," which is tantamount to considering "the Mrs." as being owned by the husband. Fortunately, the research of linguists like Janet Holmes, Robin Lakoff, and Deborah Tannen has called the attention of the public to such sexism, and we are seeing signs of the decline of this sort of language.

Research on language and gender has historically seen some theoretical shifts (Davis & Skilton-Sylvester, 2004; McKay, 2005). Reacting to views of women's language as *deficient* or inferior to men's, Robin Lakoff's (1975) work established the concept that women's language was *different* from men's language. Theoretical positions evolved to link *power* relationships to language and gender, especially power viewed as the social *domination* of women (Tannen, 1990, 1996). Current research on language and gender tends to acknowledge the *socially constructed* nature of language in any context (Cameron & Kulick, 2003). Current constructivist positions prefer to view gender as one of many factors that enter into communication: "the speaker, the setting, the cultural context, and the interactions of ethnicity, class, gender, power, sexual orientation, and a wide array of other social phenomena" (Davis & Skilton-Sylvester, 2004, p. 386).

CLASSROOM CONNECTIONS

What are some gender differences between English and any other L2 that you are familiar with? These might be words, phrases, gestures, or intonation patterns. What techniques could be used in a classroom to call the attention of students to such differences?

CORPUS ANALYSIS

A branch of discourse analysis that has experienced phenomenal growth and interest over the last decade or so is **corpus analysis** (also known as **corpus linguistics**), an approach to linguistic research that utilizes computer analyses of language. The great strength of corpus analysis, according to McEnery and Xiao (2011), "is its empirical nature, which pools together the intuitions of a great number of speakers [and writers] and makes linguistic analysis more objective" (p. 364).

A corpus is "a collection of texts—written, transcribed speech, or both—that is stored in electronic form and analyzed with the help of computer software programs" (Conrad, 2005, p. 393). The emphasis in corpus linguistics is on *naturally occurring* language, that is, texts created by users of the language for a communicative purpose. Corpora can be looked at in terms of syntax, lexicon, discourse, along with varieties of language, genres, dialects, styles, and registers. Corpora can consist of either written or spoken language and therefore offer tremendous possibilities for analysis of language across many different **genres**, or types of language use within specified contexts (Johns, 2002; Silberstein, 2011). In written form, corpora can be classified into academic, journalistic, or literary prose, for example. Speech corpora have been classified into conversations of many kinds: everyday conversation among friends, theater/television scripts, speeches, and even classroom language (Biber, Conrad, & Reppen, 1998; Kennedy, 1998; McCarthy, 1998; Biber & Conrad, 2001; Meyer, 2002; Conrad, 2005; McEnery & Xiao, 2011).

The advent of computer science presented almost endless possibilities for analysis. With data banks boasting hundreds of millions of words (Conrad, 2005, p. 394), our capacity to analyze language as it is actually used, and not as it *may* occur (e.g., in language textbooks that are sometimes guilty of manufacturing linguistic examples to illustrate a form), is greatly enhanced. We are able to identify word frequencies and co-occurrences. For example, according to the *Longman Dictionary of Contemporary English* (2004), the word *idea* co-occurs with the word *good* (as in "good idea") four times more often than with any other word, such as *great idea,* or *right idea.*

Grammatical patterns can also be identified. Biber *et al.* (1999) noted that the use of the word *get* as a passive verb rarely includes a *by* prepositional phrase that identifies an agent, and that most commonly, verbs in the *get* passive describe negative circumstances (*get hit, get stuck, get involved*) and are much more common in conversation than in fiction, news, or academic prose. And in discourse analysis, as noted by McCarthy (1998) and LoCastro (2011), such pragmatic features as discourse markers, turn-taking, and the social distance between speakers are now available for scrutiny. Even prosodic features of spoken language, such as the function of *intonation* to nominate and terminate topics, have been examined through corpus analysis (Wichmann, 2000).

For L2 teaching, the benefits of corpus analysis have been and will continue to be explored as this field grows (Conrad, 2005; Van Zante & Persiani, 2008; LoCastro, 2011; McEnery & Xiao, 2011; Silberstein, 2011). Some interesting possibilities have emerged: access by textbook writers and curriculum developers to naturally occurring language subcategorized into very specific varieties, styles, registers, and genres (O'Keefe & Farr, 2003; McEnery & Xiao, 2011); integration of grammar and vocabulary teaching (Conrad, 2000); studies of learner language (Conrad, 2005); and even corpus-based classroom activities that use concordancing and other techniques as the focus of classroom lessons (Burnard & McEnery, 2000; Aston, 2001).

For teachers who are unfamiliar with corpus analysis, Frankenberg-Garcia (2012) proposed a series of task-based, consciousness-raising exercises to help novice teachers to understand the basics of corpora. These included tips on accessing different corpora, formulating corpus queries, including queries that involve strings of words, and interpreting corpus output. Even more to the point, Bill Walker (2012) offered a textbook for ESL on academic English vocabulary that draws heavily on corpus analysis, but all framed for ease of use by both teacher and student. By systematically exposing students to numerous collocations for each item on a standard Academic Word List, Walker not only teaches vocabulary in *context*, but also connects lexical and grammatical factors in "lexicogrammatical production" (p. vi).

 CLASSROOM CONNECTIONS

What are some examples in an L2 you have taken of *collocations* (words that co-occur with other words)? For a given word, if you know a few of its collocations, how might that help you to teach the meaning and context of the word?

Of course, some cautionary statements are in order. First, frequency may not be equivalent to what Widdowson (1991) called "usefulness." Just because words, forms, and co-occurrences are highly frequent may not mean they are highly useful in a language learner's progress to proficiency. L2 curricula should therefore adopt frequency as "only *one* of the criteria used to influence instruction" (Kennedy, 1998, p. 290). Second, selection by curriculum and text-book writers on exactly what corpus data to include in a course may be the result of intuitive decisions (McEnery & Xiao, 2011). Braun (2007) asserted that the complexity of utilizing corpus data could mean that it may take a "generation of teachers for corpora to find their way into the language class-room" (p. 308).

However, others bear witness to materials and teacher training programs that are already doing so with "tips for teachers" (Chapelle & Jamieson, 2008, p. 49), student-friendly corpus-based textbook exercises (Walker, 2012), and teacher awareness-raising workshops (Frankenberg-Garcia, 2012). Corpus analysis has already enlightened not only our L2 teaching methodology, but our understanding of the nature of discourse in general.

NONVERBAL COMMUNICATION

Research on communicative competence over the last five decades has over-whelmingly been devoted to *verbal* language—that which is emitted from our mouths and our pens (or computers). Yet, every psychologist and communica-tions expert will tell you that in most face-to-face exchanges, it is not *what* you say that counts but *how* you say it—what you convey with body language, gestures, eye contact, physical distance, and other nonverbal messages.

Why the mismatch? Where is the comparable stockpile of research on *non-verbal* communication? Perhaps it is because nonverbal language is so difficult to quantify, to objectively observe, and so idiosyncratic even *within* sociocul-tural communities that it defies definition? The very *first* chapter of Norine Dresser's book, *Multicultural Manners* (2005), is on "body language." Wintergerst and McVeigh (2011) devote a whole chapter of their *Tips for Teaching Culture* to nonverbal communication. And for all of us "innocents abroad" (to borrow from Mark Twain's famous book title), communicating across cultures—and understanding our own consternation over what we see, hear, touch, and smell—is of paramount importance.

Research has identified a number of *functions* of nonverbal communica-tion (Ting-Toomey, 1999; Andersen, 2007; Kinsbourne & Jordan, 2009; Burgoon, Guerrero, & Floyd, 2011), all of which parallel the sociopragmatic and pragma-linguistic elements described in this chapter. Nonverbal functions include the following, among others, in both "sending" and "receiving" modes:

1. Managing a conversation; interpreting certain signals (initiating conversa-tion, showing interest, moving to new topic, terminating a conversation)
2. Adding emphasis or "accent" (especially with gestures) to verbal lan-guage; comprehending the meaning of such kinesic, kinesthetic, and other signals

3. Making a positive impression on another person ("putting your best foot forward"); forming impressions of those you converse with
4. Revealing your identity; "reading" another's identity (social status, professionalism, open-mindedness)
5. Expressing emotions and attitudes; understanding another's feelings and "subtexts" in a conversation ("coloring" the verbal language; candor)

Language becomes distinctly human through its nonverbal dimension, or what Edward Hall (1959) called the "silent language." The expression of culture is so bound up in nonverbal communication that the barriers to culture learning are often more nonverbal than verbal. In aural comprehension, only one of the five sensory modalities is used: hearing. But there remain in our communicative repertoire several other senses by which we communicate every day. Let's take a look at this "hidden dimension" (Hall, 1966) of language.

Kinesics

Every culture and language uses gesture, or **kinesics**, in unique but clearly interpretable ways. "There was speech in their dumbness, language in their very gesture," wrote Shakespeare in *The Winter's Tale*. All cultures throughout the history of humankind have relied on kinesics for conveying important messages. Books like Dresser's *Multicultural Manners* (2005) join a long string of manuals (e.g., Hall, 1959, 1966; Fast, 1970) offering lighthearted but provocative insights on the use of kinesics in North American and other cultures. Today, virtually every book on communication explains how you communicate—and miscommunicate—when you fold your arms, cross your legs, stand, walk, move your eyes and mouth, and so on.

But as universal as kinesic communication is, there is tremendous variation cross-culturally and cross-linguistically in the specific interpretations of gestures as McCafferty and Stam (2009) so ably demonstrated. Human beings all move their heads, blink their eyes, move their arms and hands, but the significance of these movements varies from society to society. How would you nonverbally express the following in your native language: agreement, disagreement, lack of interest, flirting, disgust?

Are those signals the same in another language and culture? Sometimes a gesture that is appropriate in one culture is obscene or insulting in another. Nodding the head, for example, means "yes" among most European language speakers. But among the Ainu of Japan, "yes" is expressed by bringing the arms to the chest and waving them. The Negritos of interior Malaya indicate "yes" by thrusting the head sharply forward, and people from the Punjab of India throw their heads sharply backward. The Ceylonese curve their chins gracefully downward in an arc to the left shoulder, whereas Bengalis rock their heads rapidly from one shoulder to the other.

Eye Contact

Is **eye contact** appropriate between two participants in a conversation? When is it polite *not* to maintain eye contact? Cultures differ widely in this particular visual modality of nonverbal communication. In American culture it is permissible, for example, for two participants of unequal status to maintain prolonged eye contact. In fact, an American might interpret lack of eye contact as discourteous lack of attention, while in Japanese culture eye contact might be considered rude.

Not only is eye *contact* itself an important category, but within eye-contact cultures, "eye gestures" (also called **oculesics**) are in keys to communication. Eyes (and surrounding anatomy—eyelids, eyebrows) signal interest, boredom, surprise, empathy, hostility, attraction, true love, understanding, misunderstanding, and other messages.

Facial Expressions

Perhaps more than any other nonverbal mode of communication, facial expressions are a rich source for conveying information, understanding feelings, and communicating emotions. "The face is far more than a window into our emotional world; it is a primary channel of interpersonal communication that has evolved as a clear and instantaneous form of human communication," writes Peter Andersen (2007, p. 36).

While intercultural variations are myriad, many experts concede that there is a basic set of facial expressions that are universal, innately acquired, and basically interpreted uniformly across cultures and languages. These are expressions happiness, sadness, fear, anger, disgust, and surprise (Guererro, Andersen, & Trost, 1998). Consider, for example, the universal power of a smile. Yes, of course, some smiles are a cover for meanness and ill will, but in normal communicative situations, a smile is universally interpreted as an expression not only of happiness, but of reaching out in friendly exchange.

Proxemics

Cultures vary widely in acceptable *distances* one can maintain in face-to-face conversation. Edward Hall (1966) calculated acceptable distances, or **proxemics**, for public, social-consultative, personal, and intimate discourse. He noted, for example, that Americans feel that a certain personal space "bubble" has been violated if a stranger stands closer than 20 to 24 inches away (unless space is restricted, such as in a subway or an elevator). However, says Hall, a typical member of a Latin American culture might feel that such a physical distance would be too great. The interesting thing is that neither party is necessarily aware of what is wrong when the distance is not right. They merely have vague feelings of discomfort or anxiety.

Sometimes objects—desks, counters, furniture—serve to maintain certain physical distances. Such objects tend to establish both the overall style and relationship of participants. Thus, a counter between two people maintains a consultative mode. Similarly, the presence of a desk or a computer monitor will set the tone of a conversation. Again, however, different cultures interpret different messages in such objects. In some cultures, objects might enhance the communicative process, but in other cases they impede it.

Artifacts

The nonverbal messages of **artifacts** such as clothing and ornamentation will signal a person's sense of self-esteem, socioeconomic class, and character. Jewelry also conveys certain messages. In a multicultural conversation group, such artifacts, along with other nonverbal signals, can be a significant factor in lifting barriers, identifying certain personality characteristics, and setting a general mood. In job interviews, the artifacts of clothing, jewelry, and (see below) smell can spell the difference between getting the job or not (Burgoon, Guerrero, & Floyd, 2011).

Kinesthetics

Tania is introduced to her new boss in the workplace. Overjoyed to have joined the company, Tania enthusiastically grasps Mr. Wilson's hand in a two-handed handshake. A minute later, on departing his office, as she expresses her thanks, she touches his shoulder and flashes a warm smile.

What's wrong with this picture? Touching, sometimes referred to as **kinesthetics**, also called **haptics**, is another culturally loaded aspect of nonverbal communication. How we touch others and where we touch them is sometimes the most misunderstood aspect of nonverbal communication. Touching in some cultures signals a very personal or intimate style, while in other cultures extensive touching is commonplace. Knowing the limits and conventions is important for clear and unambiguous communication.

Olfactory Dimensions

Our noses also receive sensory nonverbal messages. The **olfactory** modality is an important one not only for the animal kingdom, but for the human race as well, and cultures have established varying sensitivities to smells. The proliferation of cosmetics has created in most technological societies a penchant for perfumes, lotions, creams, and powders as acceptable and even necessary. Natural human odors, especially perspiration, are deemed undesirable. In some societies, of course, the smell of human perspiration is quite acceptable and even attractive. Even our cars, closets, kitchens, and bathrooms (especially bathrooms!) are the locus of many options for snuffing out (no pun intended) whatever odors might otherwise offend our nostrils.

 CLASSROOM CONNECTIONS

To what extent have you been specifically taught nonverbal language such as gestures, eye contact, and proxemics? Many language courses fail to attend to this significant mode of communication, under the mistaken assumption that verbal forms—sounds, words, phrases, and sentences—are sufficient for a learner to cope in a foreign language. Which nonverbal aspects would you teach, and how would you teach them?

We cannot underestimate the importance of nonverbal communication in second language learning and in conversational analysis (Andersen, 2007). CC includes nonverbal competence—knowledge of all the varying nonverbal semantics of the second culture, and an ability to both send and receive nonverbal signals unambiguously.

CLASSROOM APPLICATIONS: CLT AND TASK-BASED LANGUAGE TEACHING

The "push toward communication" (Higgs & Clifford, 1982) in L2 pedagogy has, for over three decades now, been relentless. Researchers have defined and redefined the construct of communicative competence (Savignon, 2005) and explored the myriad functions of language that learners must be able to accomplish. We have described spoken and written discourse, pragmatic conventions, styles, and nonverbal communication. With this storehouse of knowledge we have valiantly pursued the goal of learning how best to teach *communication*—teaching a little *about* language, but mostly focusing intently on teaching learners to *do* language.

Communicative Language Teaching

Among the shifting sands of L2 methodology since the late 1970s, one overall catch phrase to describe the prevailing approach to pedagogy has stuck with us: **communicative language teaching** (CLT). A glance at current journals in SLA reveals a huge array of material on CLT. Numerous textbooks for teachers and teacher trainers expound on the nature of communicative approaches and offer techniques for varying ages and purposes. In short, wherever you look in the literature today, you will find reference to the communicative nature of language classes.

CLT is best understood as an **approach**, rather than a method (Richards & Rodgers, 2001). It is therefore a unified but broadly based theoretical position about the nature of language and of language learning and teaching (Littlewood, 2011). It is nevertheless difficult to synthesize all of the various definitions that have been offered. From the earlier seminal works in CLT (Widdowson, 1978b; Breen & Candlin, 1980; Savignon, 1983) up to more recent work (Nunan, 2004; Ellis, 2005; Savignon, 2005; Brown, 2007; Littlewood, 2011), we have interpretations enough to send us reeling. For some, the fact that CLT has meant a multitude of different things to different people has led them to question the continued use of the term (Bax, 2003; Spada, 2007, p. 272).

William Littlewood (2011) contended, however, that the term CLT still serves a useful function as an "umbrella" term to capture the essence of classroom methodological approaches designed to "improve students' ability to communicate" (p. 542). This concept is starkly in contrast with methods that aim to teach "bits of language just because they exist, without relating them to their meaning or how they are used for communication" (p. 542).

For the sake of simplicity and directness, I offer the following four interconnected characteristics as a definition of CLT.

1. Classroom goals are focused on all of the components of CC and not restricted to grammatical or linguistic competence.
2. Language techniques are designed to engage learners in the pragmatic, authentic, functional use of language for meaningful purposes. Organizational language forms are not the central focus but rather aspects of language that enable the learner to accomplish those purposes.
3. Fluency and accuracy are seen as complementary principles underlying communicative techniques. At times fluency may have to take on more importance than accuracy in order to keep learners meaningfully engaged in language use.
4. In the communicative classroom, students ultimately have to use the language, productively and receptively, in unrehearsed contexts.

These four characteristics underscore some major departures from earlier approaches. While structurally (grammatically) sequenced curricula were a mainstay of language teaching for centuries, CLT suggests that grammatical structure might better be *subsumed* under various functional categories. A great deal of use of authentic language is implied in CLT, as teachers attempt to build fluency (Littlewood, 2011), but not at the expense of clear, unambiguous, direct communication. In order to center on "unrehearsed" communicative contexts, the mushrooming capability of technology (Internet, video, television, audio recordings, computer software) can come to the aid of teachers, especially novice teachers or nonnative speakers of the L2 being taught.

CLASSROOM CONNECTIONS

In your experiences learning languages in classrooms, did the methodology fit the description of CLT above? Completely or partially? What are some specific examples of activities you remember that were CLT-based? What would you like to have seen by way of any changes toward more communicative techniques?

Task-Based Language Teaching (TBLT)

Among recent manifestations of CLT, **task-based language teaching** (TBLT) has emerged as a major focal point of language teaching practice worldwide (Bygate, Skehan, & Swain, 2001; Skehan, 2003; Nunan, 2004; Ellis, 2005; Robinson & Gilabert, 2007; Kelch & Yang, 2008; Robinson, 2011). As the profession has continued to emphasize classroom interaction, learner-centered teaching, **authenticity**, and viewing the learner's own experiences as important contributors to learning, TBLT draws the attention of teachers and learners to tasks in the classroom. Skehan (1998, p. 95) describes a **task** as an activity or a related set of techniques in which (1) meaning is primary, (2) there is a problem to solve, (3) a relationship to real-world activities, and (4) an objective that can be assessed in terms of an outcome.

David Nunan (2004), among others (Willis, 1996; Skehan, 2003), is careful to distinguish between **target tasks** (uses of language in the world beyond the classroom) and **pedagogical tasks** (those that occur in the classroom). The latter is exemplified in a *map-oriented problem-solving task*, which might involve (1) teacher-initiated schema setting comments, (2) a review of appropriate grammar and/or vocabulary useful for the task, (3) pair or group work to propose and discuss solutions, and (4) a whole-class reporting procedure. The last two are good examples of *pedagogical* tasks designed to equip learners with the communicative language needed for accomplishing the *target* task of giving someone directions.

How is one to judge to *difficulty* of a task? Given the multifaceted nature of tasks and the observation of many practitioners that tasks widely vary in lexical, grammatical, and discourse complexity, may we posit a valid sequence of tasks in a language course?

In some research (Long, 2007; Robinson & Gilabert, 2007; Kim, 2009; Robinson, 2011) the issue of **task complexity** has begun to be unraveled, with some limited results. Long (2007) suggested a number of parameters for sequencing tasks: linguistic (grammatical, lexical) complexity, utility (usefulness), task conditions (circumstances under which the pedagogical tasks are carried out), the interactional nature of the task, and the extent to which negotiation of meaning is required (e.g., open-ended tasks are more difficult than closed-ended). Others (Garcia Mayo, 2007) suggested gauging complexity by cognitive complexity (e.g., familiarity of topic, sufficiency of information), communicative stress (e.g., time pressure, stakes), learner factors (intelligence, personal experience), and processing demands imposed by the structure of the task.

TBLT is an approach that urges teachers, in their lesson and curriculum designs, to focus on many of the communicative factors discussed in this chapter. In order to accomplish a task, a learner needs to have sufficient organizational competence, illocutionary competence to convey intended meaning, and strategic competence to choose among linguistic options and, when needed, to repair attempts to communicate. Add to these other factors in interactional competence, pragmatics, and even nonverbal ability, and you begin to glimpse the complexity of the acquisition of CC for an L2 learner.

✯   ✯   ✯   ✯   ✯

Kathy felt that her communicative progress in Thai was "almost 100% emotional." She loved everything about the Thai people and culture, and felt that her socio-cultural immersion was key. She had very few American and British friends. Her circle of friendship was almost exclusively Thai. Her strategic competence was crucial: She listened intently to how people conversed; she constantly asked people how to say things, asked for corrections, and became "almost a nuisance" with her Thai friends. She admitted she had "zero CALP" in Thai, and that all her use of Thai was BICS. Her advice to others: "Dive in! Love and respect the people you're with."

SUGGESTED READINGS

Canale, M., & Swain, M. (1980). Theoretical bases of communicative approaches to second language teaching and testing. *Applied Linguistics, 1,* 1–47.

This seminal work, the first article in the inaugural issue of Applied Linguistics, remains important reading for its historical perspective.

McEnery, T., & Xiao, R. (2011). What corpora can offer in language teaching and learning. In E. Hinkel (Ed.), *Handbook of research in second language teaching and learning: Volume II.* (pp. 364–380). New York: Routledge.

Pedagogical applications to corpus analysis are reviewed with and evaluation of the promise of the use of corpora in language classrooms.

Connor, U., Nagelhout, E., & Rozycki, W. (Eds.). (2008). *Contrastive rhetoric: Reaching to intercultural rhetoric.* Amsterdam: John Benjamins.

Multiple authors provide an update on contrastive rhetoric, with new light on the topic, suggesting "intercultural" rhetoric as a more appropriate concept.

Dresser, N. (2005). *Multicultural manners: Essential rules of etiquette for the 21st century.* Hoboken, NJ: Wiley.

A multiplicity of vignettes on communication, especially nonverbal communication, are offered for the lay person, with attention to the various faux pas we can all commit.

Littlewood, W. (2011). Communicative language teaching: an expanding concept for a changing world. In E. Hinkel (Ed.), *Handbook of research in second language teaching and learning: Volume II.* (pp. 541–557). New York: Routledge.

An updated synopsis of research and practice in CLT around the world, with references and commentary on various manifestations of CLT.

LANGUAGE LEARNING EXPERIENCE: JOURNAL ENTRY 8

Note: See Chapter 1 for general guidelines for writing a journal on a previous or concurrent language learning experience.

- In an L2 you have taken, would you say you are "communicatively competent"? Defend your response using some of the categories discussed in the first part of this chapter.
- Make two lists: activities your teacher has used (used) to promote (a) BICS and (b) CALP. Do you agree with the proportion of one to the other, given the purposes of your class?
- Are you satisfied with your progress in acquiring some of the discourse features, conversation rules, and pragmatic conventions of your foreign language? Describe what you think you can "do," in your language, in these domains.
- If you are familiar enough with writing conventions in your foreign language, describe some of the differences you perceive between your native language and the foreign language. To what extent do the differences reflect cultural points of view?
- Is your foreign language gender-loaded in any way? Describe.
- Describe the verbal and nonverbal manifestations of different styles (from intimate to oratorical) in your foreign language.

• Does your teacher engage in CLT? Evaluate the methodology of your class on the basis of the four principles of CLT. Does the teacher use what you could describe as task-based teaching? If so, describe an activity that you think was, to some extent anyway, task based.

FOR THE TEACHER: ACTIVITIES (A) & DISCUSSION (D)

Note: For each of the "Classroom Connections" in this chapter, you may wish to turn them into individual or pair-work discussion questions.

1. (A) Divide the class into small groups. Direct them to share experiences in L2 classes in terms of the extent to which *BICS* or *CALP* was the primary focus of the class in general. Then, have them identify certain activities that seemed to promote BICS and others that promoted CALP. Have each group share a couple of examples with the whole class.

2. (D) How well does *strategic competence* fit into (is it subsumed under) the overarching concept of language competence? Ask the class to share their thoughts. How do the learning and communication strategies discussed in Chapter 5 fit into strategic competence as discussed here?

3. (D) Hatch suggested (pages 218–219) that in L2 learning, one should learn how to "do" conversation and interact verbally first, and out of this interaction will emerge grammatical structures. Does this mean that language classes for adults should teach conversation rules and gambits before teaching basic grammatical or phonological structures? If not, how would Hatch's suggestion play out in an L2 course?

4. (A) To illustrate conversation rules and conventions in action, try this: In groups of five or six students each, appoint two people to be observers only. Ask the rest of the group to engage in a discussion of a controversial topic: abortion, women's rights, nonviolence, race, religion, homophobia, a current political issue, or whatever. The observers should note on a piece of paper specifically what *linguistic* (verbal) and *nonverbal* features members of the group used to accomplish the following: (a) attention getting, (b) interrupting, (c) turn taking, (d) clarification, (e) topic changing. Observers might also take note of cooperation, face-saving, and politeness conventions that were used. Ask the observers to report their findings to the rest of the class, and the group participants to make any further comments they wish.

5. (A) Split the class up into pairs, and ask each pair to brainstorm some possible contributions of *corpus linguistics* to language teaching methodology or materials. Ask a few pairs to share their ideas with the rest of the class.

6. (D) Ask your students to compare English with other languages (that they are familiar with) in terms of *gender* issues. Are there differences in verbal or nonverbal forms that one uses to address women and men? In the way women and men talk? Do other languages reflect sexism, as English does?

7. (A) Divide the class into groups in such a way that each group has members that are familiar with a variety of languages/cultures. Using the *nonverbal* categories in this chapter, compare nonverbal expressions in English-speaking culture with those of another language/culture. How might such differences be taught in a foreign language class? Have the groups share their findings afterward.

8. (D) Ask students to share, from their own L2 classes, how the principles of *CLT* and/or task-based instruction have been applied. Or, if they have not been applied, how might they develop a more communicative or task-based approach in an L2 class they have taken?

CHAPTER 9

INTERLANGUAGE

One day in the morning

It was hot continue one month ago

Look at everywhere with sad

The leaves fall down when the wind blow

On the floor full of leaves

Side by side everywhere

Anything was confusion

Look like somebody was to trouble

By pooress of mankind

This is a short essay written by an ESL student, describing a photo of an elderly man, somewhat shabbily dressed, sitting on a park bench in the fall. In the original it was written in normal essay format. I have only removed some punctuation and reframed the lines for poetic effect. Who says learner creativity is fractured and incoherent? Would you give an "A+" to this student for putting together such a vivid description? Would you correct any errors?

In this chapter we'll be looking at one of the central areas of interest in SLA over many decades: the L2 learner's *linguistic* development from a budding beginner to an advanced, competent user of the L2. What are some of the typical stepping stones in that journey, from encountering the first few words or phrases in a language to communicating effectively across modes of comprehension and production in a variety of sociocultural contexts? How does the linguistic system of the L2 become subsumed into a person's neural networks? What are some of the roadblocks? How can teachers help learners to make that journey?

In recent years researchers and teachers have come more and more to understand that second language learning is a process of the *creative* construction of a system in which learners are consciously testing hypotheses about the target language from a number of possible sources of knowledge: knowledge about language in general, the L1, the L2 itself, discernment of sociopragmatic constraints, and knowledge about life, people, and the surrounding universe. In acting upon their environment, learners construct what to them is a legitimate system of language—a structured assembly of rules that for the time being brings some order to the linguistic chaos that confronts them.

LEARNER LANGUAGE

Until the 1960s, L2 learners had been viewed for perhaps centuries as "incomplete" users of their foreign language—learners who were at best in the process of slowly and *imperfectly* "approximating" (Nemser, 1971) nativelike proficiency. Moreover, L2 learning was seen to be primarily a process of "overcoming" the interfering effects of the L1 (to be described further in this chapter). In the last few decades of the twentieth century, this view of the L2 learner's journey markedly changed. SLA began to be examined in much the same way that first language acquisition had been studied: Learners were looked on not as producers of malformed language replete with mistakes, but as intelligent beings proceeding through logical, systematic stages of acquisition, *creatively* acting upon their linguistic environment. In a hypothesis-testing process of multiple trials and errors, with many ups and downs, learners slowly internalized a constructed linguistic system as they perceived the L2.

A number of terms were coined to describe the perspective that stresses the *legitimacy* of learners' second language systems. The best known of these is **interlanguage**, a term that Larry Selinker (1972) adapted from Uriel Weinreich's (1953) term "interlingual," and that Pit Corder (1971) later popularized. Interlanguage refers to the separateness of an L2 learner's system, a system that has a structurally intermediate status between the native and target languages. William Nemser (1971) preferred to stress the successive approximation to the target language in his term **approximative system**. And Corder (1971) also used the term **idiosyncratic dialect** to connote the concept that the learner's language is unique to a particular individual, that the rules of the learner's language are peculiar to that individual alone.

While each of these designations emphasized a particular viewpoint, they shared the concept that second language learners are forming their own self-constructed linguistic systems—neither the system of the L1 nor the system of the L2, but a system based upon the best attempt of learners to bring order and structure to the linguistic stimuli surrounding them. The interlanguage hypothesis led to a new era of second language research and teaching and represented a significant breakthrough for the study of SLA.

The most obvious approach to analyzing interlanguage is to study the speech and writing of learners, or what is also called **learner language** (James, 1990; Lightbown & Spada, 2006; Adamson, 2008). *Production* (speaking and writing) data is empirically observable and is hypothesized to be reflective of a learner's underlying production competence, revealing developmental changes of linguistic forms over time. *Comprehension* (listening and reading) must, of course, not be ignored in a description of learner language, any more than considering production in child L1 acquisition as sufficient to paint a full picture. However, because of the difficulty of objectively measuring comprehension, and because of the observability of production, learner language research has relied heavily on the latter. What have several decades of observing learner language taught us?

 CLASSROOM CONNECTIONS

In your experience learning an L2, what are some examples of your developing learner language? What phonological or grammatical forms did you produce that were not quite "right"? Were any of them unique to your own "idiosyncratic dialect"? Were you aware of producing these forms? Did your teacher help you to *notice* your errors? How would you help students to learn from their mistakes?

Stages of Learner Language Development

You will recall that children acquiring their L1 proceed through a number of identifiable stages. Is it possible to specify similar stages for L2 learner language? The answer is yes and no. Yes, if you are satisfied with relatively broad strokes and fuzzy lines of distinction between stages. No, if those strokes are too broad for your liking, and if you take into consideration a great deal of variation among L2 learners. Let's pursue the "yes" side of this, with due caution.

A synthesis of models proposed by Corder (1973), Gass and Selinker (2001), and Long (2003) suggests that L2 learners progress through four stages, based on observations of learners' speech (and writing) production and on the errors they make in the process.

> **Presystematic stage.** Corder (1973) observed that in the early stages L2 learners may make a number of random errors, since they are only marginally aware of a given subset of the L2 system. Consider these actual written utterances by ESL students, in which the intended meaning is quite a mystery:
>
> > The different city is another one in the another two.
> > I want to become a physicotrafic. I will studied for six years.
> > Society has it's hard-living's bitterness way into the decaded-dragging and full troubled life.
>
> The incoherence of such sentences may have come from learners' guesses (do you have any idea what a "physicotrafic" is?) or bold attempts to express a thought, but without control of structure and/or lexicon.

Emergent stage. Now, the learner's linguistic production becomes more consistent as certain rules, words, and phrases (possibly correct in the learner's mind) are induced and applied. A hearer or reader should at this stage be able to discern what the intended meaning is. Here are more written ESL examples (that might make you smile a little):

> He was just a peony in the hands of big powders.
> All work without a play makes Jack a doornail.
> American food made me interesting to taste.
> Wars do not happen on the spot of moments.

While meaning may be interpretable, this stage may also be characterized by some **backsliding** (Selinker, 1972), in which the learner seems to have grasped a rule or principle and then regresses to a previous stage. The phenomenon of moving from a correct form to an incorrect form and then back to correctness is referred to as **U-shaped learning** (Gass & Selinker, 2001). In general the learner is still unable to correct errors when they are pointed out by someone else. Avoidance of structures and topics is typical. Consider the following conversation between a learner (L) and a native speaker (NS) of English:

> **L:** I go New York.
> **NS:** You're going to New York?
> **L:** [*doesn't understand*] What?
> **NS:** You will go to New York?
> **L:** Yes.
> **NS:** When?
> **L:** Uh, 1992.
> **NS:** Oh, you went to New York in 1992.
> **L:** Yes, uh, . . . I go 1992.

Such a conversation is reminiscent of those mentioned in Chapter 2, where children in L1 situations could not discern any error in their speech.

Systematic stage. In this third stage the learner is now able to manifest more consistency in producing the second language. The most salient difference between the second and third stages is the ability of learners to repair their errors when they are pointed out—even very subtly—to them. Consider the English learner who described a popular fishing-resort area:

> **L:** Many fish are in the lake. The fish are serving in the restaurants near the lake.
> **NS:** [*smiling*] The *fish* are serving?
> **L:** Oh, no, [*laughing*] uh, fish are *being served* in restaurants!

Postsystematic stage. In the final stage, which some researchers (Long, 2003) call **stabilization,** the learner has relatively few errors and has mastered the system to the point that fluency and intended meanings are not problematic. This fourth stage is characterized by the learner's ability to self-correct.

> In this space age when many satellites are hovering on our heads—ah, I mean, uh, *over* heads.
>
> He passed out with very high score—sorry, I mean, he *passed* test—with high score.
>
> I like Abraham Lincoln because he has known many people in Japan—um, ah, no, no, he . . . many, many Japan people know *him*!

In the fourth stage, learners can stabilize too fast, allowing minor errors to slip by undetected, and thus manifest **fossilization** (Selinker & Lamendella, 1979) of their language, a concept that will be defined and discussed later in this chapter.

 CLASSROOM CONNECTIONS

Can you recall going through any of the four stages of interlanguage development described above? What were some manifestations of your moving from one stage to another? What techniques did your teacher(s) use to help you to progress from, say, an emergent stage to a systematic stage?

It should be made clear that these four stages do not *globally* describe a learner's status in the development of the L2. For example, learners would rarely be in an emergent stage for *all* L2 subsystems. One might be in a second stage with respect to, say, the perfect tense system, and in the third or fourth stage when it comes to simple present and past tenses. Likewise, in pragmatic development, a learner could be highly adept at certain conversational gambits but at a loss to adapt to a more consultative style (Kasper, 1998). We also need to remember that production *errors* alone are inadequate measures of overall competence. They are salient features of L2 learners' interlanguage, but *correct* utterances warrant our attention and, especially in the teaching-learning process, deserve positive reinforcement.

Variation in Learner Language

Lest you be tempted to assume that all learner language is orderly and systematic, a caveat is in order. A great deal of attention has been given to the **variation** that learners manifest in their interlanguage development (N. Ellis, 1987, 2007a; Tarone, 1988; James, 1990; Bayley & Preston, 1996; Romaine, 2003; Adamson, 2008). Nick Ellis (2007b) noted that learner language development, "which is for the most part gradual and incremental, also evidences sudden changes in performance, suggesting occasional fundamental restructuring of the underlying grammar" (p. 90).

Some variation in learner language can be explained by what Gatbonton (1983) described as the "gradual diffusion" of incorrect forms of language in emergent and systematic stages of development. First, incorrect forms coexist with correct forms; then the incorrect forms are expunged. Context and style have also been identified as a source of variation, along with gender-based variation (Romaine, 1999). In classrooms, the type of task can affect variation (Tarone & Parrish, 1988). And variation can be caused, in both tutored and untutored learning, by the extent to which a learner is exposed to norms.

While one simply must expect a good proportion of learner language data to fall beyond our capacity for systematic categorization, one of the current debates in SLA theory centers on the extent to which variability can indeed be systematically explained. The essence of the problem is that learners can and do exhibit a tremendous degree of variation in the way they speak (and write) second languages, but is that variation predictable? Can we explain it? Or do we dismiss it all as "free variation"?

Notable among models of variability are Elaine Tarone's (1988) **capability continuum paradigm** and Rod Ellis's (1986, 1994a) **variable competence model**, both of which have inspired others to carry out research on the issue (Adamson, 1988; Tarone, 1988; Young, 1988; Crookes, 1989; Bayley & Preston, 1996; Foster & Skehan, 1996; Preston, 1996). Tarone (1988) focused her research on *contextual* variability, that is, the extent to which both linguistic and situational contexts may help to systematically describe what might otherwise appear simply as unexplained variation. Tarone suggested four domains of variation: (1) linguistic context; (2) psychological processing factors; (3) social context; and (4) language function.

The emphasis on context led researchers to look carefully at the conditions under which certain linguistic forms vary. For example, an English learner at two different points in the same conversation, a few minutes apart, said:

He must paid for the insurance.
He must pay the parking fee.

An examination of the linguistic *context* appears to explain the variation. Sentence 1 was uttered in the context of describing an event in the past, and sentence 2 referred to the present moment. Thus the apparent free variation of the main verb form in a modal auxiliary context is explained.

An interesting area of learner language research has focused on the variation that arises from the disparity between *classroom* contexts and *natural* situations outside language classes (R. Ellis, 1990b, 1997, 2005; Buczowska & Weist, 1991; Doughty, 1991, 2003). These studies suggest that by calling students' attention to certain linguistic features, instructional settings may actually cause some variation that is not present in the same students' output in natural contexts. Mark James (2007), for example, showed that variation could be the result of general principles of *transfer* of learning. On the other hand, the unmonitored nature of natural conversation is also cause for variation as learners "let down their guard," which spurred Rod Ellis (1994b) to hypothesize a storehouse of "variable interlanguage rules" (p. 269) depending on how *automatic* and how *analyzed* the rules are.

The bottom line? Even the tiniest of the bits and pieces of learner language, however random or variable they may appear to be at first blush, could be quite systematic if we only keep on looking. It is often tempting as a teacher or as a researcher to dismiss a good deal of learners' production as a mystery beyond explanation. Short of engaging in an absurd game of straining at linguistic gnats, we must guard against yielding to that temptation.

 CLASSROOM CONNECTIONS

In some ways, variation in learner language is the manifestation of a natural process of numerous "ups and downs" in development. What were some possible examples of variation in your own learning of an L2? If a teacher hears a student producing an error that they once spoke correctly, what should the teacher do? Ignore it, or call the student's attention to it?

LEARNERS' ERRORS: WINDOWS OF OPPORTUNITY

Learning is fundamentally a process that involves the making of mistakes. Mistakes, misjudgments, miscalculations, and erroneous assumptions form an important aspect of learning virtually any skill or acquiring information. You learn to swim by first jumping into the water and flailing arms and legs until you discover that there is a combination of movements—a structured pattern— that succeeds in keeping you afloat and propelling you through the water. The first mistakes of learning to swim are giant ones, gradually diminishing as you learn from making those mistakes. Learning to swim, to play tennis, to type, or to read all involve a process in which success comes by profiting from mistakes, by using mistakes to obtain feedback from the environment, and with that feedback to make new attempts that successively approximate desired goals.

Language learning, in this sense, is like any other learning. We have already seen in Chapter 2 that children learning their first language make countless errors from the point of view of adult grammatical language. Many of these mistakes are logical in the limited linguistic system within which children operate, but, by carefully processing feedback from others, children slowly but surely learn to produce acceptable speech. L2 learning is a process that is just like first language learning in its trial-and-error nature. Inevitably learners will make mistakes in the process of acquisition, but most *successful* learners are those who convert those "bloopers" into learning opportunities.

Researchers and teachers of second languages came to realize that the mistakes a person made in this process of constructing a new system of language needed to be analyzed carefully, for they possibly held in them some of the keys to the understanding of the process of second language acquisition (James, 1998). As Corder (1967) noted, "A learner's errors . . . are significant in [that] they provide evidence of how language is learned or acquired, what strategies or procedures the learner is employing in the discovery of the language" (p. 167).

Mistakes versus Errors

In order to analyze learner language in an appropriate perspective, it is crucial to make a distinction between two very different phenomena: mistakes and errors. A **mistake** refers to a performance error that is either a random guess or a "slip," in that it is a failure to utilize a known system correctly. All people make mistakes, in both L1 and L2 production. Proficient users of a language are normally capable of recognizing and repairing such lapses, which do not stem from a deficiency in competence but from a temporary breakdown. These hesitations, slips of the tongue, random ungrammaticalities, and other performance lapses can usually be self-corrected. Consider the following examples, all spoken by L1 English users:

> Don't make so much noise. Remember, this isn't the only house we're in.
> It was so dark you couldn't see your face in front of you.
> She just fell heads over tails!

Mistakes must be carefully distinguished from **errors** of a second language learner, idiosyncrasies in the language of the learner that are direct manifestations of a system within which a learner is operating at the time. An error, a noticeable deviation from the adult grammar of a native speaker, reflects the competence of the learner. Learners of English who ask, "Does John can sing?" are in all likelihood reflecting a competence level in which all verbs require a preposed *do* auxiliary for question formation. As such, it is an error, most likely not a mistake, and an error that reveals a portion of the learner's competence in the target language.

CLASSROOM CONNECTIONS

In some ways, mistakes in learners' speech may be a sign of prog-ress: Learners are aware of what they "should" say, and, when questioned or corrected, are cognizant of the "right" way to say it. Can you think of stages when you were in the process of "cleaning up" your errors and may have made a few random mistakes? Teachers can help students to *notice* their linguistic output in class, and slowly convert systematic errors into appropriate forms. What are some techniques that your teacher used to help you notice your "goofs" in your L2?

Can you tell the difference between an error and a mistake? Not always. An error cannot be self-corrected, according to James (1998, p. 83), while mis-takes can be repaired if the deviation is pointed out to the speaker. Because of the prevalence of *variation* in learner language (referred to above), it is diffi-cult for a teacher to discern the fine line of distinction between errors and mistakes. An immediate prompted repair by a learner, followed moments later by repetition of the same deviant form could simply be indicative of a learner's accidental vacillation in making progress from one stage to another. Perhaps these are moments for teachers and learners to be patient with the ups and downs of interlanguage development.

Error Analysis

The fact that learners make errors—and that these errors can be observed, analyzed, and classified to reveal something of the system operating within the learner—led to a surge of study, in the last few decades of the twentieth cen-tury, of learners' errors, called **error analysis** (Corder, 1971, 1973; Burt & Kiparsky, 1972). Error analysis was distinguished from previous approaches to the study of errors by its examination of *all* possible sources of error, and not just those resulting from L1 interference. Some of those alternative sources include *intra*lingual errors within the L2, the sociopragmatic context of com-munication, numerous strategic techniques, and countless affective variables. We will turn to those sources later in this chapter.

There is a danger in too much attention to learners' errors. In teachers' observation and analysis of errors—for all that they do reveal about the learner—they should beware of placing too much attention on errors, lest they lose sight of the value of positive reinforcement of clearly expressed language that is a product of the learner's progress and development. While the dimin-ishing of errors is an important criterion for increasing language proficiency, the ultimate goal of second language learning is the attainment of communicative fluency. We do well, therefore, in the analysis of learners' errors, to engage in **performance analysis** or "interlanguage analysis" (Celce-Murcia & Hawkins, 1985), a less restrictive concept that places a healthy investigation of errors within the larger perspective of the learner's total language performance.

Another shortcoming in error analysis is an overemphasis on *production* data. Language is speaking *and* listening, writing *and* reading. The comprehension of language is as important as production. It so happens that production lends itself to analysis and thus becomes the prey of researchers, but comprehension data is equally important in developing an understanding of the process of SLA.

The analysis of learners' competence is made even thornier by the variation or *instability* of learners' systems (Romaine, 2003), which are in a constant state of flux as new information flows in and, through the process of subsumption, causes existing structures to be revised. Repeated observations of a learner will often reveal apparently unpredictable or even contradictory data. In undertaking the task of performance analysis, the teacher and researcher are called upon to infer order and logic in a potentially unstable system.

Further, research (Schachter, 1974; Kleinmann, 1977; Tarone, 1981; James, 1998; R. Ellis, 2000; Gass & Selinker, 2001) has shown that error analysis fails to account for the strategy of *avoidance*. A learner who for one reason or another avoids a particular sound, word, structure, or discourse category may be assumed incorrectly to have no difficulty therewith. Schachter (1974) found, for example, that it was misleading to draw conclusions about relative clause errors among native Japanese speakers who were largely avoiding that structure and thus not manifesting nearly as many errors as some native Persian speakers.

Finally, error analysis can keep us too closely focused on specific languages rather than viewing universal aspects of language. Gass (1989) recommended that researchers pay more attention to linguistic elements that are common to all languages. The language systems of learners may have elements that reflect neither the target language nor the native language, but rather a universal feature of some kind (Celce-Murcia & Hawkins, 1985).

Identifying and Describing Errors

With those precautions in mind, we can nevertheless discern a great deal about learners' linguistic needs by careful attention to their errors. How can those errors be classified and analyzed? Here is a sketch of a few (among many) possible categories to consider, a synthesis of research from Corder (1971), Burt and Kiparsky (1972), and Lennon (1991).

> **Overt and covert errors.** Corder (1971) suggested that a distinction can be made between overt and covert errors. Overtly erroneous utterances are unquestionably ungrammatical at the *sentence* level. Covertly erroneous utterances are grammatically well formed at the sentence

level but are not interpretable within the *context* of communication. Covert errors, in other words, may not be so erroneous if you attend to surrounding discourse (before or after the utterance). Consider the following examples from learners of English:

> This men, employed in one factory, or laboratories in the country.
> Speaker 1: Who are you? Speaker 2: I'm fine, thank you.
> There are a lot of obstacles strewn with troubles lying before me.

The first utterance is unquestionably ungrammatical (and it happens to be uninterpretable), and therefore an overt error. In the second exchange, speaker 2's response is grammatically correct, but inappropriate, so it is a covert error. The third example is problematic, since it is grammatical, but even with a context might be only barely interpretable. It is by definition covert, but see the next category for a distinction between global and local errors.

Global and local errors. Not to be confused with overt and covert errors, which only refer to form and context, errors may also be viewed as either global or local (Burt & Kiparsky, 1972). **Global** errors impede communication; they are incomprehensible to the hearer (or reader). **Local errors** do not inhibit communication, usually because there is only a minor slip, allowing the hearer/reader to make an accurate guess of the intended meaning. Consider the following:

> It's a great hurry around.
> Sometimes could be must, know what happen at around the man or worker.
> Let us work for the welldone of our country!
> The teacher was so good that the students were nailed to his lips.

The first two (a and b) are global in that they are uninterpretable, while you can figure out the intended meaning of sentences (c) and (d). Yes, both might make you smile a bit, possibly because of the word pictures they evoke!

Errors of addition, omission, substitution, and permutation. These four categories simply allow a further classification of error in terms of standard mathematical categories. At times such categories help a teacher to pinpoint an error in order to ascertain potential treatment. Here are examples of each:

> Why to not from worse make a little better? (added *to* infinitive)
> I went to movie. (omitted definite article)
> I lost my road. (the word *road* is substituted for *way*)
> She have will been here two years next month. (permuted auxiliaries)

Levels or domain (Lennon, 1991**) of language.** Is the domain of the error identified as one of phonology, orthography, lexicon, grammar, or discourse? It is sometimes difficult to pinpoint exactly "where" the error occurs, and quite often several errors are made within one sentence or utterance. Consider these ESL sentences:

> We wich you an happy bird date.
> I left Boston soon for Niagara Falls to reflesh myself.
> He grow up and became an obscure typewriter at a office.
> I was so depressed. However, I felt the world was coming to end.

Sentence (a) has several obvious errors, but they are in phonology or orthography (*wich*), grammar (*an*), and lexis (*bird date*, but this could be a pronunciation/transcription error). Sentence (b) clearly has one simple phonological error (*reflesh*). Two errors are present in (c), one tense error (*grow*) and one rather amusing lexical (*typewriter*) error—that would be obscure, wouldn't it? Finally, sentence (d) has a discourse error in that the connector *however* does not fit the rest of the second sentence (which should have a meaning that is in contrast to the first clause).

Lennon (1991) suggested that another category of error is its **extent**, that is, the rank of linguistic unit that would have to be deleted, replaced, supplied, or reordered in order to repair the sentence. In sentence (d), the extent would be either to change the whole second clause to a positive connotation or simply change the connector to something like *also*.

 CLASSROOM CONNECTIONS

What are some examples of overt (sentence level) errors and covert errors in your own production of an L2? And can you remember some of the local errors (interpretable in the context) and global errors you produced? How did your teacher help you to recognize these errors? Did the teacher "coach" you to correct them or just supply the correction? Which is better?

How useful are such categories of error for the classroom teacher? Admittedly, teachers do not have enough processing time in classroom interchange to undergo a conscious analysis of the type of error committed. Decisions to treat or not to treat errors (see below in this chapter) are made intuitively and usually instantaneously. But teachers can, with some experience in the classroom, internalize these categories and use them productively. Two of the above factors are most salient: (1) Teachers are remarkably accurate in quickly determining the difference between a student's *mistakes* and *errors*, in the technical sense described here. (2) *Global* and *local* errors are also quite easily discerned without undue deliberation. Global errors call for immediate feedback, while local errors are often equivocal enough to warrant a choice on the part of the teacher to treat or not to treat.

Clearly, errors offer windows of opportunity for learners to benefit from awareness of a mistake, and for teachers to assist learners to make progress. Oddly enough, in every skill that we humans attempt to master, it is our "boo-boos" that spur us to move forward and do better next time. You are much more likely to learn a better passing shot in tennis by thinking a bit about (and correcting) the misses than about the successes, and L2 learning is no different.

SOURCES OF DIFFICULTY

A step deeper into the mind of the L2 learner takes us into the realm of "why." Why was a particular error made? What in the previous experience of the learner led to the error? By accounting for a myriad possible *sources* of error in learner language, SLA research has inched us closer and closer to identifying *difficulty* in L2 learning. And once we know something about difficulty, we can more effectively devise pedagogical techniques to help learners to become aware of error and to take action to overcome those potential roadblocks.

Let's take a quick survey of eight possible sources of difficulty that have emerged in SLA research and practice, all of which have contributed to a more sophisticated understanding of how to facilitate successful L2 acquisition.

L1 Transfer

For decades, if not centuries, L2 learning was thought to be a matter of overcoming the interference of the L1. In the 1950s, some linguists thought that the tools of structural linguistics, such as Fries's (1952) slot-filler grammar, would enable a linguist to scientifically describe first and second language systems and to determine the extent of **interlingual transfer** between them. Behaviorism contributed to the notion that human behavior is the sum of its smallest parts and components, and therefore that language learning could be described as the acquisition of all of those discrete units. The next step was a matter of examining matches and mismatches, and voilà, the difficulty of learning a given language could be accurately predicted!

The Contrastive Analysis Hypothesis

The examination of two languages in contrast, namely an L1 and L2, and the predictive validity of such a comparison, came to be known as the **Contrastive Analysis Hypothesis** (CAH), enjoying enormous popularity in the

1950s (Lado, 1957). Since human learning theories highlighted *interfering* elements of learning, the CAH concluded that where no interference could be predicted, no difficulty would be experienced since one could *transfer* positively all other items from the L1 to the L2. Likewise, greater difference or interference between the two languages would lead to greater difficulty.

Intuitively the CAH had appeal in that we commonly observe in second language learners a plethora of errors attributable to the negative transfer of the L1 to the L2. It is quite common, for example, to detect certain foreign accents and to be able to infer, from the speech of the learner alone, where the learner comes from. In the examples cited above, for example, the learner who said "reflesh" as opposed to "refresh" would immediately be pegged as an L1 speaker of Japanese. A person saying "room" with a guttural "r" and the "oo" as the short "u" as in "put" would be thought to be a French speaker. Grammatical predictions were also readily made.

Some strong claims were made of the CAH by language teaching experts and linguists. Robert Lado (1957, p. vii), for example, in the preface to *Linguistics Across Cultures*, said, "The plan of the book rests on the assumption that we can predict and describe the patterns that will cause difficulty in learning, and those that will not cause difficulty, by comparing systematically the language and the culture to be learned with the native language and culture of the student." An equally strong claim was made by Banathy, Trager, and Waddle (1966, p. 37): "The change that has to take place in the language behavior of a foreign language student can be equated with the differences between the structure of the student's native language and culture and that of the target language and culture."

Such claims were supported by what some researchers claimed to be an empirical method of prediction. A well-known model was offered by Stockwell, Bowen, and Martin (1965), who posited what they called a **hierarchy of difficulty** by which a teacher or linguist could make a prediction of the relative difficulty of a given aspect of the target language. Further, they posited eight possible degrees of difficulty for phonological systems and 16 degrees for grammar. Clifford Prator (1967) subsequently reduced those numbers to six degrees for both phonology and grammar, using English and Spanish in contrast:

> **Level 0—Transfer**. No difference or contrast. Examples: English and Spanish cardinal vowels, word order, and certain words *(mortal, inteligente, arte, americanos)*.

> **Level 1—Coalescence**. Two items in the L1 become coalesced into one item in the L2. Examples: English third-person possessives require gender distinction *(his/her)*, and in Spanish they do not *(su)*.

> **Level 2—Underdifferentiation**. An item in the L1 is absent in the L2. Examples: English learners of Spanish must "delete" English *do* as a tense carrier, possessive forms of *wh-* words *(whose)*, or the use of *some* with mass nouns.

Level 3—Reinterpretation. An item that exists in the native language is given a new shape or distribution. Example: An English speaker learning Spanish must learn new pronunciations for "j" and "x" (*baja, Mexico*) and the Spanish cardinal vowels.

Level 4—Overdifferentiation. A new item entirely, bearing little if any similarity to the native language item. Example: An English speaker learning Spanish must include determiners in generalized nominals (Man is mortal/*El hombre es mortal*).

Level 5—Split. One item in the native language becomes two or more in the target language. Example: An English speaker learning Spanish must learn the distinction between *ser* and *estar* (to be).

Prator's hierarchy was based on principles of human learning as they were understood at the time. The first, or "zero," degree of difficulty represented complete one-to-one correspondence and transfer, while the fifth degree of difficulty was the height of interference. Prator and Stockwell both claimed that their hierarchy could be applied to virtually any two languages and make it possible to predict second language learner difficulties in any language with a fair degree of certainty and objectivity.

 CLASSROOM CONNECTIONS

Today, first language effects are considered to be important—but not necessarily exclusive—factors in accounting for the learner's acquisition of a second language. In a communicative language classroom, teachers will attend to the potential effects of the first language, but will usually embed such attention in meaningful communication. To what extent have your L2 teachers focused on L1 interference? How useful was that focus?

Cross-Linguistic Influence (CLI)

Prediction of difficulty by means of contrastive procedures was eventually shown to have glaring shortcomings (Wardhaugh, 1970). The process was oversimplified. Predictions were not fulfilled in practice, mostly because those predictions were unclearly specified to begin with. Of course, the creativity of the learner was not taken into account. And in specifying L2 acquisition of *discourse*, the predictive validity of the hierarchy completely fell apart. Those weaknesses were demonstrated empirically by Whitman and Jackson (1972), whose research on Japanese learners of English showed no support whatsoever for the Stockwell/Prator predictions. In another study (Oller & Ziahosseiny, 1970) of spelling difficulty, it was suggested that, actually, *subtle* differences between two languages may present greater difficulty than vast differences.

Some attempts were made to salvage the CAH. Ronald Wardhaugh (1970) suggested that the traditional efforts to employ the CAH predictively were what he called a **strong version** of the CAH, and quipped, "Do linguists have available to them an overall contrastive system within which they can relate the two languages in terms of mergers, splits, zeroes, over-differentiations, under-differentiations, and reinterpretations?" (p. 126). Wardhaugh noted, however, that a **weak version** of the CAH might be more reasonable to adopt: a recognition of the significance of interference across languages, but a concession that linguistic difficulties may be more fruitfully pinpointed after the fact. As errors appear in learner language, teachers can utilize their knowledge of the target and native languages to understand some, but not all, sources of error.

The weak version of the CAH remains today under the label **cross-linguistic influence** (CLI) (Kellerman & Sharwood-Smith, 1986; Kellerman, 1995; Odlin, 2003; Jarvis & Pavlenko, 2008; De Angelis & Dewaele, 2011; White, 2012), suggesting that we all recognize the significant role that prior experience plays in any learning act, and that the influence of the L1 as prior experience must not be overlooked. The difference between today's emphasis on *influence*, rather than prediction, is an important one (Oostendorp, 2012). Phonology of course remains the most reliable linguistic category for predicting learner performance, but far more variation among learners is found in syntactic, lexical, discourse, and pragmatic interference (Kasper, 1992; Barron, 2012). With such variation comes the need to take cross-linguistic influence seriously, but hardly predictively.

Consider simple grammatical categories like word order, tense, or aspect, which have been shown to contain a good deal of variation. One might anticipate the following errors from French, Japanese, and Spanish speakers; however, to *predict* such utterances from learners of English is to go too far.

I am in New York since January.
I went to store yesterday.
I no understand.

Examples of subtle distinctions at the lexical level may be seen in false cognates like the French word *parent*, which in the singular means "relative" or "kin," while only the plural *(parents)* means "parents." Consider the Spanish verb *embarazar*, which commonly denotes "to make pregnant," and has therefore been the source of true "embarrassment" on the part of beginners attempting to speak Spanish! In recent years, research on CLI has uncovered a number of instances of subtle differences causing great difficulty (Sjöholm, 1995). To further complicate matters, internal learner factors such as metalinguistic awareness and external sociocultural and identity variables have been found to be significant contributors to degrees of influence across languages and cultures (De Angelis & Dewaele, 2011).

Many of the world's L2 learners are actually *multi*lingual, and may therefore be users of three or more languages, and this further muddies the CAH and CLI waters (De Angelis & Dewaele, 2011). Depending upon a number of factors, including the linguistic and cultural relatedness of the languages and the context of learning, multilinguals experience a variety of "influences" from other languages and cultures, making it difficult to pinpoint sources of error (Ringbom, 2011). In a significant number of cultures, the learning of several languages is simultaneous, thereby removing a clear-cut *time sequence* from consideration (Wunder, 2011).

All this research on CLI reinforces the principle that teachers should guard against *a priori* pigeon-holing of learners before they have even given learners a chance to perform. However, after the fact (*a posteriori*), we already have ample evidence that CLI is an important linguistic factor for teachers to attend to (Jaszczolt, 1995; Odlin, 2003; White, 2012). Sheen (1996) found, for example, that in an ESL course for speakers of Arabic, overt attention to targeted syntactic contrasts between Arabic and English reduced error rates.

CLI research has examined not only features of phonology, grammar, and lexicon (Odlin, 2003), but also L2 writing (Uysal, 2008), reading (Sparks et al., 2008), speech acts (Yu, 2004), and even nonverbal gestures (Brown & Gullberg, 2008; Choi & Lantolf, 2008). Moreover, CLI implies much more than simply the effect of one's L1 on an L2; the L2 also influences the L1 "bidirectionally" (Pavlenko & Jarvis, 2002; Brown & Gullberg, 2008).

 CLASSROOM CONNECTIONS

Many of the world's L2 learners are also learners of, or proficient in, one or more additional languages. For multilinguals, then, CLI takes on great significance since transfer can occur across several languages. Have you had experience attempting to learn more than one other language? If so, what are some examples of CLI across your L2, L3, or more? How might a teacher draw on the experience of multilinguals in the classroom?

Universals and Markedness

Linguistic universals are thought to provide *facilitative* effects in SLA, rather than difficulty, but because universals are not always unambiguous in their directionality, they bear mentioning as a potential source of difficulty (White, 2012). Fred Eckman (1977, 1981, 2004) was among the first to account for relative degrees of difficulty by means of principles of universal grammar. In his **Markedness Differential Hypothesis** (otherwise known as *markedness theory*), a *marked* member of a pair of related forms contains at least one more feature than an *unmarked* one. In addition, the unmarked (or neutral) member of the pair is the one with a wider range of distribution than the marked one (Celce-Murcia & Hawkins, 1985).

Consider the following examples. In the case of the English indefinite articles (*a* and *an*), *an* is the more complex or *marked* form (it has an additional sound) and *a* is the unmarked form with the wider distribution. Also, all languages have at least one voiceless stop (/p/, /t/, /k/); however, only some languages have voiced (/b/, /d/, /g/) *and* voiceless stops. Furthermore, no language is known to have only voiced stops without also manifesting voiceless stops (Ortega, 2009). In both examples, according to Eckman (1981), the marked *forms* (*an*; voiced + voiceless stops) are predicted to cause difficulty.

Eckman (1981) also showed that *degrees* of markedness will correspond to degrees of difficulty. Rutherford (1982) used markedness theory to explain why there seems to be a certain order of acquisition of morphemes in English: Marked structures are acquired later than unmarked structures. Major and Faudree (1996) found that the phonological performance of native speakers of Korean learning English reflected principles of markedness universals.

The attention of some SLA researchers expanded beyond markedness theory alone to the broader framework of linguistic universals in general (Gass, 1989; Carroll & Meisel, 1990; Comrie, 1990; Eckman, 1991; Major & Faudree, 1996; White, 2012). Some of these arguments focused on the applicability of tenets of universal grammar (UG) to second language acquisition (Schachter, 1988; White, 1989, 1990, 2003, 2012). As we saw in Chapter 2, many of the "rules" acquired by children learning their L1 are presumed to be universal. By extension, rules that are shared by all languages comprise this UG. Such rules are a set of limitations or parameters (Flynn, 1987) of language, and different languages set their parameters differently, thereby creating the characteristic grammar for that language.

A viable alternative to markedness theory was offered by what has come to be known as the **Competition Model** of second language acquisition (Gass & Selinker, 2001), initially proposed by Bates and MacWhinney (1982). The Competition Model suggested that when strictly formal (e.g., phonological, syntactic) options for interpreting meaning through appeal to the L1 have been exhausted, second language learners naturally look for alternative "competing" possibilities to create meaning. So, for example, if a learner's L1 grammar fails to yield a possible "translation" of an utterance, the learner turns to meaning, experience, and other *competing* strategic options in order to make sense of the utterance in question. The Competition Model serves as a reminder to teachers that learners are not exclusively dependent on formal linguistic features as their only tools for deciphering the L2.

Intralingual Transfer

One of the major contributions of learner language research has been its recognition of sources of error that extend beyond **interlingual** errors in learning a second language. It is clear that **intralingual transfer** (within a language) is a major factor in SLA, and its negative counterpart, more commonly referred to **overgeneralization,** is an ever-present source of difficulty. Evidence of intralingual overgeneralization abounds. Consider the following examples in English, excerpted from Richards (1971) and Taylor (1975):

> Does John can sing? (question formation with *do* auxiliary)
> He goed to class yesterday. (irregular past tense)
> I don't know what time is it. (indirect speech)
> He could have went to the store yesterday. (past participle)
> She can writes English very well. (main verb after modal)
> They don't singing in the choir. (simple present tense following *do)*
> She goes to bazaar every day. (definite article)
> I enjoy spending time in the nature. (definite article where none is needed)
> He was brave man. (indefinite article)

Researchers (Taylor, 1975; Jaszczolt, 1995; Odlin, 2003) have found that the early stages of language learning are characterized by a predominance of L1 interference (interlingual transfer), but once learners have begun to acquire parts of the new system, more and more overgeneralization within the L2 is manifested. This, of course, follows logically from the tenets of learning theory (James, 2007). As learners progress in the second language, their previous experience begins to include structures within the L2 itself.

 CLASSROOM CONNECTIONS

What are some examples of intralingual transfer that you have experienced? How did you eventually move to a stage where you noticed such errors and corrected them? Did your teacher ever point such errors out? Should a teacher help students to notice these errors through overt explanation or more subtly indicate such errors?

Context of Learning

A fourth major source of error, although it overlaps both types of transfer, is the context of learning. "Context" refers to a number of possibilities. The *linguistic* context includes surrounding or preceding language that could become the cause of difficulty. Consider the following conversation between two L2 learners of English:

> **Carlos:** Jean-Jacques went to the store, didn't he?
> **Kenji:** Well, no, uh, he didn't went to the store.

Carlos's correct use of the regular past tense was incorrectly repeated by Kenji, although perhaps simply as a mistake, not an error.

For classroom learning, contextual issues arise in teacher talk, materials, or focus on form, among other examples. The classroom context can lead the learner to make faulty hypotheses about the language, what Richards (1971) called "false concepts" and what Stenson (1974) termed **induced errors**. Such errors could stem from a misleading explanation from the teacher, faulty presentation in a textbook, or simply the juxtaposition of forms. Two vocabulary items presented in the same lesson—for example, *point at* and *point out*—might in later recall be confused simply because of the contiguity of presentation. And occasionally, learners resort to a more formal style than is warranted, "bookish" language that is out of place in the context, as in the following example from an English learner on the first day of class:

> Allow me to introduce myself and tell you about some of the headlights of my past.

Of course, besides being a bit too pedantic an utterance, the substitution of *headlights* for *highlights* was a source of amusement!

The sociolinguistic context of natural, untutored language acquisition can give rise to a variety of difficulties (Kasper, 1992). For example, a cross-cultural study of ritual formulas in telephone conversations revealed a number of potential misunderstandings due to interlanguage pragmatic transfer (Taleghani-Nikazm, 2002). Corder's term "idiosyncratic dialect" applies especially well here, as sources of error become difficult to identify.

 CLASSROOM CONNECTIONS

Have you had experiences in which you have misunderstood the social context of a situation? Perhaps you were too formal or too informal in using the L2 in a given context? Have any of your L2 classes focused on social settings, speech acts, and pragmatic issues? How would you teach students to grasp differences, say, between formal and informal language in your L2?

Strategies of Communication

A related contextual variable that can cause difficulty is a host of possible *strategic* techniques being employed by a learner. Communication strategies such as word coinage, circumlocution, false cognates, and prefabricated patterns can all be sources of error (Tarone, 1981). As learners employ a variety of strategies either for production or comprehension, they may draw on their L1, previous L2 knowledge, general knowledge, or simply make spur-of-the-moment intuitive guesses. Here are some examples of what were probably strategic attempts to select a lexical item:

1. The flight attendant voice *came out* through the microphone.
2. He suffers from special disease that in medicine they call it *cloudy minded*.
3. And my heart was *yeasted* with dream.
4. At Mardi Gras the streets were *undulating*.

In sentence (1), lacking a word for the particular grammatical structure that was planned, the learner creatively used what he thought was an appropriate verb; however, it didn't quite ring true in this sentence. In (2), the learner probably did not intend to be humorous in equating "cloudy" thinking with a disease! In sentence (3) the learner knew the meaning of "yeast," and made a vivid use of the word; we can make a guess at the learner's intended meaning. Sentence (4) may be an example of a learner who wanted to use a freshly learned vocabulary item, and proudly described the streets as undulating, instead of the people in the streets.

Input and Frequency

The role of **input** in SLA has been a topic of intense research since the 1970s. Most research underscores the significance of the input that a learner receives (Gor & Long, 2009), but tempers the earlier claim that input is the *sole* cause of successful language acquisition (Krashen, 1985). Without question, L2 learners derive their information about the L2 from the aggregate of all their input, which includes (in the classroom) teacher talk, textbooks and materials, the output of other students, and audio, visual/technological input, all of which are usually controlled, "positive" (Gor & Long, 2009, p. 445) samples of language. Outside the classroom, learners must filter a much wider variety of language from other speakers in natural contexts, news and entertainment media, and written sources including newspapers, magazines, and literature.

One of the issues related to input is the question of whether or not input implies an equal degree of **intake.** That is, how much of what is "put in" to a learner in the form of oral or written language is actually remembered, subsumed, and internalized (Gass & Selinker, 2001)? One of the fundamental tenets of learning theory is that we "take in" only a fraction of language that is perceived, and the burning question for teachers and researchers alike is: How can we maximize intake? The answer to that question lies in a complex amalgam of attention, cognitive style, affective disposition, general interest, and linguistic factors including L1 and L2 transfer and universal grammar constraints.

A further issue that mitigates strong claims for the primacy of input is the role of *interaction* in SLA. In recent years SLA theory has focused intently on the sociocultural nature of learning an L2 (Lantolf, 2011), as a multiplicity of interactional elements comes to bear on any linguistic input. Rarely, other than in extensive reading, is language a steady one-way stream; rather, as learners socially construct meaning through negotiation with teacher, other students, and in natural settings with various interlocutors, input is only part of the whole picture.

Closely allied with input is the all-important factor of **frequency**. How often is a learner exposed to a particular form? How significant is frequency in internalizing a form? Is function a factor in considering the frequency of input (Ellis & Ferreira-Junior, 2009)? According to some research, "frequency effects are compelling evidence for usage-based models of language acquisition" (Ellis & Collins, 2009, p. 330).

In determining difficulty of acquisition of a given form, research shows a critical distinction between **type** and **token** frequency. Type refers to the "class" of linguistic feature, while tokens are the individual members of the class. The pragmatic-type "greetings" can be realized in a number of tokens such as *hello, what's happening, how's it going*. It has been found that the learning of phonological, morphological, and syntactic rules is more a function of type than of token frequency (Bybee & Hopper, 2001). The reason for such a claim is based largely on a psychological principle: The more items that are heard (or read) in a certain linguistic position (type), the less likely it will be that the learner will remember the particular instances (tokens), and the more likely it is that a general category (type) will be internalized (Bybee & Thompson, 2000).

 CLASSROOM CONNECTIONS

In your L2 classes, have you experienced a functional curriculum where a certain *type* or *function* of language has been the focus, featuring the presentation of a number of specific linguistic *tokens* of that function? How well do you remember all those linguistic examples? How can a teacher limit the number of examples within a certain type or function?

Does the *salience* of a form override the possible effect of low frequency? Again, learning theory provides a general answer: The importance that L2 learners (as well as L1 learners) attribute to a linguistic event will greatly determine its learnability. Nick Ellis (2006b) noted that selective attention, expectation, and salience are key elements in SLA. Examples of low-salience items for many learners are grammatical particles and inflections, which bear a low semantic load in the context of the whole sentence and surrounding discourse. So, for example, in the sentence "Tomorrow I go to the store," the adverbial "tomorrow" governs the intended meaning of the sentence. The inflection of "go" is perceived as less salient, so learners are likely to attribute less importance to such word inflections.

Fossilization

Anna's grandparents emigrated with their only child from Hong Kong to San Francisco as young adults in the mid-1950s. After a few years of doing menial jobs, they opened up a grocery store on the west side of San Francisco, amidst a number of other Asian shops and restaurants. The business was successful, and was passed on to Anna's father in the 1990s, shortly after Anna was born.

Anna's English is as flawless as any native Californian's and her Cantonese is quite fluent. Her father is fluent in both Cantonese and English, with slightly accented "Chinglish" typical of "generation 1.5" Chinese in San Francisco. Anna's grandparents, now in their late 80s, handle only enough English to cater to English speakers who patronize their store, and their English is quite replete with ingrained "errors," and marked by heavy accents. Their friends are all Chinese, so they have neither need nor motivation to "progress" further in their English ability.

Annabelle's grandparents' English is a typical example of **fossilization**, the relatively permanent incorporation of nonstandard linguistic forms into a person's L2 competence. What may be a rather fluent command of a language is nevertheless characterized by persistent errors across the spectrum of domains. Fossilization is a normal and natural stage for many users of a language, and should not be viewed as flawed or the result of "failure." In fact, as Siegel (2009) notes, fossilization may represent *successful* language acquisition for those "who learn just enough to communicate what they want to communicate and no more" (p. 585).

A further misconception is captured in the forbidding metaphor of fossilization that suggests an unchangeable situation etched in stone, with no possibility of further advancement. Michael Long (2003) disagreed, saying that "the more relevant object of study for researchers becomes *stabilization*, not fossilization" (p. 521), which leaves open the possibility for further development at some point in time. For the moment we will stay with the more broadly used term of fossilization.

How do items become fossilized? Fossilization can be seen as consistent with principles of human learning already discussed in this book: conditioning, reinforcement, need, motivation, self-determination, and others. Vigil and Oller (1976) provided a formal account of fossilization as a factor of positive and negative affective and cognitive *feedback* among speakers, both of which can be either positive or negative:

> **Affective feedback** (establishes a relationship between interlocutors)
> *Positive* (maintains the conversation) "Keep talking," "I'm listening."
> *Negative* (seeks to terminate the conversation) "Well, I gotta go now."

> **Cognitive feedback** (indicates comprehension of an utterance)
> *Positive* (indicates understanding) "Uh huh," "I see," "Right."
> *Negative* (indicates lack of understanding) "What?" "Say that again."

Both affective and cognitive feedback may be encoded verbally or with kinesic mechanisms such as gesture, tone of voice, and facial expression. Various combinations of the two major types of feedback are possible. For example, a person can indicate positive affective feedback ("I want to continue this conversation") but give negative cognitive feedback to indicate that the message itself is unclear.

Vigil and Oller's model holds that fossilization is the result of a learner's utterances that gain positive affective feedback ("Keep talking") as well as positive cognitive feedback ("I understand"), the latter serving to reinforce an incorrect form of language. It is interesting that this internalization of *in*correct forms takes place by means of the same processes as the internalization of correct forms. We refer to the latter, of course, as "learning," but the same elements of input, interaction, and feedback are present. Whatever forms are produced, feedback that says "I understand you perfectly" reinforces those forms. Figure 9.1 illustrates the cause-and-effect relationship. Note that fossilization may be the result of too many green lights when there should have been some red lights.

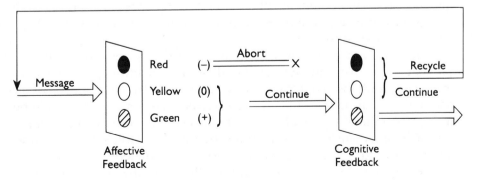

Figure 9.1   Affective and cognitive feedback

> ### 🌐 CLASSROOM CONNECTIONS
>
> In your experience learning an L2, have you ever felt that your errors were being "ignored" by your teacher, causing you to *assume* you were saying (or writing) something correctly? How might a teacher insert him or herself into your production of language to provide some negative (helping you to notice an error) cognitive feedback while still encouraging the student to speak?

Researchers have noted a number of flaws in attributing such importance to feedback alone. Selinker and Lamendella (1979) noted that Vigil and Oller's model relied on the notion of *extrinsic* feedback, and that other factors internal to the learner affect fossilization. Fossilization could be the result of the presence or absence of internal motivating factors, of seeking interaction with other people, of consciously focusing on forms, and of one's strategic investment in the learning process.

A further issue is the question of the theoretical soundness of the concept of fossilization. Long (2003) concluded that stabilization is a more appropriate construct to apply to learners whose language development has reached an apparent "plateau," arguing that "'fossilization' has simply become a general, non-technical name for non-target-like ultimate attainment, that is, . . . a broad brush method for characterizing what a learner did *not* do" (p. 513). Long contended that fossilization is an assumption at best, with insufficient supporting data.

Others (Kachru & Nelson, 1996; Siegel, 2003, 2009), point out the difficulty of distinguishing between fossilization and the development of indigenized and pidgin languages. Siegel (2009) concludes that fossilized language does not necessarily represent a speaker's failure to attain L2 competence. Han and Selinker (2005) admitted that "fossilization research is still characterized by a plurality of unresolved issues, despite the popularity of the term" (pp. 465–466).

Stabilization may well be a more appropriate term to capture plateaus in acquisition. After all, learners in all skill acquisition show uneven lines of progress, and in many cases, especially in advanced stages of learning, those lines can flatten out—or even **backslide**—for a considerable period of time. Sometimes those plateaus are rooted in motivational factors, either intrinsic or extrinsic, and sometimes by other variables: age, aptitude, input, attention, and social context. For now, the concept of stabilization does indeed appear to be safer ground—it "lightens the burden of SLA theory" (Long, 2003, p. 521).

ERROR TREATMENT: FOCUS ON FORM

Implied in all of the foregoing discussions is the difficulty of the bumpy and winding road that a language learner travels in the quest for proficiency. The metaphorical rocks in the road are best described as *difficulty* in the process of acquisition. Overcoming these difficulties requires a concerted strategic approach, and with it a degree of "trial and error." While it is important to accentuate the positive in learners' journeys to success, and not to become obsessed with error, transforming difficulty into success always seems to hinge on how learners perceive their own ability, how they process feedback around them, and how they manage to make their errors work *for* them and not against them.

In this section we will grapple first with some general background in the form of some approaches to error in the classroom, and then with some of the research surrounding the issue of focusing learners on the forms of language in the classroom.

Historical Notes

Historically, error treatment in language classrooms has been a hot topic. In the middle of the fervor over behavioral models, some of which were highly focused on the *avoidance* of error, instruction was aimed at "getting it right" from the start, by repetition, overlearning, and memorizing. One psychologist quipped that "error, like sin, must be avoided at all costs!" By the 1970s a number of new methods took a *laissez-faire* approach to error, under the assumption that natural processes within the learner would eventually lead to acquisition. Now, current approaches, including CLT and task-based instruction, advocate an optimal balance between attention to form (and errors) and attention to meaning.

Vigil and Oller's (1976) communication feedback model (described above, see Figure 9.1) offered one of the first psychologically based models for approaching error in language classrooms. The "green light" of positive affective feedback allows the speaker to continue attempting to get a message across; a "red light" causes the speaker to abort such attempts. In a classroom, most teacher feedback is affectively positive: "Okay, fine, I hear you, keep going." Cognitive feedback is the point at which error treatment becomes viable. A green light (from the teacher) says "I understand your message." A red light symbolizes corrective feedback that takes on a myriad of possible forms and causes the learner to make some kind of alteration in production.

The most useful implication of Vigil and Oller's model for a theory of error treatment is that cognitive feedback must be *optimal* in order to be effective. Too much negative cognitive feedback—a barrage of interruptions, corrections, and overt attention to malformations—leads learners to shut off their attempts at communication. On the other hand, too much positive cognitive feedback, willingness of the teacher-hearer to let errors go uncorrected, or to indicate understanding when understanding may *not* have occurred, serves to reinforce the errors of the speaker-learner. The result is the persistence of such errors.

 CLASSROOM CONNECTIONS

In your learning of an L2, have you ever felt that you were *over*-corrected by your teacher? Or *under*corrected, with your errors allowed to go unnoticed? How does a teacher reach an optimum level of encouraging a student to speak (or write) without stifling that student with overcorrection? How would you, as a teacher, *select* certain errors to treat?

In strictly behavioral terms, affective and cognitive modes of feedback are reinforcers to speakers' responses. As speakers perceive the positive "green lights" of reinforcement, they will be led to internalize certain speech patterns. Corrective feedback can still be "positive" in the Skinnerian sense, as we shall see below. However, ignoring erroneous language may be interpreted by the student as a green light; therefore, teachers must be careful to discern the possible reinforcing consequences of withholding error treatment.

In a set of practical suggestions for teachers on error treatment, Hendrickson (1980) advised teachers to try to discern the difference between *global* and *local* errors, described earlier in this chapter. Hendrickson asserted that global errors, as a rule, be treated since messages may otherwise remain garbled. Local errors require a teacher's judgment call. A learner of English was describing a quaint old hotel in Europe and said, "There is a French widow in every bedroom." The local error is clearly—and humorously—apparent. In this instance, the salient difference between a "window" and a "widow," and any possible consternation from students, begs for a teacher's feedback!

From students' perspectives, it has always been quite clear that they *expect* errors to be corrected (Cathcart & Olsen, 1976) in the classroom, whether local or global, although one study (Loewen et al., 2009) demonstrated that some L2 learners have a distaste for grammar instruction. However, in the last part of the twentieth century some pedagogical approaches advocated *no* direct treatment of error at all (Krashen & Terrell, 1983). It was argued that in natural, untutored environments, L2 speakers are usually corrected on only a small percentage of errors (Chun, Day, Chenoweth, & Luppescu, 1982). Those errors were almost always global errors and given attention not by interrupting but by waiting for transition points in conversations (Day, Chenoweth, Chun, & Luppescu, 1984).

It was a safe conclusion by the mid-1980s that a sensitive and perceptive teacher would make the language classroom an ideal optimum between some of the overpoliteness of the real world and the expectations that learners bring with them to the classroom. Kathleen Bailey (1985), for example, suggested that language teachers have a number of basic options when confronted with a student error, including:

1. to treat or ignore
2. to treat now or later
3. to stimulate other learners to initiate treatment
4. to test for the effectiveness of the treatment.

And Bailey noted that if teachers chose some form of treatment, they then had several further choices:

1. simply indicating the fact that an error occurred
2. modeling a correction
3. indicating the type of error that occurred

These basic options continued to be viable modes of error treatment in the classroom; however, in recent years, as we will see in the next section, researchers refined the options considerably.

 CLASSROOM CONNECTIONS

In L2 classrooms, learners' errors should not be classified as undesirable, but rather as natural processes of trial-and-error on the part of learners. In your experience learning L2, what were some of the specific techniques that your teachers used to treat errors made by you and your classmates? How effective were those treatments?

Form-Focused Instruction (FFI)

As methodological trends in classroom instruction shifted from an emphasis on language forms (e.g., a grammatically organized curriculum) to attention to functional language within communicative contexts (e.g., CLT), the place of **form-focused instruction** (FFI) became a burning issue. Can we teach learners to use an L2 in meaningful, communicative contexts without relinquishing responsibility to help learners to notice and refine *forms* of language? Can we direct learners to a **focus on form** (FonF) and simultaneously direct them to focus on *meaning*?

A number of varying definitions of FFI have emerged (Doughty, 2003; J. Williams, 2005; Spada & Lightbown, 2008; Pica, 2009; Spada, 2011). For the sake of simplifying a complex pedagogical issue, let's rely on Spada's (1997) definition: "any pedagogical effort which is used to draw the learners' attention to language form either implicitly or explicitly" (p. 73).

Before moving on to an explanation of FFI, let's clarify several psychological processes and constructs that are invoked—and often misused—in virtually every discussion of FFI: consciousness, awareness, attention, and the implicit/explicit dichotomy.

1. **Consciousness.** This "notoriously vague term" is used ubiquitously in the field of psychology, but, oddly enough, "quite frankly nobody really knows what consciousness is exactly" (Dörnyei, 2009, p. 132). Ellis and Larsen-Freeman (2006, p. 570) considered consciousness to be "the publicity organ of the brain," which accounts for accessing, disseminating, and exchanging information. Others refer to notions of intentionality, attention, awareness, and controlled vs. automatic processing (McLaughlin, 1990a), leaving everyone in a blur of concepts. In order to understand features of FFI, we turn to more clearly defined concepts.

2. **Awareness.** McLaughlin (1990a) cautions us not to conclude that the concept of awareness is synonymous with consciousness. A person may consciously (as opposed to *un*consciously) perceive a visual or auditory input but remain unaware of that perception. Reading a great novel in the middle of the hubbub of an airport terminal, you could be *conscious* of the surrounding noise, but unaware of it, in that you are not attending or focusing on that noise. Kennedy (2012) found that some of her L2 subjects who self-reported awareness of language demonstrated increased quality of use of specified forms.

3. **Attention.** We may be even more unambiguously served as language teachers by using the construct of attention to differentiate various options in FFI. Schmidt (2001), Dörnyei (2009), and others note that *selective* attention is the process of concentration, focus, monitoring, or control. It may be metaphorically described as a "mental spotlight," alerting one's sensors to a selected (and limited) number of perceptions. In specific reference to FFI, "focus" on form means just what it says: calling a learner's (selective) attention to a specified segment of language.

4. **Implicit/explicit dichotomy.** More to the point, as we seek to direct learners to language forms (and to their errors), should we do so implicitly or explicitly? Implicit FonF, also referred to as *incidental* focus (J.N. Williams, 2009; File & Adams, 2010) involves *non*focal attention. For example, a learner might internalize (subconsciously?) the rule for formation of the present perfect tense in the course of performing a meaning-focused task, such as describing events that began in the past and continue up to the present moment. Explicit (*intentional*) FonF directs the learner to a language form by "spotlighting" a form in the process of classroom instruction.

CLASSROOM CONNECTIONS

These four terms (which denote complex psychological concepts) are often misunderstood. In your L2 learning, what are some examples of your being *conscious*, vs. *aware*, of your language output? How did you *attend* to that output? Did your teacher favor *implicit* or *explicit* treatment, and which was more effective?

Implied in FFI are a number of basic questions about learner's errors (Sheen & Ellis, 2011). Should learner errors be corrected? If so, when, and which errors? How should they be corrected, and who should do so? Assuming that the answer to the first question is yes, the issue of *how* errors should be treated constitutes a range of approaches (Doughty, 2003; J. Williams, 2005; Sheen & Ellis, 2011; Spada, 2011). On one side of a continuum are approaches that include:

1. overt, immediate correction of errors
2. explicit, discrete-point **metalinguistic explanations** of rules
3. curricula constructed and sequenced by grammatical or phonological categories.

At the other end of the continuum are more subtle approaches to FFI:

1. implicit, **incidental** references to form
2. **noticing** (Schmidt, 1990; R. Ellis, 1997), that is, the learner's paying **attention** to specific linguistic features
3. the incorporation of forms into communicative tasks, or what Rod Ellis (1997) called **grammar consciousness raising**.

Also implied in a discussion of FFI is whether or not it is a feature that is *planned* or *spontaneous* (J. Williams, 2005). Some curricula designate certain modules or even separate courses for focus on pronunciation, grammar, or vocabulary points. In other cases, communicative lessons have built-in segments of activities in which FonF is specified in advance. These might include everything from explanatory charts and rules to grammar consciousness-raising tasks within a larger communicative task. At the other end of this continuum is an array of possible spontaneous FonF, ranging from a teacher's raised eyebrows or frowning face all the way to interruption of a learner to call attention to an error or form.

Categories of Feedback

We'll now take a brief look at some of the most common categories of feedback, along with responses to feedback that have appeared in research and pedagogical practice. The following descriptions are a synthesis of research from a number of sources (R. Ellis, 2001; Panova & Lyster, 2002; Lyster, 2004, 2007, 2011; J. Williams, 2005; Long, 2007; Loewen, 2011; Sheen & Ellis, 2011). The terms are divided into what Panova and Lyster (2002) called feedback *types* and learner *responses* to feedback. Examples are provided to show L2 learner (L) and teacher (T) utterances.

Types

Recast: An implicit type of **corrective feedback** that reformulates or expands an ill-formed or incomplete utterance in an *unobtrusive* way.

> **L:** I lost my road.
> **T:** Oh, yeah, I see, you lost your *way*. And then what happened?

Clarification request: Attention is drawn to an utterance, indicating the hearer has not understood it (Sheen & Ellis, 2011).

> **L:** We go to July 4 fireworks and crackers were very loud.
> **T:** Did you really mean "crackers"—little biscuits that you eat?

Metalinguistic feedback: Provides comments, information, or questions related to the correctness of a student's utterance (Lyster, 2004).

> **L:** I am here since January.
> **T:** Well, okay, but remember we talked about the present perfect tense?

Elicitation: A corrective technique that prompts the learner to self-correct. Elicitation and other **prompts** are more overt in their request for a response.

> **L:** [*to another student*] What means this word?
> **T:** Uh, Luis, how do we say that in English? What *does* . . .?
> **L:** Ah, what does the word mean?

Explicit correction: A clear indication to the student that the form is incorrect and provision of a corrected form.

> **L:** When I have twelve years old . . .
> **T:** No, not *have*. You mean, "when I *was* twelve years old . . ."

Repetition: The teacher repeats the ill-formed part of the student's utterance, usually with a change in intonation.

> **L:** When I have twelve years old . . .
> **T:** When I *was* twelve years old . . .

Responses to Feedback

Uptake: The learner makes a response "that immediately follows the teacher's feedback and that constitutes a reaction in some way to the teacher's intention to draw attention to some aspect of the student's initial utterance" (Lyster & Ranta, 1997, p. 49). Uptake is a general term that can have a number of manifestations, as in the example below, in which the learner's uptake confirmed comprehension, but production was still not repaired.

[*in small group work*]

> L_A: In English class I read poetry by Sherry.
> L_B: Uh, sorry, you mean "sherry" . . . that you drink? Or She*lley*?
> L_A: Ah, yes [laughing], I read Sherry!

Repair: As a result of teacher feedback, a learner corrects an ill-formed utterance, either through **self-repair** or as a result of **peer repair**.

> L_A: I was in the airport waiting for someone to pick up.
> L_B: You mean someone will pick *you* up?
> L_A: Oh, yes, I wait for someone to pick me up.

Repetition: The learner repeats the correct form as a result of teacher feedback, and sometimes **incorporates** it into a longer utterance.

> **L:**   I will be studied in school for two years to get degree.
> **T:**   Really? Someone will study *you*?
> **L:**   Oh! No, *I* must study for two years, at UCLA, for degree in MBA.

With those definitions in mind, we now turn to a brief synopsis of research on the effectiveness of FFI in its variety of possible manifestations in the classroom.

 CLASSROOM CONNECTIONS

What are some examples in your L2 learning of the *types* of feedback described here? Is one type more effective than another? If so, what causes that effectiveness? Did your teacher help you to *respond* to feedback? How? Can you think of examples of when you provided *uptake* to a teacher's feedback? How can a teacher maximize uptake in the L2 classroom?

Effectiveness of FFI

Not surprisingly, research on the effectiveness of FFI provides mixed conclusions, mostly due to a wide variety of contexts, ability levels, individual variation, sociocultural identity factors, and a multiplicity of options in providing corrective feedback (Sheen & Ellis, 2011). As a synopsis of these issues, let's look at six questions that have been addressed in the research literature:

1. Is FFI beneficial?

Almost all recent research suggests that *communicative* language instruction in general, as opposed to simple "exposure" to a language, can indeed increase learners' levels of attainment (Lightbown, 2000). Further, studies have shown (Doughty, 2003; Loewen, 2011) that, with only a few minor exceptions (Mason & Krashen, 2010), "there is a growing consensus that FonF can be beneficial for L2 learning and that it does have a place in the classroom" (Loewen, 2011, p. 580). Error treatment and FonF appear to be most effective when incorporated into a communicative, learner-centered curriculum, and least effective when error treatment is a dominant pedagogical feature (Loewen, 2005; J. Williams, 2005). The research also confirms that a primary factor in determining the effectiveness of FFI is a learner's *noticing* of form, along with the quality of the learner's *uptake*.

2. When should FonF take place?

The research generally shows that learners at all levels can benefit from various types of FFI (Doughty, 2003). Should beginning learners be given less corrective feedback than advanced learners? One study found that, from the student's perspective, more proficient students preferred feedback that focused on accuracy (Jernigan & Mihai, 2008).

Should a teacher interrupt learners in the middle of an attempt to communicate? Or wait for a "propitious" (Spada, 1997) moment? These and other related questions depend on the context. Research findings were somewhat mixed in earlier studies (Lightbown & Spada,1990; Doughty, 2003), but there has been increasing agreement more recently that "there is no clear evidence that corrective feedback needs to be provided . . . in a 'window of opportunity' in order to impact interlanguage development" (Sheen & Ellis, 2011, p. 593).

3. Are certain types of FonF more effective than others?

While Long (2007, p. 94) conceded that "the jury is still out" on the effectiveness of FonF in the classroom, quite a number of recent studies have discovered why earlier research showed conflicting results. First, whether FonF is given in the form of one of the five types listed above does not impact learners as much as what the learner *does* with the corrective feedback. For example, whether the FonF is implicit or explicit is not as important as the learner's *response* to the FonF (Long, 2007; Loewen, 2011; Sheen & Ellis, 2011). "Corrective feedback is hypothesized to facilitate acquisition if learners first *notice* the correction and second, *repair* their own erroneous utterance" (Sheen & Ellis, 2011, p. 602). In other words, a teacher's FonF that prompts some sort of intentional *uptake* from the learner—a specific focused response that attempts to repair the erroneous utterance—will be more effective than modes of FonF that are more subtle and that simply provide input.

4. Is FFI also effective in improving writing?

Approaches to teaching writing have varied between minimal, highly indirect feedback to direct, focused feedback that provides corrections (Ferris, 2012). Researchers have also looked at the efficacy of providing feedback on content as opposed to form, on how to stimulate revisions, on particular grammatical and rhetorical features, and on students' preferences for feedback, all with mixed results (Sheen, 2007; Hartshorn et al., 2010; Sheen & Ellis, 2011). Is there a conclusion? The answer, with a healthy dose of caution, is a qualified yes. One reason for the hedge is that writing, unlike speaking, is a *learned*, and not *acquired* skill, and even native users of a language exhibit extreme diversity of abilities. Having said that, following general principles of learning, all skill acquisition can benefit from "coaching," and learning to write in an L2 is no exception. Ferris (2004) and Ferris and Hedgcock (2005) remain, with a few caveats, advocates of the importance of feedback in teaching writing.

 CLASSROOM CONNECTIONS

In learning to write an L2, what approaches have your teachers taken? Did they provide minimal, direct correction or indirect comments on content? How, if at all, did they help you to notice grammatical errors? What do you think is the most effective approach to helping L2 learners to progress in their writing skills?

---

5. Does frequency make a difference?

You may remember reading in Chapters 2 and 3 that for child L1 acquisition, many studies have shown that *frequency* of input is not as important a factor in acquisition as *salience*—the meaningfulness attributed to a given form of language. Similar conclusions have been drawn by a number of SLA studies (Eubank & Gregg, 2002), with research citing innate knowledge, instantaneous acquisition, native language effects, conceptual development, and language systematicity as arguments against a positive correlation between frequency and acquisition. One study found that "input flood" (also known as enriched input, a saturation of input on specific structures) did not increase accuracy scores. Other research (N. Ellis, 2002; Gass & Mackey, 2002; Larsen-Freeman, 2002) has been equivocal on the issue of frequency.

6. Do some students benefit more than others from FFI?

The wide-ranging research on learner characteristics, styles, and strategies supports the conclusion that certain learners clearly benefit more than others from FFI. Analytic, field-independent, left-brain-oriented learners internalize explicit FFI better than relational, field-dependent, right-brain-oriented learners (Jamieson, 1992). Visual input will favor visual learners (Reid, 1987). Students who are "Js" and "Ts" on the Myers-Briggs scale will more readily be able to focus on form (Ehrman, 1989). The teacher needs to develop the intuition for ascertaining what kind of corrective feedback is appropriate for a given student at a given moment, and what forms of uptake should be expected. Principles of reinforcement theory, human learning, cognitive and sociocultural factors, and communicative language teaching all combine to form those intuitions.

✵ ✵ ✵ ✵ ✵

The "poetic" essay quoted at the beginning of this chapter is an excellent example of an L2 learner's attempt to construct meaning with limited knowledge of the L2. It's also a perfect example to highlight the sensitive and often intuitive role of the teacher in providing guidance and feedback to learners in their journey to greater language competence. The essay writer's teacher chose two sequential modes of giving feedback. The first was to highly praise the student for such a beautiful description, and to encourage further writing from the student. The second was to ask the student, in a teacher-student conference, about certain grammatical structures in the essay, and to elicit uptake from the student regarding those grammatical structures. The teacher did not recommend a revision!

SUGGESTED READINGS

De Angelis, G., & Dewaele, J-M. (Eds.). (2011). *New trends in crosslinguistic influence and multilingualism research*. Bristol, UK: Multilingual Matters.

White, L. (2012). Universal grammar, crosslinguistic variation and second language acquisition. *Language Teaching, 45*, 309–328.

De Angelis & Dewaele is a multi-authored compilation of crosslinguistic research focusing on multilingual learners and contexts. White provides an annotated bibliography of UG and crosslinguistic research from 1985–2011.

Barron, A. (2012). Interlanguage pragmatics: From use to acquisition to second language pedagogy. *Language Teaching, 45,* 44–63.

> Another in a series of "research timelines" on selected topics, this time on pragmatic considerations in interlanguage, with annotated references from 1979–2011.

Loewen, S. (2011). Focus on form. In E. Hinkel (Ed.), *Handbook of research in second language teaching and learning: Volume II.* (pp. 576–592). New York: Routledge.

Sheen, Y., & Ellis, N. (2011). Corrective feedback in language teaching. In E. Hinkel (Ed.), *Handbook of research in second language teaching and learning: Volume II.* (pp. 593–610). New York: Routledge.

> These two articles (in the same volume) contain a wealth of information on issues and controversies in FFI, an update on what SLA research has found, and extensive bibliographies.

LANGUAGE LEARNING EXPERIENCE: JOURNAL ENTRY 9

Note: See Chapter 1 for general guidelines for writing a journal on a previous or concurrent language learning experience.

- Think about some of the errors you are making (made) in learning a foreign language. List as many as you can, up to ten or so, being as descriptive as possible (e.g., the French subjunctive mood, Japanese honorifics, English definite articles, separable two-word verbs). Now, analyze where those errors came from. If they did not come from your native language, what other sources are possible?
- Make a list of some of the specific contrasts between your L1 and L2 that have been or still are difficult for you. Can you analyze why they are difficult, using the information in this chapter?
- In your list above, are there examples of "subtle differences" which nevertheless present some difficulty for you? Analyze those differences.
- Have you ever reached a stage of fossilization, or perhaps more appropriately, stabilization of progress, where you seemed to just stall for weeks or more? If so, describe that experience. Then tell about what, if anything, propelled you out of those doldrums, or determine what might have helped you if you stayed there or are still there.
- Describe your language teacher's error treatment style. Does/Did your teacher over-correct or under-correct? Did your teacher use any of the forms of feedback described in this chapter? If so, which ones and how effective do you think they were in stimulating you to *notice* them and then to *repair* or self-correct?

FOR THE TEACHER: ACTIVITIES (A) & DISCUSSION (D)

Note: For each of the "Classroom Connections" in this chapter, you may wish to turn them into individual or pair-work discussion questions.

1. (A) Divide the class into groups of three or four each. Ask each group to make a short list of examples, in languages that members of the group know, of (a) mistakes vs. errors, (b) global vs. local errors, and (c) overt vs. covert errors. Have groups share their examples with the rest of the class.

2. (D) Make an audio recording (or secure one from someone else) of a few minutes of the language of an advanced-beginning learner of English. As the class listens to the tape, ask students to listen the first time for the general gist. The second time, ask them to write down errors (phonological, grammatical, lexical, discourse) they hear. Write these on the board; then, in class discussion, identify the source of each error. Such an exercise should offer a sense of the "messiness" of real language.

3. (D) Select several languages with which students in the class are familiar, and ask them to volunteer phonological features of those languages that are most salient in "foreign-accented" English. List the features on the board and, using the hierarchy of difficulty on pages 255–256, discuss the possible reasons for the saliency of those features (why particular features get mapped onto English speech performance, and not others).

4. (D) Ask your class if anyone has learned, or attempted to learn, a third or fourth language. Ask those students to share some of the difficulties they encountered, and the extent to which there was L1–L3, L2–L3, etc., cross-linguistic influence.

5. (D) Ask the students to briefly describe someone they know whose language has fossilized, then to speculate on the *causes* of that fossilization. Ask them if they feel it's more appropriate to think of their examples as instances of *stabilization*? What evidence can they cite to support stabilization?

6. (A) In small groups of three or four, ask each group to consider all the *types* of feedback and the categories of *responses* to feedback that were defined on pages 272–273. In their own experiences learning an L2, ask them to describe examples of some of the categories and share them with their group. Then ask each group to report a few of those examples to the rest of the class.

7. (A) Divide into groups such that each group has at least two people in it who have learned or studied an L2. Ask each group to share experiences with form-focused instruction (FFI). Try to decide as a group what the features are of the *most* and least *effective* FFI.

CHAPTER 10

SORTING THROUGH PERSPECTIVES ON SLA

For every complex problem there is an answer that is short, simple, and wrong.

— H. L. Mencken

SLA is an extraordinarily complex problem. Think about it. Major disciplinary traditions are invoked in looking at the question of how, why, and when people acquire L2s: linguistics, psychology, education, anthropology, and sociology, to name some. And we have become accustomed to linking SLA research with a number of "hybrid" fields (Pica, 2005): applied linguistics, applied psychology, educational linguistics, psycholinguistics, neurolinguistics, and sociolinguistics. All of these disciplines, with myriad theories, approaches, and perspectives, are called on to "connect the dots" in explaining SLA!

So, "problems in SLA," to borrow from the title of Michael Long's (2007) book, are most certainly complex. The question is, do sixty years of serious research on SLA add up to answers that are short and simple—and *wrong*? We would have to admit that, yes, some of the answers—theories, conclusions, statistics, methods—have been shown over time to be at the very least questionable, and in the eyes of some, dead wrong. But I like to think that a significant number of findings, generalizations, approaches, and classroom techniques have been *right* in leading us slowly and surely along a pathway to a fuller understanding and appreciation of the process of learning an L2.

Furthermore, if you have been reading all the chapters of this book, you're fully aware that few if any of the major *right* answers about SLA have been short and simple. In fact, if you're not overwhelmed by now with all the questions, factors, issues, and controversies, I would be surprised! So, how can you sort through all the findings and perspectives that have been presented here? Is it possible to weed out the "wrong" answers and synthesize the "right" answers?

From time to time a book or article or keynote speech delves into the daunting task of constructing a *theory* of SLA (Long, 2007; VanPatten & Williams, 2007; Atkinson, 2011b; Ortega, 2011). Florence Myles (2010) provided a comprehensive annotated bibliography of dozens of references tracing a six-decade journey (from 1945 to 2008) of the development of theories in SLA. Scanning this list, you cannot help but be struck by a number of important milestones in that journey. Are we "there" yet? Have we identified a unified, comprehensive, all-encompassing *theory* of SLA? In the phraseology of a dictionary definition (Merriam-Webster, 2003), have we agreed on a "plausible or scientifically acceptable general body of principles offered to explain phenomena [of SLA]"?

To help in our quest for an answer to that question, Diane Larsen-Freeman (1997) suggested several lessons from chaos-complexity theory that can steer us in the right direction:

1. Beware of false dichotomies. Look for complementarity, inclusiveness, and interface.
2. Beware of linear, causal approaches to theorizing. SLA is so complex with so many interacting factors that to state that there is a single cause for an SLA effect is to go too far.
3. Beware of overgeneralization. The smallest, apparently most insignificant of factors in learning a second language may turn out to be important.
4. Conversely, beware of reductionist thinking. It is tempting to examine a small part of the whole and assume it represents the whole system.

Michael Long (1990a, pp. 659–660) also tackled the problem of theory building in a number of suggestions about "the least" a theory of SLA needs to explain. He offered eight criteria for a comprehensive theory of SLA:

1. Account for universals.
2. Account for environmental factors.
3. Account for variability in age, acquisition rate, and proficiency level.
4. Explain both cognitive and affective factors.
5. Account for form-focused learning, not just **subconscious acquisition**.
6. Account for other variables besides exposure and input.
7. Account for cognitive/innate factors which explain interlanguage systematicity.
8. Recognize that acquisition is not a steady accumulation of generalizations.

Such criteria may be a bit abstract until you actually try to apply them to a theoretical position. We'll do just that later in the chapter. Meanwhile, it may be simpler for the moment to consider that a theory is essentially an *extended definition*, as noted in Chapter 1. In this book, we have examined a multiplicity of perplexing domains in forming integrated perspectives on SLA: variables such as L1, age, cognition, intelligence, personality, identity, culture, input, interaction, and feedback. But is there an integrated, unified theory of SLA, "an *acceptable* general body of principles," that has the agreement of *all*? Not exactly.

CLASSROOM CONNECTIONS

In your experience learning an L2, to what extent do you think your course, activities, and/or your teacher's approach accounted for such factors as L1s in the class, age, personality of students, cultural issues, and construction of identities? What specific actions, words, activities, or approaches reflected a consideration of these factors? How would you, as a teacher, reflect some of these factors in your teaching?

As surely as competing models are typical of all disciplines that attempt to give **explanatory power** to complex phenomena, so this field has its fair share of claims and hypotheses, each vying for credibility and validity (Gregg, 2003; Myles, 2010; Ortega, 2011). We can be quite content with this state of affairs, for it reflects the intricacy of the acquisition process, the complexity of interdependent factors, and the variability of individuals and contexts. On the other hand, we have discovered a great deal about SLA in many languages and contexts, across age and ability levels, and within many specific purposes for acquisition. We need not be apologetic, therefore, about the remaining unanswered questions, for many of the questions posed in the short half-century of "modern" research on SLA have been effectively answered.

WEAVING A TAPESTRY OF "PERSPECTIVES" ON SLA

Having made those caveats, I would suggest that the search for a unified theory is best understood by the recognition of many *perspectives* on SLA. You may prefer to think of them as generalizations, hypotheses, or models. Whatever term you use, let's think of SLA research findings as representative of a number of possible views of this phenomenon. Remember the old John Godfrey Saxe poem about the six blind men [sic] and the elephant? Each was "right" in identifying the elephant as a wall, a tree, a rope, etc., but none perceived the whole elephant. Perhaps our many "right" perspectives on SLA are simply *one* way to view the whole?

I prefer to think of multiple perspectives on SLA as a *tapestry*—yes, another metaphor, and there are more to come in this chapter! Each thread in a tapestry is an important component of the fabric, but those threads are intricately woven together, not haphazardly or randomly, but rather, systematically, to realize the vision of the artist. When perceived as a whole, the tapestry is coherent, maybe even beautiful, and conveys a message. I don't think the field of SLA is ready yet to present one single tapestry to the academy. Nevertheless, each student of SLA, teacher, and researcher is capable of weaving threads together in his or her own coherent fashion, and each of those tapestries is potentially "acceptable."

Let's take a look at some of the ways that researchers have woven their tapestries of SLA over several decades of inquiry.

Carlos Yorio's (1976) Learner Variables

In what might have been the first published attempt to bring together a *comprehensive* classification of variables of SLA, Carlos Yorio (1976), compiled a taxonomy to represent all of the individual factors that must be considered in describing the L2 learner (see Table 10.1). This list of factors begins to give you an idea of the many different domains of inquiry that were considered important, in 1976, to constructing a theory of SLA. The implication behind each factor in the list was that each factor was *necessary* to describe the L2 learning process, and in 1976 Yorio had the wisdom *not* to claim that together the factors were *sufficient* to map the terrain.

Table 10.1 Yorio's (1976) classification of learner variables

Factors	Examples
1. Age	biological, cognitive, and social factors critical period issues parental influence schooling context peer group pressure
2. Cognition	general intelligence aptitude learning strategies
3. Native language	L1 transfer and interference phonology, syntax, semantics
4. Input	natural and instructional settings context of learning and teaching instructional variables: methods, materials, intensity, length foreign vs. second vs. bilingual language learning
5. Affect	sociocultural factors, attitudes egocentric factors: anxiety, ego permeability, self-esteem motivation: integrative, instrumental
6. Education	literate vs. nonliterate number of years of schooling educational system field of study, specialization

Long (2007) suggested that SLA theories (let's call them tapestries) must conform to traditional *logic* by fulfilling two conditions: (1) **necessity**—a condition that *must* be satisfied, and (2) **sufficiency**—the condition is *enough* to prove a point and we are therefore assured of the truth of a statement. You could make the case that each of Yorio's statements was *necessary* for your tapestry, and even that a claim for their interdependence is necessary. But certainly that also implies that (a) no single factor is *sufficient* alone, and more importantly, that (b) all of the factors together may not be sufficient to explain all of SLA.

 CLASSROOM CONNECTIONS

In L2 classes that you have taken, which of Yorio's factors made a difference in the approach that your teacher used? For example, were learning strategies encouraged? Was there reference to a first language? Were you learning a language in the context of a "foreign" or "second" language, and what difference did that make in what you did or didn't do in the classroom?

Patsy Lightbown's (1985) Hypotheses

Now let's turn the clock ahead about a decade and see how lists such as Yorio's changed. Patsy Lightbown (1985, pp. 176–180) proposed ten hypotheses regarding SLA (see Table 10.2). While they reflect some added sophistication, keep in mind these statements were made about thirty years ago—a good deal of water has gone under the bridge since.

Lightbown's list hints at how the field of SLA began to develop in both breadth and depth. "Claims" were now more likely to be viewed as "hypotheses" in view of a mushrooming of studies in all domains of SLA, some with conflicting findings, leading researchers to be more cautious. And statements about SLA reflected the refinement of questions that may have had more of a ring of certainty in the 1970s. Nevertheless, you would be right to disagree a bit with Lightbown's statements. What might those quibbles be?

 CLASSROOM CONNECTIONS

Given that you would indeed quibble with some of Lightbown's claims, which ones would they be, given your experience in an L2 classroom? In L2 classes you have taken, to what extent have intralingual errors been recognized and treated? Or has metalanguage been used to explain structural issues? How meaningful were your lessons and activities?

Table 10.2 Lightbown's (1985) SLA hypotheses

Issues	Hypotheses
1. Acquisition	Adults and adolescents can both "acquire" a second language.
2. Interlanguage	The learner creates a systematic interlanguage that is often characterized by the same systematic errors as [those of] the child learning that same language [e.g., intralingual errors], as well as errors that appear to be based on the learner's own L1 [e.g., interlingual errors].
3. Order of acquisition	There are predictable sequences in acquisition so that certain structures have to be acquired before others can be integrated.
4. Practice	Practice does not make perfect.
5. Metalinguistic knowledge	Knowing [metalinguistically] a language rule does not mean one will be able to use it in communicative interaction.
6. Error treatment	Isolated explicit error correction is usually ineffective in changing language behavior.
7. Fossilization	For most adult learners, acquisition stops—"fossilizes"—before the learner has achieved nativelike mastery of the target language.
8. Time	One cannot achieve nativelike (or near-nativelike) command of a second language in one hour a day.
9. Complexity	The learner's task is enormous because language is enormously complex.
10. Meaningfulness	A learner's ability to understand language in a meaningful context exceeds his or her ability to comprehend decontextualized language and to produce language of comparable complexity and accuracy.

Since publishing her original list of 10 generalizations in 1985, Lightbown offered several "postscripts" to the list (Lightbown, 2000, 2003; Lightbown & Spada, 2006) that modified the initial statements, urged caution in wholesale applications, related the generalizations to CLT, and provided more pedagogical relevance. For example, the "ineffectiveness" of explicit error correction (#6 above) hypothesized in 1985 was later modified to reflect two decades of research of FFI: "Teachers have a responsibility to help learners do their best, and this includes the provision of explicit, form-focused instruction and feedback on error" (Lightbown & Spada, 2006, p. 190). These kinds of revisions and modifications are excellent illustrations of the longitudinal nature of framing a comprehensive view of SLA.

Nick Ellis's (2007) Observed Findings in SLA

Move the clock forward another two decades. In one of the more recent compilations of theories of SLA (VanPatten & Williams, 2007), which described theoretical positions such as UG, input/interaction, and sociocultural approaches, Nick Ellis (2007b, pp. 88–91) posited "observed findings in SLA." Compiled from the perspective that SLA is "**C**onstruction-based, **R**ational, **E**xemplar-driven, **E**mergent, and **D**ialectic" (CREED) (p. 77), Ellis derived his observations from an input-driven model (see more on this below), but they nevertheless remain quite sweeping in their breadth. Consider his ten observations (Table 10.3).

Did you notice how Ellis's ten observations are much more full of hedges than the previous claims? Only observation 1 is *un*equivocal in claiming the condition of *necessity* (observation #4 offers a hedge in the word "often"). The rest offer considerable wiggle room, but still lay claim to certain domains as important factors in a theory of SLA. This may be the effect of a field that is more willing to identify areas of inquiry, but less willing to make strong claims on their predictability or directionality, and perhaps for good reason as the complexity of SLA is unveiled.

Table 10.3 Ellis's (2007b) Observed Findings in SLA

Topics	Observed Findings
1. Input	Exposure to input is necessary for SLA.
2. Implicit learning	A good deal of SLA happens incidentally.
3. Emergentism	Learners come to know more than what they have been exposed to in the input.
4. Predictable sequences	Learners' output (speech) often follows predictable paths with predictable stages in the acquisition of a given structure.
5. Variability	Second language learning is variable in its outcome.
6. Subsystems	Second language learning is variable across linguistic subsystems.
7. Frequency	There are limits on the effects of frequency on SLA.
8. L1	There are limits on the effect of a learner's L1 on SLA.
9. Instruction	There are limits on the effects of instruction on SLA.
10. Output	There are limits on the effects of output (learner production) on language acquisition.

CLASSROOM CONNECTIONS

Consider a few of Ellis's factors: input, implicit learning, and output. What kinds of input did you receive in your L2 classes, and how useful were those forms of input? Did your teacher give you opportunities to engage in incidental learning? How? And how much output was elicited? As a teacher, what would you do differently, if anything at all, and why?

Principles of Language Learning and Teaching

Now let's try one more of these lists, this time emerging from the issues described in this book. The major topics here are, in effect, domains of concern that lead to what I have culled as ten principal themes to weave into the fabric of an SLA tapestry (Table 10.4).

You will notice that for most statements I have chosen to go out on a limb in fulfilling the condition of *necessity*. While certain theoretical claimants may argue, as only good researchers should, I think these ten principles form a reasonably solid (but not exhaustive) foundation on which to construct your own individual tapestry. Add to them, delete some, modify others, refine them. *You*, the reader, are capable of forming your own tapestry! Do so with caution but not with undue timidity. Try it out, do some research on it, teach with it, talk about it with colleagues. That's what theory-building—or tapestry weaving—is all about.

 CLASSROOM CONNECTIONS

In this list of factors, consider individual differences and strategies. Did your L2 teacher's approach consider individual differences among you and your classmates? How so? And did the teacher encourage the use of strategies? If so, which ones and for what skills? How effective were they? As a teacher, what else would you do to reach *every* student in your classroom and facilitate strategy use?

SIX PERSPECTIVES ON SLA

Imagine a color wheel showing the six primary and secondary colors—a pie sliced into six wedges. (Yes, here comes another metaphor!) Now, imagine that each color (red, orange, yellow, green, blue, purple) represents a major cluster of

Table 10.4 Brown's Principles of SLA

Domains	Principles
1. L1 acquisition	Understanding the process of child L1 acquisition is important to understanding L2 acquisition in both adults and children.
2. Age	Age is a critical factor in SLA, with significant differences in SLA across age levels.
3. Neurolinguistics	The development and structure of the human brain is a significant factor in looking across ages as well as within any given age.
4. Learning	Models of SLA and pedagogical approaches must factor in an understanding of how human beings learn *any* skill or acquire *any* knowledge.
5. Individual differences	A wide variation in individual learning styles and personality factors is a necessary consideration in establishing the causes of success in SLA.
6. Strategies	The extent to which L2 learners utilize their strategic competence is crucial to the rate and efficiency of SLA, and to the ultimate degree of success.
7. Sociolinguistics	Sociocultural factors are crucial to a learner's success in constructing one's identity, interacting with other users of the L2, and co-constructing meaning in the context of a community of users of the L2.
8. Communicative competence	In a related principle, L2 learners are invariably called upon to internalize structural, discoursal, pragmatic, stylistic, and nonverbal properties of communication in order to effectively comprehend and produce the L2 in varying contexts.
9. Learner language	The interlanguage development of an emerging L2 involves strategically using accumulated knowledge of one's own universe, the L1, the L2, and communicative contexts, and will by the nature of human learning, involve errors, variation, and periods of stabilization.
10. Instruction	The manner/method of classroom instruction is crucial to ultimate attainment in an L2, and focus on form, whether incidental or explicit, self-stimulated or teacher-stimulated, is crucial to the acquisition of fluent use of the L2.

theoretical perspectives on SLA, but also imagine your computer's color wheel that shows *thousands* of shades of color. This may be a good metaphor for the many ways that research has depicted the process of SLA. Long's (2007) survey of the research uncovered "as many as 60 theories, models, hypotheses, and theoretical frameworks" (p. 4). Myles's (2010) annotated bibliography selected 51 seminal articles and books describing theoretical views over six decades. So, perhaps the notion of thousands of colors isn't really stretching the point?

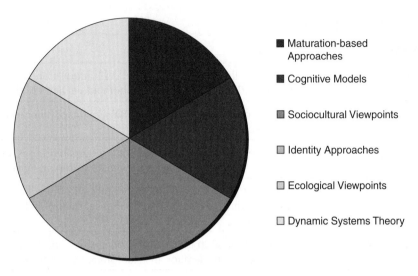

Figure 10.1   Six perspectives on SLA

My own survey of SLA findings, models, claims, and hypotheses seems to cluster theoretical perspectives into about six slices, represented in the schematic diagram in Figure 10.1. The clusters must be rather liberally defined, as some perspectives "belong" to several of the color slices (rendered here in shades of gray). And there is overlap among them, along with some very fuzzy lines of distinction. Rather than explaining each pie slice in great detail, I have provided a sketch here—a brief summary—of each perspective. I hope your own curiosity will lead you to the references provided, and to further inquiry on these perspectives.

Maturation-Based Approaches

One of the earliest claims for language acquisition, especially L1 acquisition, was made by Chomsky (1964), McNeill (1966), and others for the *innate* features of language acquisition. Proposing a hypothetical *language acquisition device*, all humans were said to possess innate abilities that led to "natural" acquisition of language. Maturation-based claims about SLA soon followed. We'll look at one perspective in a little detail, and then add some others.

The Input Hypothesis

One of the most talked-about models within this tradition was Stephen Krashen's (1977, 1981, 1982, 1985, 1992, 1997) *acquisition-learning hypothesis*, also known as the *input hypothesis* as well as the *monitor model*. Five claims were made by Krashen:

1. **Acquisition-Learning Hypothesis**: Adult learners' "fluency in L2 performance is due to what we have *acquired*, not what we have *learned*"

(1981, p. 99). Subconscious acquisition is separate from conscious learning and is superior in the long run.

2. **Monitor Hypothesis**. Monitoring, "watchdogging" one's output, and other explicit, intentional learning, ought to be largely avoided, as it presumed to hinder acquisition.

3. **Natural Order Hypothesis**. Extrapolating from morpheme order studies (Dulay & Burt, 1974b, 1976), later confirmed by Goldschneider and DeKeyser (2001), we acquire language rules in a predictable or "natural" order.

4. **Input Hypothesis**. Comprehensible input—input that is "a bit beyond" one's level of competence—is "the only *true cause* of second language acquisition" (Krashen,1984, p. 61). That input may be represented as $i + 1$, that is, neither too far beyond one's reach nor so close that it poses no challenge ($i + 0$). Further, speech will naturally "emerge" with sufficient comprehensible input.

5. **Affective Filter Hypothesis**. The best acquisition will occur in environments of low anxiety, that is, in contexts where the *affective filter* is low.

Criticisms of the Input Hypothesis

Krashen's hypotheses had some intuitive appeal to language teachers: They were, in the words of H. L. Mencken, "short and simple," easy for teachers to grasp and faithfully follow. Many researchers, however, with Mencken, have hotly disputed Krashen's claims as "wrong" (McLaughlin, 1978; Gregg, 1984; White, 1987; Brumfit, 1992; Swain & Lapkin, 1995; de Bot, 1996; Gass & Selinker, 2001; Swain, 2005). Let's look briefly at the criticisms.

1. **Consciousness.** Barry McLaughlin (1978, 1990a) sharply criticized Krashen's fuzzy distinction between subconscious (acquisition) and conscious (learning) processes, claiming that an SLA theory that appeals to conscious/subconscious distinctions is greatly weakened by our inability to identify just what that distinction is.

2. **No interface.** Kevin Gregg (1984) eloquently refuted the claim of no interface—no overlap—between acquisition and learning. Arguing that there is no evidence to back up the claim, Gregg showed that implicit and explicit learning can indeed complement each other.

3. **No explicit instruction**. Studies repeatedly showed that Krashen's "zero option" (don't ever teach grammar) cannot be supported (Long, 1983, 1988; R. Ellis, 1990b, 1997; Lightbown & Spada, 1990; Buczowska & Weist, 1991; Doughty, 1991; Doughty & Williams, 1998; Swain, 1998). Explicit strategy training (Cohen, 2011; Oxford, 2011a) and FFI, as we saw in Chapter 9, can indeed aid in successful SLA.

4. **$i + 1$**. As shown in decades of learning psychology (Ausubel, 1968) and in Vygotsky's (1987) Zone of proximal Development (ZPD), the notion of $i + 1$ is simply a reiteration of a general principle of learning. Gregg

(1984) and White (1987) also noted that we are unable to define either *i* or *1*.

5. **Speech will emerge.** In claiming that speech will naturally emerge when the learner is "ready," the input hypothesis diminishes the learner's own *initiative* in seeking input. Seliger (1983) distinguished between **High Input Generators (HIGs)**, learners who are good at initiating and sustaining interaction, and **Low Input Generators** (LIGs) who are more passive, reticent, and less assertive. HIGS were superior learners in Seliger's (1983) study.

 CLASSROOM CONNECTIONS

If HIGs are superior learners, what are some strategies you have used for generating input? Can those tricks be taught? How can a teacher nudge learners in the direction of actively generating communicative situations, rather than passively hoping that others will be the first to speak up?

---

6. **Output Hypothesis**. Claiming input as "the *only* causative variable" (Krashen, 1986, p. 62) in SLA ignores (a) the distinction between input and **intake** (Gass & Selinker, 2001), (b) the importance of *social interaction* (Dunn & Lantolf, 1998; Lantolf, 2000; Kinginger, 2001; Young, 2011) in SLA, and (c) what Merrill Swain (Swain, 1993, 1995, 2000, 2005; Swain & Lapkin, 2005), called the **Output Hypothesis**. Swain offered convincing evidence that output was at least as significant as input, if not more so. Kees de Bot (1996) argued that "output serves an important role in second language acquisition because it *generates* highly specific input the cognitive system needs to build up a coherent set of knowledge" (p. 529). Others have strongly supported the central role of output (Izumi & Bigelow, 2000; Shehadeh, 2001; Whitlow, 2001).

Universal Grammar (UG)

Another maturational set of perspectives has been offered in the claim that Universal Grammar (UG) provides at least a partial explanation for commonalities that have been found in both L1 and L2 acquisition across languages (White, 2003, 2009; Bhatia & Ritchie, 2009). Extending characteristics of language acquisition beyond language-specific constraints, UG research has been examining SLA across a number of grammatical categories, including question formation, negation, word order, embedded clauses, subject deletion, and more. UG researchers maintain that innate properties constrain both first and second language acquisition.

Emergentism

When innateness theories were first proposed in the 1960s, linguists and language teachers were swept away by the breath of fresh air after years of struggling with behavioral models. It all made eminently good sense! Of course, everyone thought, inborn genetic predispositions answered so many questions. It took some time, but by the end of the twentieth century, serious counterclaims were being mounted in the form of **emergentism**. In the words of William O'Grady (2012) "language acquisition without an acquisition device . . . [implies] not only is there no UG, there is no specialized acquisition device" (p. 116).

The shock waves of emergentism are still being felt in the SLA community, but eloquent arguments and research findings are mounting in defense of the emergent nature of language. Emergentists show that language is not some special isolated ability governed by innately predisposed rules, but rather, that "the complexity of language emerges from a relatively simple developmental process being exposed to a massive and complex environment" (N. Ellis, 2003, p. 81). Language behaves in the same way that any other complex system behaves (N. Ellis, 2007b), or what O'Grady (2012) called the Amelioration Hypothesis.

 CLASSROOM CONNECTIONS

When you took an L2 in a classroom, how was your process of learning like any other skill-learning? (Playing a sport or musical instrument, for example?) What were the *stages* of learning and how were they similar? As a teacher, how would you help people develop the *skill* of SLA?

Other Related Issues

Some other issues deserve mention under the rubric of maturationally based claims about SLA. Some of these have either been discarded or put on a back burner. *L1 interference* models and the *Contrastive Analysis Hypothesis* (CAH), for example, were due for "a period of quiescence" (Wardhaugh, 1970, p. 126) as long ago as 1970, and while no one would diminish the effect of *any* prior experience and knowledge, both positive and negative, L1-L2 contrasts remain just one among many possible factors in SLA.

Questions about "*foreign accents*" are another much less celebrated issue in SLA these days. Granted, post–critical-period SLA is indeed marked by various forms of nonnativelike accents, but in the globalization of languages, especially major languages like English, Chinese, Spanish, and French, accents are so widely varied and indigenized (Kachru, 2011), that their significance is somewhat minor.

The effect of *age* on acquisition (Birdsong, 2009) is still of intense interest, as more and more is discovered about the relationship of cognition, brain anatomy, and development across languages.

Brain-based, *neurolinguistic* inquiry into both L1 and L2 acquisition remains a topic of intense interest (Schumann et al., 2004; Urgesi & Fabbro, 2009). Some recent strides have been taken in neuro-imaging of bilinguals, along with examining the relationship of brain plasticity to SLA. However, we are in a period of infancy in identifying the precise neural networks that contribute to and impede language acquisition. Someday, perhaps, we will be able to boast the discovery of the "language gene" and other genetic, synaptic, cellular properties of language, but we're not there yet.

Cognitive Models

Let's turn the color wheel clockwise to a second collage of perspectives, one that has occupied a great deal of focused effort over perhaps half a century: cognitivism. While there is an element of cognitive perspectives in virtually every theory or model of SLA, we'll cluster a few perspectives within this parameter, as their focus is centrally on the *mental* framework for language, and on the *individual* as a learner, as opposed to more socially or affectively oriented positions (Verspoor & Tyler, 2009).

An Attention-Processing Model

In the 1960s, cognitive psychology (Ausubel, 1968) made a big splash, representing a new era of thinking that appeared to rescue educational psychology from many of the dilemmas and shortfalls of behavioral theory. While cognitive models were—and still are—more metaphorical than empirical, they accounted for conscious thinking, mental processing, and systematic storage and retrieval that was well beyond the scope of behavioral models.

One domain within cognitivism that "remains one of the key puzzles confronting the scientific worldview" (Koch, 2004, p. 1) is defining and understanding *consciousness*. Recognizing this conundrum, Barry McLaughlin (McLaughlin, 1978, 1987, 1990b; McLaughlin, Rossman, & McLeod, 1983; McLeod & McLaughlin, 1986) directed the attention of SLA researchers away from quibbling over consciousness and toward two features of human cognition: **controlled** and **automatic processing**. Controlled processing was described as typical of anyone learning a brand *new skill* (e.g., L2 beginners) in which only a very *few elements* of the skill can be retained, while automatic processes are used in more *accomplished skills* (advanced L2 learners), in which the "hard drive" of one's brain manages multiple of bits of information simultaneously.

Both ends of this continuum of processing can occur with either **focal** (intentional, explicit) or **peripheral** (incidental, implicit) *attention* to the task at hand, that is, focusing attention either centrally or on the periphery. Both focal and peripheral attention to some tasks may be quite conscious (Hulstijn, 1990). When you are driving a car, for example, your focal attention may center on cars directly in front of you as you move forward; but your peripheral attention to cars beside you and behind you, to potential hazards, and of course to the other thoughts running through your mind is all very much within your conscious awareness. In SLA your focal attention could be on *form* at times and on *meaning* at others, but an important stage to reach in SLA is to be able to focus on meaning while attending peripherally to form. Such a perspective on SLA entirely obviates the need to distinguish conscious and subconscious processing.

Let's look at some specific examples, set out in Table 10.5.

A plausible interpretation of the four processes, with some overlap among them, would place most classroom learners roughly on a line of progression from #1 (controlled/focal) to #4 (automatic/peripheral). The latter might also be known as **fluency**, an ultimate communicative goal for language learners (Wood, 2001). In FFI, for example, the ultimate goal is not to leave the learner focused on form, but rather to incorporate a correct form peripherally into the learner's automatic processing mechanisms. In the same way that right now, at this moment, you are reading these lines for meaning and understanding, you are also peripherally aware of the words, structures, and rhetorical conventions used to convey the meaning.

Table 10.5 Practical applications of McLaughlin's attention-processing model

Processes	Examples
1. Controlled/Focal	Explaining a specific grammar point Giving an example of a word usage Learning prefabricated routines Repeating after the teacher
2. Controlled/Peripheral	Giving simple greetings Playing a simple language game Using memorized routines in new situations Completing very limited conversations
3. Automatic/Focal	Monitoring output Giving brief attention to form during conversation Scanning for specific keywords Editing writing, including peer editing
4. Automatic/Peripheral	Participating in open-ended group work Skimming and rapid reading Freewriting Engaging in natural unrehearsed conversation

Implicit and Explicit Processing

Built into McLaughlin's model is a distinction between **implicit** and **explicit** attention, already explained in Chapter 9. In linguistic terms, **implicit knowledge** is information that is automatically and spontaneously used in language tasks, while **explicit knowledge** includes facts that a learner knows *about* language (J.N. Williams, 2009). Children implicitly learn phonological, syntactic, semantic, and pragmatic rules for language, but do not have access to an explicit description of those rules. Implicit processes enable a learner to perform language but not necessarily to cite rules governing the performance. Ellen Bialystok (1978, 1982, 1990a), Rod Ellis (1994a, 1997), and Nick Ellis (1994, 2007b) argued the importance of distinguishing implicit and explicit processing.

Another way of looking at the implicit/explicit dichotomy (or is it a dichotomy?) is to think of language processing as **analyzed** and **unanalyzed** knowledge (Bialystok, 1982). The former includes the verbalization of linguistic rules and facts, as in a grammar-focus exercise, while the latter is synonymous with implicit learning. Other terminology has been used to describe virtually the same dichotomy: **intentional** vs. **incidental** learning (Gass & Selinker, 2001; N. Ellis, 2007b; Dörnyei, 2009), as well as **declarative** vs. **procedural** knowledge. These terminological contrasts underscore the interplay, in all classroom learning of an L2, of directing learners' attention to form while at the same time encouraging those forms to move to the periphery. On the periphery, learners are *aware* of forms, but are not *focused* on (or overwhelmed by) those forms.

The constructs of explicit/implicit knowledge have drawn the attention of numerous researchers over the years. Arguments were raised about the definition of implicit and explicit and about how to apply both processing types in the classroom (Bialystok, 1990b; Hulstijn, 1990; Robinson, 1994, 1995, 1997). Some useful pedagogical applications emerged in Rod Ellis's (1994a, 1997; Han & Ellis, 1998) suggestions for **grammar consciousness raising**, for example, in which some explicit attention to language form is blended with implicit communicative tasks.

 CLASSROOM CONNECTIONS

In interactive classrooms, explicit instruction and structural analysis gets lost in a teacher's zeal for meaningful communication. Did you ever experience any "grammar consciousness raising" tasks in your own L2 classes? How would you as a teacher frame such awareness while still maintaining a communicative tone?

Systematicity and Variability

In this spectrum of theoretical models, one more hue should be called to your attention: interlanguage systematicity and variability (Preston & Bayley, 2009). The search for predictable sequences of acquisition, for patterns of error, for stages of progress toward a learner's goals, and for explanations of variability in that journey has been carried out mostly within a cognitive framework. The research supporting interlanguage systematicity has drawn on UG evidence, on variable competence models (R. Ellis, 1994a), and on reams of raw data from language learners across languages, ages, and contexts. In recent years we have seen less focus in SLA on attempts to discover systematicity, and more work on the importance of identity (Morgan & Clarke, 2011), interaction (Young, 2011), and on the tantalizing "ecology" of SLA (Van Lier, 2011).

Sociocultural Viewpoints

In the 1990s, momentum built around the "social turn" in SLA research, some of which was synopsized in Chapter 8. Sociocultural viewpoints differed from maturational and cognitivist perspectives in their focus on interaction, as opposed to the *individual* learner, and on language as the major tool for engaging in collaborative activity in a community of language users. As such, the previous two perspectives represented what Firth and Wagner (1997) called "SLA's general preoccupation with the *learner*, at the expense of other potentially relevant social identities" (p. 288). Drawing heavily from the earlier work of Lev Vygotsky (1978, 1987) and the linguistic perspectives of James Lantolf (2000) and many others, sociocultural theory became a "hot topic" in SLA.

Mediation and the ZPD

A key to sociocultural perspectives on SLA is the *mediating* role of language as a means to *regulate* and control communicative activity (Lantolf & Thorne, 2007; Lantolf, 2011). How do individuals use language to mediate? Children learning their L1 use language "to reshape biological perception into *cultural* perception and concepts" (Lantolf & Thorne, 2007, p. 203) in three stages that move from object-regulation to other-regulation and finally to *self-regulation*. In L2 learning, similar stages are manifested as L2 learners, through collaborative activity, create new ways of meaning.

A key to Vygotsky's research findings is his description of a **Zone of Proximal Development** (ZPD), loosely defined as the metaphorical distance between a learner's existing developmental state and his or her potential development. The ZPD is "the domain of knowledge or skill where the learner is not yet capable of independent functioning, but can achieve the desired outcome given relevant scaffolded help" (Mitchell & Myles, 2004, p. 196). Two important components of the ZPD interact to propel an L2 toward further development: (1) Scaffolding is the process of simplifying tasks for learners, of guiding learners in appropriate directions, of marking critical features of language (e.g., form-focused activity), and structuring a task for success as opposed to failure. (2) This process is a "two-way street," accomplished as a *collaborative* effort between teacher and learner, one that neither could accomplish on their own.

 CLASSROOM CONNECTIONS

In L2 classes that you have taken, in what way were tasks "scaffolded" for you, if at all? If so, how was that accomplished? If not, as a teacher, how might you scaffold a relatively difficult activity for your students?

Long's Interaction Hypothesis

A related model of SLA was developed by Michael Long (1985, 1996, 2007) who posited an **interaction hypothesis**, which essentially redefined comprehensible input and scaffolding as **modified interaction**. The latter includes the various modifications that native speakers and other interlocutors create in order to make their input comprehensible to learners. As we saw in Chapter 2, in L1 contexts, parents modify their speech to children ("Mommy go bye-bye now"). When interacting with L2 learners, native and more proficient speakers likewise modify their input in several ways:

- Slowing down speech, speaking more deliberately
- Providing comprehension checks ("Go down to the subway—do you know the word 'subway'?")
- Requesting clarification/repair ("Did you mean 'to the *right*'?")
- Giving paraphrases ("I went to a New Year's Eve party, you know, like, December 31st, the night before the first day of the new year?")

In Long's view, interaction and input are two major players in the process of acquisition, a combination emphasized by Gass (2003). In a marked departure from viewing L2 classrooms as contexts for "practicing" language forms, conversation and other interactive communication are, according to Long, the *basis* for SLA development. A number of studies supported the link between interaction and acquisition (Pica, 1987; Gass & Varonis, 1994; Loschky, 1994; Jordens, 1996; van Lier, 1996; Gass, Mackey, & Pica, 1998; Swain & Lapkin, 1998). In a strong endorsement of the power of interaction in the language curriculum, van Lier (1996) devoted a whole book to "the curriculum as interaction" (p. 188). Here, principles of awareness, autonomy, and authenticity lead the learner into Vygotsky's (1978) zone of proximal development (ZPD), where learners construct the new language through socially mediated interaction.

Long's interaction hypothesis pushed pedagogical research on SLA into a new frontier. It centered us on the language classroom not just as a place where learners of varying abilities and styles and backgrounds mingle, but also as a place where the contexts for interaction are carefully designed. It focused materials and curriculum developers on creating the optimal environments and tasks for input and interaction such that the learner will be stimulated to create his or her own learner language in a socially constructed process. Further, it continues to remind us that the many variables at work in an interactive classroom should prime teachers to expect the unexpected and to anticipate the novel creations of learners engaged in the process of discovery.

Social Constructivist Views

We can sum up sociocultural perspectives by adding another hue to this same general perspective. Social constructivist theories, discussed in Chapter 1, have been associated with current approaches to studying SLA (Siegel, 2003; Watson-Gegeo & Nielsen, 2003; Lantolf, 2005; Zuengler & Cole, 2005). They emphasize the dynamic nature of the interplay among learners, their peers, their teachers, and others with whom they interact. The interpersonal context in which a learner operates takes on great significance, and therefore, the interaction between learners and others is the focus of observation and explanation.

Identity Approaches

The next slice on the color wheel pie may quite arguably be simply an extension of sociocultural views of SLA. I'm choosing to give identity approaches their own niche for two reasons: (1) The issue of identity is deeply embedded in all human functioning, especially linguistic communication, in which a person transacts oneself to others. (2) Identity approaches are a combination of *all three* of the previously discussed maturational, cognitive, and sociocultural perspectives, and we therefore cannot overlook both age and "mind" in considering identity and its relation to SLA.

Identity approaches are not new to the field of SLA. In previous chapters we have looked at *language ego*, first studied by Guiora et al. (1972a), and the extent to which learning L2 can both positively and negatively affect one's *self-esteem* and *self-efficacy*. Schumann's (1976c) *social distance* model leaned heavily on the perception of self vis-à-vis the culture of the L2. Clarke (1976) even went so far as to suggest that L2 encounters are so threatening and traumatic that L2 learners share symptoms of schizophrenia. And then, the widely quoted Gardner and Lambert (1972) studies linking *attitudes* to motivation were predicated on L2 learners' *cultural* identity and perception of the L2 culture.

The chief spokesperson for the more recent surge of interest in identity is Bonny Norton, who has argued that "speech, speakers, and social relationships are inseparable" (1997, p. 410). A corollary to this claim is that "an individual's identity in L2 contexts is mediated by the reactions of others to that individual's social and cultural position" (Ricento, 2005, p. 899). Much of Norton's (1997, 2000, 2011) work has focused on identity issues as they relate to gender, ethnicity, race, socioeconomic status, native vs. nonnative speakers, and power. In each case, one can build strong arguments for the centrality of identity in a theory of SLA—perhaps not the *exclusivity* of identity, but its paramount importance.

Let's look at gender, as an example (Norton & Pavlenko, 2004), which takes on importance on several planes. Gender is reflected either formally (e.g., in grammar or phonology) or functionally (pragmatically) in virtually every language: from languages that dictate "female" and "male" forms (such as Thai) to the pragmatics of reference to, addressing, and attitudes toward women. According to identity theory, gender is not a static series of personal traits or attributes, but rather "a system of social relations and discursive practices" (Pavlenko & Piller, 2001, p. 23).

Another example of the role of identity is manifested in issues of native and nonnative speakers of a language and the related issues of power. Some SLA researchers maintain that the terms "native" and "nonnative" are themselves "offensive and hierarchical in that they take the native as the norm and define the 'other' negatively in relation to this norm" (Phillipson, 2000, p. 98). Especially in the context of "subtractive" SLA, by distinguishing between the two, according to Pavlenko and Lantolf (2000), learners are in jeopardy of multiple feelings of *loss*: loss of one's L1, one's L1 identity, one's "inner voice," and one's family heritage. Clearly these are not trivial concerns for the L2 learner!

 CLASSROOM CONNECTIONS

In L2 classes that you have taken, did you find that you took on a new identity? How did that process unfold? How did your interaction with others shape your identity? How would you, as a teacher, help students to recognize the importance of identity construction?

Ecological Viewpoints

As we move around the color wheel, you will note how each perspective incorporates elements (or hues) of others, a sign of the nature of SLA as a complex undertaking with many facets to examine. In this next swath of color, let's encompass a number of *unifying* views of SLA that may be thought of as *ecological* approaches. Ecology implies a relationship beyond simple cause and effect in a linear relationship (essentialism). Rather, an interdependent relationship of forces creates viability and balance. Greek historian Herodotus noted that crocodiles, for example, open their mouths to allow birds to pluck leeches out, thus providing nutrition for the birds and "natural dentistry" for the crocs! In typical food chains, we have a succession of interacting stages that ultimately nourish a number of levels of species.

In considering an ecological approach to SLA, the perspective is one that features *situated cognition* and *agency*, according to van Lier (2011). The former concept features context and the multiplicity of ways the human beings internalize our context, our environment, and then agency involves our physical, cognitive, emotional, and social interaction in whatever context we find ourselves. Agency implies our willful ability to be "agents" in our contexts, to create tools for survival in our environment. Agency means taking initiative, and linguistically, engaging in discourse to promote social relationships that are the foundation stones of survival. As van Lier (2011) noted, "an ecological stance on language learning is anchored in agency, as all of life is. Teaching, in its very essence, is promoting agency. Pedagogy is guiding this agency wisely" (p. 391).

Sociocognitive Approaches

Within this ecological perspective, Atkinson (2011a) described a *sociocognitive* approach to SLA, in which "mind, body, and world function integratively in SLA" (p. 143). A sociocognitive approach considers both physical (body) and cognitive (mental) abilities as they interact *socially* with the world around them. As already noted, human beings are, after all, adaptive organisms continually perceiving and adjusting to their environment, and ultimately *learning* from their dynamic interaction with the environment. Atkinson noted that SLA is "a natural adaptive process of ecological alignment" (2011a, p. 144).

Classical cognitivism highlighted logical thought, serial processing, and top-down rule-governed behavior—including linguistic behavior. These assumptions are challenged by sociocognitive approaches that view human behavior as embodied, adaptive intelligence that enables us to survive in our socially constructed worlds. Operating with van Lier's (2011) *situated* cognition, we humans have "a finely tuned mechanism in place that is responsive to the multifaceted and dynamic features of the physical and social environment" (Semin & Cacciopo, 2008, p. 122).

Language must be "nimble and quick" (Atkinson, 2011a, p. 146) to initiate and maintain social action. Siding with *emergentist* approaches described earlier in this chapter, and with *connectionism* described in Chapter 2, sociocognitive perspectives consider language as a major mechanism for adaptation that does not differ completely from other skills that are acquired. Further, *learning* is most certainly not confined to classrooms, as learning is a continuous adaptive process. Finally, a most productive side of this slice of the color pie is the reemergence of nonverbal communication as fundamental to our dynamic adaptation (Kinsbourne & Jordan, 2009). Nonverbal signals are empirically observable and crucial to face-to-face interaction, signaling attention, agreement, emotional responses, and other communicative acts in common with all mammalian life.

Skill Acquisition Theory

Somewhere within the hues and shades of ecological views of language lies a broadly sweeping view of SLA as the acquisition of skills that can be accounted for by a set of basic principles common to the acquisition of *all* skills. According to Robert DeKeyser (2007), skill acquisition theory "has proven to be remarkably resilient through various developments in psychology, from behaviorism to cognitivism to connectionism" (p. 97).

Psychologists have identified, in relatively broad strokes, three stages of development of skill of any kind: cognitive, associative, and autonomous (Fitts & Posner, 1967). Thus, whether you are learning to walk, play the piano, read, use apps on your iPad, or write a best-selling novel, there are predictable stages of development that apply to both natural and instructed learning. Granted, the initial stage may call upon implicit and incidental processing, but it comes in the form of perceiving others engaged in skilled behavior. The second associative stage is acting on the perceptions in "practice," or using what may be described as procedural knowledge. Finally, the autonomous stage may be reached after extensive execution of tasks in stage two, but keep in mind this stage always has its ups and downs.

 CLASSROOM CONNECTIONS

In your experience learning an L2 (or several languages), how would you characterize your learning stages in terms of cognitive, associative, and autonomous? What were some specific linguistic or psychological manifestations of such stages? As a teacher, how would you help your learners to progress from one stage to another?

Positing stages of SLA is nothing new. In fact, traditional language teaching paradigms of the mid-twentieth century featured presentation, practice, and production (Byrne, 1986), which sounds very much like stages. So does skill acquisition theory represent a new breakthrough? No, if tried-and-true pedagogical approaches are simply reenacted. Yes, if you place skill acquisition theory within a paradigm that treats language like all other skill learning, and views SLA within "the larger enterprise of cognitive science" (DeKeyser, 2007, p. 109).

A Horticultural Metaphor of SLA

Get ready for another metaphor, motivated by the notion of the *ecology* of language. But I must first issue a disclaimer about the *metaphor* that I am about to present. I intend now to stretch your mind a bit with some light-hearted, right-brained, outside-the-box musings about SLA. These thoughts are intended to entertain, amuse, and maybe even to stimulate some creative thinking.

I was moved one day in the SLA class I was teaching to create an alternative picture of SLA: one that responded not so much to rules of logic, mathematics, and physics as to botany and ecology. The germination (pun intended) of my picture was the metaphor once used by Derek Bickerton in a lecture at the University of Hawaii about his contention that human beings are "bio-programmed" for language (Bickerton, 1981) perhaps not unlike the bio-program of a flower seed, whose genetic makeup predisposes it to deliver, in successive stages, roots, stem, branches, leaves, and flowers. In a burst of right-hemisphere fireworks, I went out on a limb (another pun intended) to extend the flower-seed metaphor to SLA. My picture of the ecology of language acquisition is in Figure 10.1.

The rain clouds of input stimulate seeds of predisposition (innate, genetically transmitted processes). But the potency of that input is dependent on the appropriate styles and strategies that a person puts into action (here represented as soil). Upon the germination of language abilities, networks of competence (which, like underground roots, cannot be observed from above the ground) build and grow stronger as the organism actively interacts in its context. The resulting root system (inferred competence or intake), through the use of further strategies and affective abilities and the feedback we receive from others (note the tree trunk), ultimately gives rise to full-flowering communicative abilities. The fruit of our performance (output) is conditioned by the climate of contextual variables.

At any point the horticulturist (teacher) can irrigate to create better input, apply fertilizers for richer soil, encourage the use of effective strategies and affective enhancers, and, in the greenhouses of our classrooms, control the contextual climate for optimal growth!

Lest you scoff at these speculative images, think about how many factors in SLA theory are conceptualized and described metaphorically: *deep* and *surface* structure, language acquisition *device, pivot* and *open* words, Piaget's *equilibration,* Vygotsky's *zone* of proximal development, cognitive *pruning, transfer, prefabricated patterns,* social *distance, global* and *local* errors, *fossilization, backsliding, monitoring,* affective *filter, automatic* and *controlled* processing. How would we describe SLA without such terms?

 CLASSROOM CONNECTIONS

Can you think of some other useful metaphors that capture aspects of SLA and teaching? How did some of those metaphorical concepts play out in your own learning? Did you, for example, ever find yourself "pruning" bits and pieces of your language? Or using "prefabricated patterns" as a communication strategy? As a teacher, how would you teach your students to "monitor" their output at an optimal level?

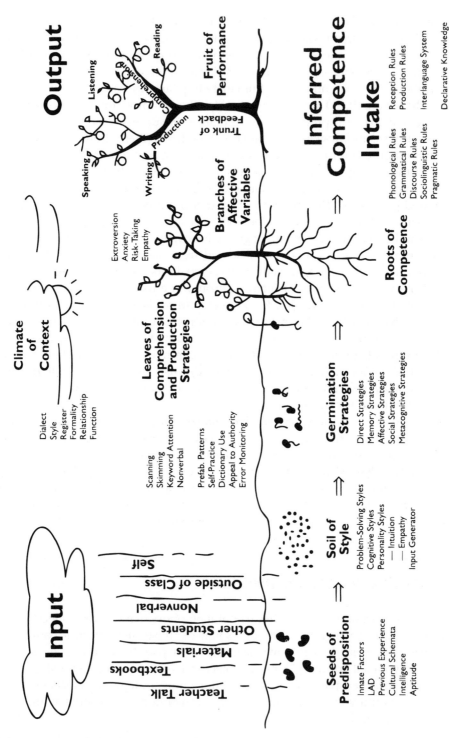

Figure 10.2   The ecology of language acquisition (Brown, 1991)

James Lantolf (1996) once made an impassioned plea for the legitimacy of metaphor in SLA theory building. Much of our ordinary language is metaphorical, whether we realize it or not, and a good many of our theoretical statements utilize metaphor. Some scholars have been less than sanguine about using metaphor in describing SLA because it gives us "license to take one's claims as something less than serious hypotheses" (Gregg, 1993, p. 291). But surely as long as one recognizes the limitations of metaphors, don't they have the power to maintain the vibrancy of theory? If a metaphor enables us to describe a phenomenon clearly and to apply it wisely—and cautiously—then it serves a purpose, as long as we understand that these word-pictures are subject to certain breakdowns when logically extended too far.

So, while you might exercise a little caution in drawing a tight analogy between Earth's botanical cycles and language learning, you might just allow yourself to think of second language learners as budding flowers—plants needing your nurture and care. When the statistical data and technical terminology of current second language research become excruciatingly difficult to understand, try creating your own metaphors!

Dynamic Systems Theory

Consider for a moment an old proverbial poem:

> For want of a nail, the shoe was lost
> For want of a shoe, the horse was lost
> For want of a horse, the rider was lost
> For want of a rider, the message was lost
> For want of a message, the battle was lost
> For want of a battle, the kingdom was lost
> And all for the want of a horseshoe nail

The message is universal: tiny little happenings can lead, step-by-step, to history-changing events. I've already mentioned in a previous chapter the quip that a butterfly flapping its wings in the Amazon could, through a progression of events, cause a hurricane in Hawaii. Chaos theory, popularized in James Gleick's 1987 book, *Chaos: Making a New Science*, was an attempt to account for seemingly random connections and presumably inexplicable phenomena in the universe around us, known as the "butterfly effect." A ping-pong ball floating down a white-water stream is viewed not as a helter-skelter scurry, but rather as a systematic, albeit complex, journey that follows laws of physics. This line of thinking, also referred to as **chaos-complexity theory** as well as **dynamic systems theory**, has now spread to many of the so-called "soft" sciences, including linguistics and SLA.

The goal of dynamic systems theory (DST) in SLA is to discover order and systematicity within all the presumed variability of millions of L2 learners across hundreds of languages worldwide. To do so, according to Michael Halliday, we need to move beyond the concept of *multi*disciplinary (and inter-disciplinary) to a *transdisciplinary* approach that supersedes the former, transcending the narrowness of disciplinary methodology (Halliday & Burns, 2006). Even with the hybrid disciplines alluded to earlier in this chapter (psycholinguistics, neurolinguistics), we are likely not to achieve complete explanatory adequacy until we move "beyond" the discipline.

DST can be described in the form of general principles, according to Diane Larsen-Freeman (2011, 2012a). These include the claim that complex systems

1. are open and dynamic
2. manifest disequilibrium
3. are adaptive to change within multiple contexts
4. have elements that interact with each other in nonlinear patterns, and
5. exhibit unexpected occurrences.

One of the most intriguing aspects of DST is the concept of the interdependency of interacting elements. Perhaps like the "murmuration" of flocks of thousands of starlings performing their amazing shadowlike dances in the sky, each element of one's L2 journey relates to other elements and causes change. An L2 learner takes in multiple inputs every day, sorts through them, organizes them, forms new meanings and hypotheses, rejects old ones, and wakes up the next morning a new, changed (linguistic) person.

 CLASSROOM CONNECTIONS

Can you think of examples in your own L2 learning of the five characteristics of DST outlined by Larsen-Freeman? How did you experience "disequilibrium"? What were some examples of "unexpected occurrences"? How could a teacher help students to accept and learn from these moments?

Five decades ago, linguist Dwight Bolinger, with Mark-Twain–like tongue in cheek, described English as "a god-awful mixture of irregularities growing out of competing regularities—a perpetual cliffhanger where one crisis resolves itself by creating another" (1966, p. 5). Perhaps Bolinger's wryness could be captured in Spivey's (2007, p. 171) somewhat more sophisticated description of language as "graded probabilistic contingencies (not logical rules) governing relationships between syntactic categories." Can we see order in the chaos? Larsen-Freeman (2011) said we can, and elaborated on adaptive qualities of successful L2 learners, their active role in achieving success, the importance—but not sufficiency—of frequency, the emergent nature of language acquisition, the pervasiveness of variability, and the primacy of agency.

Should we, with Nick Ellis (2007a), characterize DST as "the coming of age of SLA research" (p. 23)? Is DST "the quintessential future approach to human action, cognition, and behavior, including language" (van Geert, 2007, p. 47)? Or is there a downside to DST? A few caveats were offered by Zoltan Dörnyei (2009): (1) Because we are in the infancy of DST approaches, we have few specifics on "how this broad sweep would allow a better understanding of the actual processes that we observe amongst language learners." (2) DST seems to be more successful in accounting for the *un*predictable nature of SLA development than its regularities, predictable patterns, and universals. (3) Conducting empirical studies of SLA within a DST framework is problematic. Replacing quantitative research methodology with alternative tools of measurement poses a challenge (pp. 110–111).

Are we up to the challenge? I like to think we are. I've dabbled a bit in astronomy lately and have been intrigued by astronomers' search for other Earth-like planets "out there" in our vast, complex, dynamic universe. For years the prospect of finding a tiny little planet zillions of light years away, far from the prying eyes of even the finest electronic telescopes, seemed daunting if not futile.

But in recent years, by probing the complexity of the *interdependencies* of those heavenly bodies, some progress has been made. First, it was discovered that stars, or suns, with orbiting planets exhibited the tiniest of a "wobble" due to the gravitational effect of the *planet* on the sun it was spinning around! Ergo, a wobbling star equals (maybe) an accompanying orbiting planet. More recently, by measuring the light output of distant stars, it is conjectured that a planet *transiting* across a distant star actually diminishes the total light emission of the star by a few micro-millionths, which is measurable with highly sophisticated instruments. And now astronomers claim to have found several thousand Earth-sized "candidates" out there spinning around distant suns. Wow!

Now let's come back to Earth. If DST does nothing more than to expand your horizons in viewing the many facets of SLA, perhaps it deserves its place as a slice of our color wheel. Remember, no single perspective alone is *sufficient* to explain everything about SLA, but perhaps most if not all of the perspectives outlined here are *necessary* in order to maintain an open-minded, cautiously eclectic approach to SLA.

SOME FINAL COMMENTS

This chapter is intended to help you to consider the many issues, models, hypotheses, and claims discussed in the previous nine chapters and put them into a manageable framework that ultimately *informs your pedagogy*. I have chosen the color wheel as a metaphor for thinking about all these factors. You might at times want to rotate the color wheel from one slice to another to consider their prismatic effect one by one. Or maybe you'll want to blur the lines of distinction among the six color slices. Worse, you put a pin in the middle, spin it, and let fate choose which color ends up at twelve o'clock—like those games you played as a kid—then you're stuck with one facet that's too narrow to be very useful.

The point is that teachers benefit from understanding the many perspectives underlying everyday classroom practices. By putting such principles at the *foundation* of your methodological options, you facilitate making better choices among classroom techniques, valid and reliable assessments of student performance, more accurate evaluation of the effectiveness of your pedagogy, and enlightened decisions on what you will do better tomorrow. How do you bridge that gap between theoretical underpinnings and the nitty-gritty work of teaching students an L2? Let's look at some guidelines.

Theory to Practice or Cooperative Dialogue?

For a number of decades in the middle part of the twentieth century, SLA pedagogy was too often plagued by the notion of a *dichotomy* between theory and practice. Researchers in their ivory towers made issued proclamations while classroom teachers embodied those claims in the classroom. By the 1990s, the custom of leaving theory to researchers and practice to teachers became, in Clarke's (1994) words, "dysfunctional." Moreover, the unnecessary stratification of laborers in the same vineyard, a dysfunction that was perpetuated by both sides, accorded higher status to a researcher/theorist than to a practitioner/teacher. The latter was made to feel that he or she is the *recipient* of the former's findings and prognostications, with little to offer in return.

What has become clear in recent years is the importance of viewing the process of language instruction as a *cooperative dialogue* among many technicians, each endowed with special skills. Those skills vary widely: developing curricula, writing textbooks, observing and analyzing students "in action," hypothesizing parameters of acquisition, educating teachers, synthesizing others' findings, facilitating classroom learning opportunities, designing experiments, assessing student performance, enhancing learning through technology, and artfully helping learners to reach their fullest potential. There is no set of technical skills here that gets uniquely commissioned to create theory or another set allocated to "practicing" it.

We are all practitioners and we are all theorists. We are all charged with developing a broadly based conceptualization of the process of language learning and teaching. We are all responsible for understanding as much as we can about how to create contexts for optimal acquisition among learners. Whenever that understanding calls for putting together diverse bits and pieces of knowledge, you are doing some theory building. Whenever you, in the role of a teacher, ask pertinent questions about SLA, you are beginning the process of research that can lead to a "theoretical" claim. If you have some thoughts about the relevance of age factors, strategy use, identity construction, or form-focused instruction, and you're a teacher, you can become a researcher-teacher. So, the ages-old theory-practice debate has been put aside in favor of a more productive symbiotic approach.

 CLASSROOM CONNECTIONS

Do you ever feel that SLA "theory" is too far removed from classroom practices? What are some theoretical claims or hypotheses that you would like to put into practice in your own teaching? Have your L2 teachers been good examples of being both theorists and practitioners?

The Believing Game and the Doubting Game

Throughout this book, we have seen that truth is neither unitary nor unidimensional. We have seen that definitions and extended definitions are never short, never simple, and almost always complex. Just as a photographer captures many facets of the same mountain by circling around it, truth presents itself to us in many forms, and sometimes those forms seem to conflict.

The elusive nature of truth was addressed by Peter Elbow (1973), who noted that most scholarly traditions are too myopically involved in what he called the "doubting game" of truth-seeking: trying to find something *wrong* with someone's claim or hypothesis. The doubting game is seen, incorrectly, as rigorous, disciplined, rational, and tough-minded. But Elbow urged us to turn such conceptions upside down and engage in what he called the "believing game." In the believing game you try to find truths, not errors; you make acts of self-insertion and self-involvement, not self-extrication.

If you were to try to unify or to integrate everything that every second language researcher concluded, or even everything listed in the previous sections, you could not do so through the doubting game alone. But by balancing your perspective with a believing attitude toward those elements that are not categorically ruled out, you can maintain a sense of perspective. If a "doubter" were to tell you, for example, that your class of adult learners will without question experience difficulty because of the critical period hypothesis ("the younger the better"), you might throw up your hands in despair. But the "believer" in you might consider context, learner variables, teaching methodology, and other attendant factors, and spur you to a more optimistic and productive attitude.

The bottom line? Try a healthy dose of both believing and doubting games in your SLA enterprise, but when in doubt, lean toward believing.

The Art and Science of SLA

Several decades ago, Ochsner (1979) made a plea for a "poetics" of SLA research in which we use two research traditions to draw conclusions. One tradition is a **nomothetic tradition** of empiricism, scientific methodology, and prediction. On the other hand, a **hermeneutic** (or, constructivist) **tradition** provides us with a means for interpretation and understanding in which we do not look for absolute laws. "A poetics of second language acquisition lets us shift our perspectives," according to Ochsner (p. 71), who sounded very much like he had been reading Peter Elbow!

Schumann (1982a) adopted a similar point of view in suggesting the consideration of both the "art" and the "science" of SLA research. In reference to a number of controversial debates in SLA, Schumann suggested that divergent views can coexist as "two different paintings of the language learning experience—as reality symbolized in two different ways" (p. 113). His concluding remarks, however, lean toward viewing our research as art, advantageous because such a view reduces the need for closure and allows us to see our work in a larger perspective with less dogmatism and ego involvement. In short, it frees us to play the believing game more ardently and more fruitfully.

When all the well-crafted models of SLA have been considered and applied, isn't teaching the quintessential amalgamation of art and science? Teachers' behaviors in the classroom are largely guided by a course syllabus, selected materials, and a lesson plan for the day (science), but the moment-by-moment communicative transactions must be *artfully* created. Excellent teachers are competent scientists, but they are brilliant artists.

 CLASSROOM CONNECTIONS

Have your L2 teachers been good examples of combining both the art and science of teaching? In what ways? What are some classroom scenarios that you can imagine where you as a teacher could be both artistic and scientific? What scientific principles of group work, for example, might you apply, and how would your "art" become a part of the process?

The Role of Intuition

That brings us to intuition, one of the most mysterious characteristics of "the good language teacher," or should that be "the *excellent* language teacher"? Psychological research has shown us that people tend to favor either an *intuitive* or an *analytical* approach to problems. Ewing (1977) noted that "intuitive thinkers are likely to excel if the problem is elusive and difficult to define. They keep coming up with different possibilities, follow their hunches, and don't commit themselves too soon" (p. 69). Sternberg and Davidson (1982) found that insight—making inductive leaps beyond the given data—is an indispensable factor of intelligence, much of which is traditionally defined in terms of analysis. Bruner and Clinchy (1966) said that intuition is "based on a confidence in one's ability to operate with insufficient data" (p. 71).

All this suggests that intuition forms an essential component of our total cognitive endeavor—and of our teaching art. What is intuition? One of the important characteristics of intuition is its "loss for words." Often we are not able to give a verbal explanation of why we have made a decision or solution. Maybe it "felt right," or we had "a gut feeling." The implications for teaching are clear. We daily face problems in language teaching that have no ready analysis, no available language or metalanguage to capture the essence of why we said or did something. Many good teachers cannot verbalize all their classroom behaviors in a specific and analytical way, yet they remain good teachers.

Intuition involves risk taking. As we saw in Chapter 6, language learners need to take risks willingly. Language teachers must be willing to risk techniques or assessments that have their roots in a hunch that they are right. In our universe of complex theory, we still perceive vast black holes of unanswerable questions about how people best learn second languages. Intuition, "the making of good guesses in situations where one has neither an answer nor an algorithm for obtaining it" (Baldwin, 1966, p. 84), fills the void.

There is ample evidence that good language teachers have developed good intuition. In an informal study of cognitive styles among ESL learners a few years ago, I asked their teachers to predict the TOEFL score that each of their students would attain when they took the TOEFL the following week. The teachers had been with their students for only one semester, yet their predicted scores and the actual TOEFL results yielded extraordinarily high (>.90) correlations.

How do you "learn" intuition? Consider these possibilities: (1) Intuition is not developed in a vacuum. Therefore, your job is to internalize essential principles of SLA, and rely on them as firm grounding for all your classroom decisions. (2) Second, *intuitions are formed at the crossroads of knowledge and experience*. There is no substitute for the experience of "diving in" to your classroom of real learners in the real world. Learn from your victories (success) *and* your defeats (mistakes), and intuition will follow. (3) Third, be a willing risk taker. Let the creative juices within you flow freely. The wildest and craziest ideas should—with some caution—be entertained openly. In so doing, intuition will be allowed to germinate and to grow to full fruition.

If your hunches about SLA are firmly grounded in a comprehensive understanding of what SLA is and what we know about optimal conditions for learning an L2, you are well on your way to becoming an *enlightened* language teacher. You will plan a lesson, enter a classroom, and engage interactively with students, all with an optimistic attitude that you have formed a *principled* approach to your practice. You may stumble here and there, but you will use the tools of your SLA theory to *reflect* on your practice and then to learn from those reflections how to better approach the classroom on the next day. I hope you have been enabled, through digesting the pages of this book, to make that enlightened, principled, reflective journey!

SUGGESTED READINGS

Myles, F. (2010). The development of theories of second language acquisition. *Language Teaching, 43*, 320–332.

> One of a number of "research timelines" in the journal *Language Teaching*, this comprehensive annotated bibliography synopsizes theoretical works from 1945–2008.

VanPatten, B., & Williams, J. (Eds.) (2007). *Theories in second language acquisition*. Mahwah, NJ: Lawrence Erlbaum.

Atkinson, D. (Ed.). (2011b). *Alternative approaches to second language acquisition*. New York: Routledge.

> Both volumes, with separate chapters authored by renowned scholars in their fields, offer excellent discussions, summaries, and analyses of major theoretical positions in SLA, each chapter with a comprehensive set of references.

Ritchie, W., & Bhatia, T. (Eds.). (2009). *The new handbook of second language acquisition*. Bingley, UK: Emerald Group.

Hinkel, E. (Ed.). (2011). *Handbook of research in second language teaching and learning: Volume II*. New York: Routledge.

> These two volumes together comprise 1,700 pages with 84 separate chapters by leading researchers and experts in their specialized fields of SLA. Virtually every imaginable subfield is represented, and thousands of references are provided with each chapter. They are a gold mine of information for undertaking research in SLA.

Lantolf, J. (1996). SLA theory building: Letting all the flowers bloom! *Language Learning, 46*, 713–749.

> Some fascinating, mind-stretching, and rewarding reading on the place of metaphor in SLA models and hypotheses, with a balanced perspective on theories in SLA.

LANGUAGE LEARNING EXPERIENCE: FINAL JOURNAL ENTRY

Note: See journal entry directions in Chapter 1 for general guidelines for writing a journal on a previous or concurrent language learning experience.

- At the beginning of the chapter, four different lists of SLA factors were offered, representing several different points of view. Choose two or three factors that interest you the most and write about your own language learning experience in relation to the topic.

- What do you think, in your own experience as a language learner, is the most useful aspect of each of the six perspectives on SLA that were described? Describe those in terms of your actual L2 learning experiences. For example, if you think *emergentism* offers insights into your learning, how does your L2 journey seem like learning any other skill?
- How has your identity changed in the process of learning an L2? What specific "moments" do you recall when you realized that your L2 identity was either new or different? Did that bother you, or did you simply accept it as part of the natural process of SLA?
- Reflect a bit on what you think about Dynamic Systems Theory. Is it just an excuse for saying SLA is really, really, really complicated? Or does it make sense to keep probing and probing until you find a cause or answer or connection of some kind? Illustrate with examples from your L2 learning.
- If you didn't do exercise #4 or #5 below, take on that assignment of creating a largely nonverbal model of SLA. Let your mind be creative. Then write about what you learned from that experience.
- As an alternative, try outlining what you think would be the top three or four or five elements/concepts/issues in creating your theory of SLA, and briefly justify your choices.
- If you have taught already, then reflect on this one. If you have not, then project yourself into the future: What are some examples of teaching that quite clearly demand the *art* of teaching? Or *intuition* that you must rely on when all the theories and science cannot direct you? How about those moments when a student said or did something completely unpredictable?
- Given everything you now know about learning a second language, what are the characteristics of a *successful* teacher? How did your own foreign language teacher measure up?
- What did you like the most about writing this journal? The least? What benefit did you gain from the journal-writing process? How would you change the process if you were to tackle such journal writing again?

FOR THE TEACHER: ACTIVITIES (A) & DISCUSSION (D)

Note: For each of the "Classroom Connections" in this chapter, you may wish to turn them into individual or pair-work discussion questions.

1. (A) At the beginning of the chapter, four lists of generalizations about SLA were discussed (Yorio, Lightbown, Ellis, Brown). Divide the class into pairs or small groups, and assign one list of generalizations to each pair/group. Their task is to (a) evaluate their list in terms of *necessity* (is each item necessary?) and *sufficiency* (is the list as a whole sufficient for a complete theory?), (b) offer any caveats or "it depends" statements about

the list, and (c) add, change, or delete any items they wish. Ask for reports from each group.

2. (A) Divide the class into six small groups, each representing one of the six perspectives on SLA, or "slice" of the color wheel pie. Ask each group to (a) defend the importance of their perspective, and (b) note any weaknesses or drawbacks to their perspective.

3. (D) Review the five tenets of Krashen's Input Hypothesis. Ask students which ones they think are most plausible and least plausible, and why. How would they take the "best" of his theories and apply them in the classroom and yet still be mindful of the various problems inherent in his ideas about SLA?

4. (D) Direct students, as "homework," to create a model of SLA that doesn't use [much] prose and language, but rather, relies on a visual, graphic, or kinesthetic metaphor. For example, some might create an SLA board game in which players have to throw dice and pass through the "perils of puberty," the "mire of mistakes," the "falls of fossilization," and so on. Or they could create a flow chart or diagram. Or they might write a song or analogize to something kinesthetic like Aikido or a fitness routine. Ask them to bring their creations back to "show and tell" in the classroom.

5. (A) Break students into groups, perhaps according to visual, graphic, or kinesthetic preferences, and give them the same assignment as #4 above. Ask each group to present their model and explain the components.

6. (A) Divide the class into pairs or small groups. Tell each group that they are a committee that has been invited to an international symposium on SLA, the goal of which is to devise a theory of SLA. Each group must name (and explain) *three* (no more) of the most important tenets or generalizations to be included in the theory. Have each group present and defend their three factors. As a wrap-up discussion, ask the class to comment on overlap and/or a composite picture of the most important features of a theory of SLA.

7. (D) Go back to the definitions of language, learning, and teaching that were formulated at the beginning of this book (Chapter 1), and ask the class how, if at all, they might revise those definitions now, in light of all the information they have amassed in this course.

8. (A) Divide the class into pairs or groups. Ask each to make a list of a few characteristics of an "enlightened, principles-based, intuitive language teacher." Have them write their lists on the board and discuss the findings as a whole class.

BIBLIOGRAPHY

Abraham, R. (1981). *The relationship of cognitive style to the use of grammatical rules by Spanish-speaking ESL students in editing written English.* Unpublished doctoral dissertation, Champaign-Urbana, University of Illinois.

Abraham, R. (1985). Field independence-dependence and the teaching of grammar. *TESOL Quarterly, 19,* 689–702.

Abrahamsson, N., & Hyltenstam, K. (2009). Age of acquisition and nativelikeness in a second language—listener perception *vs.* linguistic scrutiny. *Language Learning, 59,* 249–306.

Abrams, Z. (2002). Surfing to cross-cultural awareness: Using Internet-mediated projects to explore cultural stereotypes. *Foreign Language Annals, 35,* 141–160.

Acton, W. (1979). *Second language learning and perception of difference in attitude.* Unpublished doctoral dissertation, University of Michigan.

Adams, C. (1997). Onset of speech after a left hemispherectomy in a nine-year-old boy. *Brain, 120,* 159–182.

Adamson, H. (1988). *Variation theory and second language acquisition.* Washington, DC: Georgetown University Press.

Adamson, H. D. (2008). *Interlanguage variation in theoretical and pedagogical perspective.* New York: Routledge.

Allaire, L. (1997). The Caribs of the Lesser Antilles. In S. Wilson (Ed.), *The indigenous people of the Caribbean* (pp. 180–185). Gainesville, Florida: University of Florida.

Allwright, R. (1980). Turns, topics, and tasks: Patterns of participation in language learning and teaching. In D. Larsen-Freeman (Ed.), *Discourse analysis in second language research.* Rowley, MA: Newbury House.

Alpert, R., & Haber, R. (1960). Anxiety in academic achievement situations. *Journal of Abnormal and Social Psychology, 61,* 207–215.

Andersen, P. (2007). *Nonverbal communication: Forms and functions* (2nd ed.). Long Grove, IL: Waveland Press.

Andersen, R. (1978). An implicational model for second-language research. *Language Learning, 28,* 221–282.

Andersen, R. (1979). Expanding Schumann's pidginization hypothesis. *Language Learning, 29,* 105–119.

Andersen, R. (1982). Determining the linguistic attributes of language attrition. In R. Lambert & B. Freed (Eds.), *The loss of language skills*. Rowley, MA: Newbury House.

Anderson, N. (1991). Individual differences in strategy use in second language reading and testing. *Modern Language Journal, 75,* 460–472.

Anderson, N. (2005). L2 learning strategies. In E. Hinkel (Ed.), *Handbook of research in second language teaching and learning* (pp. 757–771). Mahwah, NJ: Lawrence Erlbaum Associates.

Anderson, R., & Ausubel, D. (Eds.). (1965). *Readings in the psychology of cognition.* New York: Holt, Rinehart & Winston.

Andrés, V. (1999). Self-esteem in the classroom or the metamorphosis of butterflies. In J. Arnold (Ed.), *Affect in Language Learning* (pp. 87–102). Cambridge, UK: Cambridge University Press.

Arias, R., & Lakshmanan, U. (2005). Code-switching in a Spanish-English bilingual child: A communication resource? In J. Cohen, K. T. McAlister, K. Rolstad, & J. Macswan (Eds.), *Proceedings of the fourth international symposium on bilingualism* (pp. 94–109). Somerville, MA: Cascadilla Press.

Armstrong, T. (1993). *Seven kinds of smart.* New York: Penguin Books.

Armstrong, T. (1994). *Multiple intelligences in the classroom.* Philadelphia: Association for Curriculum Development.

Arnold, J. (2007). Self-concept as part of the affective domain in language learning. In F. Rubio (Ed.), *Self-esteem and foreign language learning* (pp. 13–27). Newcastle, UK: Cambridge Scholars Publishing.

Arnold, J. (Ed.). (1999). *Affect in language learning.* Cambridge, UK: Cambridge University Press.

Asher, J. (1977). *Learning another language through actions: The complete teacher's guidebook.* Los Gatos, CA: Sky Oaks Productions.

Aston, G. (Ed.). (2001). *Learning with corpora.* Houston, TX: Athelstan.

Atkinson, D. (1999). TESOL and culture. *TESOL Quarterly, 33,* 625–654.

Atkinson, D. (2000). Comments on Dwight Atkinson's "TESOL and culture": The author responds. *TESOL Quarterly, 34,* 752–755.

Atkinson, D. (2002). Toward a sociocognitive approach to second language acquisition. *Modern Language Journal, 86,* 525–545.

Atkinson, D. (2011a). A sociocognitive approach to second language acquisition. In D. Atkinson (Ed.), *Alternative approaches to second language acquisition* (pp. 143–166). New York: Routledge.

Atkinson, D. (2011c). Introduction: Cognitivism and second language acquisition. In D. Atkinson (Ed.), *Alternative approaches to second language acquisition* (pp. 1–23). New York: Routledge.

Atkinson, D. (Ed.). (2011b). *Alternative approaches to second language acquisition.* New York: Routledge.

Au, S. (1988). A critical appraisal of Gardner's social-psychological theory of second language learning. *Language Learning, 38,* 75–100.

Auerbach, E. (1995). The politics of the ESL classroom: Issues of power in pedagogical choices. In J. Tollefson (Ed.), *Power and inequality in language education* (pp. 9–33). Cambridge: Cambridge University Press.

Austin, J. (1962). *How to do things with words*. Cambridge, MA: Harvard University Press.

Ausubel, D. (1963). Cognitive structure and the facilitation of meaningful verbal learning. *Journal of Teacher Education, 14,* 217–221.

Ausubel, D. (1964). Adults vs. children in second language learning: Psychological considerations. *Modern Language Journal, 48,* 420–424.

Ausubel, D. (1965). Introduction to part one. In R. Anderson & D. Ausubel (Eds.), *Readings in the psychology of cognition* (pp. 3–17). New York: Holt, Rinehart & Winston.

Ausubel, D. (1968). *Educational psychology: A cognitive view*. New York: Holt, Rinehart & Winston.

Bachman, L. (1990). *Fundamental considerations in language testing*. New York: Oxford University Press.

Bailey, K. (1983). Competitiveness and anxiety in adult second language learning: Looking at and through the diary studies. In H. Seliger & M. Long (Eds.), *Classroom oriented research in second language acquisition* (pp. 67–102). Rowley, MA: Newbury House.

Bailey, K. (1985). Classroom-centered research on language teaching and learning. In M. Celce-Murcia (Ed.), *Beyond basics: Issues and research in TESOL*. Rowley, MA: Newbury House.

Bailey, P., Onwuegbuzie, A., & Daley, C. (2000). Correlates of anxiety at three stages of the foreign language learning process. *Journal of Language and Social Psychology, 19,* 474–490.

Bakhtin, M. (1986). *Speech genres and other late essays* (V. W. McGee, Trans.). Austin: University of Texas Press.

Bakhtin, M. (1990). *Art and answerability: Early philosophical essays* (V. Liapunov & K. Brostrom, Trans.). Austin: University of Texas Press.

Baldwin, A. (1966). The development of intuition. In J. Bruner (Ed.), *Learning about learning*. Washington, DC: U. S. Government Printing Office.

Banathy, B., Trager, E., & Waddle, C. (1966). The use of contrastive data in foreign language course development. In A. Valdman (Ed.), *Trends in Language Teaching* (pp. 35–56). New York: McGraw-Hill.

Bandura, A. (1993). Perceived self-efficacy in cognitive development and functioning. *Educational Psychologist, 28,* 117–148.

Baran, M. (2010). The immigrants' story, told through letters. http://minnesota.publicradio.org/features/2010/11/immigrant-letters-home/

Bardovi-Harlig, K. (1999a). Exploring the interlanguage of interlanguage pragmatics: A research agenda for acquisitional pragmatics. *Language Learning, 49,* 677–713.

Bardovi-Harlig, K. (1999b). From morpheme studies to temporal semantics: Tense-aspect research in SLA. *Studies in Second Language Acquisition, 21,* 341–382.

Barfield, A., & Brown, S. (Eds.). (2007). *Reconstructing autonomy in language education: Inquiry and innovation*. Basingstoke, UK: Palgrave Macmillan.

Barron, A. (2012). Interlanguage pragmatics: From use to acquisition to second language pedagogy. *Language Teaching, 45,* 44–63.

Bateman, B. (2002). Promoting openness toward culture learning: Ethnographic interviews for students of Spanish. *Modern Language Journal, 86,* 318–331.

Bates, E., & MacWhinney, B. (1982). Functionalist approach to grammar. In E. Warmer & L. Gleitman (Eds.), *Language acquisition: The state of the art* (pp. 173–218). New York: Cambridge University Press.

Bax, S. (2003). The end of CLT: A context approach to language teaching. *ELT Journal, 57,* 278–287.

Bayley, R., & Preston, D. (Eds.). (1996). *Second language acquisition and linguistic variation.* Amsterdam: John Benjamins.

Beebe, L. (1983). Risk-taking and the language learner. In H. Seliger & M. Long (Eds.), *Classroom oriented research in second language acquisition* (pp. 39–65). Rowley, MA: Newbury House.

Bell, D. (2003). Method and postmethod: Are they really so incompatible? *TESOL Quarterly, 37,* 325–336.

Bellugi, U., & Brown, R. (Eds.). (1964). The acquisition of language. *Monographs of the Society for Research in Child Development, 29* (Serial No. 92).

Belz, J., & Kinginger, C. (2003). Discourse options and the development of pragmatic competence by classroom learners of German: The case of address forms. *Language Learning, 53,* 591–647.

Benson, P. (2001). *Teaching and researching autonomy in language learning.* London: Longman.

Benson, P., & Toogood, S. (Eds.). (2002). *Learner autonomy 7: Challenges to research and practice.* Dublin, Ireland: Authentik.

Benson, P., & Voller, P. (1997). Introduction: autonomy and independence in language learning. In P. Benson & P. Voller (Eds.), *Autonomy and independence in language learning* (pp. 1–12). London: Longman.

Berko-Gleason, J. (1982). Insights from child acquisition for second language loss. In R. Lambert & B. Freed (Eds.), *The loss of language skills.* Rowley, MA: Newbury House.

Berko-Gleason, J. (1988). Language and socialization. In F. Kessel (Ed.), *The development of language and language researchers: Essays in honor of Roger Brown.* Hillsdale, NJ: Lawrence Erlbaum Associates.

Berko, J. (1958). The child's learning of English morphology. *Word, 14,* 150–177.

Berlin, B., & Kay, P. (1969). *Basic Color Terms: Their Universality and Evolution.* Berkeley: University of California Press.

Berns, M. (1984a). Functional approaches to language and language teaching: Another look. In S. Savignon & M. Berns (Eds.), *Initiatives in communicative language teaching: A book of readings.* Reading, MA: Addison-Wesley.

Berns, M. (1984b). [Review of the book *The Functional–Notional Approach: From Theory to Practice*]. *TESOL Quarterly, 18,* 325–329.

Berns, M. (1990). *Contexts of competence: Social and cultural considerations in communicative language teaching.* New York: Plenum Press.

Bhatia, T., & Ritchie, W. (2009). Language mixing, universal grammar and second language acquisition. In W. Ritchie & T. Bhatia (Eds.), *The new handbook of second language acquisition* (pp. 591–621). Bingley, UK: Emerald Group Publishing, Ltd.

Bialystok, E. (1978). A theoretical model of second language learning. *Language Learning, 28,* 69–83.

Bialystok, E. (1981). Some evidence for the integrity and interaction of two knowledge sources. In R. Andersen (Ed.), *New dimensions in second language acquisition research*. Rowley, MA: Newbury House.

Bialystok, E. (1982). On the relationship between knowing and using linguistic forms. *Applied Linguistics, 3,* 181–206.

Bialystok, E. (1983). Inferencing: Testing the "hypothesis testing" hypothesis. In H. Seliger & M. Long (Eds.), *Classroom oriented research in second language acquisition*. Rowley, MA: Newbury House.

Bialystok, E. (1985). The compatibility of teaching and learning strategies. *Applied Linguistics, 6,* 255–262.

Bialystok, E. (1990a). *Communication strategies: A psychological analysis of second language use*. Oxford, UK: Basil Blackwell.

Bialystok, E. (1990b). The dangers of dichotomy: A reply to Hulstijn. *Applied Linguistics, 11,* 46–52.

Bialystok, E. (2002). On the reliability of robustness: A reply to DeKeyser. *Studies in Second Language Acquisition, 24,* 481–488.

Biber, D., & Conrad, S. (2001). Quantitative corpus-based research: Much more than bean counting. *TESOL Quarterly, 35,* 331–336.

Biber, D., Conrad, S., & Reppen, R. (1998). *Corpus linguistics: Investigating language structure and use*. Cambridge, UK: Cambridge University Press.

Biber, D., Johansson, S., Leech, G., Conrad, S., & Finegan, E. (1999). *The Longman grammar of spoken and written English*. Harlow, UK: Longman.

Bickerton, D. (1981). *Roots of language*. Ann Arbor, MI: Karoma.

Bickerton, D. (2010). *Adam's tongue: How humans made language, how language made humans*. New York: Hill and Wang.

Birdsong, D. (2005). Nativelikeness and non-nativelikeness in L2A research. *IRAL, 43,* 319–328.

Birdsong, D. (2009). Age and the end state of second language acquisition. In W. Ritchie & T. Bhatia (Eds.), *The new handbook of Second Language Acquisition*. Amsterdam: Elsevier.

Birdsong, D. (Ed.). (1999). *Second language acquisition and the critical period hypothesis*. Mahwah, NJ: Lawrence Erlbaum Associates.

Blackledge, A., & Creese, A. (2010). *Multilingualism: A critical perspective*. New York: Continuum Press.

Bley-Vroman, R. (1988). The fundamental character of foreign language learning. In W. Rutherford & M. Sharwood-Smith (Eds.), *Grammar and second language teaching: A book of readings*. New York: Newbury House.

Block, D. (2007). The rise of identity in SLA research, post Firth and Wagner (1997). *Modern Language Journal, 91,* 863–876.

Bloom, L. (1971). Why not pivot grammar? *Journal of Speech and Hearing Disorders, 36,* 40–50.

Bloom, L. (1976). Language development. In R. Wardhaugh & H. D. Brown (Eds.), *A survey of applied linguistics* (pp. 8–43). Ann Arbor: The University of Michigan Press.

Bolinger, D. (1966). Oddments of English. *Journal of English Linguistics, 24,* 4–24.

Bolinger, D. (1975). *Aspects of language* (2nd ed.). New York: Harcourt Brace Jovanovich.

Bongaerts, T., & Poulisse, N. (1989). Communication strategies in L1 and L2: Same or different? *Applied Linguistics, 10,* 253–268.

Bongaerts, T., Planken, B., & Schils, E. (1995). Can late starters attain a native accent in a foreign language? A test of the critical period hypothesis. In D. Singleton & Z. Lengyel (Eds.), *The age factor in second language acquisition.* Clevedon, UK: Multilingual Matters.

Boroditsky, L. (2011). How language shapes thought. *Scientific American, XX,* 63–65.

Boroditsky, L., & Gaby, A. (2010). Remembrances of times east: Absolute spatial representations of time in an Australian aboriginal community. *Psychological Science, 21,* 1635–1639.

Braun, S. (2007). Integrating corpus work into secondary education: From data-driven learning to needs-driven corpora. *ReCALL, 19,* 307–328.

Breen, M., & Candlin, C. (1980). The essentials of a communicative curriculum in language teaching. *Applied Linguistics, 1,* 89–112.

Brizendine, L. (2010). *The male brain.* New York: Three Rivers Press.

Brodkey, D., & Shore, H. (1976). Student personality and success in an English language program. *Language Learning, 26,* 153–159.

Brown, A., & Gullberg, M. (2008). Bidirectional crosslinguistic influence in L1-L2 encoding of manner in speech and gesture: A study of Japanese speakers of English. *Studies in Second Language Acquisition, 30*: 225–251.

Brown, H. D. (1970). *English relativization and sentence comprehension in child language.* Unpublished doctoral dissertation, University of California, Los Angeles.

Brown, H. D. (1971). Children's comprehension of relativized English sentences. *Child Development, 42,* 1923–1936.

Brown, H. D. (1972). Cognitive pruning and second language acquisition. *Modern Language Journal, 56,* 218–222.

Brown, H. D. (1973). Affective variables in second language acquisition. *Language Learning, 23,* 231–244.

Brown, H. D. (1980). The optimal distance model of second language acquisition. *TESOL Quarterly, 14,* 157–164.

Brown, H. D. (1989). *A practical guide to language learning.* New York: McGraw-Hill.

Brown, H. D. (1990). M & Ms for language classrooms? Another look at motivation. In J. Alatis (Ed.), *Georgetown University round table on languages and linguistics 1990.* Washington, DC: Georgetown University Press.

Brown, H. D. (1991). *Breaking the language barrier.* Yarmouth, ME: Intercultural Press.

Brown, H. D. (2001). *Teaching by principles: An interactive approach to language pedagogy* (2nd ed.). White Plains, NY: Pearson Education.

Brown, H. D. (2002). *Strategies for success: A practical guide to learning English.* White Plains, NY: Pearson Education.

Brown, H. D. (2007). *Teaching by principles: An interactive approach to language pedagogy* (3rd ed.). White Plains, NY: Pearson Education.

Brown, R. (1966). The "tip of the tongue" phenomenon. *Journal of Verbal Learning and Verbal Behavior, 5,* 325–337.

Brown, R. (1973). *A first language: The early stages.* Cambridge, MA: Harvard University Press.

Brown, R., & Bellugi, U. (1964). Three processes in the child's acquisition of syntax. *Harvard Educational Review, 34,* 133–151.

Brown, R., & Hanlon, C. (1970). Derivational complexity and order of acquisition in child speech. In J. Hayes (Ed.), *Cognition and the development of language* (pp. 155–207). New York: Wiley.

Brumfit, C. (1992). Review of Stephen Krashen's *Language acquisition and language education. Applied Linguistics, 13,* 123–125.

Bruner, J., & Clinchy, B. (1966). Towards a disciplined intuition. In J. Bruner (Ed.), *Learning About Learning* (pp. 383–393). Washington, DC: U.S. Government Printing Office.

Bruner, J., Olver, R., & Greenfield, P. (Eds.). (1966). *Studies in cognitive growth.* New York: Wiley.

Buckley, L. (2000). A framework for understanding cross-cultural issues in the English as a second language classroom. *CATESOL Journal, 12,* 53–72.

Buczowska, E., & Weist, R. (1991). The effects of formal instruction on the second language acquisition of temporal location. *Language Learning, 41,* 535–554.

Budwig, N. (1995). *A Developmental–Functionalist Approach to Child Language.* Mahwah, NJ: Lawrence Erlbaum Associates.

Burgoon, J., Guerrero, L., & Floyd, K. (2011). *Nonverbal communication.* Boston: Allyn & Bacon.

Burnard, L., & McEnery, T. (Eds.). (2000). *Rethinking language pedagogy from a corpus perspective.* Frankfurt, Germany: Peter Lang.

Burt, M., & Kiparsky, C. (1972). *The gooficon: A repair manual for English.* Rowley, MA: Newbury House.

Busch, D. (1982). Introversion–extroversion and the EFL proficiency of Japanese students. *Language Learning, 32,* 109–132.

Bybee, J., & Hopper, P. (Eds.). (2001). *Frequency and the emergence of linguistic structure.* Amsterdam: John Benjamins.

Bybee, J., & Thompson, S. (2000). Three frequency effects in syntax. *Berkeley Linguistic Society, 23,* 65–85.

Bygate, M., Skehan, P., & Swain, M. (2001). *Researching pedagogic tasks: Second language learning, teaching, and testing.* Harlow, UK: Longman.

Byram, M. (2012). Language awareness and (critical) cultural awareness—relationships, comparisons, contrasts. *Language Awareness, 21,* 5–13.

Byram, M., & Feng, A. (2005). Teaching and researching intercultural competence. In E. Hinkel (Ed.), *Handbook of research in second language teaching and learning* (pp. 911–930). Mahwah, NJ: Lawrence Erlbaum Associates.

Byrne, D. (Ed.). (1986). *Teaching oral English* (2nd ed.). Harlow, UK: Longman.

Cairns, E., & Cammock, T. (1989). *The 20-item matching familiar figures test: Technical data.* Unpublished manuscript, University of Ulster, Coleraine, UK.

Cameron, D., & Kulick, D. (2003). *Language and sexuality.* Cambridge, UK: Cambridge University Press.

Campbell, D., & Fiske, D. (1959). Convergent and discriminant validation by the multitrait/multimethod matrix. *Psychological Bulletin, 56,* 81–105.

Campbell, R. (1978). Notional-functional syllabuses 1978: Part I. In C. Blatchford & J. Schachter (Eds.), *On TESOL 78: EFL policies, programs, practices* (pp. 15–19). Washington, DC: Teachers of English to Speakers of Other Languages.

Canagarajah, A. (1999). *Resisting linguistic imperialism*. Oxford: Oxford University Press.

Canale, M. (1983). From communicative competence to communicative language pedagogy. In J. Richards & R. Schmidt (Eds.), *Language and communication* (pp. 2–27). London: Longman Group, Ltd.

Canale, M., & Swain, M. (1980). Theoretical bases of communicative approaches to second language teaching and testing. *Applied Linguistics, 1,* 1–47.

Carmichael, L., Hogan, H., & Walter, A. (1932). An experimental study of the effect of language on visually perceived form. *Journal of Experimental Psychology, 15,* 73–86.

Carpenter, S. (2000). Effects of cultural tightness and collectivism on self-concept and causal attributions. *Cross-cultural Research, 34,* 38–56.

Carrell, P., Prince, M., & Astika, G. (1996). Personality types and language learning in an EFL context. *Language Learning, 46,* 75–99.

Carrier, K. (2003). Improving high school English language learners' second language listening through strategy instruction. *Bilingual Research Journal, 27,* 383–408.

Carroll, J. (Ed.). (1956). *Language, thought, and reality: Selected writings of Benjamin Lee Whorf.* Cambridge, MA: Massachusetts Institute of Technology Press.

Carroll, J., & Sapon, S. (1959). *Modern language aptitude test.* New York: The Psychological Corporation.

Carroll, L. (1872). *Through the looking glass.* Boston: Lee & Shepard.

Carroll, S., & Meisel, J. (1990). Universals and second language acquisition: Some comments on the state of current theory. *Studies in Second Language Acquisition, 12,* 201–208.

Carson, J., & Longhini, A. (2002). Focusing on learning styles and strategies: A diary study in an immersion setting. *Language Learning, 52,* 401–438.

Carter, B. (2001). From awareness to counseling in learner autonomy. *AILA Review, 15,* 26–33.

Cathcart, R., & Olsen, J. (1976). Teachers' and students' preferences for correction of classroom conversation errors. In J. Fanselow & R. Crymes (Eds.), *On TESOL 76* (pp. 41–53). Washington, DC: Teachers of English to Speakers of Other Languages.

Celce-Murcia, M., & Hawkins, B. (1985). Contrastive analysis, error analysis, and inter-language analysis. In M. Celce-Murcia (Ed.), *Beyond basics: Issues and research in TESOL* (pp. 64–66). Rowley, MA: Newbury House.

Chaika, E. (1989). *Language: The social mirror.* New York: Newbury House.

Chamot, A. (2005). Language learning strategy instruction: Current issues and research. *Annual Review of Applied Linguistics, 25,* 112–130.

Chamot, A., & El-Dinary, P. (1999). Children's learning strategies in immersion class-rooms. *Modern Language Journal, 83,* 319–341.

Chamot, A., & O'Malley, M. (1986). *A cognitive academic language learning approach: An ESL content-based curriculum.* Wheaton, MD: National Clearinghouse for Bilingual Education.

Chamot, A., & O'Malley, M. (1987). The cognitive academic language learning approach: A bridge to the mainstream. *TESOL Quarterly, 21,* 227–249.

Chamot, A., Barnhart, S., El-Dinary, P., & Robbins, J. (1999). *The learning strategies handbook.* White Plains, NY: Longman.

Chapelle, C. (1983). *The relationship between ambiguity tolerance and success in acquiring English as a second language in adult learners.* Unpublished doctoral dissertation, University of Illinois.

Chapelle, C. (1992). Disembedding "Disembedded Figures in the Landscape ...": An appraisal of Griffiths and Sheen's "reappraisal of L2 research on field dependence/independence." *Applied Linguistics, 13,* 375–384.

Chapelle, C., & Jamieson, J. (2008). *Tips for teaching CALL.* White Plains, NY: Pearson Education.

Chapelle, C., & Roberts, C. (1986). Ambiguity tolerance and field independence as predictors of proficiency in English as a second language. *Language Learning, 36,* 27–45.

Chihara, T., & Oller, J. (1978). Attitudes and proficiency in EFL: A sociolinguistic study of adult Japanese speakers. *Language Learning, 28,* 55–68.

Choi, S., & Lantolf, J. (2008). Representation and embodiment of meaning in L2 communication: Motion events in the speech and gesture of advanced L2 Korean and L2 English speakers. *Studies in Second Language Acquisition, 30,* 191–224.

Choi, Y.-J. (2003). Intercultural communication through drama in teaching English as an international language. *English Teaching, 58,* 127–156.

Chomsky, N. (1959). Review of *Verbal behavior. Language, 35,* 26–58.

Chomsky, N. (1964). Current issues in linguistic theory. In J. Fodor & J. Katz (Eds.), *The structure of language: Readings in the philosophy of language.* Englewood Cliffs, NJ: Prentice Hall.

Chomsky, N. (1965). *Aspects of the theory of syntax.* Cambridge, MA: Massachusetts Institute of Technology Press.

Christison, M. (1999). *Multiple intelligences: Theory and practice in adult ESL.* Washington, DC: National Clearinghouse for ESL Literacy Education.

Christison, M. (2005). *Multiple intelligences and language learning: A guidebook of theory, activities, inventories, and resources.* Burlingame, CA: Alta Publications.

Chun, A., Day, R., Chenoweth, N., & Luppescu, S. (1982). Types of errors corrected in native-nonnative conversations. *TESOL Quarterly, 16,* 537–547.

Clark, E. (2003). *First language acquisition.* Cambridge, UK: Cambridge University Press.

Clark, E. (2009). *First language acquisition.* (2nd ed.). Cambridge, UK: Cambridge University Press.

Clarke, M. (1976). Second language acquisition as a clash of consciousness. *Language Learning, 26,* 377–390.

Clarke, M. (1982). On bandwagons, tyranny, and common sense. *TESOL Quarterly, 16,* 437–448.

Clarke, M. (1990). Some cautionary observations on liberation education. *Language Arts, 67,* 388–398.

Clarke, M. (1994). The dysfunctions of the theory/practice discourse. *TESOL Quarterly, 28,* 9–26.

Clarke, M., Losoff, A., McCracken, M., & Rood, D. (1984). Linguistic relativity and sex/gender studies: Epistemological and methodological considerations. *Language Learning, 34,* 47–67.

Cohen, A. (1998). *Strategies in learning and using a second language.* New York: Addison Wesley Longman.

Cohen, A. (2004, November). *A web-based approach to strategic learning of speech acts.* Paper presented at San Francisco State University, San Francisco, CA.

Cohen, A. (2011). Second language learner strategies. In E. Hinkel (Ed.), *Handbook of research in second language teaching and learning: Volume II.* (pp. 681–698). New York: Routledge.

Cohen, A., & Macaro, E. (Eds.). (2007). *Language learner strategies: Thirty years of research and practice.* Oxford, UK: Oxford University Press.

Cohen, A., & Weaver, S. (2006). *Styles and strategies-based instruction: A teacher's guide.* Minneapolis: Center for Advanced Research on Language Acquisition (CARLA), University of Minnesota.

Cohen, A., Oxford, R., & Chi, J. (2003). *Language Strategy Use Inventory.* http://www.carla.umn.edu/maxsa/documents/langstratuse-inventory.pdf

Comrie, B. (1990). Second language acquisition and language universals research. *Studies in Second Language Acquisition, 12,* 209–218.

Condon, E. (1973). *Introduction to cross cultural communication.* New Brunswick, NJ: Rutgers University Press.

Connor, U. (1996). *Contrastive rhetoric: Cross-cultural aspects of second language writing.* Cambridge, UK: Cambridge University Press.

Connor, U. (2002). New directions in contrastive rhetoric. *TESOL Quarterly, 36,* 493–510.

Connor, U., & Kaplan, R. (Eds.). (1987). *Writing across languages: Analysis of L2 text.* Reading, MA: Addison-Wesley.

Connor, U., Nagelhout, E., & Rozycki, W. (Eds.). (2008). *Contrastive rhetoric: Reaching to intercultural rhetoric.* Amsterdam: John Benjamins.

Conrad, S. (2000). Will corpus linguistics revolutionize grammar teaching in the 21st century? *TESOL Quarterly, 34,* 548–560.

Conrad, S. (2005). Corpus linguistics and L2 teaching. In E. Hinkel (Ed.), *Handbook of research in second language teaching and learning* (pp. 393–409). Mahwah, NJ: Lawrence Erlbaum Associates.

Cook, V. (1973). Comparison of language development in native children and foreign adults. *International Review of Applied Linguistics, 11,* 13–28.

Cook, V. (1993). *Linguistics and second language acquisition.* New York: St. Martin's Press.

Cook, V. (1995). Multi-competence and the effects of age. In D. Singleton & Z. Lengyel (Eds.), *The age factor in second language acquisition* (pp. 52–58). Clevedon, UK: Multilingual Matters.

Cook, V. (1997). *Inside language.* London: Edward Arnold.

Cook, V. (1999). Going beyond the native speaker in language teaching. *TESOL Quarterly, 33,* 185–209.

Cook, V., & Newson, M. (1996). *Chomsky's universal grammar: An introduction.* Oxford, UK: Basil Blackwell.

Corder, S. (1967). The significance of learners' errors. *International Review of Applied Linguistics, 5,* 161–170.

Corder, S. (1971). Idiosyncratic dialects and error analysis. *International Review of Applied Linguistics, 9,* 147–159.

Corder, S. (1973). *Introducing applied linguistics.* Harmondsworth, UK: Penguin Books.

Cotterall, S., & Crabbe, D. (Eds.). (1999). *Learner autonomy in language learning: Defining the field and effecting change.* Frankfurt: Peter Lang.

Crawford, J. (1998). English only for the children? *TESOL Matters, 8,* 20–21.

Croft, W., & Cruse, D. (2004). *Cognitive linguistics.* Cambridge, UK: Cambridge University Press.

Crookes, G. (1989). Planning and interlanguage variation. *Studies in Second Language Acquisition, 11,* 367–384.

Crookes, G., & Schmidt, R. (1991). Motivation: Reopening the research agenda. *Language Learning, 41,* 469–512.

Crystal, D. (1997). *English as a global language.* Cambridge, UK: Cambridge University Press.

Crystal, D. (1999). The future of Englishes. *English Today, 58,* 15–25.

Csikszentmihalyi, M. (1990). *Flow: The psychology of optimal experience.* New York: Harper & Row.

Csikszentmihalyi, M., & Csikszentmihalyi, I. (Eds.). (1988). *Optimal experience: Psychological studies of flow in consciousness.* New York: Cambridge University Press.

Csizér, K., & Dörnyei, Z. (2005). The internal structure of language learning motivation and its relationship with language choice and learning effort. *Modern Language Journal, 89,* 19–36.

Cummins, J. (1979). Cognitive/academic language proficiency, linguistic interdependence, the optimal age question and some other matters. *Working Papers on Bilingualism, 19,* 197–205.

Cummins, J. (1980). The cross-lingual dimensions of language proficiency: Implications for bilingual education and the optimal age issue. *TESOL Quarterly, 14,* 175–187.

Cummins, J. (1981). *The role of primary language development in promoting educational success for language minority students.* Sacramento: California State Department of Education, Office of Bilingual Bicultural Education.

Curran, C. (1972). *Counseling-learning: A whole person model for education.* New York: Grune & Stratton.

Curtiss, S. (1977). *Genie: A psycholinguistic study of a modern-day "wild child."* New York: Academic Press.

D'Amico-Reisner, L. (1983). An analysis of the surface structure of disapproval exchanges. In N. Wolfson & E. Judd (Eds.), *Sociolinguistics and language acquisition.* Rowley, MA: Newbury House.

Danesi, M. (1988). Neurological bimodality and theories of language teaching. *Studies in Second Language Acquisition, 10,* 13–31.

Davies, A. (1989). Is international English an interlanguage? *TESOL Quarterly, 23,* 447–467.

Davis, K., & Skilton-Sylvester, E. (2004). Looking back, taking stock, moving forward: Investigating gender in TESOL. *TESOL Quarterly, 38,* 381–404.

Day, C. (1982). *The optimal distance model of acculturation and success in second language learning.* Unpublished doctoral dissertation, University of Illinois, Urbana-Champaign.

Day, R., Chenoweth, N., Chun, A., & Luppescu, Stuart. (1984). Corrective feedback in native-nonnative discourse. *Language Learning, 34,* 19–45.

De Angelis, G., & Dewaele, J-M. (Eds.). (2011) *New trends in crosslinguistic influence and multilingualism research.* Bristol, UK: Multilingual Matters.

de Bot, K. (1996). The psycholinguistics of the output hypothesis. *Language Learning, 46,* 529–555.

de Saussure, F. (1916). *Course in general linguistics* (W. Baskin, Trans.). New York: McGraw-Hill.

DeCapua, A., & Wintergerst, A. (2004). *Crossing cultures in the language classroom.* Ann Arbor: The University of Michigan Press.

Deci, E. (1975). *Intrinsic motivation.* New York: Plenum Press.

Deci, E., & Ryan, R. (1985). *Intrinsic motivation and self-determination in human behavior.* New York: Plenum Press.

DeKeyser, R. (2000). The robustness of critical period effects in second language acquisition. *Studies in Second Language Acquisition, 22,* 499–533.

DeKeyser, R. (2003). Implicit and explicit learning. In C. Doughty & M. Long (Eds.), *The handbook of second language acquisition* (pp. 313–348). Malden, MA: Blackwell Publishing.

DeKeyser, R. (2007). Skill acquisition theory. In D. Atkinson (Ed.), *Alternative approaches to second language acquisition* (pp. 97–113). New York: Routledge.

DeKeyser, R., & Koeth, J. (2011). Cognitive aptitudes for second language learning. In E. Hinkel (Ed.), *Handbook of research in second language teaching and learning: Volume II* (pp. 395–406). New York: Routledge.

DePalma, M. J., & Ringer, J. M. (2011). Toward a theory of adaptive transfer: Expanding disciplinary discussions of 'transfer' in second-language writing and composition studies. *Journal of Second Language Writing, 20,* 134–147.

Dewaele, J. (2009). Individual differences in second language acquisition. In. In W. Ritchie & T. Bhatia (Eds.), *The new handbook of second language acquisition* (pp. 623–646). Bingley, UK: Emerald Group Publishing, Ltd.

Dewaele, J., & Furnham, A. (1999). Extraversion: The unloved variable in applied linguistic research. *Language Learning, 49,* 509–544.

Dewaele, J., & Furnham, A. (2000). Personality and speech production: A pilot study of second language learners. *Personality and Individual Differences, 28,* 355–365.

Dewaele, J., Petrides, K., & Furnham, A. (2008). Effects of trait emotional intelligence and sociobiographical variables on communicative anxiety and foreign language anxiety among adult multilinguals: A review and empirical investigation. *Language Learning, 58,* 911–960.

Dixon, D. (2011). Recent literature concerning the support of initiatives promoting language learner autonomy around the world. *Language Teaching, 44,* 266–276.

Dlaska, A. (2000). Integrating culture and language learning in institution-wide programmes. *Language, Culture and Curriculum, 13,* 247–263.

Dogancay-Aktuna, S., & Hardman, J. (Eds.) (2008). *Global English teaching and teacher education: Praxis and possibility.* Alexandria, VA: Teachers of English to Speakers of Other Languages.

Donahue, M., & Parsons, A. (1982). The use of role play to overcome cultural fatigue. *TESOL Quarterly, 16,* 359–365.

Donne, J. (1624). *Devotions upon emergent occasions.* (Edited, with commentary by Anthony Raspa). Montreal, Canada: McGill-Queen's University Press.

Dörnyei, Z. (1995). On the teachability of communication strategies. *TESOL Quarterly, 29,* 55–84.

Dörnyei, Z. (1998). Motivation in second and foreign language learning. *Language Teaching, 31,* 117–135.

Dörnyei, Z. (2001a). *Motivational strategies in the language classroom.* Cambridge, UK: Cambridge University Press.

Dörnyei, Z. (2001b). *Teaching and researching motivation.* Harlow, England: Pearson Education.

Dörnyei, Z. (2005). *The psychology of the language learner: Individual differences in second language acquisition.* Mahwah, NJ: Lawrence Erlbaum Associates.

Dörnyei, Z. (2009). *The psychology of second language acquisition.* Oxford, UK: Oxford University Press.

Dörnyei, Z., & Csizér, K. (1998). Ten commandments for motivating language learners: Results of an empirical study. *Language Teaching Research, 2,* 203–229.

Dörnyei, Z., & Schmidt, R. (2001). *Motivation and second language acquisition.* Honolulu: University of Hawaii at Manoa.

Dörnyei, Z., & Skehan, P. (2003). Individual differences in L2 learning. In C. Doughty & M. Long (Eds.), *The handbook of second language acquisition* (pp. 589–630). Malden, MA: Blackwell Publishing.

Dörnyei, Z., & Ushioda, E. (2011). *Teaching and researching motivation.* Harlow, UK: Pearson Education, Ltd.

Doron, S. (1973). *Reflectivity-impulsivity and their influence on reading for inference for adult students of ESL.* Unpublished manuscript, University of Michigan.

Doughty, C. (1991). Second language instruction does make a difference: Evidence from an empirical study of SL relativization. *Studies in Second Language Acquisition, 13,* 431–469.

Doughty, C. (2003). Instructed SLA: Constraints, compensation, and enhancement. In C. Doughty & M. Long (Eds.), *The handbook of second language acquisition* (pp. 256–310). Malden, MA: Blackwell Publishing.

Doughty, C., & Long, M. (2003). *The handbook of second language acquisition.* Malden, MA: Blackwell Publishing.

Doughty, C., & Williams, J. (Eds.). (1998). *Focus on form in classroom second language acquisition.* New York: Cambridge University Press.

Drach, K. (1969). The language of the parent: A pilot study (Working Paper No. 14). Language Behavior Research Laboratory, University of California, Berkeley.

Dresser, N. (1996). *Multicultural manners: New rules of etiquette for a changing society.* New York: Wiley.

Dresser, N. (2005). *Multicultural manners: Essential rules of etiquette for the 21st century.* Hoboken, NJ: Wiley.

Dufeu, B. (1994). *Teaching myself.* Oxford: Oxford University Press.

Duff, P., & Talmy, S. (2011) Language socialization approaches to second language acquisition." In D. Atkinson (Ed.), *Alternative approaches to second language acquisition* (pp. 95–116). New York: Routledge.

Dulay, H., & Burt, M. (1972). Goofing: An indicator of children's second language learning strategies. *Language Learning, 22,* 235–252.

Dulay, H., & Burt, M. (1974a). Errors and strategies in child second language acquisition. *TESOL Quarterly, 8,* 129–136.

Dulay, H., & Burt, M. (1974b). Natural sequences in child second language acquisition. *Language Learning, 24,* 37–53.

Dulay, H., & Burt, M. (1976). Creative construction in second language learning and teaching. [Special issue] *Language Learning, 4,* 65–79.

Dunn, W., & Lantolf, J. (1998). Vygotsky's zone of proximal development and Krashen's *i + 1:* Incommensurable constructs; incommensurable theories. *Language Learning, 48,* 411–442.

Durkheim, E. (1897). *Le suicide*. Paris: F. Alcan.

Eckman, F. (1977). Markedness and the contrastive analysis hypothesis. *Language Learning, 27,* 315–330.

Eckman, F. (1981). On the naturalness of interlanguage phonological rules. *Language Learning, 31,* 195–216.

Eckman, F. (1991). The structural conformity hypothesis and the acquisition of consonant clusters in the interlanguage of ESL learners. *Studies in Second Language Acquisition, 13,* 23–41.

Eckman, F. (2004). From phonemic differences to constraint rankings. *Studies in Second Language Acquisition, 26,* 513–549.

Edwards, B. (1979). *Drawing on the right side of the brain*. Los Angeles: J.P. Tarcher/ St. Martin's.

Egbert, J. (2003). A study of flow theory in the foreign language classroom. *Modern Language Journal, 87,* 499–518.

Eggins, S. (2004). *An introduction to systemic functional linguistics* (2nd ed.). New York: Continuum Press.

Ehrman, M. (1989). *Ants, grasshoppers, badgers, and butterflies: Qualitative and quantitative investigation of adult language learning styles and strategies*. Unpublished doctoral dissertation, Union Institute.

Ehrman, M. (1990). The role of personality type in adult language learning: An ongoing investigation. In T. Parry & C. Stansfield (Eds.), *Language aptitude reconsidered* (pp. 126–178). New York: Prentice Hall Regents.

Ehrman, M. (1993). Ego boundaries revisited: Toward a model of personality and learning. In J. Alatis (Ed.), *Strategic interaction and language acquisition: Theory, practice, and research* (pp. 331–362). Washington, DC: Georgetown University Press.

Ehrman, M. (1996). *Understanding second language learning difficulties*. Thousand Oaks, CA: Sage.

Ehrman, M. (1999). Ego boundaries and tolerance of ambiguity in second language learning. In J. Arnold (Ed.), *Affect in language learning* (pp. 68–86). Cambridge: Cambridge University Press.

Ehrman, M., & Leaver, B. (2003). Cognitive styles in the service of language learning. *System, 31,* 393–415.

Ehrman, M., & Oxford, R. (1989). Effects of sex differences, career choice, and psychological type on adult language learning strategies. *Modern Language Journal, 73,* 1–13.

Ehrman, M., & Oxford, R. (1990). Adult language learning styles and strategies in an intensive training setting. *Modern Language Journal, 74,* 311–327.

Ehrman, M., & Oxford, R. (1995). Cognition plus: Correlates of language proficiency. *Modern Language Journal, 79,* 67–89.

El-Dib, M. (2004). Language learning strategies in Kuwait: Links to gender, language level, and culture in a hybrid context. *Foreign Language Annals, 37,* 85–95.

Elbow, P. (1973). *Writing without teachers*. New York: Oxford University Press.

Elliott, A. (1995a). Field independence/dependence, hemispheric specialization, and attitude in relation to pronunciation accuracy in Spanish as a foreign language. *Modern Language Journal, 79,* 356–371.

Elliott, A. (1995b). Foreign language phonology: Field independence, attitude, and the success of formal instruction in Spanish pronunciation. *Modern Language Journal, 79,* 530–542.

Ellis, G., & Sinclair, B. (1989). *Learning to learn English: A course in learner training.* Cambridge, UK: Cambridge University Press.

Ellis, N. (1994). Implicit and explicit language learning: An overview. In N. Ellis (Ed.), *Implicit and explicit learning of language* (pp. 1–31). London: Academic Press.

Ellis, N. (2002). Frequency effects in language processing: A review with implications for theories of implicit and explicit language acquisition. *Studies in Second Language Acquisition, 24,* 143–188.

Ellis, N. (2003). Constructions, chunking, and connectionism: The emergence of second language structure. In C. Doughty & M. Long (Eds.), *The handbook of second language acquisition* (pp. 63–103). Malden, MA: Blackwell Publishing.

Ellis, N. (2005). At the interface: Dynamic interactions of explicit and implicit language knowledge. *Studies in Second Language Acquisition, 27,* 305–352.

Ellis, N. (2006a). Language acquisition as rational contingency learning. *Applied Linguistics, 27,* 1–24.

Ellis, N. (2006b). Selective attention and transfer phenomena in SLA: Contingency, cue, salience, interference, overshadowing, blocking, and perceptual learning. *Applied Linguistics, 27,* 164–194.

Ellis, N. (2007a). Dynamic systems and SLA: The wood and the trees. *Bilingualism: Language and Cognition, 10,* 23–25.

Ellis, N. (2007b). The associative-cognitive CREED. In B. VanPatten & J. Williams (Eds.), *Theories of second language acquisition* (pp. 77–95). Mahwah, NJ: Lawrence Erlbaum.

Ellis, N., & Collins, L. (2009). Input and second language acquisition: The roles of frequency, form, and function. *Modern Language Journal, 93,* 329–335.

Ellis, N., & Ferreira-Junior, F. (2009). Construction learning as a function of frequency, frequency distribution, and function. *Modern Language Journal, 93,* 370–385.

Ellis, N., & Larsen-Freeman, D. (2006). Language emergence: Implications for applied linguistics. *Applied Linguistics, 27,* 558–589.

Ellis, R. (1986). *Understanding second language acquisition.* Oxford: Oxford University Press.

Ellis, R. (1987). *Second language acquisition in context.* New York: Prentice Hall.

Ellis, R. (1989). Sources of intra-learner variability in language use and their relationship to second language acquisition. In S. Gass, C. Madden, D. Preston, & L. Selinker (Eds.), *Variation in second language acquisition: Psycholinguistic issues.* Clevedon, UK: Multilingual Matters.

Ellis, R. (1990a). *Instructed second language acquisition: Learning in the classroom.* Cambridge, MA: Blackwell.

Ellis, R. (1990b). A response to Gregg. *Applied Linguistics, 11,* 384–391.

Ellis, R. (1994a). *The study of second language acquisition.* Oxford: Oxford University Press.

Ellis, R. (1994b). A theory of instructed second language acquisition. In N. Ellis (Ed.), *Implicit and explicit learning of language* (pp. 79–114). London: Academic Press.

Ellis, R. (1997). *SLA research and language teaching.* Oxford: Oxford University Press.

Ellis, R. (2001). Investigating form-focused instruction. *Language Learning, 51* (Suppl. 1), 1–46.

Ellis, R. (2004). The definition and measurement of L2 explicit knowledge. *Language Learning, 54,* 227–275.

Ellis, R. (2005). Instructed language learning and task-based teaching. In E. Hinkel (Ed.), *Handbook of research in second language teaching and learning* (pp. 713–728). Mahwah, NJ: Lawrence Erlbaum Associates.

Ellis, R. (Ed.). (2000). *Learning a second language through interaction.* Amsterdam: John Benjamins.

Ellis, R., Basturkmen, H., & Loewen, S. (2001). Preemptive focus on form in the ESL classroom. *TESOL Quarterly, 35,* 377–405.

Ervin-Tripp, S. (1974). Is second language learning like the first? *TESOL Quarterly, 8,* 111–127.

Eubank, L., & Gregg, K. (2002). News flash—Hume still dead. *Studies in Second Language Acquisition, 24,* 237–247.

Evans, V., & Green, M. (2006). *Cognitive linguistics: An introduction.* New York: Routledge.

Ewing, D. (1977). Discovering your problem solving style. *Psychology Today, 11,* 69–73.

Fantini, A. (1997). *New ways of teaching culture.* Alexandria, VA: Teachers of English to Speakers of Other Languages.

Fast, J. (1970). *Body language.* New York: M. Evans.

Ferris, D. (2004). The "grammar correction" debate in L2 writing: Where we are and where do we go from here. *Journal of Second Language Writing, 13,* 49–62.

Ferris, D. (2012). Written corrective feedback in second language acquisition and writing studies. *Language Teaching, 45,* 446–459.

Ferris, D., & Hedgcock, J. (2005). *Teaching ESL composition: Purpose, process, and practice.* Mahwah, NJ: Lawrence Erlbaum.

File, K., & Adams, R. (2010). Should vocabulary instruction be integrated or isolated? *TESOL Quarterly, 44,* 222–249.

Firth, A., & Wagner, J. (1997). On discourse, communication, and (some) fundamental concepts in SLA research. *Modern Language Journal, 81,* 285–300.

Fitts, P., & Posner, M. (1967). *Human performance.* Belmont, CA: Brooks/Cole.

Flege, J. (1987). A critical period for learning to pronounce foreign languages? *Applied Linguistics, 8,* 162–177.

Flynn, S. (1987). Contrast and construction in a parameter-setting model of L2 acquisition. *Language Learning, 37,* 19–62.

Ford, C. (2002). Denial and the construction of conversational turns. In J. Jybee & M. Noonan (Eds.), *Complex sentences in grammar and discourse* (pp. 1–17). Amsterdam: John Benjamins.

Foster P., & Skehan, P. (1996). The influence of planning and task type on second language performance. *Studies in Second Language Acquisition, 18,* 299–323.

Foster-Cohen, S. (2001). First language acquisition … second language acquisition: "What's Hecuba to him or he to Hecuba?" *Second Language Acquisition Research, 17,* 329–344.

Frankenberg-Garcia, A. (2012). Raising teachers' awareness of corpora. *Language Teaching 45,* 475–489.

Frawley, W. (1997). *Vygotsky and cognitive science: Language and the unification of social and computational mind.* Cambridge, MA: Harvard University Press.

Frazier, S. (2007). Continuing developments in discourse-based grammar instruction. *CATESOL Journal, 19,* 30–34.

Freire, P. (1970). *Pedagogy of the oppressed.* New York: Seabury Press.

Fries, C. (1945). *Teaching and learning English as a foreign language.* Ann Arbor: University of Michigan Press.

Fries, C. (1952). *The structure of English.* New York: Harcourt, Brace, & World.

Fushino, K. (2010). Causal relationships between communication confidence, beliefs about group work, and willingness to communicate in foreign language group work. *TESOL Quarterly, 44,* 700–724.

Gagné, R. (1965). *The conditions of learning.* New York: Holt, Rinehart & Winston.

Gan, Z., Humphreys, G., & Hamp-Lyons, L. (2004). Understanding successful and unsuccessful EFL students in Chinese universities. *Modern Language Journal, 88,* 229–244.

Ganschow, L., & Sparks, R. (1996). Anxiety about foreign language learning among high school women. *Modern Language Journal, 80,* 199–212.

Ganschow, L., Sparks, R., Anderson, R., Jovorshy, J., Skinner, S., & Patton, J. (1994). Differences in language performance among high-, average-, and low-anxious college foreign language learners. *Modern Language Journal, 78,* 41–55.

Gao, Y., Zhaoi, Y., Cheng, Y., & Zhou, Y. (2007). Relationship between English learning motivation types and self-identity changes among Chinese students. *TESOL Quarterly, 41,* 133–155.

García Mayo, M. (2007). *Investigating tasks in formal language learning.* Clevedon, UK: Multilingual Matters.

Gardner, H. (1983). *Frames of mind: The theory of multiple intelligences.* New York: Basic Books.

Gardner, H. (1999). *Intelligence reframed.* New York: Basic Books.

Gardner, H. (2004). *Changing minds.* Boston: Harvard Business School Press.

Gardner, H. (2006). *Multiple intelligences: New horizons in theory and practice.* New York: Basic books.

Gardner, H. (2011). *Frames of mind: The theory of multiple intelligences* (3rd ed.). New York: Basic Books.

Gardner, R. (1982). Social factors in language retention. In R. Lambert & B. Freed (Eds.), *The loss of language skills.* Rowley, MA: Newbury House.

Gardner, R. (1985). *Social psychology and second language learning: The role of attitudes and motivation.* London: Edward Arnold.

Gardner, R., & Lambert, W. (1972). *Attitudes and motivation in second language learning.* Rowley, MA: Newbury House.

Gardner, R., & MacIntyre, P. (1991). An instrumental motivation in language study: Who says it isn't effective? *Studies in Second Language Acquisition, 13,* 57–72.

Gardner, R., & MacIntyre, P. (1993a). A student's contributions to second language learning. Part II: Affective variables. *Language Teaching, 26,* 1–11.

Gardner, R., & MacIntyre, P. (1993b). On the measurement of affective variables in second language learning. *Language Learning, 43,* 157–194.

Gardner, R., Day, J., & MacIntyre, P. (1992). Integrative motivation, induced anxiety, and language learning in a controlled environment. *Studies in Second Language Acquisition, 14,* 197–214.

Gardner, R., Masgoret, A.-M., Tennant, J., & Mihic, L. (2004). Integrative motivation: Changes curing a year-long intermediate-level language. *Language Learning, 54,* 1–34.

Gass, S. (1989). Language universals and second language acquisition. *Language Learning, 39,* 497–534.

Gass, S. (2003). Input and interaction. In C. Doughty & M. Long (Eds.), *The handbook of second language acquisition* (pp. 224–255). Malden, MA: Blackwell Publishing.

Gass, S. (2013). *Second language acquisition: An introductory course* (4th ed.). New York: Routledge.

Gass, S., & Mackey, A. (2002). Frequency effects and second language acquisition. *Studies in Second Language Acquisition, 24,* 249–260.

Gass, S., & Selinker, L. (2001). *Second language acquisition: An introductory course* (2nd ed.). Mahwah, NJ: Lawrence Erlbaum Associates.

Gass, S., & Varonis, E. (1994). Input, interaction, and second language production. *Studies in Second Language Acquisition, 16,* 283–302.

Gass, S., Mackey, A., & Pica, T. (1998). The role of input and interaction in second language acquisition. *Modern Language Journal, 82,* 299–305.

Gatbonton, E. (1983). Patterned phonetic variability in second language speech: A gradual diffusion model. In B. Robinett & J. Schachter (Eds.), *Second language learning: Contrastive analysis, error analysis, and related aspects.* Ann Arbor: University of Michigan Press.

Genesee, F. (1982). Experimental neuropsychological research on second language processing. *TESOL Quarterly, 16,* 315–322.

Geschwind, N. (1970). The organization of language and the brain. *Science, 170,* 940–944.

Gleick, J. (1987). *Chaos: Making a new science.* New York: Penguin Books.

Gleitman, L., & Wanner, E. (1982). Language acquisition: The state of the state of the art. In E. Wanner & L. Gleitman (Eds.), *Language acquisition: The state of the art.* Cambridge, UK: Cambridge University Press.

Goldschneider, J., & DeKeyser, R. (2001). Explaining the "natural order of L2 morpheme acquisition" in English: A meta-analysis of multiple determinants. *Language Learning, 51,* 1–50.

Goldschneider, J., & DeKeyser, R. (2005). Explaining the "natural order of L2 morpheme acquisition" in English: A meta-analysis of multiple determinants. *Language Learning, 55* (Suppl. 1), 27–77.

Goleman, D. (1995). *Emotional intelligence.* New York: Bantam Books.

Goleman, D. (1998). *Working with emotional intelligence.* New York: Bantam Books.

Goleman, D. (2006). *Social intelligence: The new science of social relationships.* New York: Bantam Books.

Goleman, D. (2009). *Ecological intelligence: How knowing the hidden aspects of what we buy can change everything.* New York: Broadway business.

Goodman, K. (1970). Reading: A psycholinguistic guessing game. In H. Singer & R. Ruddell (Eds.), *Theoretical models and processes of reading.* Newark, DE: International Reading Association.

Gor, K., & Long, M. (2009). Input and second language processing. In W. Ritchie & T. Bhatia (Eds.), *The new handbook of second language acquisition* (pp. 445–472). Bingley, UK: Emerald Group Publishing, Ltd.

Gorham, J., & Christophel, D. (1992). Students' perceptions of teacher behaviors as motivating and demotivating factors in college classes. *Communication Quarterly, 40,* 239–52.

Gorsuch, G. (2009). Investigating second language learner self-efficacy and future expectancy o second language use for high-stakes program evaluation. *Foreign Language Annals, 42,* 505–540.

Gouin, F. (1880). *L'art d'enseigner et d'étudier les langues.* Paris: Librairie Fischbacher.

Grabe, W., & Kaplan, R. (1996). *Theory and practice of writing: An applied linguistic perspective.* Harlow, UK: Longman.

Graham, C. (1984, March). *Beyond integrative motivation: The development and influence of assimilative motivation.* Paper presented at the TESOL Convention, Houston, TX.

Greenberg, J. (Ed.). (1963). *Universals of language.* Cambridge, MA: Massachusetts Institute of Technology Press.

Greenberg, J. (1966). *Language universals.* The Hague: Mouton.

Gregersen, T. (2003). To err is human: A reminder to teachers of language-anxious students. *Foreign Language Annals, 36,* 25–32.

Gregersen, T., & Horwitz, E. (2002). Language learning and perfectionism: Anxious and non-anxious language learners' reactions to their own oral performance. *Modern Language Journal, 86,* 562–570.

Gregg, K. (1984). Krashen's monitor and Occam's razor. *Applied Linguistics, 5,* 79–100.

Gregg, K. (1990). The variable competence model of second language acquisition and why it isn't. *Applied Linguistics, 11,* 364–383.

Gregg, K. (1993). Taking explanation seriously: Or, let a couple of flowers bloom. *Applied Linguistics, 14,* 276–294.

Gregg, K. (2003). SLA theory: Construction and assessment. In C. Doughty & M. Long (Eds.), *The handbook of second language acquisition* (pp. 831–865). Malden, MA: Blackwell Publishing.

Grenfell, M., & Macaro, E. (2007). Claims and critiques. In A. Cohen & E. Macaro (Eds.), *Language learner strategies: Thirty years of research and practice* (pp. 9–28). Oxford, UK: Oxford University Press.

Griffiths, C., & Parr, J. (2001). Language-learning strategies: Theory and perception. *ELT Journal, 55,* 247–257.

Griffiths, R., & Sheen, R. (1992). Disembedded figures in the landscape: A reappraisal of L2 research on field dependence-independence. *Applied Linguistics, 13,* 133–148.

Grigorenko, E., Sternberg, R., & Ehrman, M. (2000). A theory-based approach to the measurement of foreign language learning ability: The CANAL-F theory and test. *Modern Language Journal, 84,* 390–405.

Guerrero, L., Andersen, P., & Trost, M. (1998). Communication and emotion: Basic concepts and approaches. In P. Andersen & L. Guererro (Eds.), *Handbook of communication and emotion: Research, theory, applications, and contexts* (pp. 3–28). San Diego, CA: Academic Press.

Guilloteaux, M., & Dörnyei, Z. (2008). Motivating language learners: A classroom-oriented investigation of the effects of motivational strategies on student motivation. *TESOL Quarterly, 42,* 55–77.

Guiora, A. (1981). Language, personality and culture, or the Whorfian Hypothesis revisited. In M. Hines & W. Rutherford (Eds.), *On TESOL '81* (pp. 169–177). Washington, DC: Teachers of English to Speakers of Other Languages.

Guiora, A., Acton, W., Erard, R., & Strickland, F. (1980). The effects of benzodiazepine (Valium) on permeability of ego boundaries. *Language Learning, 30,* 351–363.

Guiora, A., Beit-Hallami, B., Brannon, R., Dull, C., & Scovel, T. (1972a). The effects of experimentally induced changes in ego states on pronunciation ability in second language: An exploratory study. *Comprehensive Psychiatry, 13,* 421–428.

Guiora, A., Brannon, R., & Dull, C. (1972b). Empathy and second language learning. *Language Learning, 22,* 111–130.

Halbach, A. (2000). Finding out about students' learning strategies by looking at their diaries: A case study. *System, 28,* 85–96.

Hall, E. (1959). *The silent language.* New York: Doubleday.

Hall, E. (1966). *The hidden dimension.* New York: Doubleday.

Hall, J., Vitanova, G., & Marchenkova, L. (Eds.). (2005). *Dialogue with Bakhtin on second and foreign language learning.* Mahwah, NJ: Lawrence Erlbaum Associates.

Halliday, M. (1973). *Explorations in the functions of language.* London: Edward Arnold.

Halliday, M., & Burns, A. (2006). Applied linguistics: Thematic pursuits or disciplinary moorings? A conversation between Michael Halliday and Anne Burns. *Journal of Applied Linguistics, 3,* 113–128.

Han, Y., & Ellis, R. (1998). Implicit knowledge, explicit knowledge, and general language proficiency. *Language Teaching Research, 2,* 1–23.

Han, Z.-H., & Selinker, L. (2005). Fossilization in L2 learners. In E. Hinkel (Ed.), *Handbook of research in second language teaching and learning* (pp. 455–470). Mahwah, NJ: Lawrence Erlbaum Associates.

Hansen-Bede, L. (1975). A child's creation of a second language. *Working Papers on Bilingualism, 6,* 103–126.

Hansen, J., & Stansfield, C. (1981). The relationship of field dependent-independent cognitive styles to foreign language achievement. *Language Learning, 31,* 349–367.

Hansen, L. (1984). Field dependence-independence and language testing: Evidence from six Pacific island cultures. *TESOL Quarterly, 18,* 311–324.

Harley, B., & Hart, D. (1997). Language aptitude and second language proficiency in classroom learners of different starting ages. *Studies in Second Language Acquisition, 19,* 379–400.

Harlow, L. (1990). Do they mean what they say? Sociopragmatic competence and second language learners. *Modern Language Journal, 74,* 328–351.

Harris, T. (1972). *I'm OK, you're OK.* New York: Harper & Row.

Hartshorn, K. J., Evans, N., Merrill, P., Sudweeks, R., Strong-Krause, D., & Anderson, N. (2010). Effects of dynamic corrective feedback on ESL writing accuracy. *TESOL Quarterly, 44,* 84–109.

Haskell, R.E. (2001). *Transfer of learning: Cognition, instruction, and reasoning.* San Diego, CA: Academic Press.

Hatch, E., & Long, M. (1980). Discourse analysis, what's that? In D. Larsen-Freeman (Ed.), *Discourse analysis in second language research.* Rowley, MA: Newbury House.

Hedgcock, J. (2005). Taking stock of research in pedagogy in L2 writing. In E. Hinkel (Ed.), *Handbook of research in second language teaching and learning* (pp. 597–613). Mahwah, NJ: Lawrence Erlbaum Associates.

Hendrickson, J. (1980). Error correction in foreign language teaching: Recent theory, research, and practice. In K. Croft (Ed.), *Readings on English as a second language* (2nd ed.). Cambridge, MA: Winthrop.

Heyde, A. (1979). *The relationship between self-esteem and the oral production of a second language.* Unpublished doctoral dissertation, University of Michigan.

Higgins, C. (2003). "Ownership" of English in the outer circle: An alternative to the NS-NNS dichotomy. *TESOL Quarterly, 37,* 615–644.

Higgs, T., & Clifford, R. (1982). The push toward communication. In T. Higgs (Ed.), *Curriculum, competence, and the foreign language teacher.* ACTFL Foreign Language Education Series. Lincolnwood, IL: National Textbook Company.

Hilgard, E. (1963). Motivation in learning theory. In S. Koch (Ed.), *Psychology: A study of science* (Vol. 5) (p. 267). New York: McGraw-Hill.

Hill, B. (1994). Self-managed learning. *Language Teaching, 27,* 213–223.

Hill, J. (1970). Foreign accents, language acquisition, and cerebral dominance revisited. *Language Learning, 20,* 237–248.

Hill, J. (1972). *The educational sciences.* Detroit: Oakland Community College.

Hinenoya, K., & Gatbonton, E. (2000). Ethnocentrism, cultural traits, beliefs, and English proficiency: A Japanese sample. *Modern Language Journal, 84,* 225–240.

Hinkel, E. (Ed.). (2005). *Handbook of research in second language teaching and learning.* Mahwah, NJ: Lawrence Erlbaum Associates.

Hinkel, E. (Ed.). (2011). *Handbook of research in second language teaching and learning: Volume II.* New York: Routledge.

Hladik, E., & Edwards, H. (1984). A comparative analysis of mother-father speech in the naturalistic home environment. *Journal of Psycholinguistic Research, 13,* 321–332.

Hoffman, E. (1990). *Lost in translation: A life in a new language.* New York: Penguin Books.

Hofstede, G. (1986). Cultural differences in teaching and learning. *International Journal of Intercultural Relations, 10,* 301–320.

Hogan, R. (1969). Development of an empathy scale. *Journal of Consulting and Clinical Psychology, 33,* 307–316.

Holme, R. (2012). Cognitive linguistics and the second language classroom. *TESOL Quarterly 46,* 6–29.

Holmes, J. (1989). Sex differences and apologies: One aspect of communicative competence. *Applied Linguistics, 10,* 194–213.

Holmes, J. (1991). Language and gender. *Language Teaching, 24,* 207–220.

Holmes, J. (1995). *Women, men and politeness.* White Plains, NY: Longman.

Holmes, J., & Brown, D. (1987). Teachers and students learning about compliments. *TESOL Quarterly, 21,* 523–546.

Holzman, M. (1984). Evidence for a reciprocal model of language development. *Journal of Psycholinguistic Research, 13,* 119–146.

Holzman, M. (1998). *The language of children* (2nd ed.). Cambridge, MA: Blackwell.

Horwitz, E. (1990). Attending to the affective domain in the foreign language classroom. In S. Magnan (Ed.), *Shifting the instructional focus to the learner.* Middlebury, VT: Northeast Conference on the Teaching of Foreign Languages.

Horwitz, E. (2000). It ain't over 'til it's over: On foreign language anxiety, first language deficits, and the confounding variables. *Modern Language Journal, 84,* 256–259.

Horwitz, E. (2001). Language anxiety and achievement. *Annual Review of Applied Linguistics, 21,* 112–126.

Horwitz, E. (2010). Foreign and second language anxiety. *Language Teaching, 43,* 154–167.

Horwitz, E., Horwitz, M., & Cope, J. (1986). Foreign language classroom anxiety. *Modern Language Journal, 70,* 125–132.

Hsiao, T.-Y., & Oxford, R. (2002). Comparing theories of language learning strategies: A confirmatory factor analysis. *Modern Language Journal, 86,* 368–383.

Hulstijn, J. (1990). A comparison between the information-processing and the analysis/control approaches to language learning. *Applied Linguistics, 11,* 30–45.

Hulstijn, J. (2003). Incidental and intentional learning. In C. Doughty & M. Long (Eds.), *The handbook of second language acquisition* (pp. 349–381). Malden, MA: Blackwell Publishing.

Hulstijn, J. (2005). Theoretical and empirical issues in the study of implicit and explicit second-language learning: Introduction. *Studies in second language acquisition, 27,* 129–140.

Hyltenstam, K., & Abrahamsson, N. (2003). Maturational constraints in SLA. In C. Doughty & M. Long (Eds.), *The handbook of second language acquisition* (pp. 540–588). Malden, MA: Blackwell Publishing.

Hymes, D. (1972). On communicative competence. In J. Pride & J. Holmes (Eds.), *Sociolinguistics.* Harmondsworth, UK: Penguin Books.

Hymes, D. (1974). *Foundations in sociolinguistics: An ethnographic approach.* Philadelphia: University of Pennsylvania Press.

Imai, Y. (2010). Emotions in SLA: New insights from collaborative learning for an EFL classroom. *Modern Language Journal, 94,* 278–292.

Ioup, G. (2005). Age in second language development. In E. Hinkel (Ed.), *Handbook of research in second language teaching and learning* (pp. 419–435). Mahwah, NJ: Lawrence Erlbaum Associates.

Isurin, L. (2000). Deserted island or a child's first language forgetting. *Bilingualism: Language and Cognition, 3,* 151–166.

Izumi, S., & Bigelow, M. (2000). Does output promote noticing in second language acquisition? *TESOL Quarterly, 34,* 213–238.

James, C. (1990). Learner language. *Language Teaching, 23,* 205–213.

James, C. (1998). *Errors in language learning and use: Exploring error analysis.* Harlow, UK: Addison Wesley Longman.

James, M. (2006). Transfer of learning from a university content-based EAP course. *TESOL Quarterly, 40,* 783–806.

James, M. (2007). Interlanguage variation and transfer of learning. *International Review of Applied Linguistics, 45,* 95–118.

James, M. (2010). An investigation of learning transfer in English-for-general-academic-purposes writing instruction. *Journal of Second Language Writing, 19,* 183–206.

Jamieson, J. (1992). The cognitive styles of reflection/impulsivity and field independence and ESL success. *Modern Language Journal, 76,* 491–501.

Jarvis, S., & Pavlenko, A. (2008). *Crosslinguistic influence in language and cognition.* New York: Routledge.

Jaszczolt, K. (1995). Typology of contrastive studies: Specialization, progress, and applications. *Language Teaching, 28,* 1–15.

Jenkins, J., & Palermo, D. (1964). Mediation processes and the acquisition of linguistic structure. In U. Bellugi & R. Brown (Eds.), *The Acquisition of Language. Monographs of the Society for Research in Child Development,* 29 (Serial No. 92).

Jernigan, J., & Mihai, F. (2008). Error treatment preferences of adult intensive English program students: Does proficiency matter? *CATESOL Journal, 20,* 110–123.

Jessner, U. (2008). A DST model of multilingualism and the role of metalinguistic awareness. *Modern Language Journal, 92,* 270–283.

Johns, A. (Ed.). (2002). *Genre in the classroom: Multiple perspectives.* Mahwah, NJ: Lawrence Erlbaum Associates.

Johnson, J., Prior, S., & Artuso, M. (2000). Field dependence as a factor in second language communicative production. *Language Learning, 50,* 529–567.

Jones, P. (2009). Learning styles and performance in second language tasks: Instrumentation matters. *TESOL Quarterly, 43,* 721–724.

Joos, M. (1967). *The five clocks.* New York: Harcourt, Brace & World.

Jordens, P. (1996). Input and instruction in second language acquisition. In P. Jordens & J. Lalleman (Eds.), *Investigating second language acquisition.* Berlin: Mouton de Gruyter.

Joseph, R. (2012). *Right hemisphere, left hemisphere, consciousness and the unconscious, brain and mind.* New York: University Press Science Publishers.

Jun Zhang, L. (2003). Research into Chinese EFL learner strategies: Methods, findings and instructional issues. *RELC Journal, 34,* 284–322.

Jung, C. (1923). *Psychological types.* New York: Harcourt Brace.

Kachru, B. (1977, July). New Englishes and old models. *English Language Forum, 15,* 29–35.

Kachru, B. (1992). World Englishes: Approaches, issues, and resources. *Language Teaching, 25,* 1–14.

Kachru, B., & Nelson, C. (1996). World Englishes. In S. McKay & N. Hornberger (Eds.), *Sociolinguistics and language teaching* (pp. 71–102). Cambridge: Cambridge University Press.

Kachru, B. (1985). Standards, codification, and sociolinguistic realism: The English language in the outer circle. In R. Quirk & H. Widdowson (Eds.), *English in the world: Teaching and learning the language and literatures* (pp. 11–30). Cambridge, UK: Cambridge University Press.

Kachru, Y. (2005). Teaching and learning of world Englishes. In E. Hinkel (Ed.), *Handbook of research in second language teaching and learning* (pp. 149–173). Mahwah, NJ: Lawrence Erlbaum Associates.

Kachru, Y. (2011). World Englishes: Contexts and relevance for language education. In E. Hinkel (Ed.), *Handbook of research in second language teaching and learning: Volume II* (pp. 155–172). New York: Routledge.

Kagan, J. (1965). Reflection-impulsivity and reading ability in primary grade children. *Child Development, 36,* 609–628.

Kagan, J., Pearson, L., & Welch, L. (1966). Conceptual impulsivity and inductive reasoning. *Child Development, 37,* 583–594.

Kakava, C. (1995, March). *An analysis of Greek and English discourse features.* Paper presented at San Francisco State University, San Francisco, CA.

Kamwangamalu, N. (2011). Language planning: approaches and methods. In E. Hinkel (Ed.), *Handbook of research in second language teaching and learning: Volume II* (pp. 888–904). New York: Routledge.

Kaplan, R. (1966). Cultural thought patterns in inter-cultural education. *Language Learning, 16,* 1–20.

Kaplan, R. (2005). Contrastive rhetoric. In E. Hinkel (Ed.), *Handbook of research in second language teaching and learning* (pp. 375–391). Mahwah, NJ: Lawerence Erlbaum Associates.

Karpov, Y., & Haywood, H. (1998). Two ways to elaborate Vygotsky's concept of mediation. *American Psychologist, 53,* 27–36.

Kasper, G. (1992). Pragmatic transfer. *Second Language Research, 8,* 203–231.

Kasper, G. (1998). Interlanguage pragmatics. In H. Byrnes (Ed.), *Learning foreign and second languages: Perspectives in research and scholarship.* New York: The Modern Language Association of America.

Kasper, G. (2009). L2 pragmatic development. In W. Ritchie & T. Bhatia (Eds.), *The new handbook of second language acquisition* (pp. 259–293). Bingley, UK: Emerald Group Publishing, Ltd.

Kasper, G., & Roever, C. (2005). Pragmatics in second language learning. In E. Hinkel (Ed.), *Handbook of research in second language teaching and learning* (pp. 317–334). Mahwah, NJ: Lawrence Erlbaum Associates.

Kasper, G., & Rose, K. (2002). Pragmatic development in a second language. *Language Learning, 52*(Suppl. 1), 1–352.

Kaufman, D. (2004). Constructivist issues in language learning and teaching. *Annual Review of Applied Linguistics, 24,* 303–319.

Keefe, J. (1979). *Student learning styles: Diagnosing and prescribing programs.* Reston, VA: National Association of Secondary School Principals.

Keirsey, D., & Bates, M. (1984). *Please understand me: Character and temperament types.* Del Mar, CA: Prometheus Nemesis Book Company.

Kelch, J., & Yang, J. (2008). Integrating the task-based approach into content curriculum. *CATESOL Journal, 20,* 135–145.

Keller, J. (1983). Motivational design of instruction. In C. Reigelruth (Ed.), *Instructional design theories and models: An overview of their current status.* Hillsdale, NJ: Lawrence Erlbaum Associates.

Kellerman, E. (1995). Cross-linguistic influence: Transfer to nowhere? *Annual Review of Applied Linguistics, 15,* 125–150.

Kellerman, E., & Sharwood-Smith, M. (1986). *Cross-linguistic influence in second language acquisition.* New York: Pergamon Press.

Kelly, L. (1969). *Twenty-five centuries of language teaching.* Rowley, MA: Newbury House.

Kennedy, G. (1970). *Children's comprehension of English sentences comparing quantities of discrete objects.* Unpublished doctoral dissertation. Los Angeles: UCLA.

Kennedy, G. (1998). *An introduction to corpus linguistics.* Harlow, UK: Longman.

Kennedy, S. (2012). Exploring the relationship between language awareness and second language use. *TESOL Quarterly, 46,* 398–408.

Kheng, C., & Baldauf, R. (2011). Global language: (De)colonisation in the new era. In E. Hinkel (Ed.), *Handbook of research in second language teaching and learning: Volume II* (pp. 952–969). New York: Routledge.

Kim, Y. (2009). The effects of task complexity on learner-learner interaction. *System, 37,* 254–268.

Kinginger, C. (2001). i + 1 = ZPD. *Foreign Language Annals, 34,* 417–425.

Kinsbourne, M., & Jordan, J. (2009). Embodied anticipation: A neurodevelopmental interpretation. *Discourse Processes, 46,* 103–126.

Kitano, Kazu. (2001). Anxiety in the college Japanese classroom. *Modern Language Journal, 85,* 549–566.

Kleinmann, H. (1977). Avoidance behavior in adult second language acquisition. *Language Learning, 27,* 93–107.

Koch, C. (2004). *The quest for consciousness.* Englewood, CO: Roberts & Company.

Kohls, R. (1984). *Survival kit for overseas living.* Yarmouth, ME: Intercultural Press.

Kolb, D. (1999). *The Kolb learning style inventory: Version 3.* Boston: Hay Group.

Kramsch, C. (1986). From language proficiency to interactional competence. *Modern Language Journal, 70,* 366–372.

Kramsch, C. (2009). *The multilingual subject: What foreign language learners say about their experience and why it matters.* Oxford: Oxford University Press.

Kramsch, C. (2011). The symbolic dimensions of the intercultural. *Language Teaching, 44,* 354–367.

Krashen, S. (1973). Lateralization, language learning, and the critical period: Some new evidence. *Language Learning, 23,* 63–74.

Krashen, S. (1977). The monitor model for adult second language performance. In M. Burt, H. Dulay, & M. Finocchiaro (Eds.), *Viewpoints on English as a second Language.* New York: Regents.

Krashen, S. (1981). *Second language acquisition and second language learning.* Oxford: Pergamon Press.

Krashen, S. (1982). *Principles and practice in second language acquisition.* Oxford: Pergamon Press.

Krashen, S. (1985). *The input hypothesis.* London: Longman.

Krashen, S. (1986). *Bilingual education and second language acquisition theory.* In Sacramento, CA: California State Department of Education.

Krashen, S. (1992). Under what conditions, if any, should formal grammar instruction take place? *TESOL Quarterly, 26,* 409–411.

Krashen, S. (1997). *Foreign language education: The easy way.* Culver City, CA: Language Education Associates.

Krashen, S., & Terrell, T. (1983). *The natural approach: Language acquisition in the classroom.* Oxford: Pergamon Press.

Krashen, S., Seliger, H., & Hartnett, D. (1974). Two studies in adult second language learning. *Kritikon Literarum, 3,* 220–228.

Krathwohl, D., Bloom, B., & Masia, B. (1964). *Taxonomy of educational objectives. Handbook H: Affective domain.* New York: David McKay.

Kubota, R. (2004). Critical multiculturalism and second language education. In B. Norton & K. Toohey (Eds.), *Critical pedagogies and language learning* (pp. 30–52). Cambridge: Cambridge University Press.

Kubota, R. (2009). Spiritual dimensions in language teaching: A personal reflection. In M. Wong & S. Canagarajah (Eds.), *Christian and critical language educators in dialogue* (pp. 225–234). New York: Routledge.

Kuczaj, S. (Ed.). (1984). *Discourse development: Progress in cognitive development research.* New York: Springer-Verlag.

Kuhn, T. (1970). *The structure of scientific revolutions.* Chicago: University of Chicago Press.

Kumaravadivelu, B. (2001). Toward a postmethod pedagogy. *TESOL Quarterly, 35,* 537–560.

Kumaravadivelu, B. (2003). Problematizing cultural stereotypes in TESOL. *TESOL Quarterly, 37,* 709–718.

Kumaravadivelu, B. (2008). *Cultural globalization and language education.* New Haven: Yale University Press.

Labov, W. (1970). The study of language in its social context. *Studium Generale, 23,* 30–87.

Lado, R. (1957). *Linguistics across cultures.* Ann Arbor: University of Michigan Press.

LaForge, P. (1971). Community language learning: A pilot study. *Language Learning, 21,* 45–61.

Lai, Y.-C. (2009). Language learning strategy use and English proficiency of university freshmen in Taiwan. *TESOL Quarterly, 43,* 255–280.

Lakoff, G. (1987). *Women, fire, and dangerous things: What categories reveal about the mind.* Chicago: Chicago University Press.

Lakoff, G. (2004). *Don't think of an elephant: Know your values and frame the debate.* White River Junction, VT: Chelsea Green Publishing.

Lakoff, G., & Johnson, M. (1980). *Metaphors we live by.* Chicago: University of Chicago Press.

Lakoff, G., & Johnson, M. (2003). *Metaphors we live by* (2nd ed.). Chicago: University of Chicago Press.

Lakoff, R. (1975). *Language and woman's place.* New York: Harper Colophon.

Lakoff, R. (1976). Language and society. In R. Wardhaugh & H. D. Brown (Eds.), *A survey of applied linguistics* (pp. 207–228). Ann Arbor: University of Michigan Press.

Lakshmanan, U. (1995). Child second language acquisition of syntax. *Studies in Second Language Acquisition, 17,* 301–329.

Lakshmanan, U. (2009). Child second language acquisition. In W. Ritchie & T. Bhatia (Eds.), *The new handbook of second language acquisition* (pp. 377–399). Bingley, UK: Emerald Group Publishing, Ltd.

Lamb, M. (2004). Integrative motivation in a globalizing world. *System, 32,* 3–19.

Lamb, T., & Reinders, H. (Eds.). (2008). *Learner and teacher autonomy: Concepts, realities, and responses.* Amsterdam: John Benjamins.

Lambert, R., & Freed, B. (Eds.). (1982). *The loss of language skills.* Rowley, MA: Newbury House.

Lambert, W. (1967). A social psychology of bilingualism. *The Journal of Social Issues, 23,* 91–109.

Lambert, W. (1972). *Language, psychology, and culture: Essays by Wallace E. Lambert.* Palo Alto, CA: Stanford University Press.

Landes, J. (1975). Speech addressed to children: Issues and characteristics of parental input. *Language Learning, 25,* 355–379.

Lantolf, J. (1996). SLA theory building: "Letting all the flowers bloom!" *Language Learning, 46,* 713–749.

Lantolf, J. (2000). Second language learning as a mediated process. *Language Teaching, 33,* 79–96.

Lantolf, J. (2005). Sociocultural and second language learning research: An exegesis. In E. Hinkel (Ed.), *Handbook of research in second language teaching and learning* (pp. 335–353). Mahwah, NJ: Lawrence Erlbaum Associates.

Lantolf, J. (2011). The sociocultural approach to second language acquisition: soiciocultural theory, second language acquisition, and artificial L2 development. In D. Atkinson (Ed.), *Alternative approaches to second language acquisition* (pp. 24–47). New York: Routledge.

Lantolf, J. (Ed.). (2000). *Sociocultural theory and second language learning.* Oxford: Oxford University Press.

Lantolf, J., & Beckett, T. (2009). Sociocultural theory and second language acquisition. *Language Teaching, 42,* 459–475.

Lantolf, J., & Thorne, S. (2007). Sociocultural theory and second language acquisition. In B. VanPatten & J. Williams (Eds.), *Theories of second language acquisition* (pp. 201–224). Mahwah, NJ: Lawrence Erlbaum.

Larsen-Freeman, D. (1976). An explanation for the morpheme acquisition order of second language learners. *Language Learning, 26,* 125–134.

Larsen-Freeman, D. (1997). Chaos/complexity science and second language acquisition. *Applied Linguistics, 18,* 141–165.

Larsen-Freeman, D. (2002). Making sense of frequency. *Studies in Second Language Acquisition, 24,* 275–285.

Larsen-Freeman, D. (2004). CA for SLA: It all depends. *Modern Language Journal, 88,* 603–607.

Larsen-Freeman, D. (2011). A complexity theory approach to second language development/acquisition. In D. Atkinson (Ed.), *Alternative approaches to second language acquisition* (pp. 48–72). New York: Routledge.

Larsen-Freeman, D. (2012a). Complex, dynamic systems: A new transdisciplinary theme for applied linguistics? *Language Teaching, 45,* 202–214.

Larsen-Freeman, D. (2012b). *Exploring the fractal dimension of language.* Paper presented at CATESOL, April 14.

Larson, D., & Smalley, W. (1972). *Becoming bilingual: A guide to language learning.* New Canaan, CN: Practical Anthropology.

Lawrence, G. (1984). *People types and tiger stripes: A practical guide to learning styles.* Gainesville, FL: Center for Applications of Psychological Type.

Lee, K., & Oxford, R. (2005, March). *English learning, self-image, strategy awareness, and strategy use.* Paper presented at TESOL, San Antonio, TX.

Leki, I. (1991). Twenty-five years of contrastive rhetoric: Text analysis and writing pedagogies. *TESOL Quarterly, 25,* 123–144.

Leki, I. (2000). Writing, literacy, and applied linguistics. *Annual Review of Applied Linguistics, 20,* 99–115.

Lenneberg, E. (1967). *The biological foundations of language.* New York: Wiley.

Lennon, P. (1991). Error: Some problems of definition, identification, and distinction. *Applied Linguistics, 12,* 180–196.

Lett, J., & O'Mara, F. (1990). Predictors of success in an intensive foreign language learning context: Correlates of language learning at the Defense Language Institute Foreign Language Center. In T. Parry & C. Stansfield (Eds.), *Language aptitude reconsidered.* New York: Prentice Hall Regents.

Levine, D., Baxter, J., & McNulty, P. (1987). *The culture puzzle.* New York: Prentice Hall.

Levine, G. (2003). Student and instructor beliefs and attitudes about target language use, first language use, and anxiety: Report of a questionnaire study. *Modern Language Journal, 87,* 343–364.

Li, X. (1996). *"Good writing" in cross-cultural context.* Albany, NY: State University of New York Press.

Liddicoat, A. (2011). Language teaching and learning from an intercultural perspective. In E. Hinkel (Ed.), *Handbook of research in second language teaching and learning: Volume II* (pp. 837–855). New York: Routledge.

Lightbown, P. (1985). Great expectations: Second language acquisition research and classroom teaching. *Applied Linguistics, 6,* 173–189.

Lightbown, P. (2000). Classroom SLA research and second language teaching. *Applied Linguistics, 21,* 431–462.

Lightbown, P. (2003). SLA research in the classroom/SLA research for the classroom. *Language Learning Journal, 28,* 4–13.

Lightbown, P., & Spada, N. (1990). Focus-on-form and corrective feedback in communicative language teaching: Effects on second language learning. *Studies in Second Language Acquisition, 12,* 429–448.

Lightbown, P., & Spada, N. (2000). Do they know what they're doing? L2 learners' awareness of L1 influence. *Language Awareness, 9,* 198–217.

Lightbown, P., & Spada, N. (2006). *How languages are learned (3rd ed.).* Oxford, UK: Oxford University Press.

Littlewood, W. (2001). Cultural awareness and the negotiation of meaning in intercultural communication. *Language Awareness, 10,* 189–199.

Littlewood, W. (2011). Communicative language teaching: an expanding concept for a changing world. In E. Hinkel (Ed.), *Handbook of research in second language teaching and learning: Volume II* (pp. 541–557). New York: Routledge.

Liu, J. (1999). Nonnative-English-speaking professionals in TESOL. *TESOL Quarterly, 22,* 85–102.

Liu, M., & Jackson, J. (2008). An exploration of Chinese EFL learners' unwillingness to communicate and foreign language anxiety. *Modern Language Journal, 92,* 71–76.

LoCastro, V. (1997). Politeness and pragmatic competence in foreign language education. *Language Teaching Research, 1,* 239–267.

LoCastro, V. (2008). Long sentences and floating commas: Mexican students' rhetorical practices and the sociocultural context. In U. Connor, E. Nagelhout, & W. Rozycki (Eds.), *Contrastive rhetoric: Reaching to intercultural rhetoric* (pp. 195–218). Amsterdam: John Benjamins.

LoCastro, V. (2011). Second language pragmatics. In E. Hinkel (Ed.), *Handbook of research in second language teaching and learning: Volume II* (pp. 319–344). New York: Routledge.

Lock, A. (1991). The role of social interaction in early language development. In N. Krasegnor, D. Rumbaugh, R. Schliefelbusch, & M. Studdert-Kennedy (Eds.), *Biological and behavioral determinants of language development*. Hillsdale, NJ: Lawrence Erlbaum Associates.

Loew, R. (1997). Attention, awareness, and foreign language behavior. *Language Learning, 47,* 467–505.

Loewen, S. (2005). Incidental focus on form and second language learning. *Studies in Second Language Acquisition, 27,* 361–386.

Loewen, S. (2011). Focus on form. In E. Hinkel (Ed.), *Handbook of research in second language teaching and learning: Volume II* (pp. 576–592). New York: Routledge.

Loewen, S., Li, S., Lei, F., Thompson, A., Nakatsukasa, K., Ahn, S., & Chen, X. (2009). Second language learners' beliefs about grammar instruction and error correction. *Modern Language Journal, 93,* 91–104.

Loftus, E. (1976). Language memories in the judicial system. Paper presented at the NWAVE Conference, Georgetown University. Washington, DC.

Long, M. (1983). Does second language instruction make a difference? A review of research. *TESOL Quarterly, 17,* 359–382.

Long, M. (1985). Input and second language acquisition theory. In S. Gass & C. Madden (Eds.), *Input in second language acquisition* (pp. 377–393). Rowley, MA: Newbury House.

Long, M. (1988). Instructed interlanguage development. In L. Beebe (Ed.), *Issues in second language acquisition: Multiple perspectives* (pp. 115–141). New York: Newbury House.

Long, M. (1990a). The least a second language acquisition theory needs to explain. *TESOL Quarterly, 24,* 649–666.

Long, M. (1990b). Maturational constraints on language development. *Studies in Second Language Acquisition, 12,* 251–285.

Long, M. (1996). The role of the linguistic environment in second language acquisition. In W. Ritchie & T. Bhatia (Eds.), *Handbook of second language acquisition* (pp. 413–468). San Diego: Academic Press.

Long, M. (2003). Stabilization and fossilization in interlanguage development. In C. Doughty & M. Long (Eds.), *The handbook of second language acquisition* (pp. 487–535). Malden, MA: Blackwell Publishing.

Long, M. (2007). *Problems in SLA*. New York: Lawrence Erlbaum Associates.

Long, M., & Doughty, C. (2003). SLA and cognitive science. In C. Doughty & M. Long (Eds.), *The handbook of second language acquisition* (pp. 866–870). Malden, MA: Blackwell Publishing.

Long, M., & Robinson, P. (1998). Focus on form: Theory, research, and practice. In C. Doughty & J. Williams (Eds.), *Focus on form in classroom second language acquisition* (pp. 15–41). New York: Cambridge University Press.

Loschky, L. (1994). Comprehensible input and second language acquisition: What is the relationship? *Studies in Second Language Acquisition,* 16, 303–323.

Lukmani, Y. (1972). Motivation to learn and language proficiency. *Language Learning, 22,* 261–274.

Lybeck, K. (2002). Cultural identification and second language pronunciation of Americans in Norway. *Modern Language Journal, 86,* 174–191.

Lyster, R. (2004). Differential effects of prompts and recasts in form-focused instruction. *Studies in Second Language Acquisition, 26,* 399–432.

Lyster, R. (2007). *Learning and teaching languages through content: A counterbalanced approach.* Amsterdam: John Benjamins.

Lyster, R. (2011). Content-based second language teaching. In E. Hinkel (Ed.), *Handbook of research in second language teaching and learning: Volume II* (pp. 611–630). New York: Routledge.

Lyster, R., & Ranta, L. (1997). Corrective feedback and learner uptake: Negotiation of form in communicative classrooms. *Studies in Second Language Acquisition, 19, 37–66.*

Macaro, E. (2000). Learner strategies in foreign language learning. *Tuttitalia, 22,* 9–18.

Macaro, E. (2001). *Learning strategies in foreign and second language classrooms.* London: Continuum Press.

MacCorquodale, K. (1970). On Chomsky's review of Skinner's *Verbal behavior. Journal of the Experimental Analysis of Behavior, 13,* 83–99.

MacIntyre, P. (1995a). How does anxiety affect second language learning? A reply to Sparks and Ganschow. *Modern Language Journal, 79,* 90–99.

MacIntyre, P. (1995b). On seeing the forest and the trees: A rejoinder to Sparks and Ganschow. *Modern Language Journal, 79,* 245–248.

MacIntyre, P. (2007). Willingness to communicate in the second language: Understanding the decision to speak as a volitional process. *Modern Language Journal, 91,* 5645–576.

MacIntyre, P., & Gardner, R. (1988). *The measurement of anxiety and applications to second language learning: An annotated bibliography.* (Research Bulletin No. 672). London, Ontario: The University of Western Ontario.

MacIntyre, P., & Gardner, R. (1989). Anxiety and second language learning: Toward a theoretical clarification. *Language Learning, 39,* 251–275.

MacIntyre, P., & Gardner, R. (1991a). Investigating language class anxiety using the focused essay technique. *Modern Language Journal, 75,* 296–304.

MacIntyre, P., & Gardner, R. (1991b). Language anxiety: Its relationship to other anxieties and to processing in native and second languages. *Language Learning, 41,* 513–534.

MacIntyre, P., & Gardner, R. (1991c). Methods and results in the study of anxiety and language learning: A review of the literature. *Language Learning, 41,* 85–117.

MacIntyre, P., & Gardner, R. (1994). The subtle effects of language anxiety on cognitive processing in the second language. *Language Learning, 44,* 283–305.

MacIntyre, P., & Legatto, J. (2011). A dynamic system approach to willingness to communicate: Developing an idiodynamic method to capture rapidly changing affect. *Applied Linguistics, 32,* 149–171.

MacIntyre, P., & Noels, K. (1996). Using social-psychological variables to predict the use of language learning strategies. *Foreign Language Annals, 29,* 373–386.

MacIntyre, P., Baker, S., Clément, R., & Conrod, S. (2001). Willingness to communicate, social support, and language-learning orientations of immersion students. *Studies in Second Language Acquisition, 23,* 369–388.

MacIntyre, P., Baker, S., Clément, R., & Donovan, L. (2002). Sex and age effects on willingness to communicate, anxiety, perceived competence, and L2 motivation among junior high school French immersion students. *Language Learning, 52,* 537–564.

MacIntyre, P., Dörnyei, Z., Clément, R., & Noels, K. (1998). Conceptualizing willingness to communicate in a L2: A situational model of L2 confidence and affiliation. *Modern Language Journal, 82,* 545–562.

MacIntyre, P., Noels, K., & Clément, R. (1997). Biases in self-ratings of second language proficiency: The role of anxiety. *Language Learning, 47,* 265–287.

Macnamara, J. (1975). Comparison between first and second language learning. *Working Papers on Bilingualism, 7,* 71–94.

MacWhinney, B. (Ed.). (1999). *The emergence of language.* Mahwah, NJ: Lawrence Erlbaum Associates.

Major, R., & Faudree, M. (1996). Markedness universals and acquisition of voicing contrasts by Korean speakers of English. *Studies in Second Language Acquisition, 18,* 69–90.

Major, R., Fitzmaurice, S., Bunta, F., & Balasubramanian, C. (2005). Testing the effects of regional, ethnic, and international dialects of English on listening comprehension. *Language Learning, 55,* 37–69.

Malinowski, B. (1923). The problem of meaning in primitive languages. In C. Ogden & I. Richards (Eds.), *The Meaning of meaning.* London: Kegan Paul.

Malotki, E. (1983). *Hopi time: A linguistic analysis of temporal concepts in the Hopi language.* Berlin: Mouton.

Maratsos, M. (1988). Crosslinguistic analysis, universals, and language acquisition. In F. Kessel (Ed.), *The development of language and language researchers: Essays in honor of Roger Brown.* Hillsdale, NJ: Lawrence Erlbaum Associates.

Marchenkova, L. (2005). Language, culture, and self: The Bakhtin-Vygotsky encounter. In J. Hall, G. Vitanova, & L. Marchenkova (Eds.), *Dialogue with Bakhtin on second and foreign language learning* (pp. 171–188). Mahwah, NJ: Lawrence Erlbaum Associates.

Marckwardt, A. (1972). Changing winds and shifting sands. *MST English Quarterly, 21,* 3–11.

Marinova-Todd, S., Marshall, D., & Snow, C. (2000). Three misconceptions about age and L2 learning. *TESOL Quarterly, 34,* 9–34.

Markee, N. (2004). Zones of interactional transitions in ESL classes. *Modern Language Journal, 88,* 583–596.

Markee, N. (2005). Conversation analysis for second language acquisition. In E. Hinkel (Ed.), *Handbook of research in second language teaching and learning* (pp. 355–374). Mahwah, NJ: Lawrence Erlbaum Associates.

Markee, N., & Kasper, G. (2004). Classroom talks: An introduction. *Modern Language Journal, 88,* 491–500.

Marshall, T. (1989). *The whole world guide to language learning.* Yarmouth, ME: Intercultural Press.

Masgoret, A.-M., & Gardner, R. (2003). Attitudes, motivation, and second language learning: A meta-analysis of studies conducted by Gardner and associates. *Language Learning, 53,* 123–163.

Maslow, A. (1970). *Motivation and personality* (2nd ed.). New York: Harper & Row.

Mason, B., & Krashen, S. (2010). A reader response to File and Adams. *TESOL quarterly, 44,* 790–793.

Matsumoto, D. (2000). *Culture and psychology: People around the world.* Belmont, CA: Wadsworth.

Matsumoto, D., & Juang, L. (2013). *Culture and psychology.* (5th ed.). Stamford, CT: Wadsworth Publishing.

Maubach, A.-M., & Morgan, C. (2001). The relationship between gender and learning styles among A-level modern language students. *Language Learning Journal, 23,* 41–47.

McArthur, T. (2001). World English and world Englishes: Trends, tensions, varieties, and standards. *Language Teaching, 34,* 1–20.

McCafferty, S., & Stam, G. (Eds.). (2009). *Gesture: Second language acquisition and classroom research.* New York: Routledge.

McCarthy, M. (1998). *Spoken language and applied linguistics.* Cambridge, UK: Cambridge University Press.

McClelland, N. (2000). Goal orientations in Japanese college students learning EFL. In S. Cornwell & P. Robinson (Eds.), *Individual differences in foreign language learning: Effects of aptitude, intelligence, and motivation* (pp. 99–115). Tokyo: Japan Association for Language Teaching.

McDonough, S. (1999). Learner strategies. *Language Teaching, 32,* 1–18.

McEnery, T., & Xiao, R. (2011). What corpora can offer in language teaching and learning. In E. Hinkel (Ed.), *Handbook of research in second language teaching and learning: Volume II* (pp. 364–380). New York: Routledge.

McGinn, L., Stokes, J., & Trier, A. (2005). *Does music affect language acquisition?* Paper presented at TESOL, San Antonio, TX.

McGroarty, M. (1984). Some meanings of communicative competence for second language students. *TESOL Quarterly, 18,* 257–272.

McGroarty, M., & Galvan, J. (1985). Culture as an issue in second language teaching. In M. Celce-Murcia (Ed.), *Beyond basics: Issues and research in TESOL.* Rowley, MA: Newbury House.

McKay, S. (2002). *Teaching English as an international language: Rethinking goals and approaches.* Oxford: Oxford University Press.

McKay, S. (2005). Sociolinguistics and second language learning. In E. Hinkel (Ed.), *Handbook of research in second language teaching and learning* (pp. 281–299). Mahwah, NJ: Lawrence Erlbaum Associates.

McKay, S. (2011). English as an international lingua franca pedagogy. In E. Hinkel (Ed.), *Handbook of research in second language teaching and learning: Volume II* (pp. 122–139). New York: Routledge.

McLaughlin, B. (1978). The monitor model: Some methodological considerations. *Language Learning, 28,* 309–332.

McLaughlin, B. (1987). *Theories of second language learning.* London: Edward Arnold.

McLaughlin, B. (1990a). "Conscious "versus" unconscious" learning. *TESOL Quarterly, 24,* 617–634.

McLaughlin, B. (1990b). Restructuring. *Applied Linguistics, 11,* 113–128.

McLaughlin, B., Rossman, T., & McLeod, B. (1983). Second language learning: An information-processing perspective. *Language Learning, 33,* 135–158.

McLeod, B., & McLaughlin, B. (1986). Restructuring or automaticity? Reading in a second language. *Language Learning, 36,* 109–123.

McNeill, D. (1966). Developmental psycholinguistics. In F. Smith & G. Miller (Eds.), *The genesis of language: A psycholinguistic approach* (pp. 69–73). Cambridge, MA: Massachusetts Institute of Technology Press.

McNeill, D. (1968). On the theories of language acquisition. In T. Dixon & D. Horton (Eds.), *Verbal behavior and general behavior theory* (p. 416). Englewood Cliffs, NJ: Prentice Hall.

McTear, M. (1984). Structure and process in children's conversational development. In S. Kuczaj (Ed.), *Discourse development: Progress in cognitive development research*. New York: Springer-Verlag.

Medgyes, P. (1994). *Non-natives in ELT*. London: Macmillan.

Mellow, J.D. (2002). Toward principled eclecticism in language teaching: The two-dimensional model and the centering principle. *TESL-EJ, 5*, 1–20.

Meredith, K. (2011). Identity and language learning: Multiple critical perspectives. *Language Teaching, 44*, 551–561.

Merlevede, P., Bridoux, D., & Vandamme, R. (2001). *Seven steps to emotional intelligence*. New York: Crown House Publishing.

Merriam-Webster's collegiate dictionary (11th ed.). (2003). Springfield, MA: Merriam-Webster.

Mestre, J. P. (Ed.) (2005). *Transfer of learning: From a modern multidisciplinary perspective*. Greenwich, CT: Information Age Publishing.

Meyer, C. (2002). *English corpus linguistics*. Cambridge, UK: Cambridge University Press.

Miller, G. (1956). The magical number seven, plus or minus two: Some limits on our capacity for processing information. *Psychological Review, 63*, 81–97.

Miller, W. (1963). The acquisition of formal features of language. *American Journal of Orthopsychiatry, 34*, 862–867.

Mills, N., Pajares, F., & Herron, C. (2006). A reevaluation of the role of anxiety: Self-efficacy, anxiety, and their relation to reading and listening proficiency. *Foreign Language Annals, 39*, 276–295.

Milon, J. (1974). The development of negation in English by a second language learner. *TESOL Quarterly, 8*, 137–143.

Mitchell, C., & Vidal, K. (2001). Weighing the ways of the flow: Twentieth century language instruction. *Modern Language Journal, 85*, 26–38.

Mitchell, R., & Myles, F. (1998). *Second language learning theories*. New York: Oxford University Press.

Mitchell, R., & Myles, F. (2004). *Second language learning theories* (2nd ed.). London: Hodder Arnold.

Moerk, E. (1985). Analytic, synthetic, abstracting, and word-class defining aspects of verbal mother-child interactions. *Journal of Psycholinguistic Research, 14*, 263–287.

Mondada, L., & Doehler, S. (2004). Second language acquisition as situated practice: Task accomplishment in the French second language classroom. *Modern Language Journal, 88*, 501–518.

Montrul, S. (2002). Incomplete acquisition and attrition of Spanish tense/aspect distinctions in adult bilinguals. *Bilingualism: Language and Cognition, 5*, 39–68.

Montrul, S. (2008). *Incomplete acquisition in bilingualism: Re-examining the age factor*. Amsterdam: John Benjamins.

Montrul, S. (2011). Spanish heritage speakers: Bridging formal linguistics, psycholinguistics and pedagogy. *Heritage Language Journal, 8,* i–vi.

Moody, R. (1988). Personality preferences and foreign language learning. *Modern Language Journal, 72,* 389–401.

Morgan, B., & Clarke, M. (2011). Identity in second language teaching and learning. In E. Hinkel (Ed.), *Handbook of research in second language teaching and learning: Volume II* (pp. 817–836). New York: Routledge.

Mori, J. (2004). Negotiating sequential boundaries and learning opportunities: A case from a Japanese language classroom. *Modern Language Journal, 88,* 536–550.

Morris, B., & Gerstman, L. (1986). Age contrasts in the learning of language-relevant materials: Some challenges to critical period hypotheses. *Language Learning, 36,* 311–352.

Moyer, A. (1999). Ultimate attainment in L2 phonology: The critical factors of age, motivation, and instruction. *Studies in Second Language Acquisition, 21,* 81–108.

Moyer, A. (2004). *Age, accent, and experience in second language acquisition.* Clevedon, UK: Multilingual Matters.

Muñoz, C., & Singleton, D. (2011). A critical review of age-related research on L2 ultimate attainment. *Language Teaching, 44,* 1–35.

Murphey, T. (2006). *Language Hungry! An introduction to language learning fun and self-esteem.* London: Helbling Languages.

Myers, I. (1962). *The Myers-Briggs type indicator.* Palo Alto, CA: Consulting Psychologists Press.

Myles, F. (2010). The development of theories of second language acquisition. *Language Teaching, 43,* 320–332.

Naiman, N., Fröhlich, M., Stern, H., & Todesco, A. (1978). *The good language learner.* Toronto: Ontario Institute for Studies in Education. (Reprinted by Multilingual Matters, Clevedon, UK.)

Nakatani, Y. (2005). The effects of awareness-raising training on oral communication strategy use. *Modern Language Journal, 89,* 76–91.

Nakuma, C. (1998). A new theoretical account of "fossilization": Implications for L2 attrition research. *International Review of Applied Linguistics, 36,* 247–256.

Nassaji, H., & Cumming, A. (2000). What's in a ZPD? A case study of a young ESL student and teacher interacting through dialogue journals. *Language Teaching Research, 4,* 95–121.

Natalicio, D., & Natalicio, L. (1971). A comparative study of English pluralization by native and non-native English speakers. *Child Development, 42,* 1302–1306.

Nayar, P. (1997). ESL/EFL dichotomy today: Language politics or pragmatics? *TESOL Quarterly, 31,* 9–37.

Nekvapil, J. (2011). The history and theory of language planning. In E. Hinkel (Ed.), *Handbook of research in second language teaching and learning: Volume II* (pp. 871–887). New York: Routledge.

Nelson, G., Carson, J., Al Batal, M., & El Bakary, W. (2002). Cross-cultural pragmatics: Strategy use in Egyptian Arabic and American English refusals. *Applied Linguistics, 23,* 163–189.

Nemser, W. (1971). Approximative systems of foreign language learners. *International Review of Applied Linguistics, 9,* 115–123.

Neufeld, G. (1977). Language learning ability in adults: A study on the acquisition of prosodic and articulatory features. *Working Papers on Bilingualism, 12,* 45–60.

Neufeld, G. (1979). Towards a theory of language learning ability. *Language Learning, 29,* 227–241.

Neufeld, G. (1980). On the adult's ability to acquire phonology. *TESOL Quarterly, 14,* 285–298.

Neufeld, G. (2001). Non-foreign-accented speech in adult second language learners: Does it exist and what does it signify? *ITL Review of Applied Linguistics, 133–134,* 185–206.

Ney, J., & Pearson, B. (1990). Connectionism as a model of language learning: Parallels in foreign language teaching. *Modern Language Journal, 74,* 474–482.

Nilsen, A., Bosmajian, H., Gershuny, H., & Stanley, J. (1977). *Sexism and language.* Urbana, IL: National Council of Teachers of English.

Noels, K., & Giles, H. (2009). Social identity and language learning. In W. Ritchie & T. Bhatia (Eds.), *The new handbook of second language acquisition* (pp. 647–670). Bingley, UK: Emerald Group Publishing, Ltd.

Noels, K., Clément, R., & Pelletier, L. (1999). Perceptions of teachers' communicative style and students' intrinsic and extrinsic motivation. *Modern Language Journal, 83,* 23–34.

Noels, K., Pelletier, L., Clément, R., & Vallerand, R. (2000). Why are you learning a second language? Motivational orientations and self-determination theory. *Language Learning, 50,* 57–85.

Norton, B. (1997). Language, identity, and the ownership of English. *TESOL Quarterly, 31,* 409–430.

Norton, B. (2000). *Identity and language learning.* Harlow, UK: Pearson Education.

Norton, B., & McKinney, C. (2011). An identity approach to second language acquisition. In D. Atkinson (Ed.), *alternative approaches to second language acquisition* (pp. 73–94). London: Routledge.

Norton, B., & Pavlenko, A. (2004). *Gender and English language learners.* Alexandria, VA: TESOL.

Norton, B., & Toohey, K. (2001). Changing perspectives on good language learners. *TESOL Quarterly, 35,* 307–322.

Norton, B., & Toohey, K. (2011). Identity, language learning, and social change. *Language Teaching, 44,* 412–446.

Nunan, D. (1989). *Understanding language classrooms: A guide for teacher-initiated action.* Englewood Cliffs, NJ: Prentice Hall.

Nunan, D. (2003). The impact of English as a global language on educational policies and practices in the Asia-Pacific region. *TESOL Quarterly, 37,* 589–613.

Nunan, D. (2004). *Task-based language teaching.* Cambridge, UK: Cambridge University Press.

Nuttall, C. (1996). *Teaching reading skills in a foreign language* (2nd ed.). Oxford: Heinemann.

O'Grady, W. (1996). Language acquisition without Universal Grammar: A general nativist proposal for L2 learning. *Second Language Research, 12,* 374–397.

O'Grady, W. (1999). Toward a new nativism. *Studies in Second Language Acquisition, 21,* 621–633.

O'Grady, W. (2003). The radical middle: Nativism without universal grammar. In C. Doughty & M. Long (Eds.), *The handbook of second language acquisition* (pp. 43–103). Malden, MA: Blackwell Publishing.

O'Grady, W. (2005). *How children learn language.* New York: Cambridge University Press.

O'Grady, W. (2012). Language acquisition without an acquisition device. *Language Teaching, 45,* 116–130.

O'Grady, W., Lee, M, & Kwak, H.-Y. (2009). Emergentism and second language acquisition. In W. Ritchie & T. Bhatia (Eds.), *The new handbook of second language acquisition* (pp. 69–88). Bingley, UK: Emerald Group Publishing, Ltd.

O'Hara, M. (2003). Cultivating consciousness: Carl R. Rogers's person-centered group process as transformative androgogy. *Journal of Transformative Education, 1,* 64–79.

O'Keefe, A., & Farr, F. (2003). Using language corpora in initial teacher education: Pedagogic issues and practical applications. *TESOL Quarterly, 37,* 389–418.

O'Malley, J., & Chamot, A. (1990). *Learning strategies in second language acquisition.* New York: Cambridge University Press.

O'Malley, J., Chamot, A., & Kupper, L. (1989). Listening comprehension strategies in second language acquisition. *Applied Linguistics, 10,* 418–437.

O'Malley, J., Chamot, A., & Walker, C. (1987). Some applications of cognitive theory to second language acquisition. *Studies in Second Language Acquisition, 9,* 287–306.

O'Malley, J., Chamot, A., Stewner-Manzanares, G., Kupper, L., & Russo, R. (1985a). Learning strategies used by beginning and intermediate ESL students. *Language Learning, 35,* 21–46.

O'Malley, J., Chamot, A., Stewner-Manzanares, G., Russo, R., & Kupper, L. (1985b). Learning strategy applications with students of English as a second language. *TESOL Quarterly, 19,* 557–584.

O'Malley, J., Russo, R., & Chamot, A. (1983). A review of the literature on learning strategies in the acquisition of English as a second language: The potential for research applications. Rosslyn, VA: InterAmerica Research Associates.

Obler, L. (1981). Right hemisphere participation in second language acquisition. In K. Diller (Ed.), *Individual differences and universals in language learning aptitude.* Rowley, MA: Newbury House.

Obler, L. (1982). Neurolinguistic aspects of language loss as they pertain to second language acquisition. In R. Lambert & B. Freed (Eds.), *The loss of language skills.* Rowley, MA: Newbury House.

Obler, L., & Gjerlow, K. (1999). *Language and the brain.* Cambridge, UK: Cambridge University Press.

Ochsner, R. (1979). A poetics of second language acquisition. *Language Learning, 29,* 53–80.

Odlin, T. (2003). Cross-linguistic influence. In C. Doughty & M. Long (Eds.), *The handbook of second language acquisition* (pp. 436–486). Malden, MA: Blackwell Publishing.

Oller, J. (1981a). Language as intelligence? *Language Learning, 31,* 465–492.

Oller, J. (1981b). Research on the measurement of affective variables: Some remaining questions. In R. Andersen (Ed.), *New dimensions in second language acquisition research.* Rowley, MA: Newbury House.

Oller, J., & Ziahosseiny, S. (1970). The contrastive analysis hypothesis and spelling errors. *Language Learning, 20,* 183–189.

Oller, J., Baca, L., & Vigil, A. (1978). Attitudes and attained proficiency in ESL: A sociolinguistic study of Mexican-Americans in the Southwest. *TESOL Quarterly, 11,* 173–183.

Oller, J., Hudson, A., & Liu, P. (1977). Attitudes and attained proficiency in ESL: A sociolinguistic study of native speakers of Chinese in the United States. *Language Learning, 27,* 1–27.

Olshtain, E. (1989). Is second language attrition the reversal of second language acquisition? *Studies in Second Language Acquisition, 11,* 151–165.

Olshtain, E., & Cohen, A. (1983). Apology: A speech-act set. In N. Wolfson & E. Judd (Eds.), *Sociolinguistics and language acquisition.* Rowley, MA: Newbury House.

Oltman, P., Raskin, E., & Witkin, H. (1971). *Group embedded figures test.* Palo Alto, CA: Consulting Psychologists Press.

Oostendorp, M. (2012). New perspectives on cross-linguistic influence: Language and cognition. *Language Teaching, 45,* 389–398.

Ortega, L. (2009). *Understanding second language acquisition.* London: Hodder Education.

Ortega, L. (2011). SLA after the social turn. In D. Atkinson (Ed.), *Alternative approaches to second language acquisition* (pp. 167–180). New York: Routledge.

Osgood, C. (1953). *Method and theory in experimental psychology.* New York: Oxford University Press.

Osgood, C. (1957). *Contemporary approaches to cognition.* Cambridge, MA: Harvard University Press.

Oxford, R. (1990a). *Language learning strategies: What every teacher should know.* New York: Newbury House.

Oxford, R. (1990b). Styles, strategies, and aptitude: Connections for language learning. In T. Parry & C. Stansfield (Eds.), *Language aptitude reconsidered* (pp. 67–125). New York: Prentice Hall Regents.

Oxford, R. (1995). Style analysis survey (SAS): Assessing your own learning and working styles. In J. Reid (Ed.), *Learning styles in the ESL/EFL classroom* (pp. 208–215). New York: Heinle & Heinle.

Oxford, R. (1999). Anxiety and the language learner: New insights. In J. Arnold (Ed.), *Affect in language learning* (pp. 58–67). Cambridge UK: Cambridge University Press.

Oxford, R. (2011a). Strategies for learning a second or foreign language. *Language Teaching, 44,* 167–180.

Oxford, R. (2011b). *Teaching and researching language learning strategies.* Harlow, UK: Pearson Education Ltd.

Oxford, R. (Ed.). (1996). *Learning strategies around the world: Cross-cultural perspectives.* Honolulu: University of Hawaii Press.

Oxford, R., & Anderson, N. (1995). A crosscultural view of learning styles. *Language Teaching, 28,* 201–215.

Oxford, R., & Crookall, D. (1989). Research on language learning strategies: Methods, findings, and instructional issues. *Modern Language Journal, 73,* 404–419.

Oxford, R., & Ehrman, M. (1988). Psychological type and adult language learning strategies: A pilot study. *Journal of Psychological Type, 16,* 22–32.

Ozeki, N. (2000). *Listening strategy instruction for female EFL college students in Japan.* Tokyo: Macmillan Language House.

Pakir, A. (1999). Connecting with English in the context of internationalism. *TESOL Quarterly, 33,* 103–114.

Palfreyman, D. (2003). The representation of learner autonomy and learner independence in organizational culture. In D. Palfreyman & R. Smith (Eds.), *Learner autonomy across cultures: Language education perspectives* (pp. 183–200). Basingstoke, England: Palgrave Macmillan.

Panetta, C. (2001). *Contrastive rhetoric revisited and redefined.* Mahwah, NJ: Lawrence Erlbaum Associates.

Panova, I., & Lyster, R. (2002). Patterns of corrective feedback and uptake in an adult ESL classroom. *TESOL Quarterly, 36,* 573–595.

Parry, T., & Child, J. (1990). Preliminary investigation of the relationship between VORD, MLAT, and language proficiency. In T. Parry & C. Stansfield (Eds.), *Language aptitude reconsidered* (pp. 30–66). New York: Prentice Hall Regents.

Paulston, C. (1974). Linguistic and communicative competence. *TESOL Quarterly, 8,* 347–362.

Pavlenko, A., & Jarvis, S. (2002). Bidirectional transfer. *Applied Linguistics, 23,* 190–214.

Pavlenko, A., & Lantolf, J. (2000). Second language learning as participation in the (re)construction of selves. In J. Lantolf (Ed.), *Sociocultural theory and second language learning* (pp. 155–177). Oxford, UK: Oxford University Press.

Pavlenko, A., & Norton, B. (2007). Imagined communities, identity, and English language learners. In J. Cummins & C. Davison (Eds.), *International handbook of English language teaching* (pp. 669–680). New York: Springer.

Pavlenko, A., & Piller, I. (2001). New directions in the study of multilingualism, second language learning, and gender. In A. Pavlenko, A. Blackledge, I. Piller, & M. Teutsch-Dwyer (Eds.), *Multilingualism, second language learning, and gender* (pp. 17–52). Berlin: Mouton de Gruyter.

Pemberton, R. (1996). *Taking control: Autonomy in language learning.* Hong Kong: Hong Kong University Press.

Pemberton, R., Toogood, S., & Barfield, A. (Eds.). (2009). *Maintaining control: Autonomy and language learning.* Hong Kong: Hong Kong University Press.

Pennycook, A. (1997). Cultural alternatives and autonomy. In P. Benson & P. Voller (Eds.), *Autonomy and independence in language learning* (pp. 35–53). London: Longman.

Peters, A. (1981). Language learning strategies: Does the whole equal the sum of the parts? In K. Diller (Ed.), *Individual differences and universals in language learning aptitude.* Rowley, MA: Newbury House.

Petersen, C., & Al-Haik, A. (1976). The development of the Defense Language Aptitude Battery. *Educational and Psychological Measurement, 36,* 369–380.

Phillipson, R. (1992). *Linguistic imperialism.* London: Oxford University Press.

Phillipson, R. (2000). English in the new world order. In T. Ricento (Ed.), *Ideology, politics, and language policies: Focus on English* (pp. 87–106). Amsterdam: John Benjamins.

Phillipson, R. (2009). English in globalization: A lingua franca or a lingua franken-steinia? *TESOL Quarterly, 43*, 335–339.

Piaget, J. (1954). *The construction of reality in the child.* New York: Basic Books.

Piaget, J. (1955). *The language and thought of the child.* New York: Meridian.

Piaget, J. (1970). *The science of education and the psychology of the child.* New York: Basic Books.

Piaget, J. (1972). *The principles of genetic epistemology.* New York: Basic Books.

Piaget, J., & Inhelder B. (1969). *The psychology of the child.* New York: Basic Books.

Pica, T. (1987). Second language acquisition, social interaction, and the classroom. *Applied Linguistics, 8,* 3–21.

Pica, T. (2005). Second language acquisition research and applied linguistics. In E. Hinkel (Ed.), *Handbook of research in second language teaching and learning* (pp. 263–280). New York: Routledge.

Pica, T. (2009). Second language acquisition in the instructional environment. In W. Ritchie & T. Bhatia (Eds.), *The new handbook of second language acquisition* (pp. 473–501). Bingley, UK: Emerald Group Publishing, Ltd.

Pike, K. (1967). *Language in relation to a unified theory of the structure of human behavior.* The Hague: Mouton.

Pimsleur, P. (1966). *Pimsleur language aptitude battery.* New York: Harcourt, Brace & World.

Pinker, S. (1994). *The language instinct: How the mind creates language.* New York: William Morrow.

Pinker, S. (2007). *The language instinct: How the mind creates language (P.S.).* New York: Harper Perennial Modern Classics.

Pitchford, N., & Mullen, K. (2006). The developmental acquisition of basic colour terms. In N. Pitchford & C. Biggam (Eds.), *Progress in Colour Studies: Volume II. Psychological Aspects* (pp. 139–158). Philadelphia: John Benjamins Publishing Company.

Porte, G. (1999). English as a forgotten language. *ELT Journal, 53,* 28–35.

Prator, C. (1967). *Hierarchy of difficulty.* Unpublished classroom lecture, University of California, Los Angeles.

Prator, C., & Celce-Murcia, M. (1979). An outline of language teaching approaches. In M. Celce-Murcia & L. McIntosh (Eds.), *Teaching English as a second or foreign language.* Rowley, MA: Newbury House.

Pressley, M. (2000). What should comprehension instruction be the instruction of? In M. Kamil, P. Mosenthal, P. Pearson, & R. Barr (Eds.), *Handbook of reading research, Volume III* (pp. 545–561). Mahwah, NJ: Lawrence Erlbaum Associates.

Preston, D. (1996). Variationist perspectives on second language acquisition. In R. Bayley & D. Preston (Eds.), *Second language acquisition and linguistic variation.* Amsterdam: John Benjamins.

Preston, D., & Bayley, R. (2009). Variationist linguistics and second language acquisition. In W. Ritchie & T. Bhatia (Eds.), *The new handbook of second language acquisition* (pp. 89–113). Bingley, UK: Emerald Group Publishing, Ltd.

Priven, D. (2002). The vanishing pronoun: A case study of language attrition in Russian. *Canadian Journal of Applied Linguistics, 5,* 131–144.

Quirk, R. (1988). The question of standard in the international use of English. In P. Lowenberg (Ed.), *Georgetown University round table on languages and linguistics. 1987* Washington, DC: Georgetown University Press.

Raimes, A. (1998). Teaching writing. *Annual Review of Applied Linguistics, 18,* 142–167.

Ramage, K. (1990). Motivational factors and persistence in foreign language study. *Language Learning, 40,* 189–219.

Ramirez, A. (1995). *Creating contexts for second language acquisition: Theory and methods.* White Plains, NY: Longman.

Ravem, R. (1968). Language acquisition in a second language environment. *International Review of Applied Linguistics, 6,* 175–185.

Reid, J. (1987). The learning style preferences of ESL students. *TESOL Quarterly, 21,* 87–111.

Reid, J. (1995). *Learning styles in the ESL/EFL classroom.* Boston: Heinle & Heinle.

Reynolds, A. (1991). The cognitive consequences of bilingualism. *ERIC/CLL News Bulletin, 14,* 1–8.

Ricento, T. (1994). [Review of the book *Linguistic Imperialism*]. *TESOL Quarterly, 28,* 421–427.

Ricento, T. (2005). Considerations of identity in L2 learning. In E. Hinkel (Ed.), *Handbook of research in second language teaching and learning* (pp. 895–910). New York: Routledge.

Richards, J. (1971). A non-contrastive approach to error analysis. *English Language Teaching, 25,* 204–219.

Richards, J. (1979). Rhetorical styles and communicative styles in the new varieties of English. *Language Learning, 29,* 1–25.

Richards, J., & Rodgers, T. (1982). Method: Approach, design, and procedure. *TESOL Quarterly, 16,* 153–168.

Richards, J., & Rodgers, T. (2001). *Approaches and methods in language teaching* (2nd ed.). New York: Cambridge University Press.

Riddiford, N., & Joe, A. (2010). Tracking the development of sociopragmatic skills. *TESOL Quarterly, 44,* 195–205.

Riley, P. (1988). The ethnography of autonomy. In A. Brookes & P. Grundy (Eds.), *Individualisation and autonomy in language learning* (pp. 12–34). London: British Council.

Ringbom, H. (2011). Perceived redundancy or crosslinguistic influence? What L3 learners' material can tell us about the causes of errors. In G. De Angelis & J.-M. Dewaele (Eds.), *New trends in crosslinguistic influence and multilingualism research* (pp. 19–24). Bristol, UK: Multilingual Matters.

Risager, K. (2011). The cultural dimensions of language teaching and learning. *Language Teaching, 44,* 485–499.

Ritchie, W., & Bhatia, T. (Eds.). (2009). *The new handbook of second language acquisition.* Bingley, UK: Emerald Group.

Rivers, W. (1964). *The psychologist and the foreign language teacher.* Chicago: University of Chicago Press.

Robinson-Stuart, G., & Nocon, H. (1996). Second culture acquisition: Ethnography in the foreign language classroom. *Modern Language Journal, 80,* 431–449.

Robinson, P. (1994). Implicit knowledge, second language learning, and syllabus construction. *TESOL Quarterly, 28,* 161–166.

Robinson, P. (1995). Attention, memory, and the "noticing" hypothesis. *Language Learning, 45,* 283–331.

Robinson, P. (1997). Individual differences and the fundamental similarity of implicit and explicit adult second language learning. *Language Learning, 47,* 45–99.

Robinson, P. (2001). Individual differences, cognitive abilities, aptitude complexes and learning conditions in second language acquisition. *Second Language Research, 17,* 368–392.

Robinson, P. (2003). Attention and memory during SLA. In C. Doughty & M. Long (Eds.), *The handbook of second language acquisition* (pp. 631–678). Malden, MA: Blackwell Publishing.

Robinson, P. (2005). Aptitude and L2 acquisition. *Annual Review of Applied Linguistics, 25,* 46–73.

Robinson, P. (Ed.) (2011). *Second language task complexity: Researching the cognition hypothesis of language learning and performance.* Amsterdam: John Benjamins.

Robinson, P. (Ed.). (2002). *Individual differences and instructed language learning.* Amsterdam: John Benjamins.

Robinson, P., & Ellis, N. (2008). *Handbook of cognitive linguistics and second language acquisition.* New York: Routledge.

Robinson, P., & Gilabert, R. (2007). Task complexity, the cognition hypothesis, and second language learning and performance. *International Review of Applied Linguistics, 45,* 161–176.

Rodríguez, M., & Abreu, O. (2003). The stability of general foreign language classroom anxiety across English and French. *Modern Language Journal, 87,* 365–374.

Rogers, C. (1951). *Client-centered therapy.* Boston: Houghton Mifflin.

Rogers, C. (1977). *Carl Rogers on personal power.* New York: Delacorte.

Rogers, C. (1983). *Freedom to learn for the eighties.* Columbus, OH: Charles E. Merrill.

Romaine, S. (1999). *Communicating gender.* Mahwah, NJ: Lawrence Erlbaum Associates.

Romaine, S. (2003). Variation. In C. Doughty & M. Long (Eds.), *The handbook of second language acquisition* (pp. 409–435). Malden, MA: Blackwell Publishing.

Rosa, E., & Leow, R. (2004). Awareness, different learning conditions, and second language development. *Applied Psycholinguistics, 25,* 269–292.

Rosansky, E. (1975). The critical period for the acquisition of language: Some cognitive developmental considerations. *Working Papers on Bilingualism, 6,* 92–102.

Rosansky, E. (1976). Methods and morphemes in second language acquisition research. *Language Learning, 26,* 409–425.

Rost, M., & Ross, S. (1991). Learner use of strategies in interaction: Typology and predictability. *Language Learning, 41,* 235–273.

Roth, W.-M., & Lawless, D. (2002). When up is down and down is up: Body orientation, proximity, and gestures and resources. *Language in Society, 31,* 1–28.

Rubin, J. (1975). What the "good language learner" can teach us. *TESOL Quarterly, 9,* 41–51.

Rubin, J. (1976). How to tell when someone is saying "no." *Topics in Culture Learning* (Vol. 4). Honolulu: East-West Culture Learning Institute. (Reprinted in N. Wolfson & E. Judd, Eds., *Sociolinguistics and language acquisition,* Rowley, MA: Newbury House.)

Rubin, J., & Thompson, I. (1982). *How to be a more successful language learner.* Boston: Heinle & Heinle.

Rubin, J., & Thompson, I. (1994). *How to be a more successful language learner* (2nd ed.). Boston: Heinle & Heinle.

Rubin, J., Chamot, A., Harris, V., & Anderson, N. (2007). Intervening in the use of strategies. In A. Cohen & E. Macaro (Eds.), *Language learner strategies: Thirty years of research and practice* (pp. 141–160). Oxford, UK: Oxford University Press.

Rubio, F. (Ed.). (2007). *Self-esteem and foreign language learning.* Newcastle, UK: Cambridge Scholars Publishing.

Rumelhart, D., & McClelland, J. (Eds.). (1986). *Parallel distributed processing: Explorations in the microstructure of cognition.* Cambridge, MA: Massachusetts Institute of Technology Press.

Rutherford, W. (1982). Markedness in second language acquisition. *Language Learning, 32,* 85–108.

Saleemi, A. (1992). *Universal grammar and language learnability.* Cambridge, UK: Cambridge University Press.

Sasaki, M. (1993a). Relationships among second language proficiency, foreign language aptitude, and intelligence: A protocol analysis. *Language Learning, 43,* 469–505.

Sasaki, M. (1993b). Relationships among second language proficiency, foreign language aptitude, and intelligence: A structural equation modeling approach. *Language Learning, 43,* 313–344.

Saslow, J., & Ascher, A. (2011) *Top Notch 1.* (2nd ed.). White Plains, NY: Pearson Longman.

Savignon, S. (1972). *Communicative competence: An experiment in foreign language teaching.* Philadelphia: Center for Curriculum Development.

Savignon, S. (1983). *Communicative competence: Theory and classroom practice.* Reading, MA: Addison-Wesley.

Savignon, S. (2005). Communicative language teaching: Strategies and goals. In E. Hinkel (Ed.), *Handbook of research in second language teaching and learning* (pp. 635–651). Mahwah, NJ: Lawrence Erlbaum Associates.

Savignon, S., & Sysoyev, P. (2002). Sociocultural strategies for a dialogue of cultures. *Modern Language Journal, 86,* 508–524.

Saville-Troike, M. (1989). *The ethnography of communication: An introduction* (2nd ed.). Malden, MA: Blackwell.

Saxton, Matthew. (2010). *Child language: Acquisition and development.* London: Sage Publications, Ltd.

Scarino, A. (2009). Assessing intercultural capability in learning languages: Some issues and considerations. *Language Teaching, 42,* 67–80.

Schachter, J. (1974). An error in error analysis. *Language Learning, 24,* 205–214.

Schachter, J. (1988). Second language acquisition and its relationship to Universal Grammar. *Applied Linguistics, 9,* 219–235.

Schecter, S., & Bayley, R. (2002*). Language as cultural practice: Mexicanos en el norte.* Mahwah, NJ: Lawrence Erlbaum Associates.

Schinke-Llano, L. (1989). Early childhood bilingualism. *Studies in Second Language Acquisition, 11,* 223–240.

Schinke-Llano, L. (1993). On the value of a Vygotskian framework for SLA theory. *Language Learning, 43,* 121–129.

Schmenk, B. (2005). Globalizing learner autonomy. *TESOL Quarterly, 39,* 107–118.

Schmidt, R. (1990). The role of consciousness in second language learning. *Applied Linguistics, 11,* 129–158.

Schmidt, R. (2001). Attention. In P. Robinson (Ed.), *Cognition in second language acquisition* (pp. 3–32). New York: Cambridge University Press.

Schumann, J. (1975). Affective factors and the problem of age in second language acquisition. *Language Learning, 25,* 209–235.

Schumann, J. (1976a). Second language acquisition research: Getting a more global look at the learner. *Language Learning,* Special Issue Number 4, 15–28.

Schumann, J. (1976b). Second language acquisition: The pidginization hypothesis. *Language Learning, 26,* 391–408.

Schumann, J. (1976c). Social distance as a factor in second language acquisition. *Language Learning, 26,* 135–143.

Schumann, J. (1978). *The pidginization process: A model for second language acquisition.* Rowley, MA: Newbury House.

Schumann, J. (1982). Art and science in second language acquisition research. In M. Clarke & J. Handscombe (Eds.), *On TESOL '82: Pacific perspectives on language learning and teaching.* Washington, DC: TESOL.

Schumann, J. (1997). *The neurobiology of affect in language.* Cambridge, MA: Blackwell.

Schumann, J. (1998). The neurobiology of affect in language. [Special issue]. *Language Learning, 48* (Suppl. 1).

Schumann, J. (1999). A neurobiological perspective on affect and methodology in second language learning. In J. Arnold (Ed.), *Affect in language learning* (pp. 28–42). Cambridge, UK: Cambridge University Press.

Schumann, J., Crowell, S., Jones, N., Lee, N., Schuchert, S., & Wood, L. (2004). *The neurobiology of language: Perspectives from second language acquisition.* Mahwah, NJ: Lawrence Erlbaum Associates.

Schwartz, B. (1999). Let's make up your mind: "Special nativist" perspectives on language, modularity of mind, and nonnative language acquisition. *Studies in Second Language Acquisition, 21,* 635–655.

Scollon, R. (2004). Teaching language and culture as hegemonic practice. *Modern Language Journal, 88,* 271–274.

Scovel, T. (1969). Foreign accents, language acquisition, and cerebral dominance. *Language Learning, 19,* 245–254.

Scovel, T. (1978). The effect of affect on foreign language learning: A review of the anxiety research. *Language Learning, 28,* 129–142.

Scovel, T. (1979). Review of *Suggestology and Outlines of Suggestopedy. TESOL Quarterly, 13,* 255–266.

Scovel, T. (1982). Questions concerning the application of neurolinguistic research to second language learning/teaching. *TESOL Quarterly, 16,* 323–331.

Scovel, T. (1984, January). *A time to speak: Evidence for a biologically based critical period for language acquisition.* Paper presented at San Francisco State University, San Francisco, CA.

Scovel, T. (1988). *A Time to speak: A psycholinguistic inquiry into the critical period for human speech.* New York: Newbury House.

Scovel, T. (1999). "The younger the better" myth and bilingual education. In R. Gonzalez & I. Melis (Eds.), *Language ideologies: Critical perspectives on the English Only movement.* Urbana, IL: National Council of Teachers of English.

Scovel, T. (2000). A critical review of the critical period hypothesis. *Annual Review of Applied Linguistics, 20,* 213–223.

Scovel, T. (2001). *Learning new languages: A guide to second language acquisition.* Boston: Heinle & Heinle.

Seargeant, P. (2009). *The idea of English in Japan: Ideology and the evolution of a global language.* Buffalo, NY: Multilingual Matters.

Seargeant, P. (2011). *The idea of English in Japan: Ideology and the evolution of a global language.* Buffalo, NY: Multilingual Matters.

Seedhouse, P. (2004). *The interactional architecture of the language classroom: A conversation analysis perspective.* Hoboken, NJ: Wiley-Blackwell.

Seedhouse, P. (2011). Conversation analytic research into language teaching and learning. In E. Hinkel (Ed.), *Handbook of research in second language teaching and learning: Volume II* (pp. 345–363). New York: Routledge.

Seelye, H. (1974). *Teaching culture: Strategies for foreign language educators.* Skokie, IL:

Seliger, H. (1983). Learner interaction in the classroom and its effects on language acquisition. In H. Seliger & M. Long (Eds.), *Classroom oriented research in second language acquisition.* Rowley, MA: Newbury House.

Selinker, L. (1972). Interlanguage. *International Review of Applied Linguistics, 10,* 201–231.

Selinker, L., & Lamendella, J. (1979). The role of extrinsic feedback in interlanguage fossilization: A discussion of "Rule fossilization: A tentative model." *Language Learning, 29,* 363–375.

Shatz, M., & McCloskey, L. (1984). Answering appropriately: A developmental perspective on conversational knowledge. In S. Kuczaj (Ed.), *Discourse development: Progress in cognitive development research.* New York: Springer-Verlag.

Sheen, R. (1996). The advantage of exploiting contrastive analysis in teaching and learning a foreign language. *International Review of Applied Linguistics, 34,* 183–197.

Sheen, Y. (2007). The effect of focused written corrective feedback and language aptitude on ESL learners' acquisition of articles. *TESOL Quarterly, 41,* 255–283.

Sheen, Y., & Ellis, N. (2011). Corrective feedback in language teaching. In E. Hinkel (Ed.), *Handbook of research in second language teaching and learning: Volume II* (pp. 593–610). New York: Routledge.

Shehadeh, A. (2001). Self- and other-initiated modified output during task-based instruction. *TESOL Quarterly, 35,* 433–457.

Shenk, D. (2011). *The genius in all of us: New insights into genetics, talent, and IQ.* New York: Anchor Books.

Siegal, M. (2000). Comments on Dwight Atkinson's "TESOL and culture": A reader reacts. *TESOL Quarterly, 34,* 744–747.

Siegel, J. (2003). Social context. In C. Doughty & M. Long (Eds.), *The handbook of second language acquisition* (pp. 178–223). Malden, MA: Blackwell Publishing.

Siegel, J. (2009). Language contact and second language acquisition. In W. Ritchie & T. Bhatia (Eds.), *The new handbook of second language acquisition* (pp. 569–589). Bingley, UK: Emerald Group Publishing, Ltd.

Silberstein, S. (2011). Constrained but not determined: Approaches to discourse analysis. In E. Hinkel (Ed.), *Handbook of research in second language teaching and learning: Volume II* (pp. 274–290). New York: Routledge.

Simard, D., & Wong, W. (2004). Language awareness and its multiple possibilities for the L2 classroom. *Foreign Language Annals, 37,* 96–110.

Sinclair, J., & Coulthard, R. (1975). *Towards an analysis of discourse: The English used by teachers and pupils.* Oxford: Oxford University Press.

Singleton, D. (2001). Age and second language acquisition. *Annual Review of Applied Linguistics, 21,* 77–89.

Singleton, D., & Lengyel, Z. (Eds.). (1995). *The age factor in second language acquisition.* Clevedon, UK: Multilingual Matters.

Singleton, D., & Muñoz, C. (2011). Around and beyond the critical period hypothesis. In E. Hinkel (Ed.), *Handbook of research in second language teaching and learning: Volume II* (pp. 407–425). New York: Routledge.

Singleton, D., & Ryan, L. (2004). *Language acquisition: The age factor* (2nd ed.). Clevedon, UK: Multilingual Matters.

Sjöholm, K. (1995). *The influence of crosslinguistic, semantic, and input factors in the acquisition of English phrasal verbs: A comparison between Finnish and Swedish learners at an intermediate and advanced level.* Abo, Finland: Abo Akademi University Press.

Skehan, P. (1989). *Individual differences in second language learning.* London: Edward Arnold.

Skehan, P. (1991). Individual differences in second language learning. *Studies in Second Language Acquisition, 13,* 275–298.

Skehan, P. (1998). *A cognitive approach to language learning.* Oxford: Oxford University Press.

Skehan, P. (2002). Theorising and updating aptitude. In P. Robinson (Ed.), *Individual differences and instructed language learning* (pp. 69–93). Amsterdam: John Benjamins.

Skehan, P. (2003). Task-based instruction. *Language Teaching, 36,* 1–14.

Skinner, B. F. (1938). *Behavior of organisms: An experimental analysis.* New York: Appleton-Century-Crofts.

Skinner, B. F. (1953). *Science and human behavior.* New York: Macmillan.

Skinner, B. F. (1957). *Verbal behavior.* New York: Appleton-Century-Crofts.

Skinner, B. F. (1968). *The technology of teaching.* New York: Appleton-Century-Crofts.

Skutnabb-Kangas, T. (2000). *Linguistic genocide in education—or worldwide diversity and human rights?* Mahwah, NJ: Lawrence Erlbaum Associates.

Skutnabb-Kangas, T. (2009). What can TESOL do in order not to participate in crimes against humanity? *TESOL Quarterly, 43,* 340–344.

Skutnabb-Kangas, T., & Phillipson, R. (Eds.). (1994). *Linguistic human rights: Overcoming linguistic determination.* Berlin: Mouton de Gruyter.

Slavin, R. (2003). *Educational psychology: Theory and practice* (7th ed.). Boston: Allyn and Bacon.

Slavin, R. (2011). *Educational psychology: Theory and practice* (10th ed.). White Plains, NY: Pearson Education.

Slavoff, G., & Johnson, J. (1995). The effects of age on the rate of learning a second language. *Studies in Second Language Acquisition, 17,* 1–16.

Slobin, D. (1971). *Psycholinguistics.* Glenview, IL: Scott, Foresman.

Slobin, D. (Ed.). (1986). *The crosslinguistic study of language acquisition: Vols. 1–2.* Hillsdale, NJ: Lawrence Erlbaum Associates.

Slobin, D. (Ed.). (1992). *The crosslinguistic study of language acquisition: Vol. 3.* Hillsdale, NJ: Lawrence Erlbaum Associates.

Slobin, D. (Ed.). (1997). *The crosslinguistic study of language acquisition. Vol. 5: Expanding the contexts.* Mahwah, NJ: Lawrence Erlbaum Associates.

Smith, F. (1975). *Comprehension and learning: A conceptual framework for teachers.* New York: Holt, Rinehart & Winston.

Sokolik, M. (1990). Learning without rules: PDP and a resolution of the adult language learning paradox. *TESOL Quarterly, 24,* 685–696.

Sonaiya, R. (2002). Autonomous language learning in Africa: A mismatch of cultural assumptions. *Language, Culture and Curriculum, 15,* 106–116.

Sorenson, A. (1967). Multilingualism in the Northwest Amazon. *American Anthropologist, 69,* 670–684.

Spada, N. (1997). Form-focused instruction and second language acquisition: A review of classroom and laboratory research. *Language Teaching, 30,* 73–87.

Spada, N. (2007). Communicative language teaching: Current status and future prospects. In J. Cummins & C. Davison (Eds.), *International handbook of English language teaching* (pp. 271–288). Boston: Springer Science and Business Media.

Spada, N. (2011). Beyond form-focused instruction: Reflections on past, present and future research. *Language Teaching, 44,* 225–236.

Spada, N., & Lightbown, P. (2008). Form-focused instruction: Isolated or integrated? *TESOL Quarterly, 42,* 181–207.

Sparks, R., & Ganschow, L. (1991). Foreign language learning differences: Affective or native language aptitude differences? *Modern Language Journal, 75,* 3–16.

Sparks, R., & Ganschow, L. (1993a). The impact of native language learning problems on foreign language learning: Case study illustrations of the linguistic deficit coding hypothesis. *Modern Language Journal, 77,* 58–74.

Sparks, R., & Ganschow, L. (1993b). Searching for the cognitive locus of foreign language learning difficulties: Linking first and second language learning. *Modern Language Journal, 77,* 289–302.

Sparks, R., & Ganschow, L. (1995). A strong inference approach to causal factors in foreign language learning: A response to MacIntyre. *Modern Language Journal, 79,* 235–244.

Sparks, R., & Ganschow, L. (2001). Aptitude for learning a foreign language. *Annual Review of Applied Linguistics, 21,* 90–111.

Sparks, R., & Young, D. (Eds.). (2009). *Language learning and disabilities, anxiety and special needs:* Special issue of *Foreign Language Annals, 42.*

Sparks, R., Ganschow, L., & Javorsky, J. (2000). Déjà vu all over again: A response to Saito, Horwitz, and Garza. *Modern Language Journal, 84,* 251–255.

Sparks, R., Patton, J., Ganschow, L., Humbach, N., & Javorsky, J. (2008). Early first-language reading and spelling skills predict later second-language reading and spelling skills. *Journal of Educational Psychology, 100,* 162–174.

Sparrow, L. (2000). Comments on Dwight Atkinson's "TESOL and culture": Another reader reacts. *TESOL Quarterly, 34,* 747–752.

Speilmann, G., & Radnofsky, M. (2001). Learning language under tension: New directions from a qualitative study. *Modern Language Journal, 85,* 259–278.

Spielberger, C. (1983). *Manual for the state-trait anxiety inventory.* Palo Alto, CA: Consulting Psychologists Press.

Spivey, M. (2007). *The continuity of mind*. Oxford, UK: Oxford University Press.

Spolsky, B. (1969). Attitudinal aspects of second language learning. *Language Learning, 19,* 271–283.

Spolsky, B. (1989). Communicative competence, language proficiency, and beyond. *Applied Linguistics, 10,* 138–156.

Spratt, M., Humphreys, G., & Chan, V. (2002). Autonomy and motivation: Which comes first? *Language Teaching Research, 6,* 245–266.

Stansfield, C., & Hansen, J. (1983). Field dependence independence as a variable in second language cloze test performance. *TESOL Quarterly, 17,* 29–38.

Stenson, N. (1974). Induced errors. In J. Schumann & N. Stenson (Eds.), *New frontiers of second language learning*. Rowley, MA: Newbury House.

Stern, H. (1970). *Perspectives on second language teaching*. Toronto: Ontario Institute for Studies in Education.

Stern, H. (1975). What can we learn from the good language learner? *Canadian Modern Language Review, 34,* 304–318.

Sternberg, R. (1985). *Beyond IQ: A triarchic theory of human intelligence*. New York: Cambridge University Press.

Sternberg, R. (1988). *The triarchic mind: A new theory of human intelligence*. New York: Viking Press.

Sternberg, R. (1997). *Successful intelligence: How practical and creative intelligence determine success in life*. New York: Plume.

Sternberg, R. (2003). *Wisdom, intelligence, and creativity synthesized*. New York: Cambridge University Press.

Sternberg, R. (2007). *Wisdom, intelligence, and creativity synthesized*. New York: Cambridge University Press.

Sternberg, R., & Davidson, J. (1982). The mind of the puzzler. *Psychology Today, 16,* 37–44.

Stevick, E. (1976a). Teaching English as an alien language. In J. Fanselow & R. Crymes (Eds.), *On TESOL 76* (pp. 225–238). Washington, DC: Teachers of English to Speakers of Other Languages.

Stevick, E. (1976b). *Memory, meaning and method*. Rowley, MA: Newbury House.

Stevick, E. (1982). *Teaching and learning languages*. New York: Cambridge University Press.

Stevick, E. (1989). *Success with foreign languages: Seven who achieved it and what worked for them*. New York: Prentice Hall.

Stockwell, R., Bowen, J., & Martin, J. (1965). *The grammatical structures of English and Spanish*. Chicago: University of Chicago Press.

Stubbs, M. (1996). *Text and corpus analysis*. Oxford, UK: Basil Blackwell.

Sullivan, E. (1967). *Piaget and the school curriculum: A critical appraisal*. Toronto: Ontario Institute for Studies in Education.

Sunderland, J. (2000). Issues of language and gender in second and foreign language education. *Language Teaching, 33,* 203–223.

Svanes, B. (1987). Motivation and "cultural distance" in second language acquisition. *Language Learning, 37,* 341–359.

Svanes, B. (1988). Attitudes and "cultural distance" in second language acquisition. *Applied Linguistics, 9,* 357–371.

Swain, M. (1984). Large-scale communicative language testing. In S. Savignon & M. Berns (Eds.), *Initiatives in communicative language teaching: A book of readings.* Reading, MA: Addison-Wesley.

Swain, M. (1993). The output hypothesis: Just speaking and writing aren't enough. *Canadian Modern Language Review, 50,* 158–164.

Swain, M. (1995). Three functions of output in second language learning. In G. Cook & B. Seidlhofer (Eds.), *Principle and practice in applied linguistics: Studies in honour of H. G. Widdowson* (pp. 125–144). Oxford, UK: Oxford University Press.

Swain, M. (1998). Focus on form through conscious reflection. In C. Doughty & J. Williams (Eds.), *Focus on form in classroom second language acquisition* (pp. 64–81). New York: Cambridge University Press.

Swain, M. (2000). The output hypothesis and beyond: Mediating acquisition through collaborative dialogue. In J. Lantolf (Ed.), *Sociocultural theory and second language learning* (pp. 97–114). Oxford, UK: Oxford University Press.

Swain, M. (2005). The output hypothesis: Theory and research. In E. Hinkel (Ed.), *Handbook of research in second language teaching and learning* (pp. 471–483). Mahwah, NJ: Lawrence Erlbaum Associates.

Swain, M., & Lapkin, S. (1995). Problems in output and the cognitive process they generate: A step towards second language learning. *Applied Linguistics, 16,* 371–391.

Swain, M., & Lapkin, S. (1998). Interaction and second language learning: Two adolescent French immersion students working together. *Modern Language Journal, 82,* 320–337.

Taguchi, T. (2002). Learner factors affecting the use of learning strategies in cross-cultural contexts. *Prospect, 17,* 18–34.

Taleghani-Nikazm, C. (2002). A conversational analytic study of telephone conversation openings between native and nonnative speakers. *Journal of Pragmatics, 34,* 1807–1832.

Talmy, L. (2003). *Toward a cognitive semantics: Concept structuring systems.* Vol. 1. Cambridge, MA: Bradford Books, MIT Press.

Tannen, D. (1986). *That's not what I meant! How conversational style makes or breaks your relations with others.* New York: William Morrow.

Tannen, D. (1990). *You just don't understand: Women and men in conversation.* New York: William Morrow.

Tannen, D. (1996). *Gender and discourse.* New York: Oxford University Press.

Tarone, E. (1981). Some thoughts on the notion of "communication strategy." *TESOL Quarterly, 15,* 285–295.

Tarone, E. (1988). *Variation in interlanguage.* London: Edward Arnold.

Tarone, E. (1990). On variation in interlanguage: A response to Gregg. *Applied Linguistics, 11,* 392–400.

Tarone, E., & Parrish, B. (1988). Task related variation in interlanguage: The case of articles. *Language Learning, 38,* 21–44.

Taylor, B. (1975). The use of overgeneralization and transfer learning strategies by elementary and intermediate students in ESL. *Language Learning, 25,* 73–107.

Thomas, L. (1996). Language as power: A linguistic critique of U.S. English. *Modern Language Journal, 80,* 129–140.

Thomas, M. (1998). Programmatic ahistoricity in second language acquisition theory. *Studies in Second Language Acquisition, 20,* 387–405.

Thorndike, E. (1932). *The fundamentals of learning*. New York: Teachers College, Columbia University.

Tieger, P., & Barron-Tieger, B. (2007). *Do what you are: Discover the perfect career for you through the secrets of personality type*. New York: Little, Brown, and Company.

Ting-Toomey, S. (1999). *Communicating across cultures*. New York: Guilford Press.

Tollefson, J. (2011). Ideology in second language acquisition. In E. Hinkel (Ed.), *Handbook of research in second language teaching and learning: Volume II* (pp. 801–816). New York: Routledge.

Tollefson, J. (Ed.). (1995). *Power and inequality in language education*. Cambridge, UK: Cambridge University Press.

Tomiyama, M. (2000). Child second language attrition: A longitudinal case study. *Applied Linguistics, 21,* 304–332.

Torrance, E. (1980). *Your style of learning and thinking, Forms B and C*. Athens: University of Georgia Press.

Triandis, H. (1972). *The analysis of subjective culture*. New York: Wiley.

Tsui, A., & Tollefson, J. (Eds.). (2007). *Language policy, culture, and identity in Asian contexts*. Mahwah, NJ: Lawrence Erlbaum.

Turner, K. (1995). The principal principles of pragmatic inference: Cooperation. *Language Teaching, 28,* 67–76.

Turner, K. (1996). The principal principles of pragmatic inference: Politeness. *Language Teaching, 29,* 1–13.

Twaddell, F. (1935). *On defining the phoneme*. Language Monograph Number 166.

Twain, M. (1869). *The innocents abroad* (Vol. 1). New York: Harper & Brothers.

Twain, M. (1880). *A tramp abroad*. Hartford, CT: American Publishing Company.

Uber Grosse, C. (2004). The competitive advantage of foreign languages and cultural knowledge. *Modern Language Journal, 88,* 351–373.

Urgesi, C., & Fabbro, F. (2009). Neuropsychology of second language acquisition. In W. Ritchie & T. Bhatia (Eds.), *The new handbook of second language acquisition* (pp. 357–376). Bingley, UK: Emerald Group Publishing, Ltd.

Ushioda, E. (2009). A person-in-context relational view of emergent motivation, self, and self-identity. In Z. Dörnyei & E. Ushioda (Eds.), *Motivation, language identity and the L2 self* (pp. 215–228). Bristol, UK: Multilingual Matters.

Uysal, H. (2008). Tracing the culture behind writing: Rhetorical patterns and bidirectional transfer in L1 and L2 essays of Turkish writers in relation to educational context. *Journal of Second Language Writing, 17,* 183–207.

Vallerand, R. (1997). Towards a hierarchical model of intrinsic and extrinsic motivation. In M. Zanna (Ed.), *Advances in experimental social psychology. Vol. 29* (pp. 271–360). San Diego, CA: Academic Press.

Van Buren, P. (1996). Are there principles of Universal Grammar that do not apply to second language acquisition? In P. Jordens & J. Lalleman (Eds.), *Investigating second language acquisition*. Berlin: Mouton de Gruyter.

Van Ek, J., & Alexander, L. (1975). *Threshold level English*. Oxford: Pergamon Press.

Van Geert, P. (2007). Dynamic systems in second language learning: Some general methodological reflections. *Bilingualism: Language and Cognition, 10,* 47–49.

Van Lier, L. (1996). *Interaction in the language curriculum: Awareness, autonomy and authenticity*. London: Longman.

Van Lier, L. (2011). Language learning: An ecological-semiotic approach. In E. Hinkel (Ed.), *Handbook of research in second language teaching and learning: Volume II* (pp. 383–394). New York: Routledge.

Van Zante, J., & Persiani, R. (2008). Using corpus linguistics findings in the classroom: A rationale with practical applications. *CATESOL Journal, 20,* 95–109.

Vandergrift, L. (2003). Orchestrating strategy use: Toward a model of the skilled L2 listener. *Language Learning, 53,* 461–494.

Vann, R., & Abraham, R. (1990). Strategies of unsuccessful language learners. *TESOL Quarterly, 24,* 177–198.

VanPatten, B., & Williams, J. (Eds.) (2007). *Theories in second language acquisition.* Mahwah, NJ: Lawrence Erlbaum.

Verspoor, M., & Tyler, A. (2009). Cognitive Linguistics and second language learning. In W. Ritchie & T. Bhatia (Eds.), *The new handbook of second language acquisition* (pp. 160–177). Bingley, UK: Emerald Group Publishing, Ltd.

Vigil, N., & Oller, J. (1976). Rule fossilization: A tentative model. *Language Learning, 26,* 281–295.

Vygotsky, L. (1962). *Thought and language.* Cambridge, MA: Massachusetts Institute of Technology Press.

Vygotsky, L. (1978). *Mind in society: The development of higher psychological processes.* Cambridge, MA: Harvard University Press.

Vygotsky, L. (1987). *The collected works of L.S. Vygotsky: Volume 1. Thinking and speaking.* New York: Plenum Press.

Wagner-Gough, J. (1975). Comparative studies in second language learning. *CAL-ERIC/CLL Series on Languages and Linguistics, 26.*

Wakamoto, N. (2000). Language learning strategy and personality variables: Focusing on extroversion and introversion. *International Review of Applied Linguistics, 38,* 71–81.

Wakamoto, N. (2009). *Extroversion/introversion in foreign language learning.* New York: Peter Lang.

Walker, B. (2012). *English vocabulary for academic success.* Eugene, OR: Bill Walker.

Walsh, T., & Diller, K. (1981). Neurolinguistic considerations on the optimum age for second language learning. In K. Diller (Ed.), *Individual differences and universals in language learning aptitude.* Rowley, MA: Newbury House.

Warden, C., & Lin, H. (2000). Existence of integrative motivation in an Asian EFL setting. *Foreign Language Annals, 33,* 535–547.

Wardhaugh, R. (1970). The contrastive analysis hypothesis. *TESOL Quarterly, 4,* 123–130.

Wardhaugh, R. (1971). Theories of language acquisition in relation to beginning reading instruction. *Language Learning, 21,* 1–26.

Wardhaugh, R. (1976). *The contexts of language.* Rowley, MA: Newbury House.

Wardhaugh, R. (1992). *An introduction to sociolinguistics* (2nd ed.). Cambridge, MA: Blackwell.

Watson-Gegeo, K. (2004). Mind language, and epistemology: Toward a language socialization paradigm for SLA. *Modern Language Journal, 88,* 331–350.

Watson-Gegeo, K., & Nielsen, S. (2003). Language socialization in SLA. In C. Doughty & M. Long (Eds.), *The handbook of second language acquisition* (pp. 155–177). Malden, MA: Blackwell Publishing.

Watson, J. (1913). Psychology as the behaviorist views it. *Psychological Review, 20,* 158–177.

Weiner, B. (1986). *An attributional theory of motivation and emotion.* New York: Springer.

Weiner, B. (1992). *Human motivation: Metaphors, theories and research.* Newbury Park, CA: Sage.

Weiner, B. (2000). Intrapersonal and interpersonal theories of motivation from an attributional perspective. *Educational Psychology Review, 12,* 1–14.

Weinreich, U. (1953). *Languages in contact: Findings and problems.* New York: Linguistic Circle of New York.

Weir, R. (1962). *Language in the crib.* The Hague: Mouton.

Weltens, B. (1987). The attrition of foreign language skills: A literature review. *Applied Linguistics, 8,* 22–38.

Weltens, B., & Cohen, A. (1989). Language attrition research: An introduction. *Studies in Second Language Acquisition, 11,* 127–133.

Wen, W., & Clément, R. (2003). A Chinese conceptualisation of willingness to communicate in ESL. *Language, Culture and Curriculum, 16,* 18–38.

Wenden, A. (1985). Learner strategies. *TESOL Newsletter, 19,* 1–7.

Wenden, A. (1992). *Learner strategies for learner autonomy.* Englewood Cliffs, NJ: Prentice Hall Regents.

Wenden, A. (2002). Learner development in language learning. *Applied Linguistics, 23,* 32–55.

Wenger, E. (1998). *Communities of practice: Learning, meaning, and identity.* Cambridge, UK: Cambridge University Press.

Wharton, G. (2000). Language learning strategy use of bilingual foreign language learners in Singapore. *Language Learning, 50,* 203–243.

White, C., Schramm, K., & Chamot, A. (2007). In A. Cohen & E. Macaro (Eds.), *Language learner strategies: Thirty years of research and practice* (pp. 93–116). Oxford, UK: Oxford University Press.

White, L. (1987). Against comprehensible input: The input hypothesis and the development of second language competence. *Applied Linguistics, 8,* 95–110.

White, L. (1989). *Universal grammar and second language acquisition.* Amsterdam: John Benjamins.

White, L. (1990). Second language acquisition and universal grammar. *Studies in Second Language Acquisition, 12,* 121–133.

White, L. (2003). *Second language acquisition and universal grammar.* Cambridge, UK: Cambridge University Press.

White, L. (2009). Grammatical theory: Interfaces and L2 knowledge. In W. Ritchie & T. Bhatia (Eds.), *The new handbook of second language acquisition* (pp. 49–68). Bingley, UK: Emerald Group Publishing, Ltd.

White, L. (2012). Universal grammar, crosslinguistic variation and second language acquisition. *Language Teaching, 45,* 309–328.

Whitlow, J. (2001). Comments on Shinichi Izumi and Martha Bigelow's "Does output promote noticing in second language acquisition?": Some methodological and theoretical considerations. *TESOL Quarterly, 35,* 177–181.

Whitman, R., & Jackson, K. (1972). The unpredictability of contrastive analysis. *Language Learning, 22,* 29–41.

Whorf, B. (1956). Science and linguistics. In J. Carroll (Ed.), *Language, thought, and reality: Selected writings of Benjamin Lee Whorf.* Cambridge, MA: Massachusetts Institute of Technology Press.

Wichmann, A. (2000). *Intonation in text and discourse: Beginnings, middles and endings.* Harlow, UK: Longman.

Widdowson, H. (1978a). *Notional-functional syllabuses 1978: Part IV.* In C. Blatchford & J. Schachter (Eds.), *On TESOL '78: EFL Policies, Programs, Practices* (pp. 33–35). Washington, DC: Teachers of English to Speakers of Other Languages.

Widdowson, H. (1978b). *Teaching language as communication.* Oxford: Oxford University Press.

Widdowson, H. (1991). The description and prescription of language. In J. Alatis (Ed.), *Linguistics and language pedagogy: The state of the art* (Georgetown University Round Table on Languages and Linguistics 1991). Washington, DC: Georgetown University Press.

Wilkins, D. (1976). *Notional syllabuses.* London: Oxford University Press.

Williams, J. (2005). Form-focused instruction. In E. Hinkel (Ed.), *Handbook of research in second language teaching and learning* (pp. 671–691). Mahwah, NJ: Lawrence Erlbaum Associates.

Williams, J. N. (2005). Learning without awareness. *Studies in Second Language Acquisition, 27,* 269–304.

Williams, J. N. (2009). Implicit learning in second language acquisition. In W. Ritchie & T. Bhatia (Eds.), *The new handbook of second language acquisition* (pp. 319–353). Bingley, UK: Emerald Group Publishing, Ltd.

Williams, M., & Burden, R. (1997). *Psychology for language teachers: A social constructivist approach.* Cambridge, UK: Cambridge University Press.

Willis, J. (1996). *A framework for task-based learning.* Essex, UK: Longman.

Wintergerst, A., & McVeigh, J. (2011). *Tips for teaching culture: Practical approaches to intercultural communication.* White Plains, NY: Pearson Education.

Wintergerst, A., DeCapua, A., & Itzen, R. (2001). The construct validity of one learning styles instrument. *System, 29,* 395–403.

Wintergerst, A., DeCapua, A., & Verna, M. (2002). An analysis of one learning styles instrument for language students. *TESL Canada Journal, 20,* 16–37.

Witkin, H. (1962). *Psychological differentiation.* New York: Wiley.

Witkin, H., & Goodenough, D. (1981). *Cognitive styles: Essence and origins.* New York: International Universities Press.

Witkin, H., Oltman, P., Raskin, E., & Karp, S. (1971). *Embedded figures test. Manual for the embedded figures test.* Palo Alto, CA: Consulting Psychologists Press.

Wodak, R. (2012). Language, power, and identity. *Language Teaching, 45,* 215–233.

Wolfson, N. (1981). Compliments in cross-cultural perspective. *TESOL Quarterly, 15,* 117–124.

Wolfson, N., D'Amico-Reisner, L., & Huber, L. (1983). How to arrange for social commitments in American English: The invitation. In N. Wolfson & E. Judd (Eds.), *Sociolinguistics and language acquisition.* Rowley, MA: Newbury House.

Wong, J., & Waring, H. (2011). *Conversation analysis and second language pedagogy: A guide for ESL/EFL teachers.* New York: Routledge.

Wong, R. (1986). Instructional considerations in teaching pronunciation. In J. Morley (Ed.), *Current perspectives on pronunciation: Practices anchored in theory.* Washington, DC: Teachers of English to Speakers of Other Languages.

Wood, D. (2001). In search of fluency: What is it and how can we teach it? *Canadian Modern Language Review, 57,* 573–589.

Wright, D. (2000). Culture as information and culture as affective process: A comparative study. *Foreign Language Annals, 33,* 330–341.

Wu, W. (2003). Intrinsic motivation and young language learners: The impact of the classroom environment. *System, 31,* 501–517.

Wunder, E-M. (2011). Crosslinguistic influence in multilingual language acquisition: Phonology in third or additional language acquisition. In G. De Angelis & J.-M. Dewaele (Eds.), *New trends in crosslinguistic influence and multilingualism research* (pp. 105–128). Bristol, UK: Multilingual Matters.

Yashima, T., Zenuk-Nishide, L., & Shimizu, K. (2004). The influence of attitudes and affect on willingness to communicate and second language communication. *Language Learning, 54,* 119–152.

Yorio, C. (1976). Discussion of "Explaining sequence and variation in second language acquisition." *Language Learning,* Special Issue Number 4, 59–63.

Young, D. (1992). Language anxiety from the foreign language specialist's perspective: Interviews with Krashen, Omaggio-Hadley, Terrell, and Rardin. *Foreign Language Annals, 25,* 157–172.

Young, R. (1988). Variation and the interlanguage hypothesis. *Studies in Second Language Acquisition, 10,* 281–302.

Young, R. (2008). *Language and interaction: An advanced resource book.* New York: Routledge.

Young, R. (2011). Interactional competence in language, teaching, and testing. In E. Hinkel (Ed.), *Handbook of research in second language teaching and learning: Volume II* (pp. 426–443). New York: Routledge.

Yu, M.-C. (2004). Interlinguistic variation and similarity in second language speech act behavior. *Modern Language Journal, 88,* 102–119.

Yule, G., & Tarone, E. (1990). Eliciting the performance of strategic competence. In R. Scarcella, E. Andersen, & S. Krashen (Eds.), *Developing communicative competence in a second language.* New York: Newbury House.

Zangwill, O. (1971). The neurology of language. In N. Minnis (1971), *Linguistics at large.* New York: Viking Press.

Zimmerman, B. (1990). Self-regulated learning and academic achievement: An overview. *Educational Psychologist, 25,* 3–17.

Zimmerman, B. (2000). Attaining self-regulation: A social cognitive perspective. In M. Boekaerts, P. Pintrich, & M. Zeidner (Eds.), *Handbook of self-regulation* (pp. 13–39). San Diego: Academic Press.

Zobl, H., & Liceras, J. (1994). Functional categories and acquisition orders. *Language Learning, 44,* 159–180.

Zuengler, J., & Cole, K.-M. (2005). Language socialization and second language learning. In E. Hinkel (Ed.), *Handbook of research in second language teaching and learning* (pp. 301–316). Mahwah, NJ: Lawrence Erlbaum Associates.

GLOSSARY

acculturation   the process of adjusting and adapting to a new culture, usually when one is living in the new culture, and often with the resultant creation of a new cultural identity

affect   emotion or feeling

affective domain   emotional issues and factors in human behavior, often compared to the cognitive domain

affective strategy   one of three categories of metastrategy, strategies and tactics that help the learner to employ beneficial emotional energy, form positive attitudes toward learning, and generate motivation

ambiguity intolerance   a style in which an individual is relatively ill-equipped to withstand or manage a high degree of uncertainty in a linguistic context, and as a result may demand more certainty and structure

ambiguity tolerance   a style in which an individual is relatively well suited to withstand or manage a high degree of uncertainty in a linguistic context

amotivation   the absence of any motivation entirely

analyzed knowledge   the general form in which we know most things with awareness of the structure of that knowledge (see **explicit knowledge**)

anomie   feelings of social uncertainty, dissatisfaction, or "homelessness" as individuals lose some of the bonds of a native culture but are not yet fully acculturated in the new culture

anxiety   the subjective feeling of tension, apprehension, and nervousness connected to an arousal of the autonomic nervous system, and associated with feelings of uneasiness, frustration, self-doubt, apprehension, or worry

appeal to authority   a direct appeal for help from a more proficient user of the language

approach   a unified but broadly based theoretical position about the nature of language and of language learning and teaching that forms the basis of methodology in the language classroom

approximative system   learner language that emphasizes the successive approximation of the learner's output to the target language

366

artifacts in nonverbal communication, factors external to a person, such as clothing and ornamentation, and their effect on communication

attention the psychological process of focusing on certain stimuli to the exclusion of others

attention getting securing the attention of one's audience in a conversation

attitude a set of personal feelings, opinions, or biases about races, cultures, ethnic groups, classes of people, and languages

attribution theory how people explain the causes of their own successes and failures

attrition the loss or forgetting of language skills

Audiolingual Method (ALM) a language teaching method, popular in the 1950s, that placed an extremely strong emphasis on oral production, pattern drills, and conditioning through repetition

auditory learning style the tendency to prefer listening to lectures and audiotapes, as opposed to visual and/or kinesthetic processing

authentic (referring to pronunciation) oral production judged by a speech community to be correct, native or nativelike, and appropriate within that speech community

authenticity a principle emphasizing real-world, meaningful language used for genuine communicative purposes

automatic processes relatively permanent cognitive efforts, as opposed to controlled processes

automaticity the act of processing input and giving output without deliberation or hesitation in real-time speed

autonomy individual effort and action through which learners initiate language, problem solving, strategic action, and the generation of linguistic input

avoidance (of a topic) in a conversation, steering others away from an unwanted topic; (of a language form) a strategy that leads to refraining from producing a form that speaker may not know, often through an alternative form; as a strategy, options intended to prevent the production of ill-formed utterances, classified into such categories as syntactic, lexical, phonological, and topic avoidance

awareness cognizance of linguistic, mental, or emotional factors through attention and focus; conscious attention

awareness-raising usually, in foreign language classes, calling a learner's attention to linguistic factors that may not otherwise be noticed

backsliding (in learner language) a phenomenon in which the learner seems to have grasped a rule or principle and then regresses to a previous stage

basic interpersonal communicative skills (BICS) the communicative capacity that all humans acquire in order to be able to function in daily interpersonal exchanges; context-embedded performance

behavioral science a paradigm that studies the behavior of organisms (including humans) by focusing centrally on publicly observable responses that can be objectively and scientifically perceived, recorded, and measured

behaviorism the study of human behavior using strictly scientific, empirical evidence, often linked with conditioning, stimulus-response, and reinforcement paradigms

bilingualism relatively equal simultaneous proficiency in two languages. **Compound** bilingualism refers to the use of two languages in one context, with one meaning set, while **coordinate** bilingualism refers to using two languages in two separate contexts (e.g., home and school), and a presumed separate storage of meanings.

capability continuum paradigm see **variable competence model**

chaining acquiring a chain of two or more stimulus-response connections

chaos-complexity theory an approach to describing a phenomenon that emphasizes its dynamic, complex, nonlinear, and unpredictable nature

clarification request an elicitation of a reformulation or repetition from a student

classical conditioning psychological learning paradigm associated with Pavlov, Thorndike, Watson, and others which highlights the formation of associations between stimuli and responses that are strengthened through rewards

Classical Method a language teaching method in which the focus is on grammatical rules, memorization of vocabulary and other language forms, translation of texts, and performing written exercises

code-switching in bilinguals, the act of inserting words, phrases, or even longer stretches of one language into the other

cognitive constructivism a branch of constructivism that emphasizes the importance of individual learners constructing their own representation of reality

cognitive linguistics a theoretical position that asserts that language is not an autonomous faculty, but rather is interwoven into conceptualization, knowledge, and language use

cognitive pruning the elimination of unnecessary clutter and a clearing of the way for more material to enter the cognitive field

cognitive psychology a school of thought in which meaning, understanding, and knowing are significant data for psychological study, and in which one seeks psychological principles of organization and mental and emotional functioning, as opposed to behavioral psychology, which focuses on overt, observable, empirically measurable behavior

cognitive strategies strategic options relating to specific learning tasks that involve direct manipulation of the learning material itself

cognitive strategy one of three categories of metastrategy, strategies, and tactics that help the learner to construct, transform, and apply L2 knowledge

cognitive style the way a person learns material or solves problems

cognitive/academic language proficiency (CALP) the dimension of proficiency in which a learner manipulates or reflects on the surface features of language in academic contexts, such as test-taking, writing, analyzing, and reading academic texts; context-reduced performance

collectivism a cultural worldview that assumes the primacy of community, social groups, or organizations and places greater value on harmony within such groups than on one's individual desires, needs, or aspirations

communication strategies   strategic options relating to output, how one productively expresses meaning, and how one effectively delivers messages to others (see **learning strategies**)

communicative competence (CC)   the cluster of abilities that enable humans to convey and interpret messages and to negotiate meanings interpersonally within specific contexts

Communicative Language Teaching (CLT)   an approach to language teaching methodology that emphasizes authenticity, interaction, student-centered learning, task-based activities, and communication for real-world, meaningful purposes

communities of practice (CoP)   a group of people who share a common interest in a particular domain, characterized by mutual engagement, joint enterprise, and shared repertoire

Community Language Learning (CLL)   language teaching method that emphasizes interpersonal relationships, inductive learning, and views the teacher as a "counselor"

compensatory strategies   strategic options designed to overcome self-perceived weaknesses, such as using prefabricated patterns, code-switching, and appeal to authority

competence   one's underlying knowledge of a system, event, or fact; the unobservable ability to perform language, but not to be confused with performance

Competition Model   the claim that when strictly formal (e.g., phonological, syntactic) options for interpreting meaning through appeal to the first language have been exhausted, second language learners naturally look for alternative "competing" possibilities to create meaning

compound bilingualism   see **bilingualism**

comprehension   the process of receiving language; listening or reading; input

conditioned response   in behavioral learning theory, a response to a stimulus that is learned or elicited by an outside agent

connectionism   the belief that neurons in the brain are said to form multiple connections

conscious learning   see **awareness** and **focal attention**

constructivism   the integration of various paradigms with an emphasis on social interaction and the discovery, or construction, of meaning

context-embedded language   language forms and functions that are embedded in a set of schemata within which the learner can operate, as in meaningful conversations, real-life tasks, and extensive reading (see **basic interpersonal communicative skills**)

context-reduced language   language forms and functions that lack a set of embedded schemata within which the learner can operate, as in traditional test items, isolated reading excerpts, and repetition drills (see **cognitive academic language proficiency**)

Contrastive Analysis Hypothesis (CAH)   the claim that the principal barrier to second language acquisition is first language interference, and that a scientific analysis of the two languages in question enables the prediction of difficulties a learner will encounter

contrastive rhetoric   naturally occurring discourses, usually written, across different languages and cultures

controlled processes capacity limited and temporary cognitive efforts, as opposed to automatic processes

coordinate bilingualism see **bilingualism**

corpus linguistics an approach to linguistic research that relies on computer analyses of a collection, or corpus, of texts—written, transcribed speech, or both—stored in electronic form and analyzed with the help of computer software programs

corrective feedback responses to a learner's output that attempt to repair or call attention to an error or mistake

covert error an error that is grammatically well formed at the sentence level but not interpretable within the context of communication; a discourse error

creative construction the hypothesis, in child second language acquisition, that claims the rarity of L1 interference, the emergence of common acquisition orders, perception of systematic features of language, and the production of novel utterances

critical period a biologically determined period of life when language can be acquired more easily and beyond which time language is increasingly difficult to acquire

Critical Period Hypothesis the claim that there is a biological timetable before which and after which language acquisition, both first and second, is more successfully accomplished

cross-linguistic influence (CLI) a concept that replaced the contrastive analysis hypothesis, recognizing the significance of the role of the first language in learning a second, but with an emphasis on the facilitating and interfering effects both languages have on each other

culture the ideas, customs, skills, arts, and tools that characterize a given group of people in a given period of time

culture shock in the process of acculturation, phenomena involving mild irritability, depression, anger, or possibly deep psychological crisis due to the foreignness of the new cultural milieu

debilitative anxiety feelings of worry that are perceived as detrimental to one's self-efficacy or that hinder one's performance

declarative knowledge consciously known and verbalizable facts, knowledge, and information (in linguistics, about language)

deductive reasoning moving from a generalization to specific instances in which subsumed facts are inferred from a general principle

demotivation losing interest and drive that once was present

descriptive adequacy satisfying scientific or empirical principles for describing a phenomenon such as language

descriptive school of linguistics see **structural school of linguistics**

Direct Method a language teaching method popular in the early twentieth century that emphasized direct target language use, oral communication skills, and inductive grammar, without recourse to translation from the first language

discourse a language (either spoken or written) beyond the sentence level; relationships and rules that govern the connection and interrelationship of sentences within communicative contexts

discourse analysis the examination of the relationship between forms and functions of language beyond the sentence level

discourse competence the ability to connect sentences in stretches of discourse and to form a meaningful whole out of a series of utterances

dynamic systems theory (DST) an amalgamation of claims, based on chaos theory and complexity theory, that language acquisition is a dynamic process involving nonlinear individual variations

egocentricity characteristic of very young children in which the world revolves around them, and they see all events as focusing on themselves

elicitation a corrective technique that prompts the learner to self-correct

elicited response behavior resulting from a preceding outside stimulus

emergent stage (of learner language) one in which the learner grows in consistency in linguistic production

emergentism a perspective that questions nativism and holds that the complexity of language, like any other human ability, emerges from relatively simple developmental processes being exposed to a massive and complex environment

emitted response behavior freely offered without the presence of an outside stimulus

emotional intelligence associated with Goleman, a mode of intelligence that places emotion, and/or the management of emotions, at the seat of intellectual functioning

empathy "putting yourself into someone else's shoes," reaching beyond the self to understand what another person is thinking or feeling

English as a foreign language (EFL) generic term for English learned as a foreign language in a country or context in which English is not commonly used as a language of education, business, or government, e.g., expanding circle countries

English as a second language (ESL) generic term for English learned as a foreign language within the culture of an English-speaking (inner circle) country

English as an international language (EIL) English as a *lingua franca* worldwide

English only a political movement in the United States arguing for a language policy that compels institutions to use English in ballots, driver's regulations, education, etc., to the exclusion of other languages

EQ see **emotional intelligence**

equilibration progressive interior organization of knowledge in a stepwise fashion; moving from states of doubt and uncertainty (disequilibrium) to stages of resolution and certainty (equilibrium)

error an idiosyncrasy in the language of the learner that is a direct manifestation of a system within which a learner is operating at the time

error analysis the study of learners' ill-formed production (spoken or written) in an effort to discover systematicity

explanatory adequacy satisfying a principled basis, independent of any particular language, for the selection of a descriptively appropriate grammar of a language

explanatory power a theoretical claim that is completely adequate to account for a multiplicity of cause-and-effect elements within it, that is, to explain *why* a phenomenon (such as language) behaves in specified ways

explicit correction   an indication to a student that a form is incorrect and providing a corrected form

explicit knowledge   information that a person knows *about* language, and usually, the ability to articulate that information

explicit learning   acquisition of linguistic competence with conscious awareness of, or focal attention on, the forms of language, usually in the context of instruction

extent   (in error analysis) the rank of linguistic unit that would have to be deleted, replaced, supplied, or reordered in order to repair the sentence

extrinsic motivation   choices made and effort expended on activities in anticipation of a reward from outside and beyond the self

extroversion   the extent to which a person has a deep-seated need to receive ego enhancement, self-esteem, and a sense of wholeness from other people, as opposed to receiving that affirmation within oneself, as opposed to introversion

eye contact   nonverbal feature involving what one looks at and how one looks at another person in face-to-face communication

facilitative anxiety   "helpful" anxiety, euphoric tension, or the beneficial effects of apprehension over a task to be accomplished

field dependence   the tendency to be "dependent" on the total field so that the parts embedded in the field are not easily perceived, although that total field is perceived more clearly as a unified whole

field independence   ability to perceive a particular, relevant item or factor in a "field" of distracting items

field sensitivity   the same as field dependence, with an emphasis on the positive aspects of the style (see **field dependence**)

Flow theory   school of thought that highlights the importance of an experiential state characterized by intense focus and involvement that leads to improved performance on a task

fluency   the unfettered flow of language production or comprehension usually without focal attention on language forms

focal attention   giving central attention to a stimulus, as opposed to peripheral attention

form-focused instruction (FFI)   any pedagogical effort used to draw a learner's attention to language form either implicitly or explicitly

forms   (of language) the "bits and pieces" of language, such as morphemes, words, grammar rules, discourse rules, and other organizational elements of language

fossilization   the relatively permanent incorporation of incorrect linguistic forms into a person's second language competence; also referred to as **stabilization**

framing   conceptualizing the universe around us with linguistic symbols that shape the way people think—through words, phrases, and other verbal associations

frequency   (of input) number of occurrences of a form, in either input or output, in a given amount of time

functional syllabus   see **notional-functional syllabus**

function   (of language) a meaningful, interactive purpose within a social (pragmatic) context, which we accomplish with forms of language

generative-transformational linguistics description of language or language acquisition, originally associated with Noam Chomsky, that views language as a system of principled rules, independent of any particular language, that governs its use; human language forms are thus "generated" by these rules and "transformed" through conventional constraints

global error an error that hinders communication or prevents a hearer (or reader) from comprehending some aspect of a message

global self-esteem see **self-esteem**

grammar consciousness raising the incorporation of forms into communicative tasks

Grammar Translation Method a language teaching method in which the central focus is on grammatical rules, paradigms, and vocabulary memorization as the basis for translating from one language to another

grammars descriptions of linguistic systems; rules that account for linguistic performance

grammatical competence an aspect of communicative competence that encompasses knowledge of lexical items and of rules of morphology, syntax, sentence-level grammar, semantics, and phonology

haptics see **kinesthetics**

hemisphere the left or right "half" of the brain, each performing different categories of neurological functions

heritage language a language of one's parents, grandparents, or family lineage, usually acquired (or learned through instruction) by individuals raised in homes where the dominant language of the region, such as English in the United States, is not spoken or not exclusively spoken in that home

hermeneutic tradition a constructivist research approach that specifies a means for interpreting and understanding the universe without necessarily searching for absolute laws, as opposed to a **nomothetic tradition**

heterogeneous competence multiple abilities, often unsystematic, that are in the process of being formed

hierarchy of difficulty a scale by which a teacher or linguist could make a prediction of the relative difficulty of a given aspect of a target language

High Input Generators (HIGs) people who are adept at initiating and sustaining interaction, or "generating" input from teachers, peers, and other speakers of the language in the arena, as opposed to **Low Input Generators**

ideology the body of assertions, beliefs, and aims that constitute a sociopolitical system within a group, culture, or country

idiosyncratic dialect learner language that emphasizes the notion that a learner's language and the rules that govern it are unique to a particular individual

illocutionary competence the ability to send and receive intended meanings

illocutionary force the intended meaning of the utterance or text within its context

implicit knowledge information that is automatically and spontaneously used in language tasks

implicit learning   acquisition of linguistic competence without intention to learn and without focal awareness of what has been learned, as opposed to **explicit learning**

impulsive style   the tendency to make quick decisions in answer to problems; sometimes, but not always, those decisions involve risk-taking or guessing

incidental learning   learning without central attention to form (see **implicit learning**)

individualism   a cultural worldview that assumes the primacy of attending to one's own interests and/or the interests of one's immediate family, and places value on the uniqueness of the individual

induced errors   errors caused by something in the learner's environment, such as the teacher, a textbook, or the classroom methodology

inductive reasoning   recalling a number of specific instances in order to induce a general law or rule or conclusion that governs or subsumes the specific instances

inhibition   apprehension over one's self-identity or fear of showing self-doubt, leading to building mechanisms of protective self-defense

inner circle   countries traditionally considered to be dominated by native speakers of English, e.g., United States, United Kingdom, Australia, New Zealand

input   the process of comprehending language (listening and reading)

instrumental orientation   acquiring a language as a means for attaining instrumental goals, such as acquiring a degree or certificate in an academic institution, furthering a career, reading technical material, translation, etc.

intake   what is actually remembered, subsumed, and internalized from various inputs to the learner, especially teacher input

integrative orientation   learning a language in order to integrate oneself into the culture of a second language group and become involved in social interchange in that group

intentional learning   see **explicit learning**

interaction hypothesis   the claim, by Long, that language competence is the result not only of input, but also of interaction between a learner's input and output

interactional competence   the ability to interact communicatively with a focus on such interactional factors as participant identity, construction of interpersonal meanings, turn-taking, and sociopragmatics

interference   negative transfer in which a previous item is incorrectly transferred or incorrectly associated with an item to be learned

interlanguage   learner language that emphasizes the separateness of a second language learner's system, a system that has a structurally intermediate status between the native and target languages

interlingual   the effect of language forms on each other across two or more languages

interlingual transfer   the effect of one language (usually the first) on another (usually the second)

intralingual transfer   the effect of forms of one language (usually the target language) on other forms within the same language

intrinsic motivation   choices made and effort expended on activities for which there is no apparent reward except the activity itself

introversion   the extent to which a person derives a sense of wholeness and fulfillment from "within," apart from a reflection of this self from other people, as opposed to **extroversion**

kinesics   body language, gesture, eye contact, and other physical features of nonverbal communication

kinesthetic learning style   the tendency to prefer demonstrations and physical activity involving bodily movement

kinesthetics   in nonverbal communication, conventions for how to touch others and where to touch them

language   a systematic means of communicating ideas or feelings by the use of conventionalized signs, sounds, gestures, or marks having understood meanings

language acquisition device (LAD)   an innate, metaphorical "mechanism" in young children's brains that predisposes them to acquire language

language anxiety   a feeling of worry experienced in relation to a foreign language, either trait or state in nature (see **anxiety**)

language aptitude   inherent ability, either learned or innate, and separate from knowledge of a particular language, to acquire foreign languages

language ego   the identity a person develops in reference to the language he or she speaks

language policy   the stated position of a government on the official or legal status of a language (or languages) in a country, often including the role of a language in educational, commercial, and political institutions

lateralization   the assigning of specified neurological functions to the left hemisphere of the brain, and certain other functions to the right hemisphere

Law of Effect   Thorndike's theory hypothesizing that stimuli that occur after a behavior have an influence on future behaviors

learner language   generic term used to describe a learner's interlanguage or interlanguage system

learning   acquiring knowledge of a subject or a skill by study, experience, or instruction

learning strategies   strategic options relating to input, processing, storage, and retrieval, or taking in messages from others, as opposed to **communication strategies**

learning style   cognitive, affective, and physiological traits that are relatively stable indicators of how learners perceive, interact with, and respond to the learning environment

left-brain dominance   a style that favors logical, analytical thought, with mathematical and linear processing of information

Linguistic Coding Deficit Hypothesis (LCDH)   the claim that anxiety in a foreign language class could be the result of first language deficits, namely, difficulties that students may have with language "codes" (phonological, syntactic, lexical, semantic features)

linguistic determinism   the claim that one's language determines and shapes the way one thinks, perceives, and feels within the culture of the speech community

linguistic relativity not as strong a claim as linguistic determinism; rather, the acknowledgement of the effect that language has on one's cultural worldview and thought pattern, but also the interaction of language and culture

local error an error that does not prevent a message from being understood, usually due to a minor violation of one segment of a sentence, allowing the hearer/reader to make an accurate guess about the intended meaning

Low Input Generators (LIGs) relatively passive learners who do little to create opportunities for input to be directed toward them, as opposed to **High Input Generators**

Markedness Differential Hypothesis an accounting of relative degrees of difficulty of learning a language by means of principles of universal grammar, also known as markedness theory

meaningful learning anchoring and relating new items and experiences to knowledge that exists in the cognitive framework (see **subsumption**)

mentalism an approach to scientific description that allows for the possibility of the veracity of unobservable guesses, hunches, and intuition

metacognitive [strategies] strategic options that relate to one's "executive" functions; strategies that involve planning for learning, thinking about the learning process as it is taking place, monitoring of one's production or comprehension, and evaluating learning after an activity is completed

metalinguistic explanation in the classroom, linguistic explanations of rules or patterns in a language

metalinguistic feedback responses to a learner's output that provide comments, information, or questions related to the linguistics form(s) of the learner's utterance

method a coherent, prescribed group of activities and techniques for language teaching, unified by a homogeneous set of principles or foundations; sometimes proclaimed to be suitable for all foreign language teaching contexts

mistake a performance error that is a random guess or a failure to utilize a known system correctly

modified interaction the various modifications that native speakers and other interlocutors create in order to render their input comprehensible to learners, similar to Krashen's comprehensible input

monitor hypothesis in Krashen's theory, the assumption of the existence of a device for "watchdogging" one's output, for editing and making alterations or corrections

motivation the anticipation of reward, whether internally or externally administered; choices made about goals to pursue and the effort exerted in their completion

motivational intensity the strength of one's motivational drives and needs

multiple discrimination learning to make a number of different identifying responses to many different stimuli

multiple intelligences associated with Gardner, the hypothesis that intelligence is not unitary, but has multiple modes

native English-speaking teacher (NEST) a teacher teaching his or her native language as a foreign language

native speaker one who uses the language as a first language

nativist a school of thought that rests on the assertion that language acquisition is innately (genetically) determined, and that human beings are therefore predisposed to a systematic perception of language

nativization indigenization of a language; what was once a second language in a culture evolves into a language accepted as "native" or standard

Natural Approach a language teaching method that simulates child language acquisition by emphasizing communication, comprehensible input, kinesthetic activities, and virtually no grammatical analysis

necessity a criterion for legitimizing the conditions of a theory in which a component part *must* be included, and if not, the theory is rendered inadequate, as opposed to **sufficiency**

neobehaviorism behavioral psychological school of thought associated with Skinner and others that asserted the importance of emitted behavior and operant conditioning

nomothetic tradition a research approach that relies on empiricism, scientific methodology, and prediction, as opposed to a **hermeneutic tradition**

nonnative speaker one who uses the language as a second or foreign language

noticing the learner's paying attention to specific linguistic features in input

notional-functional syllabus a language course that attends primarily to functions as organizing elements of a foreign language curriculum

oculesics nonverbal communication involving eye contact and eye "gestures" to signal meaning

olfactory pertaining to one's sense of smell; in nonverbal communication the effect of natural and artificial odors on communication

operant a response (e.g., an utterance of some kind) emitted without prior elicitation or stimulation

operant conditioning conditioning in which an organism (in the case of language acquisition, a human being) emits a response (an utterance, for example), or operant, without necessarily observable stimuli; that operant is maintained (learned) by reinforcement

optimal distance model the hypothesis that an adult who fails to master a second language in a second culture may have failed to synchronize linguistic and cultural development

organizational competence the ability to use rules and systems that dictate what we can do with the forms of language

outer circle countries that use English as a common *lingua franca* and in which English is for many people nativized, e.g., India, Singapore, the Philippines, Nigeria, Ghana

Output Hypothesis the claim, originating with Swain, that output serves as important a role in second language acquisition as input because it generates highly specific input that the cognitive system needs to build up a coherent set of knowledge

overgeneralization the process of generalizing a particular rule or item in the second language, irrespective of the native language, beyond conventional rules or boundaries

overt error an error that is unquestionably ungrammatical at the sentence level

paradigm   in Thomas Kuhn's theory, within "normal science," a prevailing or widely accepted method of explaining or examining a phenomenon within a scientific field of inquiry

parallel distributed processing (PDP)   the receiving, storing, or recalling of information at several levels of attention simultaneously

parameters   characteristics of human language (in Universal Grammar) that vary across languages; built-in options, settings, or values that allow for cross-linguistic variation

pedagogical tasks   activities or techniques that occur in the classroom

peer pressure   encouragement, often among children, to conform to the behavior, attitudes, language, etc., of those around them

perceived social distance   the cognitive and affective proximity that one perceives, as opposed to an objectively measured or "actual" distance between cultures (see **social distance**)

performance   one's actual "doing" of language in the form of speaking and writing (production) and listening and reading (comprehension), as opposed to **competence**

performance analysis   analysis of a learner's performance, with emphasis on investigating errors within the larger perspective of the learner's total language performance, including the "positive" or well-formed aspects of a learner's performance

peripheral attention   attending to stimuli that are not in focal, central attention, but rather on the "periphery," as opposed to **focal attention**

perlocutionary force   the effect and importance of the consequences of communicative speech acts

phatic communion   defining oneself and finding acceptance in expressing that self in relation to valued others

post-structuralism   schools of thought that emerged after the structural schools of the mid-twentieth century, e.g. constructivism

postsystematic stage   a stage in which the learner has relatively few errors and has mastered the system to the point that fluency and intended meanings are not problematic; stabilization

power distance   the extent to which a culture accepts hierarchical power structures and considers them to be normal

pragmalinguistic   the intersection of pragmatics and linguistic forms

pragmatic competence   the ability to produce and comprehend functional and sociolinguistic aspects of language; illocutionary competence

pragmatics   conventions for conveying and interpreting the meaning of linguistic strings within their contexts and settings

prefabricated patterns   memorized chunks of language—words, phrases, short sentences—the component parts of which the speaker is unaware

presystematic [error]   an error in which the learner is only vaguely aware that there is some systematic order to a particular class of items; random error

proactive inhibition   failure to retain material because of interfering effects of similar material learned *before* the learning task, as opposed to **retroactive inhibition**

procedural knowledge implicitly known knowledge that is incidentally available but not consciously verbalizable

prompt see **elicitation**

proxemics in nonverbal communication, conventions for acceptable physical distance between persons

punishment withdrawal of a positive reinforcer or presentation of an aversive stimulus

rationalism seeking to discover underlying motivations and deeper structures of human behavior by using an approach that employs the tools of logic, reason, extrapolation, and inference in order to derive explanations for human behavior; exploring "why" questions

recast an implicit type of corrective feedback that reformulates or expands an ill-formed or incomplete utterance in an unobtrusive way

reflective style the tendency to take a relatively long time to make a decision or solve a problem, sometimes in order to weigh options before making a decision

register a set of language variants commonly identified by certain phonological features, vocabulary, idioms, and/or other expressions that are associated with an occupational or socioeconomic group

reinforcement in behavioral learning theory, events or stimuli that follow a response or behavior and serve to reward the response or behavior

repair correction by the learner of an ill-formed utterance, either through self-initiated repair, or in response to feedback

repetition (in error treatment) the sequential reiteration of an ill-formed part of a student's utterance by a teacher; reiteration by a student of the correct form as a result of teacher feedback, sometimes including incorporation of the correct form in a longer utterance

respondent conditioning in behavioral learning theory, behavior that is elicited by a preceding stimulus

respondent conditioning training in which sets of responses are elicited by identifiable stimuli

response in behavioral learning theory, any elicited or emitted behavior by an organism

retroactive inhibition failure to retain material because of interfering effects of similar material learned *after* the learning task, as opposed to **proactive inhibition**

right-brain dominance a style in which one favors visual, tactile, and auditory images and is more efficient in processing holistic, integrative, and emotional information

risk taking willingness to gamble, to try out hunches about a language with the possibility of being wrong

rote learning the process of mentally storing facts, ideas, or feelings having little or no association with existing cognitive structure

S^{2}R model Oxford's (2011) concept of strategic self-regulated learning (see **self-regulation**)

scientific method   a process of describing verifiable, empirically assessable data; accepting as fact only those phenomena that have been subjected to empirical observation or experimentation

second identity   an alternate ego, different from one's first language ego, that develops in reference to a second language and/or culture (see **language ego**)

self-actualization   reaching the pinnacle of one's potential; the culmination of human attainment

self-efficacy   belief in your own capabilities to perform an activity

self-esteem   self-appraisal, self-confidence, knowledge of oneself, usually categorized into **global** (overall), **situational/specific** (in a general context), and **task** (particular activities within a context) self-esteem

self-regulation   deliberate, self-stimulated, goal-directed management, control, and application of cognitive, affective, and sociocultural-interactive strategies to aid in learning a foreign language

Series Method   language teaching method created by Gouin, in which learners practiced a number of connected "series" of sentences, which together formed a meaningful story or sequence of events

shifting   (of a topic) changing the subject in a conversation

signal learning   learning to make a general diffuse response to a signal

situated learning   within communities of practice, pedagogy that is tailored for a particular group of learners in a particular context

situational self-esteem   see **self-esteem**

social constructivism   a branch of constructivism that emphasizes the importance of social interaction and cooperative learning in constructing both cognitive and emotional images of reality

social distance   the cognitive and affective proximity of two cultures that come into contact within an individual

socioaffective strategies   strategic options relating to social-mediating activity and interacting with others

sociobiological critical period   social and biological explanations for a critical period for language acquisition (see **critical period**)

sociocultural-interactive (S-I) strategy   one of three categories of metastrategy, strategies and tactics that help the learner to interact and communicate, to compensate for knowledge gaps, and to deal effectively with culture

sociolinguistic competence   ability to use or apply sociocultural rules of discourse in a language

sociopragmatics   the interface between pragmatics and social organization

speech acts   communicative behaviors used systematically to accomplish particular purposes

stabilization   see **postsystematic stage**, and **fossilization**

state anxiety   a relatively temporary feeling of worry experienced in relation to some particular event or act, as opposed to trait anxiety

stereotype   an overgeneralized, oversimplified view or caricature of another culture or a person from the culture, as perceived through the lens of one's own culture

stimulus   in behavioral learning theory, an agent that directly evokes a behavior (activity, emotion, thought, or sensory excitation)

stimulus–response learning   acquiring a precise response to a discriminated stimulus

strategic competence   (according to Canale & Swain) the ability to use strategies to compensate for imperfect knowledge of rules or performance limitations; (according to Bachman) the ability to assess a communicative context and plan and execute production responses to accomplish intended purposes

strategic self-regulation   (see **self-regulation**)

strategies-based instruction (SBI)   teaching learners with an emphasis on the strategic options that are available for learning; usually implying the teacher's facilitating awareness of those options in the learner and encouraging strategic action

strategy   any number of specific methods or techniques for approaching a problem or task; modes of operation for achieving a particular end; planned designs for controlling and manipulating certain information

strong version   (of the critical period hypothesis; of the contrastive analysis hypothesis) hypotheses or models that make broad generalizations with few (if any) exceptions, and that make claims, *a priori,* of the application of a model to multiple contexts

structural school of linguistics   a school of thought prevailing in the 1940s and 1950s, in which the linguist's task was to identify the structural characteristics of human languages by means of a rigorous application of scientific observation of the language, and using only "publicly observable responses" for the investigation

structural syllabus   a language course that attends primarily to forms (grammar, phonology, lexicon) as organizing elements of a foreign language curriculum, as opposed to a **functional syllabus**

style   (in psychological functioning) consistent and rather enduring tendencies or preferences within an individual; general characteristics of intellectual and emotional functioning that differentiate one person from another

styles   (in speech discourse) conventions for selecting words, phrases, discourse, and nonverbal language in specified contexts, such as intimate, casual, and consultative styles

subconscious acquisition   see **peripheral attention**

subsumption   the process of relating and anchoring new material to relevant established entities in cognitive structure (see **meaningful learning**)

subtractive bilingualism   proficiency in two languages in which learners rely more and more on a second language, which eventually diminishes their native language

sufficiency   a criterion for legitimizing the conditions of a theory in which a component part is "adequate" to meet the specifications of the theory, as opposed to **necessity**

sustained deep learning (SDL)   the kind of learning that requires an extended period of time to achieve goals

sympathy   understanding what another person is thinking or feeling, but agreement or harmony between individuals is implied, as opposed to **empathy**, which implies more possibility of detachment

systematicity   consistency and predictability in learner language

tactics   specific manifestations or techniques within a metastrategy (or category of strategy) by a learner in a given setting for a particular purpose

target tasks   uses of language in the world beyond the classroom

task   a classroom activity in which meaning is primary; there is a problem to solve, a relationship to real-world activities, with an objective that can be assessed in terms of an outcome

task self-esteem   see **self-esteem**

task-based language teaching   an approach to language instruction that focuses on tasks (see **task**)

teaching   showing or helping someone to learn, giving instructions; guiding; providing with knowledge; causing to know or understand

tension   a neutral concept that includes both dysphoric (detrimental) and euphoric (beneficial) effects in learning a foreign language (see **debilitative** and **facilitative anxiety**)

termination   (of a topic) in a conversation, the process of ending the conversation

token   specific words or structures that are classified within a **type**, or class of features

tolerance of ambiguity   see **ambiguity tolerance**

topic clarification   in a conversation, asking questions to remove perceived ambiguities in another's utterance

topic development   maintaining a topic in a conversation

topic nomination   proposing a topic for discussion in a conversation

Total Physical Response (TPR)   a language teaching method relying on physical or kinesthetic movement accompanied by language practice

trait anxiety   a relatively permanent predisposition to be anxious about a number of things, as opposed to state anxiety

transaction   a social interaction through which one "reveals" thoughts, ideas, or feelings to another person

transfer   the carryover of previous performance or knowledge to previous or subsequent learning

triarchic theory   associated with Sternberg, the hypothesis that intelligence consists of componential, experiential, and contextual abilities

turn-taking   in a conversation, conventions in which participants allow appropriate opportunities for others to talk, or "take the floor"

type   a general class of linguistic features, within which a number of specific words or structures may be used (vs. **token**)

U-shaped learning   the phenomenon of moving from a correct form to an incorrect form and then back to correctness

unanalyzed knowledge   the general form in which we know most things without being aware of the structure of that knowledge (see **implicit knowledge**)

uncertainty avoidance   the extent to which people within a culture are uncomfortable with situations they perceive as unstructured, unclear, or unpredictable; cultural ambiguity intolerance

unconditioned response   in behavioral learning theory, a natural biological response to a stimulus, not elicited by an outside agent

universal grammar (UG)   a system of linguistic rules that hypothetically apply to all human languages

uptake   a student utterance that immediately follows a teacher's feedback and that constitutes a reaction in some way to the teacher's intention to draw attention to some aspect of the student's initial utterance

variable competence model   a model of second language learner development that recognizes and seeks to explain variability in terms of several contextual factors; also called the capability continuum paradigm

variation   instability in learners' linguistic systems

verbal association   learning of chains of responses that are linguistic

visual learning style   the tendency to prefer reading and studying charts, drawings, and other graphic information

weak version   (of the contrastive analysis hypothesis, and other models) the belief in the possibility, *a posteriori*, that a model might apply to a specified context, once contextual variables are taken into account, as opposed to a claim for predictive validity (**strong version**) across broad contexts

Whorfian Hypothesis   the argument that one's language is not merely a reproducing instrument for voicing ideas but rather is itself the shaper of ideas, the program and guide for the individual's mental activity

willingness to communicate (WTC)   an underlying continuum representing the predisposition toward or away from communicating, given the choice

world Englishes   varieties of English spoken and written in many different countries, especially those not in the traditional "inner circle"

worldview   a comprehensive conception of the world—especially culturally and socially—from one's specific cultural norms; *weltanschauung*

zone of proximal development (ZPD)   the distance between a learner's existing developmental state and his or her potential development

AUTHOR INDEX

Numbers followed by *n* refer to a figure or table caption or source note.

384

SUBJECT INDEX

Numbers followed by *n* refer to a figure or table caption or source note.